Outdoor Recreation
for 21st Century America

Outdoor Recreation for 21st Century America

A Report to the Nation:
The National Survey on
Recreation and the Environment

H. Ken Cordell
Principal Author

Contributing Authors

Carter J. Betz
Analysis and Writing

Gary T. Green
Data Collection and Writing

Shela Mou
Production and Editing

Vernon R. Leeworthy and Peter C. Wiley
Chapter 10

James J. Barry and Daniel Hellerstein
Chapter 9

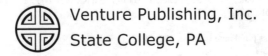
Venture Publishing, Inc.
State College, PA

Production Manager: Richard Yocum
Manuscript Editing: Valerie Fowler, Michele L. Barbin, and Richard Yocum
Cover: Venture Publishing, Inc.

Library of Congress Catalogue Card Number 2003113628
ISBN 1-892132-45-1

Acknowledgments

The studies documented in this publication were supported in part by funds allocated by the USDA Forest Service for preparation of the periodic national resource assessments required under the Forest and Rangeland Renewable Resources Planning Act of 1974, as amended (RPA). The RPA requires an analysis of present and anticipated uses of, demand for, and supply of the various renewable resources on all forest and rangelands in the United States. The most recent RPA Assessment was published by the USDA Forest Service in 2001. The Strategic Planning and Resource Assessment Staff in the national head-quarters office of the USDA Forest Service administers funds for the RPA Assessment, and they have provided sustained support and encouragement over many years for the National Survey on Recreation and the Environment (NSRE). We would like to thank the USDA Forest Service's Recreation, Heritage, and Wilderness Resources Staff, the Resource Valuation and Use Research Staff, and the following personnel: Deborah Shields, Greg Super, Floyd Thompson, Linda Langner, and David Darr.

We also express deep appreciation for major funding and technical input from Dr. Vernon R. Leeworthy of the National Oceanic and Atmospheric Administration. His colleagues and administrative leaders of that agency are also acknowledged. Dr. Leeworthy is the sponsor and sole scientist responsible for the marine recreation questions in the NSRE. Other agencies have supported and continue to support NSRE in many ways. Sponsoring agencies include the Environmental Protection Agency (EPA), the Economic Research Service (USDA), the National Park Service (USDI), and the Bureau of Land Management (USDI). Agencies supporting NSRE in other ways include the Natural Resources Conservation Service (USDA), the U.S. Army Corps of Engineers (DOD), and the Tennessee Valley Authority.

Special acknowledgment is extended to the University of Georgia and the Warnell School of Forest Resources, the Department of Recreation and Leisure Studies, and the Department of Agricultural and Applied Economics. We acknowledge the essential and sustained contributions of Drs. Gary T. Green, Michael A. Tarrant, and John Bergstrom. A very special acknowledgment goes to the University of Tennessee in Knoxville and the Department of Forestry, Wildlife, and Fisheries. Under that department's leadership, the Human Dimensions Research Laboratory is the primary data collection arm of the NSRE and its wide array of survey questions of interest to the survey's sponsors and users. Dr. Mark Fly and Rebecca Stephens manage the Human Dimensions Laboratory and interact daily with the Forest Service NSRE staff in Athens, Georgia.

Table of Contents

List of Figures and Tables

Foreword

Participation in outdoor recreation emerged as an increasingly important part of American life in the post–World War II era for many reasons. Rising incomes, increased free time over the life span, better access to transportation, the post–World War II baby boom, lifestyles that valued the out-of-doors and contact with nature, and the creation of more outdoor recreation sites all contributed. Government manages one third of the landmass of the United States, and such land is increasingly valued and used for recreation, regardless of its original intended function. As outdoor recreation participation has grown, it has become a more important component of our health, our economy, our impact on the environment, and our happiness.

This book provides an authoritative look at outdoor recreation in America. It provides cutting-edge information about trends. It is perhaps the only source that provides comprehensive coverage of both long-term and short-term trends and comparison of state to national participation statistics. While many previous attempts have been made by the federal government to measure outdoor recreation participation and its impacts, partisan politics have intervened repeatedly to prevent the three attempted Nationwide Outdoor Recreation Plans from accurately identifying the scope and trends of outdoor recreation participation. Similarly, much of the survey work done by various outdoor recreation industries is suspect for numerous reasons, including self-interest.

The problem of understanding the scope of outdoor recreation in America has been largely resolved by placing responsibility for gathering such information with the USDA Forest Service, the University of Tennessee, and the University of Georgia. Dr. Ken Cordell, the primary author of this book, heads the Outdoor Recreation Trends Assessment Group, a research unit of the Forest Service Research and Development Branch located on the campus of the University of Georgia in Athens. Cordell's group has been able to repeatedly conduct large-scale scientific surveys to provide an accurate picture of outdoor recreation in America and how it is changing.

Outdoor Recreation for 21st Century America provides a unique understanding of Americans in the great outdoors. Using a critical mass of original data, a definitive portrait of outdoor recreation in America emerges, answering the questions a journalist might ask: who, what, when, where, and sometimes why and how. The portrait is compelling, full of surprises, and devoid of the political and ideological baggage from which so many other attempts to understand this subject suffer. Read on. This book will tell you what is happening in the great outdoors.

—Geoffrey Godbey

Introduction: The Purpose of This Book

The primary purpose of this book is to provide recreation planners, public land managers, academicians, media, students, industry, and others interested in outdoor recreation with a resource describing trends and contemporary Americans' participation in outdoor recreation. The 2nd section (Chapters 1–4) describes long-term and short-term trends, going back to 1960 and linking to earlier nationwide recreation surveys. The 3rd section (Chapters 5–7) describes participation in different groupings of outdoor activities. The 4th section (Chapters 8–11) describes participation and trends by type of outdoor resource or setting (e.g., forest, farm, marine). The final section (Chapters 12–15) provides comparisons across major metropolitan areas, across regions and states, and between enthusiasts and others.

This book is not designed to be read from cover to cover in front of a warm fire over a cup of hot chocolate on a brisk Sunday morning. It is a professional information resource to be used in planning, decision making, marketing, and documentation. While this book was designed for as wide an audience as possible, the data provided is broken out to suit many different, specific interests and needs. For example, a chapter on farm recreation is included for agencies and interests in rural agricultural lands.

Survey Implementation

The National Survey on Recreation and the Environment (NSRE) is administered through a partnership between the Forest Service Research Group on the University of Georgia campus in Athens, and the Human Dimensions Research Laboratory at the University of Tennessee in Knoxville. Financial organization, survey and sampling design, data analysis, and data interpretation (such as reported through this book) are the responsibility of the Athens Forest Service research group. The Athens research group designs survey questions and protocols and specifies sampling distributions, not only for the home agency's needs but also to meet the needs of other survey sponsors. Other sponsors include the National Oceanic and Atmospheric Administration, the Economic Research Service, the Environmental Protection Agency, the National Park Service, the Bureau of Land Management, and a variety of nongovernmental and private sector interests. The Human Dimensions Research Laboratory in the Department of Forestry, Wildlife, and Fisheries at the University of Tennessee in Knoxville obtains samples of phone numbers, programs Computer Assisted Telephone Interview (CATI) protocols, implements interviewing, monitors interview results, and transmits cleaned data files to the Athens Forest Service Group.

The Data in This Book

NSRE surveying proceeds in phases, each aimed at obtaining approximately 5,000 completed interviews. Each phase is referred to as a version. Each version contains the core questions of activity participation and demographics. Added to the core questions for each version are modules of questions sponsored by other agencies or organizations, including various offices of the Forest Service. Surveying continues until the targeted 5,000 completed interviews are obtained. This book is based on data from versions 1 through 9, conducted from 1999 to 2001. In total there were 42,868 interviews completed for versions 1 through 9 analyzed for this book. Total sample size for any given chapter or table within a chapter varies according to how many completed interviews were available for the specific "cut" of the data being made for that chapter or table. Thus, confidence intervals vary from chapter to chapter and table to table because of varying sample size. Intervals based on the full sample typically range between 2% and 3%.

A confidence interval is a statistical estimate based on sample data. At some designated level of confidence (usually 95%), the interval is believed to contain the true estimate in repeated samples. That is, if 100 separate samples were drawn, the true estimate or population parameter would lie within the interval in 95 of those samples, or 95% of the time. Most of the confidence intervals that appear in this book report a proportion or percentage of recreation participants. A few others report mean or average values, for example, annual days of participation in a specific activity.

The United States' National Recreation Surveys

When the Outdoor Recreation Resources Review Commission (ORRRC) conducted the first of this nation's outdoor recreation participation surveys in 1960, transistor radios, Chevy Impala V8 convertibles, the Beatles, Vietnam, President Kennedy, Russia in Cuba, Buddy Holly and the Crickets, Elvis and pink Cadillacs, suede shoes and family vacations were among the many thoughts in people's minds. Just over 40% of the country's population were living in rural areas. Almost 90% was non-Hispanic White, 56% did not graduate from high school, and most of the 45 million families had just one car. Picnicking, driving for pleasure, and swimming were the most popular outdoor activities, and few others came close (ORRRC, 1962).

As will be discussed in the history section that follows, ORRRC left quite a legacy to this country. Not only did it inspire numerous significant congressional acts that set up management and protection of some of the world's greatest outdoor settings but also it started a system of national assessments of the demand and supply of outdoor recreation. ORRRC commissioned 27 reports ranging from an examination of the wildland resource to a look at urban open space and a study of recreation supply financing options. One of the more important of those 27 reports was Report 19, the National Recreation Survey (NRS). Under the leadership of Abbott Ferriss, the first U.S. NRS sampled 15,609 persons 12 years or older over a year's time through seasonal samples covering summer/fall of 1960 and winter/spring of 1961. This book focuses on findings from one of the legacies ORRRC left us, the 7th of the U.S. federal government's nationwide recreation participation surveys—the National Survey on Recreation and the Environment (NSRE).

Since ORRRC and prior to the current NSRE, 5 additional national surveys existed: 1965, 1972, 1977, 1982–1983, and 1994–1995. The surveys done in the 1970s were problematic for many reasons and not often referenced. The 1965 through 1982–1983 surveys were managed within the Department of the Interior and conducted by the U.S. Bureau of the Census. Since the 1982–1983 survey, the last that the Department of the Interior managed, the U.S. national recreation surveys have been managed by the USDA Forest Service. The Outdoor Recreation Trends Assessment Group, a research unit of the Forest Service Research and Development Branch located at the University of Georgia in Athens, now houses the survey. The current NSRE includes a nearly identical set of core outdoor activity participation questions in an attempt to be as comparable to the original 1960 and subsequent Interior surveys as possible.

The two most recent NSRE surveys differ slightly from the earlier NRS surveys in that individuals ages 16 and older (instead of 12 and older) were interviewed. To allow direct comparisons with earlier surveys, people ages 12–15 years were assumed to participate in recreation activities at the same rate as those ages 16–20. The total number of participants from the 1995 and 2000 NSRE was then adjusted to reflect participation by people ages 12 and older.

The name selected for the most recent of the United States' national recreation surveys (in 1995 and in 2000)—the National Survey on Recreation and the Environment (NSRE)—reflects not only continuing interest in this country in outdoor recreation but also growing interest in the natural environment and the management of public lands. In addition to questions about recreation participation, constraints, and demographics, many questions now deal with knowledge of natural land issues, environmental attitudes, preferences for public land objectives, and values of wilderness. Also, because NSRE has multiple sponsors, a variety of other questions asked of the public make the survey complex but diverse in design.

NSRE Design

The NSRE's principal purpose is to describe and to explore participation in a wide range of outdoor recreation activities by people 16 or older in the United States. It also explores their lifestyles and demographic characteristics. NSRE is designed explicitly to estimate proportions and numbers of the population participating in outdoor recreation activities. The Forest Service uses these participation data in a number of ways, but the principal use is to report demand trends for the National Assessment of Outdoor Recreation and Wilderness, completed every 10 years with updates in the intervening 5 years (Cordell et al., 1999). This assessment is required by the Forest and Rangeland Renewable Resources Planning Act (RPA), a law enacted by the U.S. Congress in 1974 (USDA Forest Service, 2001). NSRE data are also used to assist recreation planners and managers in other federal and state agencies in recreation planning and for guidance in evaluating land and water management issues. Other uses of the data include assessing the roles of local, state, federal, and private providers of outdoor recreation, and evaluating alternative methods for financing outdoor recreation services and facilities.

The NSRE is an in-home telephone survey of persons ages 16 or over applied across all ethnic groups and throughout the urban and rural areas of the United States. It is administered as an ongoing number of versions, each having a different mix of question sets or modules. Core questions for NSRE are included in all versions, including activity participation, demographics, and household structure. Where appropriate, questions collect information about disabled persons' access to recreation areas. These questions are asked only of respondents who indicate that they have a disability. Other modules of questions are added as different versions are administered. These modules include sets of questions covering environmental attitudes, objectives for public land management, attitudes toward and values gained from protected wilderness, knowledge of the National Wilderness Preservation System, lifestyle indicators, uses of leisure, rural land ownership, interest in farm-based recreation, and other more specific questions.

NSRE focuses on 78 outdoor recreation activities. Not all of these activities are asked in every version of the survey, although a majority of them are. For each activity included in a particular version, respondents are asked whether or not they participated at least once during the past 12 months. In some versions, questioning about participation goes further. For a subset of the full list of activities, the number of participation days and the number of trips, where an activity was the primary purpose for such trips, are also collected. This further questioning about some of the activities is turned on by a respondent's indicating they indeed had participated in one of those activities. For that small subset of activities for which trip profiles are collected, yet more detailed data are collected, including number of trips of 15 or more minutes away from home where an activity of interest was the primary purpose for the trip.

Modules of Questions

As described earlier, the NSRE is a multifaceted survey focusing on a variety of issues related to outdoor recreation. While only recreation participation data are summarized in this book, we thought it useful to list other modules of questions dealt with in the NSRE. Short descriptions of a number of such issues follow.

Persons With Disabilities

A significant issue in the United States, as elsewhere, is whether persons with challenging conditions are inappropriately restricted from access to outdoor recreation areas. In addition to concerns about general access, NSRE includes a section asking about the nature of disabilities and opinions on availability of access. Access questions address both legislatively mandated and policy-driven programs, which seek to improve access for all United States citizens. Because the subsample of disabled respondents is asked the full breadth of NSRE questions as well as those in the disabilities module, the survey provides an in-depth national profile of persons with disabilities that goes well beyond data typically available.

Wilderness

Despite numerous studies of actual wilderness users, the general American public (i.e., wilderness nonusers) has been little studied with regard to its values, opinions, and awareness of protected wilderness. In NSRE, perhaps the most comprehensive coverage ever assembled about wilderness in the eyes of the public is underway. Coupled with other sections of the questionnaire (e.g., participation profiles, lifestyles, and demographics), specifically tailored questions about wilderness can be examined in the full social context in which opinions about wilderness are formed and held.

Trip Profiles and Valuation Objectives

Resource economics literature dating back a number of decades describes a method generally referred to as travel-cost modeling. This methodology focuses on recreational trips taken to different types and qualities of destination sites. Although refined over the years by other economists, an early and basic premise was that persons taking recreation trips incur and are willing to pay costs for travel and access, and in so doing, provide the researcher an opportunity to observe a relationship between cost and number of trips taken. From this relationship, a formal trip-demand function can be estimated, as can the amount the trip taker is willing to pay for that recreational trip over and above what they actually do pay. This over-and-above willingness to pay is the economist's way to derive an estimate of the economic value of the trip and of the place visited during that trip.

Favorite Activities

Because individuals vary in what they enjoy and commit themselves to in outdoor recreation, a section of the survey asks about favorite activities. Included is a measure of commitment and the preferred setting or environment for the identified favorite activities. Asking respondents about favorite activities serves a number of purposes. First, it tracks trends in most favored activities from generation to generation and from decade to decade. Often participation data alone is not sufficient to identify activities favored most, even though participation percentages may point to popularity. Second, it sets up the respondent for the constraints module (see Barriers and Constraints). Preceding national surveys found that asking about constraints to participation has more meaning to respondents if asked in the context of their favorite outdoor pursuits. Third, it identifies differences in preferences between different groups in American society—by age, gender, race, or any other characteristic.

Barriers and Constraints

Reasons for nonparticipation in outdoor recreation are of particular interest to outdoor recreation managers. The NSRE replicates and adds to the list of barriers and constraints from previous national surveys and allows open-ended responses to capture any new or previously unidentified barriers and constraints. This section was asked in 1 of 2 situations: for respondents who reported that they did not participate in any outdoor recreation, and for respondents who reported that they did not participate in their favorite activity as often as they would have liked.

Environmental Issues

Within political and public arenas, information on how we use and value our environment and natural lands is useful in forming or reforming environmental policy. In particular, it is useful where policy focuses on public lands. Often, organized interests, natural resource professionals, political interests, commodity interests, and local communities are at the table and their voices are heard. Usually, the voice of the public is not at the table and is not heard. The emphasis people place on different environmental resources and services is growing in importance in the United States and the world. We developed a number of tailored scales for NSRE to describe how people across American society view and value our natural lands and other environmental resources.

Lifestyles

New for national surveys in the United States is a scale of 36 lifestyle indicators. The intention is to identify lifestyle activities (e.g., using a computer and the Internet at home) that respondents participate in regularly. The dimensions in this lifestyle scale include hobbies, chores, family activities, sport spectatorship, community and church, vacations and travel, self-learning, health and exercise, environmental involvement, fads, socializing, and going out. Together with recreation participation, environmental attitudes, and demographics, lifestyle information adds enormously to the breadth of profiling done for any particular group of interest in American society. Adding lifestyles provides a new level of opportunity for cluster analysis and other approaches for segmenting people by interests, behaviors and/or attitudes. These segmentation results are used to make more efficient programs for outreach, education, and involvement aimed at the American people.

Implementation and Bias Management
Computer Assisted Telephone Interview System

NSRE telephone interviews are conducted with a Computer Assisted Telephone Interview (CATI) system employed by the Human Dimensions Research Laboratory at the University of Tennessee in Knoxville. The CATI system has 3 primary functions: (1) it facilitates dialing and interviewing, (2) it manages the administrative functions associated with interviewing, and (3) it organizes and stores the data for later processing. As quickly as an interview is completed, the CATI system randomly selects another telephone number, making delays minimal. It then instructs the computer to dial the selected number, and if successful in reaching an eligible person (i.e., a person 16 or older with the most recent birthday in the household) and receiving their approval to continue with the interview, the interviewer reads the survey questions as they appear on the computer screen and enters responses.

Using a computer to control the survey assures question skip and branching patterns are executed as intended, responses are within range, there are no unintended missing data, and data entry occurs in real time as the survey is being administered. If the CATI system and the interviewer are not able to establish contact with a potential interviewee, then a code is entered (e.g., busy, no answer). If the timing of the call is inconvenient, a call back is scheduled for another date and time. If an answering machine is reached, we will endeavor to reach them at another time and date. Overall, the CATI system is of great assistance to interviewers executing the NSRE telephone survey. Given exponentially expanding phone numbers, voice mail, caller ID, call screening, and many other innovations in telephone communications, CATI might even be viewed as essential.

Sampling

Because the NSRE serves the needs of different sponsors, its sampling framework had to be designed accordingly. Interests in rural Americans, coastal recreation participation, and other special interests required oversampling in some parts of the country and among some groups within the overall population. As well, to obtain sufficient data on activities with very low participation rates, sufficient sampling proportions were needed to assure sufficient sample sizes for analysis and crosstabulations.

Issues of Bias

Many potential sources of bias exist in any large survey of human subjects. The principal ones are response and nonresponse biases. Included under response biases are recall and digit preference. Under nonresponse biases are refusal, avidity, incomplete telephone listings, and language barriers. Recall bias is simply an inability of a respondent to recall accurately, or to recall at all, whether he or she participated in recreational activities. There is disagreement among survey scientists as to an optimum recall period (e.g., 1 week, 1 month, 6 months) or methods for correcting recall bias. For the NSRE, we simply accept that some recall bias occurs, and except for telescoping assume this source of bias is balanced between recalling low and recalling high. Telescoping is recalling participation longer ago than the recall period of design. Digit preference bias relates to recall bias. It results from rounding (usually upward) responses about frequency of participation. For example, for activities of frequent participation, such as walking or running/jogging, respondents often round to the nearest 5 or 10 (e.g., 25, 30, or 40) rather than reporting actual number of occasions, such as 28 times during the last 12 months.

Principal sources of nonresponse bias include avidity, incomplete telephone listings, and refusal to participate. Avidity bias is the tendency of persons who participate in outdoor leisure activities to accept being interviewed more readily than those who participate only infrequently or not at all. Often people who participate very little refuse an interview because they feel it does not pertain to them. Thus we end up oversampling those who participate more. Left unaccounted for, avidity bias can result in seriously inflated estimates of population participation rates and biased estimates of participation differences by social group. Another source of nonresponse bias, incomplete telephone listings, like any other incomplete sampling frame, can occur for many reasons. More frequently encountered reasons include institutionalization, not having a phone, and access only to pay phones or other nonindividualistic arrangements.

Of all sources of bias, however, nonresponse bias potentially caused by some households and individuals refusing to participate in an interview is of most concern in administering the NSRE. Increasingly, in today's fast moving, high-tech world, it is difficult to make contact to set up and complete telephone interviews. First, the expansion of telephone numbers that has been occurring over the last 2 decades makes it much more difficult today to identify a potential interviewee. Cell phones, pagers, fax machines, and the growing number of businesses and households create more demands for new telephone numbers. As this need expands and the numbers grow, more area codes must be created.

More numbers is only a part of the growing challenge. Once a legitimate phone number is obtained and a household identified, the process then must focus on making voice contact and gaining the responding person's confidence and cooperation. Technology is putting a greater strain on attempts to reach and interview persons in a typical household. Just a few years ago, interviewers only had to deal with answering machines. With today's technology, there is now caller ID, call blocking, and privacy managers. Households using any or all of these devices can easily choose whether to accept a call based on recognition of who is calling.

Much of today's society is fast paced and time conscious. Keeping a potential respondent on the phone is more difficult. Competition with telemarketers, charitable organizations, political polling, and other survey research affects our ability to entice a respondent to complete an interview. Usually, unless the survey is viewed as interesting or important, a respondent is not willing to give up 15–20 minutes. Willingness to cooperate tends to vary by state and between urban and/or rural. For the NSRE in general, households in urban areas of the country are more easily contacted, but they are less likely to stay with and complete an interview. People in rural areas are more likely to cooperate, but they are more difficult to contact.

Another source of bias comes from language barriers and the inadvertent exclusion of non-English speaking U.S. residents. According to the 2000 census, 12.5% of the U.S. population and 14.2% of the U.S. metropolitan population is Hispanic. For the non-English speaking segment of the Hispanic population, the NSRE is conducted in Spanish. The most difficult part of this process is wording the translation to enable overall comprehension by all the various Hispanic dialects.

For the NSRE, a concerted effort to estimate avidity, listing bias, and refusals is being made by asking 2 key questions of persons who refuse to participate in the survey. Those questions are age and whether or not the respondent participated in outdoor recreation in the last 12 months. Additionally, the gender of the respondent is recorded when recognizable. The estimated proportions of nonrespondents, relative to respondents, was combined with weights derived from the 2000 census of the United States population to weight each observation to correct for overrepresentation or underrepresentation by that respondent's social group in the sample. As with any survey, regardless of scope or complexity, bias is a reality to be recognized and dealt with early on, to the extent affordable, through design of the sample, and the questionnaire content.

Section I

History of Outdoor Recreation in the United States

There has been a steadily increasing trend in outdoor recreation participation throughout the history of this country. As later chapters will show, this upward trend continues into the 21st century. Outdoor recreation not only is a deeply entrenched part of Americans' lifestyles but also is a growing part of those lifestyles. In 1999 we published Outdoor Recreation in American Life (Cordell et al., 1999). In that book, Dr. Robert Douglass wrote a brief history of outdoor recreation in the United States. This section adapts his contribution to that earlier book (Douglass, 1999). We felt that including some of his write-up of the history of outdoor recreation, although brief, is an important part of the story of outdoor recreation for 21st century America. Without the creation of the opportunities this history portrays, outdoor participation as we know it would not exist.

Outdoor recreation has been developing in America for more than 100 years. The formative years defined the roles of the public and private sectors and were rooted in the evolution of the management of federal, state, and local public lands. With the ending of World War II and the economic and population growth that followed, an era of growth and the development of infrastructure to support nature-based recreation commenced. Following and overlapping this infrastructure development was the modern period of the late 1980s and 1990s—like nothing in the past.

The Formative Years

Recreation has played both direct and indirect roles in the evolution of how America cares for its natural resources. Many public recreation areas and parks were established to supply recreation opportunities directly. Indirectly, outdoor recreation demands precipitated changes in land management well beyond the areas and parks established specifically for outdoor recreation. Recreation was not formally recognized during this nation's formative years in natural resource and public land management. During the late 19th and early 20th centuries, the romanticism and conservation movements were at their peaks, and President Theodore Roosevelt rode those peaks in a grand way. But then, with 90% of the population living in rural areas, politicians did not seem to care much about a national stewardship of natural lands or recreation policy. People of the time were busy carving a living from the landscape and had little leisure time.

With time, society and our collective view of natural lands changed. Eventually, nature and wild lands were seen in a friendlier light—as things of beauty and no longer the enemy. Authors such as James Fennimore Cooper produced novels that presented a romantic view of the natural landscape, and Albert Bierstadt produced magnificent paintings of the western mountains that influenced many to consider and act on preserving tracts of land for their naturalness and beauty. But early on Americans exerted little or no pressure on federal and state governments to provide outdoor recreation opportunities. Why would they? Natural lands surrounded them and were abundant in their rural habitats.

At the turn of the 20th century, recreation opportunities abounded in this country, but not as a result of government or other collective policy. Hunting, fishing, boating, and many other activities were common. The playground movement gave rise to city-oriented recreation activities, and American railroads made excursions to distant parks and resorts possible. As the federal estate was being developed and its policies shaped, including national forests and national parks, little initial thought was given to outdoor recreation as a primary use of those federal lands. Local needs for recreation were addressed directly by municipal governments. For example, New York's Central Park was designed in 1850 by Frederick L. Olmstead. Central Park and others, along with village greens, commons, plazas, and other institutional open spaces, were used by city dwellers as de facto parks, even though these open spaces were not a direct result of recreation planning. However, no popular, broad-based support existed for outdoor recreation prior to the close of the 19th century at any level of government. Yellowstone was established as a federal park in 1872 because some farsighted individuals held out for its public ownership at a time when that land appeared to be valueless. The Yosemite Grant to California and the reservation of Yellowstone Park were carved from public domain land when there was no opposition from profit interests.

With creation of the National Park System in the 20th century, recreation became a major component of federal land management for the first time. Introducing the concept of national parks for public use and education started a movement that spread to almost every other country in the world by the end of the 20th century. With the establishment of the National Forest System, another federal agency, the Forest Service, became destined to become the nation's largest host to outdoor recreation. Americans quickly recognized the potential in national forests, and in 1921 Chief William Greeley declared outdoor recreation a major use of the national forest system. In all, the federal government manages 761 million acres of land—691 million acres available for recreation. Seven federal agencies care for approximately 34% of the nation's land and host hundreds of millions of visits per year for recreation.

State governments have only 6% of the country's forest and park land, but offer impressive opportunities, mostly in the East. As national parks and national forests were getting their start in the West, state land conservation also was being launched. Several northeastern states organized agencies to care for natural land during the late 19th century. New York began the Adirondack and Catskill Preserves in 1885. Pennsylvania followed by creating state forests and wildlife and watershed protection areas in 1889. As with the federal government, preservation and conservation were the driving forces behind these state programs. State parks were given a big boost in 1921 when the National Park

Access to the National Forest was different in the early 1900s. Photo dated before 1910 and courtesy of USDA Forest Service, Clearwater National Forest.

Service hosted the first National Conference on State Parks. That conference, now the National Society for Park Resources, has been meeting on a regular basis ever since. States realized early on that their role was to provide balanced outdoor recreation opportunities to their citizens.

The Years of Definition and Expansion

After the Great Depression and World War II, recreation became a major component of American life. After World War II, Americans took to the open road to see and to experience the great outdoors. They did so in such numbers as to overwhelm existing recreation facilities, many of which were outmoded in design and capacity. Pent up demand for recreation that had been put off by World War II and the Korean conflict were straining an outdated infrastructure. Recognizing a need to improve the situation, Congress passed legislation to conduct a national study of outdoor recreation. The Outdoor Recreation Resources Review Commission (ORRRC) was established in 1958 and charged with studying the present and future needs for outdoor recreation. Releasing its findings in early 1962, the ORRRC Report stimulated a massive federal movement to create more recreation opportunities in the United States (ORRRC, 1962). ORRRC commissioned a nationwide recreation participation survey administered in 1960, the 1st of this nation's participation surveys. The National Survey on Recreation and the Environment (NSRE), reported in this book, is the nation's 7th such survey.

A major breakthrough for outdoor recreation came concurrently as ORRRC was surfacing its findings. In 1960 Congress passed the Multiple Use–Sustained Yield Act to establish a policy for managing the national forests. This legislation intended to place recreation on the same level of importance as timber, water, wildlife, and range. In the vast national forest system, outdoor recreation opportunities were to have the same footing as timber and other uses of the forest. The multiple-use concept extended to the Bureau of Land Management's national resource lands, approximately 175 million acres in 11 western states and 165 million acres in Alaska. Historically, the great recreation potential of this land was slow to develop because the bureau had been dispersing and leasing land rather than providing outdoor recreation or otherwise managing it. Congress provided a new charter through the Federal Land Policy and Management Act of 1976, which led to opening much BLM land to recreation.

The release of the Outdoor Recreation Resources Review Commission Report in 1962 set off a chain of related activities that defined the national and state policies on outdoor recreation and began a large transfer of land from the private to the public sector. As a direct result of that report, Congress passed a series of acts, including the creation of the National Wilderness Preservation System, the National Wild and Scenic Rivers System, the National Trails System, and a system of National Recreation Areas. Legislation funded acquisition of recreation land under the Land and Water Conservation Fund Act of 1965 and provided a method of encouraging state involvement in the push to address the recommendations of the ORRRC Report.

The Outdoor Recreation Act of 1963 was one outcome of ORRRC. It required the newly created Bureau of Outdoor Recreation to conduct a continuous federal inventory and evaluation of the outdoor recreation needs and resources in the United States. State plans came about when required by the Bureau of Outdoor Recreation as a condition for grant eligibility. Three 5-year comprehensive nationwide outdoor recreation plans were produced by the Department of the Interior—the last in 1979. That last plan sought to establish continuous recreation planning and assessment rather than periodic efforts.

Assessment of outdoor recreation was discontinued by the Department of the Interior after the 1979 effort. The Bureau of Outdoor Recreation was downsized, renamed, then eliminated. All its functions, including the Nationwide Recreation Survey, were transferred to the National Park Service. The function of conducting a national assessment and the Nationwide Outdoor Recreation Plan was eliminated eventually, but the Park Service did conduct one more nationwide participation survey in 1982–1983 (see Chapter 2). Under authority of the Forest and Rangeland Renewable Resources Planning Act (RPA), the nationwide survey and responsibility for assessing outdoor recreation in America became the responsibility of the Forest Service. The first full national recreation assessment under the RPA was completed by the Forest Service in 1989. The nationwide recreation survey was transferred to the Forest Service in the early 1990s with the next survey commencing in 1994, following a lag of almost a dozen years between surveys.

Federal and state responses to the ORRRC Report brought about significant changes in outdoor recreation. In some ways, the success of that report also brought about its obsolescence. As time passed, people's outdoor recreation involvement changed. By 1980 many national leaders were again concerned about the overall recreation situation. Twenty years after the ORRRC Report was published, the Outdoor Recreation Policy Review Group published a private assessment of the outdoor recreation situation, Outdoor Recreation for America—1983. That report pushed Congress and the President into ordering another serious study to update the 1958 ORRRC project. The President's Commission on Americans Outdoors (PCAO) was established by executive order in 1985 and produced its report, Americans Outdoors: The Legacy, the Challenge, in 1987. This new study produced a new approach by the government in its role of providing a national policy for recreation. Instead of concentrating on supply and demand numbers, the new policy focused on societal concepts. The need for an outdoor recreation ethic, private property rights, landowner liability, cooperative partnerships, and environmental quality were the topics forming the new federal policy for outdoor recreation.

Since the 1970s state parks have rearranged their priorities so that outdoor recreation, rather than just park protection, defines their mission. Increased use of state parks between 1960 and 1990 has fueled development of facilities and recreation programs. Today, every state has a park system, on about 13 million acres of state-owned public land. They were visited an estimated 766 million times in 2001. Land acquisition for state parks rose rapidly through the 1970s but tapered off since then. Even though use of state parks has continued to grow, expansion of parkland area has not, because of slow to no-growth state appropriations. State park systems have had to depend less on tax support and turn to revenue generation and more high-end development, such as resorts.

Private land has always been a significant part of the American outdoor recreation story as well. During the years of economic and population expansion, private land provided many of the opportunities for outdoor recreation. Much of this land is in the East where it helps to balance the lack of sufficient federal land. In the past, one of the major reasons for closing private land to public recreation was the fear of liability. States wanting the private land to be open to public use had to pass legislation to shield landowners from suits. All 50 states have passed some form of recreation user statute to limit liability of landowners. Now, liability is less of a concern, but less private land is being made available because of landowners' desires for privacy, pursuit of their own personal recreation, and avoidance of damage from careless users.

As both federal and state land systems have begun facing serious tax support deficits, it is becoming more common to see a partnership with the private sector. Now private capital and private management of facilities are common on public land. Stephen Mather introduced this concept in a modest way while director of the National Park Service in 1916. But demands for more expensive and elaborate facilities and services have surpassed the public sector's ability to meet their growing demand. Now lodging, ski resorts, and similar developments as concessions are common on public land.

The 1990s

Outdoor recreation and nature-based tourism have been adjusting to new realities which became clearly evident in the 1990s. Technological innovations and economic and social structural changes have been profound. The unprecedented affluence and economic advancement of the 1990s saw more people investing their time, energy, and money in recreation pursuits. Tourism is moving people to all corners of the earth—even to places where the attractions only recently have been defined. Recreation participation has been increasing in this country for over 100 years, and that trend continues, but in numbers never seen before or predicted by the best models. Many of those looking for fulfilling leisure are going to computer games and the Internet, which often now accompany them on outdoor recreation trips. Personal watercraft, mountain bikes, portable

DVD players, and hundreds of new concepts enhance vacation activities. Where safe drinking water is scarce, tiny, portable water filtration systems now allow serious backpackers to stay out longer than they once could. Lightweight clothing and related gear provide warmth, waterproofing, and safety.

Pursuit of an activity appears to have replaced the vacation as the primary means for outdoor recreation. Soccer leagues, adult golf outings and tournaments, triathlon camps, specialized theme cruises, and nature-based tourism are small parts of the new wave of outdoor recreation involvement. Today's outdoor recreationist can begin their activities in such far away bases as Tahiti or Bora Bora. In today's marketplace "green" sells. Environmental interest is high and it attracts paying visitors. Nature-based tourism implies travel to interact with a natural environment for education, observation, or recreation. Visiting an area to appreciate its natural attributes has been the rationale for nature-based tourism as we commonly accept the term. In the 1990s, a new term, ecotourism, was introduced. Ecotourism is defined by the Ecotourism Society as "…socially and environmentally responsible travel to natural areas that conserves the environment and improves the welfare of the local people." Ecotourism has developed from the desire of nature-based tourism in the 1990s to benefit from unique environments while contributing to their protection and improvement.

New equipment and the desire to learn something new drove much of the 1990s, as they drive much of today's outdoor recreation participation. An all-terrain vehicle driving school is available for people who have purchased such a vehicle. Bicycle tours of European countries attract Americans who want to pedal around while looking at wineries, art, castles, or some other theme. Many Asians come to this country to climb its mountains using the equipment that new technologies provide. Hand-held global positioning satellite (GPS) receivers and cellular telephones have changed the way people interface with the wilderness experience. Today, it is possible to be in touch with the office while camping in the middle of a wilderness area.

Different technologies have created different situations—not all of them good or bad in the long run. These technologies will enable people to enjoy the out-of-doors in ways unknown to their parents. Anglers can use the GPS systems to determine their location, mark a fishing spot for a return visit, have an automatic course plotted for home or the next fishing site, and have a standby man-overboard locator. As the price per unit has dropped, GPS receivers have become a popular method of traveling in backcountry areas because they give all the directions needed to get where one wants to go. However, they are best used when backed up with a compass and a map. And then there's night vision. Adapted from military uses, night vision has opened up a whole new venue and expanded the times during which outdoor recreation can take place.

Internet users gather all sorts of information about their destinations well before leaving home. Maps, trail conditions, camping availability, snow conditions, and costs of events are just a few things learned from the Internet. Reservations, tickets, and equipment use can be arranged electronically. Completing the recreation planning and obtaining all the required information in advance fits into the new style that demands time efficiency.

The changes in outdoor recreation taking place today may depend more on attitude than on toys. People are willing to pay to recreate, but they want quality. Public sector recreation helped to meet the country's recreational needs when ideas of what constituted quality outdoor experiences were simple. Now, with ideas of quality and excitement much more complex, and in some ways unrealistic, and with public money and management infrastructure becoming more scarce, public lands are being stressed to meet the multitude of demands that now occur everywhere—not just in the most accessible areas. Recreation opportunities still exist on the public estate, but now many must occur in partnership with the private sector simply to stay open. Where outdoor recreation will go in the future will be linked in complex ways to political winds, wars, conservatism, the economy, population growth and diversification, immigration, and many other factors. If the past is a predictor of the future, however, one trend is clear, and persistent: Outdoor recreation participation will continue to rise.

Section II

Trends Over Time

Population has been, is, and will be the major driver of outdoor recreation participation growth in this country. Since the 1960s, when the population was at 180 million, the number legally living in this country expanded to over 280 million. This section is dedicated to an examination of trends in outdoor recreation participation over time, driven by population growth and to lesser extent by other factors. The 1st chapter looks at long-term trends, from 1960 to now. During that period, the activities found to be growing fastest were bicycling, camping, canoeing/kayaking, and swimming. The 2nd chapter looks at more recent trends—that is, since the 1982–1983 National Recreation Survey. In that 2nd chapter we see that viewing or photographing birds was the activity that had been growing fastest in this country, since the early 1980s. Birding alone added more than 50 million participants and grew an unprecedented 231% in just under 20 years. Chapter 3 compares how people's recreation participation patterns changed since the 1994–1995 National Survey on Recreation and the Environment. The most popular activities in 2000–2001 (i.e., those with the greatest number of participants) included walking for pleasure, outdoor family gatherings, and visiting a beach. These are the same activities at the top in 1994–1995, 6 years earlier. Finally, the last chapter in this section questions whether there were any detectable effects of September 11, 2001, on outdoor participation. This chapter examines short-term trends and changes in people's outdoor recreation participation before, just after, and one year after September 11, 2001. Interesting insights were gained from surveying a modest sample of Americans 16 or older regarding their short-term travel plans and any changes resulting from the attacks on the Pentagon and World Trade Center. Surprising to many who had forecast substantial reductions in recreation travel, only a very modest near-term decrease in recreation and vacation travel could be detected.

Section II

Trends Over Time

Chapter 1
Long-Term Trends—1960 to 2001

This country's 1st nationwide outdoor recreation survey was done in 1960. We thought it would be interesting to examine how not only recreation participation but also our country's population has changed in the last 43 years. Most notable and obvious about these years, of course, has been the dramatic growth of population. A doubling of the current population is projected by the year 2100. Native Americans might have the view that population has been dramatically growing (and changing in composition) for much longer than just 43 years—since well before 1500 perhaps. Contemporary population growth, however, more than any other factor, now drives most things in this country, including changes in outdoor recreation.

Highlights

From the 1960 population of around 180 million, the number of people legally living in this country has expanded to over 280 million—growth of about 100 million in just over 40 years. Obviously population growth is not the full story behind recreation participation change. Some activities have grown faster, and some slower, than population. This shift in the popularity hierarchy among activities means that the influence of changes in tastes, incomes, wealth, technology, and the supply of opportunities have also been felt. One can note relative differences among activities between 1960 and 2000–2001, as shown in Figure 1.1 (p. 24).

Activities growing fastest since 1960 include bicycling, camping, canoeing/ kayaking, and swimming. The technological advancement of bicycles has transformed what was once a close-to-home, slow-paced activity into one involving many different styles of bicycles with a wide variety of equipment, competition, and outdoor venues for testing new technology. The appearance of mountain bikes in the late 1970s—and especially their more affordable availability beginning in the early 1980s—was a significant development. Mountain bikes and "hybrids" that combined features of both mountain bikes and street bikes introduced a whole new style of bicycling. They also opened up myriad off-road opportunities previously inaccessible to street bikes. By the 1990s mountain bikes had become mainstream, outselling many of the designs of more traditional street bicycles.

Technology and changing lifestyles have impacted camping as well. Campgrounds now serve the tent camper of the 1960s less and serve travelers with large, high-tech motor homes and towed residence trailers more. Electrical, water, sewage, cable television, and phone hookups are no longer considered just nice-to-have amenities—for many they have become the norm and for some they are viewed as necessities. The aging U.S. population and larger numbers of retirees have increased the market for amenity-based camping experiences, especially those centered around recreational vehicles. Families also increasingly demand campground services that feature some of the comforts and conveniences of home, such as hot showers, television hookups, computer games, and other entertainment for children. For the more traditional tent campers, primitive camping opportunities are still plentiful, especially on public lands but in many private campgrounds as well.

Participation in canoeing and kayaking grew from 2.6 million in 1960 to approximately 15 million in 1982–1983 and then to 27.7 million in 2000–2001. Here, too, technology has had a profound impact. Today's kayaks include hole-riding boats, surfing boats, boofing boats, squirting boats, beginner boats, intermediate boats, advanced boats, and boats for large and small paddlers. Swimming, unlike other fast growing activities, is not especially driven by technology. Its growth has been driven by persistent popularity and by population growth. From 1995–2001, the proportion of people who said they went swimming outdoors in the past year held constant at about 55%. Due to population growth, however, this steady percentage of participation has meant an increase from about 109 million swimmers to approximately 125 million. Water to be near, in, or under continues to be a major outdoor attractant. The proximity of outdoor swimming opportunities to where people live, including pools and

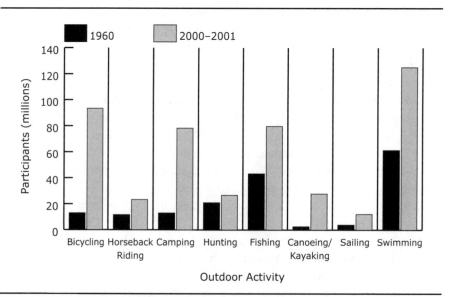

Figure 1.1 Participants in outdoor activities, age 12 and older, 1960 and 2001 (NSRE, 2001; ORRRC, 1962)

natural and man-made water bodies, is another major reason for the continuing popularity of swimming. Detailed descriptions of these long-term outdoor recreation participation trends follow.

Population Growth: The Dominant Driver of Participation Trends

At the close of the 1950s and into 1960, the Outdoor Recreation Resources Review Commission conducted the United States' first nationwide outdoor recreation participation survey. The U.S. population had reached 179 million (U.S. Bureau of the Census, 1993). Alaska, the state with the smallest population, had only 224,000 residents in 1960. By comparison, the population of New York, the most heavily populated state, was almost 75 times that of Alaska, having reached 16.8 million in 1960. Across the United States more than 30% of the 1960 population lived in rural areas. Almost three quarters of the population at that time lived in either rural areas or in towns and cities of less than 1 million people. In the post–World War II and Korean War years, population growth accelerated beyond anything this country had previously experienced or expected. The most popular outdoor recreation activities of this growing population throughout the summer of 1960 were picnics, driving for pleasure, swimming, sightseeing, walking for pleasure, and playing outdoor games and sports (Outdoor Recreation Resources Review Commission, 1962).

Between 1960 and 1980 the U.S. population increased by another 26% to a total of over 226 million—an average growth of 2.36 million per year. From 1980 to 1990 population again increased substantially, growing almost 10% and reaching about 249 million (Gibson & Jung, 2002). The growth rate, however, had slowed slightly to just over 2.2 million per year. This led many people to a short-lived forecast of a future that featured declining population growth rates, ultimately reaching a zero growth rate around the middle of the 21st century (USDA Forest Service, 1989). Most of the population growth of the 1980s occurred in urban areas. On average population in urban counties grew by 15%, compared to only about 4% in rural counties (Cordell & Overdevest, 2001). Between January 1990 and January 2000 U.S. population grew from around 249 to more than 281 million, a decade's increase of 32 million as compared to just over 22 million in the preceding decade. This growth of around 3.2 million persons per year indicated an acceleration of growth and caused forecasters to abandon their earlier forecasts of declining growth rates that would result in zero population growth. For example, Alaska's population grew to almost 627,000 in this period.

In the 3 years since the 2000 census, population in the United States (as of November 2002) increased by about 7 million to approximately 288.4 million persons (Figure 1.2). Projections based on 1990 census data indicate that U.S.

population is expected to more than double by the end of this century. By 2020, population is projected to be 325 million, by 2050 almost 404 million, by 2075 nearly 481 million, and by 2100, 571 million! If it occurs, this growth—almost 300 million more men, women, and children in just 10 decades—will exceed the total growth of population over the last 10,000 years within the geographic area we now call the United States. Growth by 300 million is more than the total population currently living in the United States. Between now and 2020, growth will average 2.4 million per year. In the last year of the 21st century, almost 4 million new residents will be added (about the number of people who currently reside in the entire state of South Carolina). As stated earlier, population growth (now and in the future) is one of the major drivers of growth in outdoor recreation in the United States. But, as we shall see, there is more to it than that.

Outdoor Recreation Participation Trends (1960–Present)

Rate of growth of outdoor recreation participation for the most part has paralleled population growth from 1960 to 1980. To track this growth, the primary statistics used are changes in percentages of the population and numbers of participants across selected activities. In Chapters 5 through 7, analysis of number of days of participation will also be reported.

The source of data for tracking long-term trends is the United States' ongoing National Recreation Survey (NRS) series. The first of these serial surveys

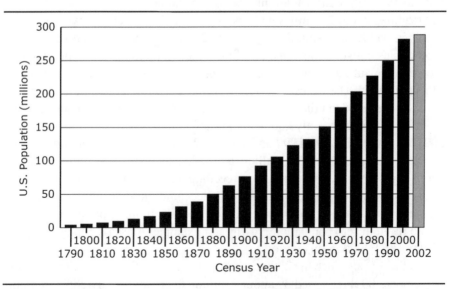

Figure 1.2 Population growth in the United States, 1790–2002 (U.S. Bureau of the Census, 1993)

reported in 1960 (ORRRC, 1962). A number of repetitions of the National Recreation Survey were done in following years (Cordell, McDonald, Lewis, Miles, Martin & Bason, 1996). This chapter references the 1965 and the 1982–1983 NRS surveys, as well as more recent editions in 1995 and 2000–2001. (Interviewing for the current survey continues.) The name of these latter two surveys has been changed to the National Survey on Recreation and the Environment (NSRE) to bring attention to the addition of a wide band of environmental opinion questions and issues (Cordell, Betz & Green, 2002).

The most recent of the National Recreation Surveys represents phone interviews of people age 16 years or older. The first few national surveys, however, also included adolescents between 12 and 15 years of age. (Federal and university regulations now do not permit interviewing anyone under 16 years of age unless in the company of a responsible adult.) To make comparisons across surveys from 1960–2001, the NSRE estimates of numbers and percentages of the population 16 and older participating in outdoor activities were adjusted to reflect assumed participation by adolescents 12–15 years old. People ages 12–15 at the time of the 1995 and 2001 national surveys were assumed to participate at the same rates as people ages 16–20.

The estimated millions of noninstitutionalized people ages 12 years or older in the United States during annual periods covered by the 5 National Recreation Surveys referenced in this chapter include

1960	131 million
1965	144 million (10% more than 1960)
1982–1983	188 million (44% more than 1960)
1994–1995	211 million (61% more than 1960)
2000–2001	229 million (75% more than 1960)

The following sections examine long-term trends in number and percentage of U.S. population age 12 and older who participate in outdoor activities common to the 1960, 1965, 1982–1983, 1994–1995, and 2000–2001 national surveys. Following chapters present recent trends for a longer and more comprehensive set of activities common to the 1982–1983 and 1994–1995 surveys.

Land-Based Activities

Four land-based activities have been tracked since the original National Recreation Survey in 1960: bicycling, horseback riding, camping, and hunting. These 4 land activities are the only ones reported here because they are the only activities defined in that original survey in such a way that direct comparisons can be made with more recent surveys. Two of these 4 activities (i.e., bicycling and camping) have experienced highly significant growth in the numbers of people who participate (Figure 1.3). When the 1960 survey was conducted, multiple-speed bikes were just beginning to appear. In all likelihood, only a few of the almost 13 million people 12 years or older who had reported doing "some bicycling during the past year" used what were then considered advanced technology bikes. By 1965, the number of bicyclists had jumped to nearly 26 million ages 12 and older—a doubling of participants in just 5 years.

Almost 20 years later in 1982–1983, just over 60 million Americans reported participating in bicycling at some point during the previous year—more than double the number that participated in 1965. Since that 1980s survey, especially in the 1990s, the technological advancement in bicycles has transformed what was once a homogeneous, slow-paced activity confined to paved surfaces into an activity involving many different types of bikes with a wide variety of equipment, technology, paces, and outdoor venues. Advances toward lighter bicycles, more efficient gearing and shifting, off-trail tires, and a number of other features are quite obvious when one visits a bicycle shop and compares bikes on the sales floor with the old single-speed, big-tired Schwinn Cruiser exhibited on the wall. Mountain bikes are among the more notable advancements. Mountain bikes and hybrids between mountain and touring bikes, with their lightweight, tough construction, extended gear ratios, and all-terrain tires enable riders to both traverse very difficult terrain, as well use them for commuting or in other riding venues.

The slight dip in bicycling participation to 29% in 1994–1995 was no doubt influenced by the inadvertent omission of a question specific to mountain biking in that survey. Although survey respondents were asked, "Did you go bicycling in the past 12 months?" it is likely that some respondents who participated only in mountain biking answered no to this question, thinking that the question referred only to bicycling on streets. In the 2000–2001 NSRE, the bicycling question was reworded as: "Did you do any type of bicycling for fun or exercise?" If a person responded yes, this question was followed up with one specific to mountain or hybrid bicycles. Consequently, the 2000–2001

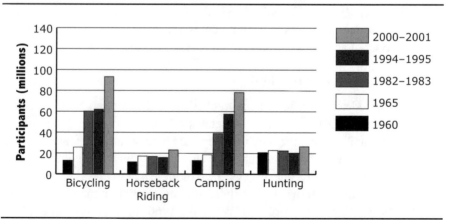

Figure 1.3 Participation in land-based activities listed in each National Recreation Survey, 1960–2001

participation rate (41%) is much more in line with expectations. This rate produces an estimate of more than 93 million bicyclists in the United States, from the most casual neighborhood cruiser to long-distance touring cyclists to the spectrum of mountain bikers that ranges from recreational weekend riders to the most avid backcountry adventurers.

Camping is another activity whose long-term growth has been tracked. It is likely that in most people's minds, camping is an activity for families with children and a tent or camper set up in a peaceful, forested campground with campfire smoke drifting lazily across a lake. But like bicycling, the technology, styles, and some of the venues of camping have changed since the 1960s. In the 1960s most campgrounds were designed to accommodate small groups, usually family sized, and their tents. At that time, about 13 million people ages 12 or older reported camping 1 or more times. In 1965, as the equipment and options for camping were beginning to change, participation had grown to nearly 19 million participants—a 44% increase in what then was called the "family camping market." By 1982–1983, camping had nearly tripled the 1960 numbers of participants and more than doubled the percentage of the population reporting they went camping during the year. Campgrounds served the tent camper less and served travelers with their large, luxurious motor homes and towed residence trailers more. These types of campers see electrical and water hookups for their recreational vehicles as essentials—not just nice-to-have amenities. Now, computer and cable TV hookups are in vogue. Stores, restaurants, video game pavilions, and laundry facilities became the norm for commercial campgrounds and some state park campgrounds. Hot showers were viewed as essentials.

In 1994–1995, almost 58 million people age 12 or older participated in camping—roughly a 340% growth in the 35 years since the first national survey in 1960. The nature of camping also continued to change. Family camping is still popular, but the composition of a camping party is more likely to be retirees, singles, or groups of 2 or more unrelated individuals. The most recent NSRE reveals that more than 78 million people—just over one third of the population age 12 or older—camped 1 or more times in the last year. This is a growth of 20.7 million people in just over 6 years. Given that in 960 a total of about 13 million camped, this growth is nothing short of phenomenal.

The other 2 land activities comparable with those in the 1960 survey are horseback riding and hunting. Both of these activities require relatively large areas of land with backcountry roads and trails. Between 1960 and 1965, horseback riding increased in both percentage of population and total number of participants. From 1965 through 1995 the activity decreased in both percentage of the population and number of people participating. The number of people horseback riding per year between 1960 and 1995 seems to have peaked somewhere around or shortly after 1965, when an estimated 17.2 million participated. Currently, there is a modest resurgence of growth in horseback riding. Participation in horseback riding grew to 10% and topped any previous total number of participants by reaching 23.3 million in 2001. It is likely that the prominence of the equestrian events in the 1996 summer Olympics in Atlanta, Georgia, and rising income levels may have helped to drive this increase.

Participation in hunting had been stable to slightly declining up until 1995. The estimated number of hunters in 1994–1995 was slightly smaller than the estimated number in the 1960s. The proportion of the population that hunted decreased from 16% in 1960 to around 10% in the 1990s. Since 1995, hunting participation has seen a slight resurgence to 11.6% participation. With the population age 12 and older growing by almost 20 million during that time, however, the number of participants has now reached over 26 million. Over 8% hunt big game, 7.2% hunt small game, and 2.4% hunt migratory birds (e.g., ducks, geese). Additionally, many hunters participate in all 3 forms of hunting.

Suitable areas for hunting are increasingly difficult to find. In earlier decades, there was substantially more undeveloped land in all regions of the country with fewer people looking to use those areas. In the 1960s, few landowners required people to obtain permission to hunt on their land, even people they did not know. In more recent decades, however, a larger population is competing for a smaller available private-land base for hunting and other activities (Cordell & Tarrant, 2002; Teasley, Bergstrom, Cordell, Zarnoch & Gentle, 1999). Access to hunt or to participate in any other outdoor activity on private lands has declined steadily as owners have closed more of their land to the general public. This is likely a major factor in the slow growth of hunting, and its lack of growth between 1960 and 1995.

Water-Based Activities

Among the 4 water-based activities with comparable statistics across the 5 National Recreation Surveys referenced in this chapter—fishing, canoeing/kayaking, sailing, and swimming—all increased in number of participants during the period from 1960 to 2001 (Figure 1.4). For canoeing/kayaking this resulted in a nearly tenfold increase in participants, from about 2.6 million to more than 27 million. There was a significant jump in participation between 1965 and 1983 and a smaller but substantial increase between 1995 and 2001. Fishing participation has also steadily increased since 1960. The percentage growth in the number of anglers in the United States between 1960 and 2001 was roughly 85%. The number of swimmers during that same time period more than doubled, showing slow but steady growth that has leveled off at 55% of Americans 12 or older. Participation growth in sailing, a relatively expensive activity, occurred up to the early 1980s then decreased by almost a million participants by 1995. More recently, as with horseback riding and hunting, the number of participants has risen, although the percentage of the population participating has not. Costs for storing and servicing a boat, finding open water for sailing, and having the necessary skills to sail are likely the major reasons for slow growth in this activity.

Canoeing and kayaking are activities done in both quiet, still water and turbulent whitewater. Participation in canoeing and kayaking grew from an estimated 2.6 million in 1960 to approximately 15 million in 1982–1983 (Figure 1.4). The estimated number of participants in 1994–1995 rose to about 17 million. In 1995, the estimated proportion of canoeists and kayakers who used their boats in whitewater was 21.1%. In 2000–2001, nearly 28 million people 12 or older went canoeing or kayaking, representing an impressive increase in the population participating from 8% in 1995 to 12% in 2001.

Figure 1.4 shows that the percentage of the population age 12 and older who participated increased appreciably for the water-based activities of canoeing/kayaking and swimming. The percentage of the population that participated in canoeing/kayaking in 1960 was approximately 2%, a very small segment of the population. In 1960, canoes were made primarily of wood or aluminum. Now, 6 times the 1960 percentage canoe or kayak, and the materials used range from aluminum to fiberglass to carbon fiber. The versatility and resiliency of modern boats have advanced vastly in 43 years. Today's kayaks are made of materials such as crosslinked, linear, or high molecular weight extruded polyethylene (Wipper, 1999).

Swimming, too, has grown in popularity. In 1960 this low-cost, easy-access activity was enjoyed by almost one half of the population age 12 and older. This activity's popularity continued to grow, both as a percentage of the population and in overall numbers of participants. By 1965, the percentage participating in swimming climbed to one half of the population, and almost 72 million 12 or older escaped from the summer's heat by going swimming. By 1983, 53% (just under 100 million people) participated and by 1995, 55% participated. With both a growth of percentage participating and growth of population, by

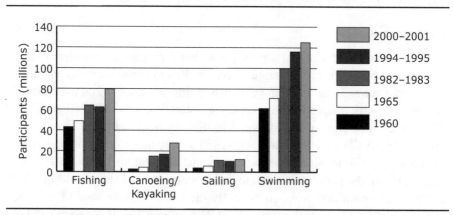

Figure 1.4 Participation in water-based activities listed in each National Recreation Survey, 1960–2001

1995 numbers engaged had risen to over 116 million—almost double the number in 1960.

Currently the proportion of the U.S. population 12 or older who participate in swimming to some extent during any given 12-month period has stabilized at around 55%. The growth of the number in our population who participate has been driven largely by overall population growth, but also by the continuing availability of local outdoor swimming opportunities. For millions of Americans, frequent trips to the pool, lake, or beach has become a ritual of summer. In 1982–1983, 80 million went swimming in a pool and 59 million went swimming in a lake, pond, stream, or ocean—a ratio of 1.36 to 1.00. By 2000–2001, the number of people who went swimming in a pond, lake, river, or ocean (95.7 million) slightly exceed the number who went pool swimming (93.9 million)—trending toward a ratio near 1:1.

In 1960 fishing was one of the more popular of all activities. About 33% of the population reported some form of fishing in 1960, amounting to over 43 million participants. While the number of people who fish has continued to grow, for the most part the percentage who fish has not. In 1960, 33% went fishing; today, the percentage is just barely over 34%. Because proportions of the population who fish have remained at around one third, the numbers of people fishing has risen only modestly. Fishing is done across a number of venues and employs a wide array of equipment. Beach, pier, boat, tournament, trout, salmon, fly, ice, and many other forms of fishing are pursued. While the technology of fishing (e.g., sonic lures, depth finders, powerful bass boats) has advanced, this technology has not seemed to spur participation growth nearly as much as in other activities such as biking and canoeing/kayaking. Currently, 34.7% of the population participates in some form of fishing, amounting to nearly 80 million people. By setting, 10% fish in saltwater, 23% fish in warm freshwater, and 14% fish in cold freshwater. These 3 percentages do not sum to 34.7% because many people do more than 1 type of fishing.

Snow Skiing

In the 1960 and 1965 national surveys, downhill skiing and cross-country skiing were not distinguished as separate activities. Respondents were asked simply if they had snow skied. In the 5 years separating these surveys the estimated percentage participating in snow skiing doubled from 2% to 4% (Figure 1.5). This represented an increase of over 3 million participants from 2.6 to 5.7 million. In the 17 years up to the 1982–1983 survey, the number of skiers rose to almost 17 million—a number 6.5 times that of 1960. In 1982–1983, an estimated 9% of the population participated in some form of skiing—12 million downhill and 6 million cross-country. By the 1994–1995 survey, 11% of the U.S. population age 12 and older—about 22.5 million people—participated in either downhill skiing or cross-country skiing or both. Including snowboarding in the 1994–1995 skiing numbers raises the total number of snow skiers to 25.4 million (12% of the population). These 3 skiing styles do not sum to the total participants because some people participated in more than one. Between 1982–1983 and 1994–1995 there was a 48% increase in the number of downhill skiers and about a 15% increase in cross-country skiers. Snowboarding was not included in the 1982–1983 survey.

By 2001, the NSRE showed that the percentage of Americans age 12 and older who snow skied (not counting snowboarding) stayed essentially the same at approximately 11%. The increase in number of these snow skiers was primarily due to population gains since 1995. The real story from the 2000–2001 NSRE is the rapid growth in snowboarding, which more than doubled from 2.3% participating in 1995 to 4.9% in 2000–2001. With snowboarding included, the percentage who said they did any form of snow skiing increased from 12.1% in 1994–1995 to 14.5% in 2000–2001. This resulted in a 31% gain in all snow skiers between 1995 and 2001—from 25.4 million to 33.3 million. This contrasts with a gain of just 13% between those years if snowboarders are not included. Part of the reason for the substantial increase in snowboarders is that more downhill skiers also participate in snowboarding. In 2001, 20.5% of downhill skiers also went snowboarding compared to 10.5% in 1995. The same is true for cross-country skiers, but to a lesser extent. In 2001, 16.5% also snowboarded compared to 9% in 1995. The percentage who participated in snowboarding but did no other type of snow skiing increased from 1.9% in 1995 to 3.3% in 2001. Further information regarding participation trends in snow- and ice-based activities is provided in Chapter 2.

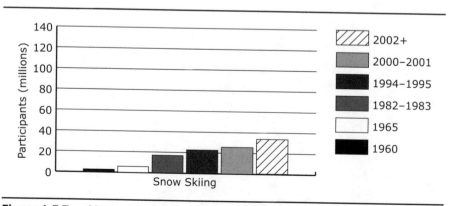

Figure 1.5 Trend in percentage and numbers of people ages 12 and older participating in snow skiing as reported across U.S. National Recreation Surveys, 1960–2001

Chapter 2
Recent Trends—1982 to 2001

As hard as it is for some of us to believe, as of the writing of this chapter it is has been 20 years since interviewing for the 1982–1983 National Recreation Survey (NRS) was conducted. The 1982–1983 NRS was managed by the National Park Service, under the competent leadership of Merle van Horne, formerly with the Heritage Conservation and Recreation Service. Publication of that survey's results marked the close of the highly successful and widely used 5th Nationwide Recreation Survey (U.S. Department of Interior, 1986). Our office, the Forest Service Research Unit in Athens, Georgia, worked closely with Merle, as did a number of other agency representatives to design and implement that national survey. Donald Hodel was Secretary of Interior and William P. Mott was the National Park Service Director.

In 1982 the population of the country was around 232 million, 83% of which was White. Population was growing at about 2.2 million per year. In the NCAA basketball tournament that year, a little known freshman by the name of Michael Jordan led perennial power North Carolina past Georgetown for the national title. In football, legend Paul William (Bear) Bryant stayed unemotional long after the final ceremony, long after his Alabama players had given more than their best and then carried him from the sideline in a tidal wave of victory—The Bear was retiring— It had been a good year and an outstanding career. The year 1982 also turned out to be an exceptionally fine year for wine. A bountiful, and in some places, extraordinary harvest across Europe's major wine producing regions had winemakers, importers, distributors, and consumers optimistic that 1982 would be the 4th exceptional vintage for European wines in just 5 years. In late fall 1982, Mother Nature was throwing a tantrum by dumping rain and snow on the sun-lovers of California, while leaving the ski slopes of New England warm and barren of snow.

In economic developments, steel imports totaled 1.26 million tons in November, an increase of 9% over October. In 1982, foreign steel accounted for almost 24% of the steel supply in the United States and fears were rising over too much dependence on foreign steel. In 1982, General Motors was touting a 10.9% low interest rate program—The company was about to raise rates to a more profitable 11.9% for new car loans. In the stock market, money market mutual funds lost $6.5 billion in assets in a week, but various funds were preparing to fight competition from the newly established money market deposit accounts offered by banks and savings institutions. As mutual funds and CDs fought it out, the government's index of leading economic indicators showed a modest improvement for November, stirring hopes within the Reagan Administration of an economic recovery from the recent recession. At the same time, the Federal Reserve Board was moving to ease monetary strains by lowering interest rates. In 1982 Greenspan's predecessor, Chairman Paul A. Volcker, oversaw cutting the federal funds rate from 12% to 8.5%.

On the international scene, Soviet Union leader Yuri V. Andropov was preparing to meet with President Reagan in an effort to improve Soviet-American relations. According to the Soviet News Agency (Tass) Andropov was looking to reach agreements with the United States at the upcoming Soviet-American nuclear arms talks in Geneva. The Reagan administration, however, indicated that the Soviet Union would have to improve its international behavior and demonstrate good faith in arms control before President Reagan would agree to anything. The Soviet Union was sharply attacking Pope John Paul II, asserting that the Vatican was involved in "subversive" activities in Poland and in anticommunist propaganda. At this time, Iraq was considering restoring diplomatic relations with Egypt after a break of nearly 4 years, provoked by Egypt's signing of a peace treaty with Israel. The world was changing, but the wine was good, Coach Smith was still winning, as was outdoor recreation in the United States.

Highlights

Viewing or photographing birds (i.e., birding) has remained the activity growing fastest in the United States since the early 1980s. The activity has added more than 50 million participants to its 1982–1983 base of 22 million and grew over 231% (Figure 2.1). Following birding was day hiking and backpacking at 193% and 182% growth respectively. Snowmobiling grew 125% in the 19 years between surveys. The 2nd motorized activity in this list of fastest growing activities was driving motorized vehicles off-road, including all-terrain and other 4-wheel drive vehicles. Growing 2nd fastest, but still between 50% and 100% since 1982, were attending outdoor concerts, plays, and other events; walking for pleasure; camping at developed sites; canoeing or kayaking (kayaking is now the fastest short-term growth activity; see Chapter 3); running or jogging; downhill skiing; and swimming in natural waters (e.g., streams, lakes, and oceans). Five of these 7 activities are physically active. Growing at between 25% and 50% were the activities of ice skating, visiting nature centers/museums, picnicking, horseback riding, sightseeing, and driving for pleasure. Most of these activities are relatively passive and are done within the confines of development or vehicles.

Because generally men participate in most activities at higher rates than women, the trends men set tend to have more influence on overall activity trends. Trends in participation in walking for pleasure, running/jogging, driving motor vehicles off-road, primitive camping, backpacking, fishing, and snowmobiling have been greatly influenced by men over the last 19 years. For a few activities, namely horseback riding, pool swimming, fishing, and sailing, the participation trend for women was counter to the overall trend.

Regarding age-related trends, participation by the oldest age group (persons 60 or older) was up for a number of activities, making older Americans the outdoor trendsetters. Regarding race, Whites' trends in participation was a major driver of population-wide trends for most activities. Especially strong contributions by Whites were seen for attending outdoor sporting events, day hiking, viewing/photographing birds, golfing, primitive camping, swimming, motorboating, canoeing/kayaking, and snowmobiling. Blacks contributed especially to the overall trends for attending outdoor concerts and dramas, camping, and hunting. As trends differ by activity across demographic segments of American society, the profile of participants will continue to shift.

Participation Trends

Tables 2.1, 2.2, and 2.3 show 32 activities included in both the 1982–1983 Nationwide Recreation Survey and in that survey's successor, the most current nationwide survey, the National Survey on Recreation and the Environment (NSRE). Activities in Table 2.1 (pp. 40–41) are listed by rate of growth in numbers of people 12 or older participating in them since 1982. Activities in Table 2.2 (pp. 42–43) and Table 2.3 (pp. 44–45) are listed in descending order of percentage of the population who participate in them.

As used here and elsewhere in this book, participation means undertaking an activity at least once in the 12 months prior to a person's being interviewed. To be comparable with the 1982–1983 survey, which interviewed persons 12 or older, the 2000–2001 data, which was from persons 16 or older, had to be adjusted. Table 2.4 (p. 46) displays percentages of activity participants by

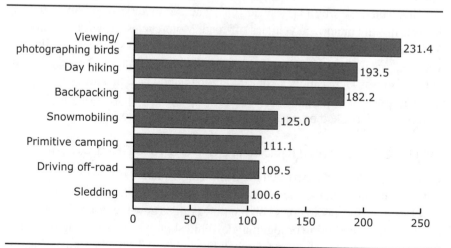

Figure 2.1 Fastest growing activities in the United States since 1982

number of days in the previous 12 months during which respondents to the
1982–1983 and the 2000–2001 surveys participated in the activities listed.

Activities Growing Over 100%

Table 2.1 shows that viewing or photographing birds remained in the top spot
as the activity growing fastest overall since the early 1980s. This was a
prominent finding from the earlier 1994–1995 NSRE in which we found that
number of participants in birding had grown over 240% between 1982–1983
and 1994–1995. Although not as high a percentage as this earlier growth trend,
growth of over 231% from the baseline of 1982–1983 to 2000–2001 is still
nothing short of astounding. As will be seen in the next chapter, this activity
did not grow as fast as a few others in the short term from 1995 to 2001, but
as a long-term trend, this rate of growth was substantially above that for any
other activity. From just about 22 million participants in the early 1980s, the
number of birding participants grew to almost 73 million 12 or older by
2000–2001. Following not far behind birding was day hiking and backpacking
at 194% and 182% growth respectively. While the people adding these activities
to their recreation agendas may not have been highly committed to spending
a lot of time in these activities, these growth rates in number of people participating, nevertheless, represent substantial growth.

Snowmobiling, as 1 of 2 motorized activities growing over 100%, grew at
125% in the 19 years between surveys. From just 3% of the population 12 or
older in 1982–1983 to almost 6% in 2000–2001, this is rapid growth. Demand
for snowmobiling in Yellowstone is a good example of this growth. Following
snowmobiling is primitive camping, which is for the most part, tent camping
that occurs outside of developed campgrounds where facilities and services are
not provided. Over 16% of the population in 2000–2001 participated in this
activity, which grew by 111% since 1982. The 2nd motorized activity in this top
list was driving motorized vehicles off-road. Motorcycles, all-terrain vehicles,
and other 4-wheel drive vehicles, including pickup trucks and sport utility
vehicles, are included in this growth. (Growing use of motorized vehicles on
natural lands is increasingly a concern among public land managers.) Sledding
grew at just over 100%, attesting to the influence that the growing number of
sled designs have had on participation in this traditional winter activity.

Activities Growing Between 50% and 100%

Growing 2nd fastest at between 50% and 100% since 1982 were attending
outdoor concerts, plays, and other events; walking for pleasure; camping in
developed sites; canoeing or kayaking (kayaking is now the fastest short-term
growth activity); running or jogging; downhill skiing; and swimming in natural
waters (e.g., streams, lakes, and oceans). Five of these 7 activities are physically
active, a good thing given recent reports of obesity among Americans. The

market for downhill skiing has been sluggish in recent years, but apparently in the longer term, is growing substantially.

Rounding out the list of 2nd fastest growing activities are golfing at 65%, motorboating at 62%, attending outdoor sports events at 55%, bicycling (all forms) at 53%, and cross-country skiing at 50%. Golf continues to grow and is particularly popular with retirees. Attending college, professional, and amateur sporting events such as baseball has been growing faster than population growth. The same is true for bicycling, where technology has played a heavy hand in the popularity and growth of the activity.

Activities Growing Between 25% and 50%

Six of the activities in Table 2.1 have grown between 25% and 50%. They include ice skating, visiting nature centers/museums, picnicking, horseback riding, sightseeing, and driving for pleasure. Most of these activities are relatively passive, except for ice skating, and most are done within the confines of development or vehicles. Percentage growth of these activities is nowhere near those covered in the preceding sections. However, 4 of these activities—visiting nature centers and museums, picnicking, sightseeing, and driving for pleasure—have a large participant base at almost 50% of the population 12 and older. Thus, even modest percentage increases in participation represent many millions of additional persons participating in these activities, each of which has grown by about 1.8 million participants per year.

Activities Growing Slowest

At the bottom of Table 2.1 are playing outdoor team sports, fishing, outdoor pool swimming, hunting, waterskiing, sailing, and tennis. In previous surveys, hunting had actually been decreasing and has only recently begun to rise again, probably due to the healthy economy of the late 1990s. Waterskiing is being replaced by jetskiing, which is growing rapidly. Tennis is waning, but tends to be cyclical.

Trends by Sex, Age, Race, and Region of Residence

Table 2.2 shows trends in percentages of men and women, and persons in different age groups, participating in land, water, and snow/ice activities in 2000–2001, with comparable percentages for 1982–1983 in parentheses. Because generally men participate in most activities at higher rates than women, the trends men set tend to have more influence on the overall trend in any given activity. For example, in Table 2.2, the trend in walking for pleasure, running/jogging, driving motor vehicles off-road, primitive camping, backpacking, fishing, and snowmobiling was greatly influenced by the trend in men's participation. While women's participation percentages tended to follow the same upward or downward trend as men's, in a few instances, namely horseback

Table 2.1 Trends in estimated percentages and numbers of persons age 12 and older who participated 1 or more times in the last 12 months by activity, 1982–1983 and 2000–2001

Activity	Percent Participating 1982–1983	Millions Participating 1982–1983	Percent Participating 2000–2001	Millions Participating 2000–2001	Percent change 1982–1983 to 2000–2001
Viewing/photographing birds	12	22	31.8	72.9	231.4
Day hiking	14	26	33.3	76.3	193.5
Backpacking	5	9	11.1	25.4	182.2
Snowmobiling	3	6	5.9	13.5	125.0
Primitive camping	10	18	16.6	38.0	111.1
Driving off-road	11	20	18.3	41.9	109.5
Sledding	10	18	15.7	36.1	100.6
Outdoor concerts	25	48	40.7	93.4	94.6
Walking for pleasure	53	100	83.1	190.5	90.5
Developed camping	17	33	26.8	61.5	86.4
Canoeing or kayaking	8	15	12.1	27.7	84.7
Running or jogging	26	49	37.3	85.5	74.5
Downhill skiing	6	12	9.1	20.8	73.3
Swimming in natural water	32	59	42.8	98.0	66.1
Golfing	13	24	17.2	39.5	64.6
Motorboating	19	35	24.8	56.8	62.3
Attending sports events	40	75	50.7	116.3	55.1
Bicycling	32	61	40.7	93.3	53.0
Cross-country skiing	3	6	3.9	9.0	50.0
Ice skating	6	12	7.7	17.6	46.7
Visiting nature centers or museums	50	95	57.1	130.9	37.8
Picnicking	48	90	53.9	123.6	37.3
Horseback riding	9	17	10.2	23.3	37.1
Sightseeing	46	86	51.4	117.7	36.9
Driving for pleasure	48	90	51.0	116.8	29.8
Outdoor team sports	24	45	24.5	56.2	24.9

Table 2.1 Trends in estimated percentages and numbers of persons age 12 and older who participated 1 or more times in the last 12 months by activity, 1982–1983 and 2000–2001 *continued*

Activity	Percent Participating 1982–1983	Millions Participating 1982–1983	Percent Participating 2000–2001	Millions Participating 2000–2001	Percent change 1982–1983 to 2000–2001
Fishing	34	64	34.7	79.6	24.4
Outdoor pool swimming	43	80	42.6	97.6	22.0
Hunting	12	22	11.6	26.6	20.9
Waterskiing	9	17	8.8	20.2	18.8
Sailing	6	11	5.3	12.1	10.0
Tennis outdoors	17	32	12.7	29.1	-9.1

Note: Based on 229 million people age 12 and older in 2001 (U.S. Bureau of the Census, 2000) and 188 million people age 12 and older in 1983 (U.S. Department of the Interior, 1986).

Table 2.2 Estimated percentages of persons 12 or older who participated 1 or more times in the last 12 months by activity, gender, and age, 2000–2001 and 1982–1983 (in parentheses)

Activity	Population	Male	Female	Ages 12–24	Ages 25–39	Ages 40–59	Ages 60+
Land Activities							
Walking for pleasure	83.1 (53)	79.8 (45)	86.0 (61)	84.7 (57)	83.8 (58)	84.6 (53)	78.8 (42)
Visiting nature centers/museums	57.1 (50)	57.7 (50)	56.6 (51)	57.1 (65)	66.9 (62)	60.1 (41)	39.8 (26)
Picnicking	53.9 (48)	51.2 (45)	56.4 (51)	46.1 (52)	60.8 (59)	59.6 (46)	46.0 (29)
Sightseeing	51.4 (46)	49.7 (45)	53.0 (46)	45.4 (46)	53.9 (54)	56.7 (47)	46.7 (31)
Driving for pleasure	51.0 (48)	51.1 (47)	51.0 (49)	47.8 (48)	53.1 (59)	55.7 (46)	43.7 (35)
Attending outdoor sports	50.7 (40)	56.0 (44)	46.1 (36)	62.7 (55)	53.6 (44)	49.1 (36)	35.9 (16)
Attending outdoor concerts	40.7 (25)	40.6 (25)	40.7 (26)	53.7 (34)	39.4 (29)	38.8 (22)	30.6 (12)
Bicycling	40.7 (32)	45.3 (33)	36.5 (32)	56.9 (55)	46.9 (37)	37.3 (22)	19.1 (7)
Running or jogging	37.3 (26)	44.7 (30)	30.6 (23)	73.9 (51)	38.1 (31)	23.4 (13)	12.3 (2)
Day hiking	33.3 (14)	37.0 (15)	29.9 (13)	33.8 (19)	40.3 (17)	35.5 (12)	19.2 (5)
Viewing/photographing birds	31.8 (12)	29.3 (11)	34.1 (12)	24.1 (10)	30.1 (12)	38.4 (12)	35.6 (13)
Developed camping	26.8 (17)	28.7 (18)	25.1 (16)	32.7 (24)	31.1 (22)	27.1 (15)	14.3 (5)
Outdoor team sports	24.5 (24)	33.0 (30)	17.0 (18)	49.8 (50)	27.0 (26)	15.4 (11)	4.7 (2)
Driving off-road	18.3 (11)	23.2 (14)	13.8 (8)	28.9 (20)	20.9 (11)	15.1 (6)	6.3 (2)
Golfing	17.2 (13)	25.3 (20)	9.8 (7)	22.3 (16)	18.7 (13)	16.3 (13)	10.2 (7)
Primitive camping	16.6 (10)	22.0 (11)	11.7 (8)	24.2 (17)	18.6 (11)	15.1 (6)	6.0 (2)
Tennis outdoors	12.7 (17)	13.9 (18)	11.7 (16)	28.1 (32)	11.7 (20)	7.4 (10)	2.9 (1)
Hunting	11.6 (12)	20.3 (22)	3.7 (3)	15.3 (15)	12.3 (13)	11.3 (13)	6.8 (5)
Backpacking	11.1 (5)	14.6 (6)	7.9 (3)	16.4 (9)	13.8 (5)	9.7 (2)	2.5 (*)
Horseback riding	10.2 (9)	10.6 (8)	9.8 (10)	16.3 (18)	11.6 (10)	9.1 (5)	2.7 (1)

* indicates less than one half of 1%

Note: Numbers from 1982–1983 source report were reported in integers only.

Table 2.2 Estimated percentages of persons 12 or older who participated 1 or more times in the last 12 months by activity, gender, and age, 2000–2001 and 1982–1983 (in parentheses) *continued*

Activity	Population	Male	Female	Ages 12–24	Ages 25–39	Ages 40–59	Ages 60+
Water Activities							
Swimming in natural waters	42.8 (32)	45.5 (34)	40.5 (30)	56.4 (49)	50.1 (40)	41.7 (21)	17.8 (7)
Outdoor pool swimming	42.6 (43)	41.0 (43)	44.0 (42)	63.5 (67)	48.5 (49)	37.0 (33)	18.0 (11)
Fishing	34.7 (34)	45.1 (47)	25.4 (23)	42.4 (43)	37.6 (40)	34.9 (31)	22.1 (17)
Motorboating	24.8 (19)	29.4 (22)	20.7 (16)	29.6 (25)	27.8 (23)	24.9 (17)	14.5 (7)
Canoeing or kayaking	12.1 (8)	14.6 (10)	9.9 (7)	19.2 (14)	12.9 (9)	11.2 (6)	3.8 (1)
Waterskiing	8.8 (9)	11.1 (11)	6.8 (7)	17.7 (17)	10.1 (12)	5.6 (4)	0.8 (*)
Sailing	5.3 (6)	5.5 (7)	5.2 (5)	7.6 (9)	5.3 (7)	5.2 (5)	2.8 (2)
Snow and Ice Activities							
Sledding	15.7 (10)	16.6 (12)	14.8 (9)	30.5 (22)	19.7 (11)	10.9 (5)	2.3 (*)
Downhill skiing	9.1 (6)	11.1 (8)	7.3 (5)	16.1 (12)	10.6 (8)	7.0 (3)	1.3 (1)
Ice skating	7.7 (6)	7.6 (6)	7.7 (6)	18.2 (15)	8.2 (6)	4.4 (3)	0.6 (*)
Snowmobiling	5.9 (3)	7.6 (4)	4.5 (2)	10.5 (6)	6.8 (3)	4.3 (2)	1.3 (*)
Cross-country skiing	3.9 (3)	4.3 (4)	3.6 (3)	5.3 (5)	3.9 (4)	4.7 (3)	1.4 (*)

* indicates less than one half of 1%
Note: Numbers from 1982–1983 source report were reported in integers only.

Table 2.3 Estimated percentages of persons 12 or older who participated 1 or more times in the last 12 months by activity, race, and census region, 2000–2001 and 1982–1983 (in parentheses)

Activity	Population	White, non-Hispanic	Black, non-Hispanic	Northeast	Midwest	South	West
Land Activities							
Walking for pleasure	83.1 (53)	85.9 (54)	83.1 (49)	86.4 (54)	84.5 (59)	81.5 (49)	81.5 (52)
Visiting nature centers or museums	57.1 (50)	61.3 (51)	41.6 (40)	57.2 (48)	61.2 (57)	53.4 (44)	58.8 (55)
Picnicking	53.9 (48)	56.5 (49)	46.6 (42)	54.5 (45)	56.4 (56)	49.5 (40)	57.4 (55)
Sightseeing	51.4 (46)	57.2 (47)	43.7 (36)	51.7 (44)	52.3 (50)	50.6 (41)	51.4 (49)
Driving for pleasure	51.0 (48)	57.7 (50)	40.2 (35)	51.2 (45)	53.4 (54)	50.1 (43)	50.0 (53)
Attending outdoor sports	50.7 (40)	56.7 (41)	43.1 (33)	47.8 (35)	58.7 (44)	49.2 (37)	48.2 (42)
Attending outdoor concerts	40.7 (25)	43.9 (26)	41.3 (21)	45.7 (28)	43.5 (26)	36.8 (20)	39.6 (31)
Bicycling	40.7 (32)	42.5 (33)	35.9 (29)	43.2 (34)	44.4 (38)	35.7 (27)	42.8 (31)
Running or jogging	37.3 (26)	35.7 (26)	43.4 (30)	35.7 (25)	36.8 (24)	37.5 (26)	38.8 (31)
Day hiking	33.3 (14)	34.5 (15)	10.5 (3)	32.6 (13)	30.2 (15)	26.8 (9)	45.8 (23)
Viewing/photographing birds	31.8 (12)	36.1 (13)	20.1 (5)	34.5 (12)	34.3 (15)	29.9 (8)	30.1 (12)
Developed camping	26.8 (17)	30.8 (19)	13.7 (4)	23.2 (13)	29.9 (19)	22.0 (14)	33.4 (25)
Outdoor team sports	24.5 (24)	22.9 (23)	27.9 (27)	24.2 (22)	24.4 (26)	24.7 (24)	24.8 (23)
Driving off-road	18.3 (11)	21.0 (12)	11.2 (3)	15.2 (9)	17.8 (12)	18.0 (9)	21.4 (14)
Golfing	17.2 (13)	20.9 (14)	6.8 (3)	15.5 (14)	23.7 (17)	14.2 (9)	16.8 (14)
Primitive camping	16.6 (10)	20.1 (11)	5.4 (2)	13.2 (7)	16.2 (10)	13.6 (7)	24.0 (16)
Tennis outdoors	12.7 (17)	12.7 (17)	11.0 (13)	16.2 (16)	12.5 (17)	11.5 (16)	11.9 (19)
Hunting	11.6 (12)	14.6 (12)	4.7 (7)	8.0 (9)	14.5 (13)	12.6 (15)	10.4 (9)
Backpacking	11.1 (5)	12.7 (5)	3.4 (1)	12.2 (5)	9.0 (3)	7.7 (3)	16.9 (9)
Horseback riding	10.2 (9)	11.7 (10)	5.3 (4)	7.8 (7)	10.6 (10)	10.3 (8)	11.5 (13)

* indicates less than one half of 1%

Note: Numbers from 1982–1983 source report were reported in integers only.

Table 2.3 Estimated percentages of persons 12 or older who participated 1 or more times in the last 12 months by activity, race, and census region, 2000–2001 and 1982–1983 (in parentheses) *continued*

Activity	Population	White, non-Hispanic	Black, non-Hispanic	Northeast	Midwest	South	West
Water Activities							
Swimming in natural waters	42.8 (32)	50.5 (34)	19.8 (11)	50.6 (36)	42.7 (33)	40.6 (30)	40.1 (27)
Outdoor pool swimming	42.6 (43)	48.6 (45)	30.2 (27)	46.7 (48)	41.8 (40)	43.8 (40)	38.5 (44)
Fishing	34.7 (34)	39.3 (35)	26.6 (27)	28.6 (25)	37.7 (37)	37.9 (39)	32.2 (32)
Motorboating	24.8 (19)	31.2 (21)	8.4 (3)	22.6 (15)	30.5 (24)	24.6 (18)	21.8 (18)
Canoeing or kayaking	12.1 (8)	15.3 (9)	3.6 (1)	16.1 (12)	15.5 (11)	9.6 (5)	9.7 (6)
Waterskiing	8.8 (9)	11.3 (11)	2.5 (*)	5.9 (7)	11.3 (10)	8.6 (10)	9.3 (9)
Sailing	5.3 (6)	6.3 (7)	3.0 (1)	8.1 (8)	4.7 (6)	4.5 (4)	5.0 (7)
Snow and Ice Activities							
Sledding	15.7 (10)	20.7 (12)	6.4 (2)	22.9 (15)	26.7 (13)	8.0 (6)	11.1 (9)
Downhill skiing	9.1 (6)	11.1 (7)	3.0 (*)	12.1 (9)	9.6 (5)	5.6 (3)	11.7 (12)
Ice skating	7.7 (6)	8.3 (7)	6.5 (1)	12.9 (11)	10.8 (8)	4.2 (3)	5.6 (5)
Snowmobiling	5.9 (3)	7.7 (3)	1.7 (*)	7.9 (5)	10.7 (6)	1.9 (*)	6.0 (2)
Cross-country skiing	3.9 (3)	4.9 (4)	1.0 (*)	6.2 (4)	5.5 (5)	1.3 (*)	4.5 (5)

* indicates less than one half of 1%
Note: Numbers from 1982–1983 source report were reported in integers only.

Table 2.4 Percentage of persons 12 or older participating in the last 12 months by activity and number of days of participation, 2000–2001 and 1982–1983 (in parentheses)[1]

Activity	1 to 2 Days	3 to 10 Days	11 to 25 Days	25+ Days
Land Activities				
Horseback riding	45.3 (47)	30.1 (27)	8.5 (8)	16.0 (17)
Backpacking	31.5 (39)	48.9 (47)	13.4 (9)	6.2 (6)
Primitive camping	31.0 (36)	49.5 (47)	13.1 (12)	6.4 (6)
Developed camping	27.6 (26)	53.6 (51)	13.2 (16)	5.7 (7)
Motorboating	27.5 (33)	42.9 (39)	16.5 (17)	13.1 (12)
Driving off-road	23.6 (23)	38.2 (39)	17.9 (21)	20.3 (17)
Viewing/photographing birds	20.9 (15)	32.2 (29)	11.8 (14)	35.2 (42)
Fishing	20.4 (21)	40.4 (43)	20.0 (21)	19.2 (15)
Day hiking	19.4 (28)	39.3 (47)	16.7 (14)	24.5 (12)
Hunting	14.7 (19)	40.2 (42)	25.7 (22)	19.5 (17)
Mountain biking	14.6 (12)[2]	35.5 (32)	19.7 (19)	30.2 (38)
Water Activities				
Sailing	46.8 (56)	38.1 (30)	9.0 (6)	6.2 (8)
Canoeing or kayaking	46.1 (51)	40.6 (39)	8.5 (8)	4.8 (3)
Swimming in natural water	18.0 (19)	48.3 (42)	19.5 (20)	14.2 (19)
Outdoor pool swimming	12.7 (14)	41.0 (38)	19.9 (19)	26.4 (29)
Snow and Ice Activities				
Snowmobiling	40.3 (40)	37.5 (36)	11.3 (14)	10.8 (10)
Cross-country skiing	39.0 (51)	46.1 (35)	10.0 (10)	4.9 (4)
Downhill skiing	33.5 (34)	47.1 (44)	14.8 (16)	4.6 (7)

[1] Data from NSRE 2000–2001 is for respondents ages 16 and older. The process used to convert participation rates for the total sample to ages 12 and older was not practical to do for each demographic subgroup.
[2] Bicycling days are not directly comparable. NSRE 2000–2001 refers to mountain biking only and 1982–1983 NRS refers to all bicycling.

riding, pool swimming, fishing, and sailing, women's participation trend was counter to the overall trend.

The pattern of age group participation trends was also interesting. As seen in Table 2.2, generally participation by the oldest age group (persons 60 or older) was strongly up, contributing significantly to the overall trend. This pattern was similar for the next age group, persons 40 to 59. For walking, visiting nature centers/museums, picnicking, sightseeing, attending outdoor sports and concert events, day hiking, camping, off-road driving, backpacking, and swimming, the older age groups strongly contributed to the trend shown in the overall population. For younger age groups, generally the reverse is evident. Participation for persons 12 to 24 have trended modestly with or counter to the overall trend. While population-wide participation in visiting nature centers, picnicking, horseback riding, and fishing are substantially up, the trend for persons 12 to 24 is down. Over a number of years, different trends by sex and age will have highly significant effects on the overall profile of participants in different activities. For example, the profile of participants in driving motor vehicles off-road is shifting toward greater proportions of older males.

For the 1982–1983 survey, the only racial groupings were White and Black. Asians and Hispanics were not shown separately for that survey's report. In Table 2.3, trends for Whites and Blacks are shown. Generally, being the most numerous as participants in the activities listed, Whites' trends in participation was the major driver of overall activity trends. Especially strong contributions by Whites to activity trends can be seen for attending outdoor sporting events, day hiking, viewing/photographing birds, golfing, primitive camping, swimming, motorboating, canoeing/kayaking and snowmobiling. Blacks contributed especially to the overall trends for attending outdoor concerts and dramas, developed and primitive camping, and hunting. Trends for Blacks ran counter to overall activity trends for pool swimming, fishing, waterskiing, and sailing.

Regional trends, as a contribution to national trends, can also be seen in Table 2.3. Generally, direction and magnitude of regional trends were consistent with the overall national trend. For a number of activities, however, the South contributed strongly. These included visiting nature centers and museums, picnicking, sightseeing, driving for pleasure, birdwatching, and driving off-road. On the other hand, the South's trends ran counter to national activity trends for outdoor pool swimming and sailing. Trends in the West generally were also consistent with the overall national trend. Especially strong contributions to the national trends were evident in the West, however, for bicycling, day hiking, tennis (trending downward), backpacking, swimming, and sailing (also trending downward). Notable counter trends in the West including both downhill and cross-country skiing and horseback riding. The Northeast contributed especially to birding, attending outdoor concerts, swimming, and motorboating growth.

Trends in Days per Year

For some of the activities in Tables 2.1 through 2.3, days of participation were asked in both 1982–1983 and 2000–2001. These activities are listed in Table 2.4 along with percentages of participants by number of days per year on which participation occurred. Trends in days of participation per year are important because they reflect the overall quantity of an activity in demand by the recreating public. A day of participation as we have defined it does not mean spending all day doing an activity; rather, it means the activity was undertaken for any amount of time during a single day. Other activities also could have been undertaken on that same day. Thus, activity days are not additive across activities, except as an index.

As a general observation, distributions of participants (percentages) by number of days per year across the activities listed have changed little since 1982. The 2000–2001 percentages are shown first in Table 2.4 with the 1982–1983 percentages following in parentheses. Exceptions to this general observation representing increasing days of participation include backpacking, day hiking, sailing, and cross-country skiing. For backpacking, the shift has been to fewer participants spending just 1 to 2 days to more spending 11 to 25 days. For day hiking, the shift has been from a sizeable percentage of participants spending just 1 to 2 days per year to more who spend over 25 days per year. For sailing and cross-country skiing, the shift has been from more participants putting in just 1 to 2 days to more putting in 3 to 10 days.

Activities where the shift was from more to fewer days per participant per year include birdwatching, bicycling, and swimming in natural bodies of water. For birding, the shift was from a sizeable percentage of participants spending more than 25 days per year in the activity to a larger percentage spending just 1 to 2 days, representing a large influx of novice birders. For bicycling, the shift was from approximately 38% spending more than 25 days participating to more participants spending fewer days across the lesser 3 categories of days per year. For swimming in natural water bodies, the shift has been from swimming on more than 25 days to more people who swim 3 to 10 days per year.

Chapter 3
Current Trends—1994 to 2001

In 1994 the 6th of this nation's outdoor recreation surveys began. That year, as did all the years of the 1990s, gave witness to numerous events and changes—both good and bad—around the world and in the United States. For example, as 1994 drew to a close, the United States and North Korea signed the Geneva Accord, which directly aided the release of U.S. Army aviator Bobby Hall from captivity. A Sri Lankan mother, Chandraki Kumaratunga, joined the ranks of the few female prime ministers in the world. In the wake of the signing of the Jordan-Israel peace treaty, his Holiness the Dalai Lama called for peace at the World Peace Summit in Spain. Meanwhile, Russia continued to oppose Chechen rebels in their ongoing war for independence. In a different battle, although in many ways a much bigger one, President Clinton declared December 1st World AIDS Day, an initiative to reenergize the ongoing fight against HIV and AIDS.

Closer to home, and on a lighter note, fans of the National Hockey League sighed in relief as the player lockout ended, while University of Arkansas basketball fans cheered as their team beat perennial power Duke in the NCAA championship. As 1996 ended, America was still basking in the glory of another special event, one that had occurred earlier that summer. Atlanta hosted the 1996 Olympic games and Athens played host to the Olympic women's soccer event. Using the University of Georgia's sports facilities, thousands of soccer fans from around the world descended on Athens and, without incident, watched the U.S. women's team take the Gold in a final match with China.

These were but a few of the happenings of the 1990s—a truly incredible decade. Massive economic growth, population growth, unprecedented immigration, and widespread land development marked an astonishing decade of social and environmental change in the United States. The 1990s also saw tremendous growth and diversification in Americans' outdoor recreation participation. This chapter looks at this growth. The focus is on trends in outdoor recreation participation since the earlier application of the National Survey on Recreation and the Environment in 1994–1995. Having a good feel for these trends is necessary for sound decision making as a provider of outdoor opportunities, whether public or private. It is also just simply interesting.

As administered in both 1994–1995 and 2000–2001, applications of the National Survey on Recreation and the Environment were designed to be directly comparable. In planning the 2000–2001 survey, every effort was made to maintain the definitions, sampling designs, interviewing protocols, and analytical approaches implemented in 1994–1995. Weighting the resulting data to correct for nonresponse or sampling biases was highly similar. This chapter shows trends since that previous NSRE in 1994–1995. Those earlier NSRE results were published in Outdoor Recreation in American Life (Cordell et al., 1999).

Highlights

The most popular activities in 2000–2001 (those having the most participants) included walking for pleasure, outdoor family gatherings, and visiting nature centers, museums or zoos.

Walking and family gatherings were also the top two activities in 1994–1995 with sightseeing in third place. (Visiting a beach was another popular activity in both surveys, but because of a difference in the question wording it is not directly comparable and does not appear in this chapter.) A sizable difference between these two periods in our history, however, is the percentage and sheer numbers of people participating in the top activities. For example, walking had a 67% participation rate (percentage participating) in 1994–1995. By 2000–2001 that rate had climbed to 83%. Visiting nature centers, museums, zoos, and similar "learning sites" also showed an increase in percentage of persons 16 or older participating, as did other activities. Comparing relative rankings of popularity of activities among males shows that visiting nature centers rose from 4th in 1994–1995 to 3rd in 2000–2001, attending outdoor spectator sports events went from 5th to 4th, and picnicking from 6th to 5th. Viewing wildlife and bicycling joined the top 10 list for males for the first time, while pool swimming dropped off men's list. Picnicking and attending sports events both climbed the females' list. Similar to males, viewing wildlife appeared in the female top 10 activities for the first time.

Looking at race and ethnicity, visiting nature centers, museums or zoos moved up slightly in popularity for White and Hispanics. Walking and family gatherings reversed spots for Blacks, and the biggest change for Asians/Pacific Islanders was the rise in picnicking 2 spots to 3rd place. The rise in the popularity of viewing wildlife, from 12th overall in 1994–1995 to 8th in 2000–2001, was mostly the result of a rise in interest among Whites. Between urban and rural residents, there were many more similarities than differences with a few exceptions. Visiting nature centers, zoos, or museums rose as a more popular activity among urban dwellers compared to a decline in position for rural dwellers.

In addition to speculation about the "vast differences" between urban and rural people's outdoor recreation, we also hear about differences in lifestyles, politics, cultural values, and recreation choices between different regions of the country. But when examined, it was found that people across the 9 divisions delineated by the Bureau of Census differed little in what they chose as their most popular outdoor recreation activities. The differences that did appear were in rates of growth in activity participation. The slowest growth occurred in the aging band of central states, particularly among those in the East North

Central, West South Central, and East South Central regions. Growth was vigorous in both Mountain and Pacific Coast states, as it was in the New England and South Atlantic states.

Examining growth by activity revealed a remarkable story for outdoor recreation in America. Of the 61 activities examined, many at the top of the list when ranked by percentage growth from 1994–1995 to 2000–2001 are physically demanding. They reflect a continuing shift in the mix of activities people are turning to in the United States. In all likelihood, these activities also reflect a change in the composition of the people participating in outdoor activities. Physically challenging sports, such as kayaking, snowboarding, backpacking, and mountain climbing, typically require specialized equipment and skills that not everyone possesses. Together with larger numbers of people participating in outdoor activities, this means very noticeable differences between what one would have witnessed at a "typical" outdoor area in earlier times versus now. Numbers, types of clothing and equipment, and participation styles have changed dramatically. While many of the activities at or near the top of this list do not represent large numbers of added people (e.g., kayaking participation increased by just 4.8 million between 1994 and 2001), others not much further down the list have increased more substantially in numbers. The number of people reporting viewing/photographing wildlife, for example, has risen by over 34 million, viewing/photographing fish has risen by 26 million, and viewing/photographing birds has increased by around 16 million. The sections that follow examine trends in activity participation since 1994 in detail.

Top 10 Most Popular Activities 1994 to 2001

One way of looking at participation trends is to examine time-series data for shifts in the order or popularity of activities when ranked from highest to lowest by rate of participation. In Table 3.1 (p. 52) the 10 activities with the highest participation rates in 2000–2001 are listed from 1st (the highest percentage of population participating) to 10th highest. Walking for pleasure and outdoor family gatherings top the list as they did in 1994–1995. A difference between then and now, however, is the percentage of the population participating in, for example, walking and family gatherings. Walking went from an approximate 67% participation rate in 1994–1995 to an 83% participation rate in 2000–2001. This growth is highly significant considering not only that the percentage of persons 16 or older participating increased but also that the population to which that percentage applies increased. Family gatherings went from about 62% to nearly 74%. This too is highly significant growth.

Visiting nature centers, zoos, museums, and similar learning sites rose from 4th to 3rd most popular in the last few years. It also showed a roughly 4% gain in participation rate. These changes reflect a trend in public interest in activities that focus on viewing and learning about nature and culture. This trend is

Table 3.1 Ten most popular activities in 2000–2001 and popularity ranking in 1994–1995

Activities	% of Population 16+ Participating (2000–2001)	Rank of Popularity (1994–1995)	% of Population (1994–1995)
Walking for pleasure	83.0	1	66.7
Family gatherings	73.5	2	61.8
Visiting nature centers	57.1	4	53.4
Picnicking	54.5	5	49.1
Sightseeing	51.8	3	56.6
Attending outdoor sports events	49.9	6	47.5
Visiting historic sites	46.2	8	44.1
Viewing/photographing wildlife	44.7	12	31.2
Swimming (lakes, streams)	41.8	9	39.0
Swimming (outdoor pools)	41.0	7	44.2

substantiated by the rise of wildlife viewing from not being in the list of the top 10 in 1994–1995 to a rank of number 8 in 2000–2001. This ranking is the result of a rise in participation from around 31% in 1994–1995 to almost 45% in 2000–2001. Swimming in outdoor pools dropped from 7th place in 1994–1995 to 10th in 2000–2001. Swimming in natural water, however, remained constant on the list of most popular activities at number 9.

Picnicking rose slightly from 5th to 4th in 2000–2001, but sightseeing, which had been at number 3, ended up as number 5. The percentage of people reporting participation in sightseeing dropped from nearly 57% in 1994–1995 to just under 52% in 2000–2001. Visiting historic sites stayed at number 7 with participation increasing slightly from 44% to 46%. Attending outdoor sports events also kept its same position (6th) and likewise added over 2 percentage points to its participation rate.

Shifts in Most Popular Activities by Demographic Group

Males

Table 3.2 lists the 10 most popular activities for males in 1994–1995 and in 2000–2001. The most important comparisons in this table are the relative positions of activities from 1 through 10 between time periods. Comparing relative positions of activities for males shows that visiting nature centers (shifting from 4 to 3), attending outdoor spectator sports events (5 to 4), picnicking (6 to 5), and viewing wildlife and bicycling (which joined the top 10 list) each rose in popularity. Falling from their former relative levels of popularity for males were sightseeing, swimming in outdoor pools, and yard games. Activities for which the participation rates rose the most included walking (65% to almost 80%), bicycling (31% to 44%), and attending family gatherings (64% to 73%).

Females

Table 3.2 also lists the 10 most popular activities for females in 1994–1995 and in 2000–2001. Walking and attending outdoor family gatherings were number 1 and number 2, respectively, in both time periods. Picnicking rose from number 5 to number 3 for females while yard games dropped off the list (as was the case for males). Other activities rising on the list of females' most popular activities were attending outdoor spectator sports events (8 to 6) and viewing wildlife (debuting at number 8). Activities falling to lower levels on the list include sightseeing (3 to 5) and swimming in outdoor pools (6 to 9). Activities for which participation rates rose the most included walking (68% to 86%), attending outdoor family gatherings (60% to 74%), and picnicking (51% to 57%). Participation rates for sightseeing and swimming in pools fell between 1994 and 2001.

Table 3.2 Ten most popular activities and participation rates, males and females, 1994–1995 and 2000–2001 (with abbreviated activity names)

Males

1994–1995		2000–2001	
Walking	65.0	Walking	79.7
Family gathering	63.7	Family gathering	72.7
Sightseeing	57.7	Nature centers	57.7
Nature centers	54.5	Sports events	55.1
Sports events	53.6	Picnicking	51.8
Picnicking	47.1	Sightseeing	50.1
Historic sites	46.0	Historic sites	48.0
Swimming (pools)	45.5	View wildlife	45.7
Swimming (lakes)	42.7	Swimming (lakes)	44.3
Yard games	40.9	Bicycling	44.0

Females

1994–1995		2000–2001	
Walking	68.3	Walking	85.9
Family gathering	60.0	Family gathering	74.2
Sightseeing	55.6	Picnicking	57.0
Nature centers	52.5	Nature centers	56.6
Picnicking	50.8	Sightseeing	53.4
Swimming (pools)	42.9	Sports events	45.4
Historic sites	42.5	Historic sites	44.6
Sports events	41.9	View wildlife	43.8
Swimming (lakes)	35.6	Swimming (pools)	42.3
Yard games	32.8	Swimming (lakes)	39.8

Race

Racial diversity in this country continues its trend toward a smaller proportion of non-Hispanic Whites relative to proportions of other races or ethnic origins. In Table 3.3 rankings of the top 10 activities in 2000–2001 are listed for each of 4 major racial/ethnic groups in this country (i.e., White, Black, Hispanic, and Asian/Pacific Islander) for the periods 1994–1995 and 2000–2001. The list of activities in the 1st column is ordered top to bottom in order of popularity for the entire population of persons 16 or older.

Starting with the most popular activity, walking for pleasure, it is obvious that this activity is popular broadly and that in 2000–2001 it is the top listed activity for all races. This represents a very slight shift from 1994–1995 when walking trailed family gatherings by less than 1.0 percentage point for Blacks. Family gatherings is the 2nd most popular activity across the board in 2000–2001. Visiting nature centers rose in popularity for Whites and Hispanics going from 4th most popular in 1994–1995 to 3rd in 2000–2001 for both groups. For Blacks, this activity declined from 5th to 6th.

Picnicking, for the most part, occupies the middle tier of most popular activities, as does sightseeing and attending outdoor spectator sports. Picnicking moved up the list for Blacks and Asians, while sightseeing moved down the list across the board. Attending outdoor sports declined in popularity for Hispanics and has remained at a relatively low level for Asian/Pacific Islanders.

Visiting nature centers, museums, or zoos moved up for both Whites and Hispanics. Viewing wildlife is another learning-oriented activity that showed gains between the two surveys. Both of these activities represent interest in seeing and learning about nature and wildlife. But as can be seen in Table 3.3,

Table 3.3 Ten most popular activities by racial/ethnic group, 1994–1995 and 2000–2001

Ten Most Popular Activities for Total U.S. Population	Racial/Ethnic Group			
	White, Non-Hispanic	Black, Non-Hispanic	Hispanic	Asian/Pacific Islander
	Activity's Popularity Ranking (1994–1995/2000–2001)			
Walking	1/1	2/1	1/1	1/1
Family gatherings	2/2	1/2	2/2	2/2
Nature centers	4/3	5/6	4/3	4/4
Picnicking	5/5	4/3	3/4	5/3
Sightseeing	3/4	3/4	6/9	3/5
Sports events	6/6	6/5	5/8	7/7
Historic sites	8/8	8/9	9/10	6/6
Viewing wildlife	–[1]/7	–/–	–/–	–/–
Swimming (lakes)	9/9	–/–	9/–	10/10
Swimming (pools)	7/–	10/–	8/–	8/–

[1] Dash denotes that the activity was not among the top 10 at the time of the survey.

the rise of wildlife viewing is the result of a rise in interest among Whites. No other racial group has shown this level of increased interest. Likewise, the level of popularity of swimming in lakes, streams and oceans is due primarily to high participation rates among Whites.

Urban and Rural

Growth of the country's urban population and urban sprawl continue as persistent trends in the United States. Table 3.4 shows the 10 most popular activities for both urban and rural residents and compares trends in most popular activities between 1994–1995 and 2000–2001. For both urban and rural residents almost all of the most popular activities posted gains in the percentage of the population ages 16 and older who participated, especially the top two activities, walking for pleasure and attending outdoor family gatherings.

For urban residents, walking, attending family gatherings, and sightseeing have remained popular through the mid- and late-1990s into the early part of the 21st century. Sightseeing, however, was one of the few activities with a declining participation rate. The popularity of visiting nature centers, museums, or zoos

Table 3.4 Ten most popular activities and percentages participating for urban and rural residents, 1994–1995 and 2000–2001

Urban

1994–1995		2000–2001	
Walking	67.2	Walking	83.3
Family gathering	61.7	Family gathering	73.2
Sightseeing	57.5	Nature centers	58.7
Nature centers	55.0	Picnicking	54.5
Picnicking	49.2	Sightseeing	51.2
Sports events	47.7	Sports events	49.3
Swimming (pools)	45.9	Historic sites	47.4
Historic sites	44.9	Viewing wildlife	43.0
Swimming (lakes)	39.5	Swimming (pools)	42.8
Yard games	36.6	Swimming (lakes)	42.4

Rural

1994–1995		2000–2001	
Walking	65.1	Walking	81.6
Family gathering	62.1	Family gathering	74.6
Sightseeing	53.4	Picnicking	54.5
Picnicking	48.8	Sightseeing	54.0
Nature centers	48.2	Sports events	52.2
Sports events	46.9	Viewing wildlife	51.6
Historic sites	41.4	Nature centers	50.8
Swimming (pools)	38.4	Historic sites	41.6
Swimming (lakes)	37.2	Yard games	39.9
Yard games	37.1	Swimming (lakes)	39.1

rose from the 4th most popular activity to 3rd with a substantial increase in percentage who participate. Picnicking also edged up a spot, going from 5th in 1994–1995 to 4th in 2000–2001. About 55% of urbanites reported having gone on one or more picnics sometime during the last year. Visiting historic sites is another activity which rose slightly, from 8th to 7th. Swimming in pools dropped in popularity from 7th in 1994–1995 to 9th in 2000–2001. Viewing wildlife entered the list of 10 most popular activities at number 8 in the latest survey.

For rural residents, walking and family gatherings held the top two spots of most popular activities in both 1994–1995 and in 2000–2001. Sightseeing and picnicking exchanged the 3rd and 4th spots, with picnicking edging sightseeing by less than 1 percentage point in 2000–2001. Attending sports events rose from 6th to number 5, increasing in participation from about 47% to more than 52%. Visiting nature centers was not quite as popular among rural residents as urban residents in 1994–1995. It dropped from 5th most popular to 7th even though the participation rate increased more than 2%. Pool swimming dropped off rural residents' list in 2000–2001, while viewing wildlife appeared as the 6th most popular activity with nearly 52% participating.

Comparison of urban and rural residents' most popular activities in 2000–2001 shows more similarity than differences except for level of popularity of visiting nature centers and viewing wildlife. Visiting nature centers, museums or zoos is considerably more popular among urban dwellers than rural dwellers, sitting at number 3 among urbanites and number 7 among rural dwellers. Viewing wildlife, on the other hand, is more popular among rural than urban residents, at number 6 versus number 8. For each of these activities, the difference in urban and rural participation rate is roughly 8%.

Regions of the Country

One often hears about differences in lifestyles, politics, and cultural values between different regions of the country. Without doubt some such differences exist and in fact appear to be getting greater as different ethnic groups settle in different regions. But as Table 3.5 (p. 58) shows, people across the 9 census divisions differ little in what they chose as their most popular outdoor recreation activities.

Walking for pleasure, in both 1994–1995 and 2000–2001, was the most popular of all outdoor activities across the differing climates, terrains, and cultures of the 9 regions listed in Table 3.5. Walking is a low-cost, low-skill activity in which almost anyone can—in fact, almost everyone does—participate. The popularity of attending outdoor family gatherings is also consistently high, placing 2nd across all regions. Like walking, it is a pervasive activity in which the majority of Americans participate each year. Visiting nature centers, museums, or zoos rose in 6 of the 9 census regions which explains its ascent from 4th most popular in the United States as a whole in 1994–1995 to 3rd in

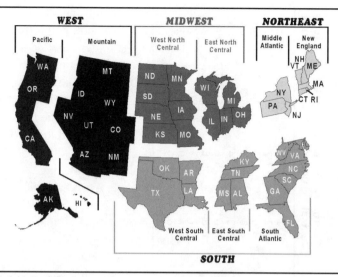

Figure 3.1 United States census regions and divisions

2000–2001. Picnicking and sightseeing, traditional outdoor activities if ever there were any, have remained popular, holding fast to the middle positions of the lists of most popular activities for all regions. Picnicking has moved up somewhat while sightseeing has dipped in ranking in all but one region.

Attending outdoor sporting events and visiting historic sites have remained in the lower ranks of the 10 most popular activities, as the trends in Table 3.5 show. At number 8 for the U.S. population overall, viewing wildlife as an activity appears on the list of most popular activities in 7 of the 9 regions in 2001–2002. Although much higher on the list for people living in the New England states, for the other regions swimming in lakes, streams, and oceans occupies the number 9 ranking or lower. Swimming in outdoor pools fell from 7th to the 10th most popular activity in the U.S. in 2000–2001. It appears in the top 10 in just 4 regions, no higher than 8th place.

Education

Table 3.6 (p. 59) tabulates rankings of the top 10 activities for different levels of education between 1994–1995 and 2000–2001. Across all levels of education walking is the top listed activity in both 1994–1995 and in 2000–2001. Attending outdoor family gatherings maintained its number 2 status during this same period among those without a college degree while it rose to 2nd place from the 3rd position among college graduates and 4th position among those with advanced degrees. Visiting nature centers and other nature learning facilities rose for all education levels except for postgraduates—most notably among people with less than a high school education. The end result is that visiting nature centers now is the 3rd most popular activity across people of almost all

Table 3.5 Ten most popular activities by census region, 1994–1995 and 2000–2001

Top 10 Activities for Total U.S. Population	Census Region[1]								
	New England	Mid Atlantic	East North Central	West North Central	South Atlantic	East South Central	West South Central	Rocky Mountains	Pacific Coast
Walking	1/1	1/1	1/1	1/1	1/1	1/1	1/1	1/1	1/1
Family gatherings	2/2	2/2	2/2	2/2	2/2	2/2	2/2	2/2	2/2
Nature centers	4/3	5/3	4/3	3/4	4/3	4/4	4/3	4/4	4/3
Picnicking	6/5	4/4	5/4	5/5	8/4	6/5	6/5	5/3	5/4
Sightseeing	3/6	3/5	3/6	4/6	3/5	3/3	3/4	3/5	3/5
Sports events	9/8	6/7	6/5	6/3	5/7	5/6	5/6	6/7	6/6
Historic sites	7/7	8/6	8/9	7/8	7/6	8/8	8/8	7/8	7/8
Viewing wildlife	–[2]/9	–/–	–/7	–/7	–/10	–/7	–/7	10/6	–/–
Swimming (lakes/streams)	5/4	9/9	10/–	10/–	9/9	10/–	9/10	–/–	9/10
Swimming (pools)	8/–	7/8	7/–	9/–	6/8	7/9	7/9	8/–	8/–

1 See Figure 3.1 for regions.
2 Activity not among the top 10 for the region at the time of the survey.

education levels. In 1994–1995 its popularity was 4th or lower for all but the most educated group.

Picnicking also rose in popularity across all educational levels. This rise was especially pronounced among those with less than high school education and for those with a college degree. Sightseeing was one of the activities that fell in overall popularity from the mid-1990s to the start of the 2000s. While staying generally in the middle range, sightseeing has dropped in its popularity position across all levels of education. Attending spectator sports events, as an outdoor activity, remained at about the same levels across educational levels as it had been in the mid-1990s with the exception of people without a high school education where it dipped 2 spots despite a decline in participation of less than 1.0 percentage point.

Visiting historic sites was not among the top 10 activities for those who had not finished high school in the mid-1990s or in the 2000–2001 period. Across all other levels of education visiting historic sites held constant or rose slightly. In the mid-1990s, visiting historic sites was already considerably more popular for those who had a college degree or had done graduate work than for the general population. This remained true in 2000–2001, edging to 4th place for postgraduates.

Viewing/learning activities—that is, activities that offer the opportunity to sightsee, observe, photograph, or otherwise take in natural views, historic sites, wildlife, birds, or other attractions—have always been popular. In the mid-1990s, 3 of these activities—visiting nature centers, sightseeing, and visiting historic sites—were among the top 10 most popular activities. In 2000–2001, viewing wildlife (other than birds) rose to the status of one of the 10 most popular outdoor activities in the country across all educational levels, except for those without a

Table 3.6 Ten most popular activities by education level, 1994–1995 and 2000–2001

Ten Most Popular Activities	Education				
	Less Than High School	High School Graduate	Some College	College Graduate	Postgraduate Study
	Activity's Popularity Ranking (1994–1995/2000–2001)				
Walking	1/1	1/1	1/1	1/1	1/1
Family gatherings	2/2	2/2	2/2	3/2	4/2
Nature centers	6/3	5/4	4/3	4/3	3/3
Picnicking	7/4	4/3	5/4	7/4	6/5
Sightseeing	5/8	3/5	3/5	2/6	2/6
Sports events	3/5	6/6	6/6	6/7	7/7
Historic sites	–/–[1]	9/9	8/7	5/5	5/4
Viewing wildlife	–/–	–/7	–/8	–/9	–/8
Swimming (lakes)	9/–	10/10	9/9	9/8	9/9
Swimming (pools)	4/9	7/–	7/10	8/10	8/–

[1] Activity not among the top 10 at the time of the survey.

high school education. It rose to number 7 among those who had earned a high school diploma but had chosen not to go further with their education. This group includes a large number of retirees, among whom we have observed a rapid increase in recent years of participation in viewing and learning activities such as viewing wildlife.

Swimming in lakes, streams, or the ocean (i.e., natural water bodies), the 9th most popular activity in the U.S. in 2000–2001, held similar positions across all education levels although it did drop out of the top 10 for the least educated group. Pool swimming, which fell from 7th to 10th place nationally between 1994–1995 and 2000–2001, showed a decline in rank for all education levels and dropped out of two. It plummeted from 4th to 9th place for people with less than a high school education; however, this represented a relatively small decrease in the percentage participating.

Income

Table 3.7 shows the popularity rankings of activities in 1994–1995 and 2000–2001 for 6 categories of annual family income. Walking maintained its number 1 status for all income levels. Likewise, attending outdoor family gatherings was number 2 for all income levels by rising one notch for the 2nd highest income group. Visiting nature centers, museums or zoos gained one place in the rankings for all income levels, rising to number 3 in the income levels over $25,000 and to number 4 for lower incomes. Picnicking also showed an increase across all levels, although its rank was considerably lower at the two highest income levels in both survey years. Sightseeing, attending sports events, and visiting historic sites for the most part maintained their popularity ratings, occupying the middle

Table 3.7 Ten most popular activities by annual family income, 1994–1995 and 2000–2001

Ten Most Popular Activities	Annual Family Income					
	<$15,000	$15,000– $24,999	$25,000– $49,999	$50,000– $74,999	$75,000– $99,999	$100,000+
	Activity's Popularity Ranking (1994–1995/2000–2001)					
Walking	1/1	1/1	1/1	1/1	1/1	1/1
Family gatherings	2/2	2/2	2/2	2/2	3/2	2/2
Nature centers	5/4	5/4	4/3	4/3	4/3	4/3
Picnicking	4/3	4/3	5/4	6/4	8/7	9/7
Sightseeing	3/5	3/5	3/5	3/5	2/4	3/6
Sports events	6/10	6/10	6/6	5/7	5/6	5/4
Historic sites	7/8	7/8	7/7	7/6	7/5	6/5
Viewing wildlife	–[1]/6	–/6	–/8	–/8	–/9	–/10
Swimming (lakes)	9/–	10/–	9/9	9/9	9/8	8/8
Swimming (pools)	8/–	8/–	8/–	8/10	6/10	7/9

[1] Activity not among the top 10 at the time of the respective survey.

of the pack. Sightseeing did, however, fall in the rankings in every income category, and attending sports events dropped sharply among the lowest income group—perhaps reflecting increasing ticket prices. Visiting historic sites tended to increase its rank among the higher income levels and drop slightly in the lower. The addition of viewing wildlife to the top 10 list is mostly due to its rise in popularity among lower and middle income levels. Swimming in natural waters pretty much held steady toward the bottom of the top 10 lists for all groups. Meanwhile, swimming in outdoor pools dropped in each income level, foreshadowing its change from 7th nationally in 1994–1995 to 10th in 2000–2001.

Age

Table 3.8 provides activity rankings in 1994–1995 and 2000–2001 by age groupings. For all age groups walking maintained its top position. Family gatherings outdoors maintained the 2nd place rank or rose from number 3 to 2. Visiting nature centers, museums, or zoos gained one spot for the two middle-aged groups but fell one place in the two oldest and the youngest category. The large population of the two baby boomer groups, however, was enough to push this activity from 4th to 3rd nationally. Picnicking showed a steady but modest rise across age groups with the exception of the youngest group. The opposite was true for sightseeing, which witnessed a drop in rank of 2 places or more for all but the oldest group. Attending outdoor sports events had mostly modest gains, while visiting historic sites posted an increase in only the 35–44 year old age group. Viewing wildlife made substantial jumps in the oldest age groups and appears for the first time in the top 10 activities among the 35–44 year olds. A related viewing and learning activity, viewing birds, also appeared in the top 10 for the 3 oldest age groups; however, it does not appear in Table 3.8

Table 3.8 Ten most popular activities by age, 1994–1995 and 2000–2001

Ten Most Popular Activities	Age Group					
	16–24	25–34	35–44	45–54	55–64	65+
	Activity's Popularity Ranking (1994–1995/2000–2001)					
Walking	1/1	1/1	1/1	1/1	1/1	1/1
Family gatherings	2/2	2/2	2/2	3/2	3/2	3/2
Nature centers	5/6	3/3	4/3	4/3	4/5	4/5
Picnicking	9/–[1]	5/4	5/4	5/4	5/3	5/4
Sightseeing	6/–	4/6	3/5	2/5	2/4	2/3
Sports events	4/5	7/5	6/6	7/8	7/8	8/7
Historic sites	10/–	8/9	8/7	6/6	6/6	6/9
Viewing wildlife	–/–	–/–	–/8	10/7	10/7	10/8
Swimming (lakes)	7/7	9/7	9/9	9/9	–/–	–/–
Swimming (pools)	3/4	6/10	7/10	8/–	9/–	–/–

[1]Activity not among the top 10 for the region at the time of the survey.

because it was not among the top 10 activities for the entire U.S. population in 2000–2001. Swimming in natural waters maintained its position toward the bottom of the top 10 activities. Swimming in outdoor pools ranks much higher (4th in 2000–2001) for the youngest age group than for any other. It barely made the rankings for ages between 25 and 44 and did not appear among the top 10 activities for those age 45 and older. Overall, there appear to be important age differences in trends for these most popular activities.

Number of Activities Over the Course of a Year

Table 3.9 shows the mean, median, and percentiles from the 75th through the 99th of the number of population-wide activities in which people 16 or older participated during the 12-month reporting periods covered by each of the 2 NSRE surveys (i.e., 1994–1995 and 2000–2001). In the 6 years between these 2 surveys, little detectable change can be seen in number of activities in which people chose to engage. None of the numbers compared between the 2 columns are significant, even at the 0.1 level.

Even so, from observing the median and 75th percentile, it is obvious that some slight shift downward may have occurred—but this shift is slight indeed. Overall, people during the 1990s and at the beginning of the 21st century are choosing to participate in about the same number of activities. As seen earlier in this chapter, in some ways the U.S. population on average shifted the activities they chose, but not the number of activities they put on their leisure agenda.

Table 3.9 Mean, median, and upper range percentiles of number of population-wide activities, 1994–1995 and 2000–2001

Measure	1994–1995	2000–2001
Mean	8.7	8.9
Median (50th Percentile)	9	8
75th Percentile	13	12
90th Percentile	17	17
95th Percentile	19	19
99th Percentile	24	24

Participation by Type of Outdoor Activity

Table 3.10 (p. 64) lists 13 types or groups of related recreational activities. The individual activities are classified into the following types:

Type/Group	Individual Activities
Trail/street/road	Running/jogging, bicycling, walking for pleasure
Viewing/learning	Visiting nature centers, prehistoric sites, or historic sites; viewing/photographing birds, other wildlife, flora or fish; sightseeing
Camping	Developed camping, primitive camping
Hunting	Hunting
Fishing	Fishing (including ice fishing)
Boating	Any boating
Outdoor adventure	Day hiking, orienteering, backpacking, mountain climbing, rock climbing, caving, driving off-road, horseback riding
Social	Picnicking, family gathering, yard games (e.g., croquet), visiting a beach
Individual sports	Golfing, tennis outdoors, handball outdoors
Team sports	Outdoor team sports
Spectator	Attending outdoor concerts, attending outdoor sports events
Snow/ice	Snow/ice activities
Swimming	Swimming in lakes, streams, ponds or oceans; swimming in an outdoor pool; snorkeling; surfing

The rate of growth from 1994–1995 to 2000–2001 (percentage growth of number of participants 16 or older participating at least once during the previous 12 months) was greatest for snow- and ice-based winter activities at about 48%. Across regions (census divisions; see Figure 3.1, p. 57) this growth ranged from 29% in the Middle Atlantic states to 90% in the West South Central region. Obviously the high growth in these states reflects travel to destinations outside of the West South Central region by that region's residents and probably represents a relatively modest numerical increase above a comparably small base in snow/ice activity participants. The next highest activity type growth rates, both roughly 38%, were for camping and trail/street/road activities (e.g., bicycling, running, walking). Camping grew slowest in the West South Central region and fastest in the South Atlantic. Trail/street/road activities also had the highest growth in the South Atlantic and lowest in the East North Central region, which still amounted to a 30% increase. Outdoor adventure activities followed closely in 4th place with 36% growth in participants between 1994–1995 and 2000–2001. The New England states paced the change in outdoor adventure participants with almost 50% growth.

Table 3.10 Trends in number of participants and percentage change by type of activity, 1994–1995 to 2000–2001, with highest and lowest change for regions[1]

Activity Type[2]	Millions 1994–1995	Millions 2000–2001	% Change 1994–1995 to 2000–2001[3]	Lowest Regional % Change	Highest Regional % Change
Snow/ice	38	56	48.1	28.9 (MA)	90.1 (WSC)
Camping	52	71	37.9	22.6 (WSC)	51.2 (SA)
Trail/street/road	134	184	37.8	30.2 (ENC)	50.5 (SA)
Outdoor adventure	72	98	35.6	24.4 (ESC)	49.6 (NE)
Boating	59	77	31.8	20.9 (ESC)	67.6 (Mtn)
Hunting	18	24	30.4	7.6 (ENC)	48.9 (WNC)
Social	139	180	29.5	22.0 (ENC)	42.5 (SA)
Fishing	57	73	27.7	14.4 (NE)	43.0 (Mtn)
Viewing/learning	142	177	25.0	19.7 (ENC)	34.8 (SA)
Individual sports	49	61	24.3	4.0 (WSC)	39.2 (SA)
Spectator	115	136	18.5	5.7 (WSC)	26.5 (WNC)
Team sports	48	48	0.1	-12.6 (ENC)	13.3 (Pac)
Swimming	106	103	-2.7	-10.5 (WSC)	9.1 (NE)

[1] Regions include New England (NE), Middle Atlantic (MA), East North Central (ENC), West North Central (WNC), South Atlantic (SA), East South Central (ESC), West South Central (WSC), Mountain (Mtn), and Pacific (Pac). See Figure 3.1, p. 57.
[2] An activity type represents a combination of several individual activities that have the setting or style of participation in common.
[3] Percent change is based on the nonrounded number of participants.

Across the 13 groupings of similar activities, swimming (both pool and natural water bodies) and participating in team sports (e.g., soccer, baseball) had the slowest growth from 1994 to 2001. For swimming, the West South Central showed a sharp decline in participation of −10.5%, while in the New England states it grew just 9%. For team sports, the range across regions was from about −13% in the East North Central states to 13% in the Pacific states. These were the only types of outdoor activity with losses of participants.

Over all activity types, the greatest incidence of slow growth occurred in the Central states, particularly among those in the East North Central, West South Central and East South Central regions. Neither the Mountain states nor the Pacific Coast states were associated with slow growth for any of the activity types. In fact, these regions were among those showing the fastest growth rates across activity types, along with the South Atlantic, New England and West North Central states.

Trends in Participation by Type of Outdoor Resource

To take a different view of participation trends, the natural resource-based activities tracked by both the 1994–1995 and the 2000–2001 NSREs were aggregated into land, water, and snow/ice resource-based activities. The trends in participation among these activity aggregations were examined across the 9 census divisions (see Figure 3.2, p. 67) and across areas of the country distinguished by population density (persons per square mile). These activity aggregations distinguish outdoor recreation participation by the broadly defined type of natural setting upon which they primarily occur and depend. For the nation as a whole, growth in numbers participating in land, water, and snow/ice activities was considerable. Activities included within each aggregation include the following:

Land		
	Biking	Horseback riding
	Picnicking	Family gathering
	Visiting nature centers	Visiting prehistoric sites
	Visiting historic sites	Walking for pleasure
	Day hiking	Backpacking
	Developed camping	Primitive camping
	Viewing/photographing birds	Mountain climbing
	Viewing/photographing wildlife	Rock climbing
	Big game hunting	Small game hunting
	Migratory bird hunting	Sightseeing
	Driving off-road	Running or jogging
	Orienteering	Caving

Water	Viewing/photographing fish	Ice fishing
	Coldwater fishing	Warmwater fishing
	Saltwater fishing	Anadromous fishing
	Sailing	Canoeing
	Kayaking	Rowing
	Motorboating	Waterskiing
	Jetskiing	Rafting
	Windsurfing	Surfing
	Swimming in lakes, ponds	Snorkeling
	Swimming in outdoor pool	
Snow/Ice	Skiing	Sledding
	Snowmobiling	Ice skating
	Snowshoeing	

Land-Based Activities

In 1994 there were just over 144 million people age 16 and older who reported participating in land activities. By 2001, that number had grown to almost 206 million, reflecting both population growth and a vigorously growing economy up to 2001. Thus, the number of participants grew by almost 62 million—nearly a 43% increase.

Water-Based Activities

In 2001, there were just over 148 million who participated in water activities, up almost 24 million from 1994. This represented an increase of about 19%, which is substantial, yet less than half the rate of growth of land-based activities.

Snow/Ice Activities

The most rapid growth between 1994 and 2001 was in snow and ice-based activities, at over 47%. From 38 million in 1994, the number of snow/ice participants grew to just over 56 million, an increase of more than 18 million in 6 years.

Growth by Region of the Country

Figure 3.2 shows growth between 1994 and 2001 for each of the 9 census regions of the country, both in millions of new participants and percentage of the population ages 16 or older participating. Growth in number of participants is plotted with solid lines and growth percentages participating are shown as broken lines. To create some sense of order in the figure, regions are listed from left to right in descending order of millions of participants in land-resource activities.

There is considerable difference in the number of new participants in land-resource activities across the 9 regions. The greatest growth in millions of participants in land-based activities was in the South Atlantic, followed in order by the Pacific, East North Central, Middle Atlantic, and West South Central. Greater growth in the South Atlantic reflects the high rates of population and economic growth in the southeastern coastal states of that region, especially Florida, Georgia, and Virginia. Highest percentage growth in land-based participation was also in the South Atlantic, followed closely by the Mountain, East South Central, and West South Central regions.

The South Atlantic also led all other regions in millions of new water activity participants. Following the South Atlantic in added participants were the Pacific, East North Central, and Middle Atlantic regions. Growth in participants in the remaining regions was somewhat below, but near the level of the Middle Atlantic. As was also true for land activities, the South Atlantic led all regions in percentage growth of water participation, followed closely by the Mountain and New England regions. Next in growth percentage of water activities among regions was the East South Central, Pacific, and West South Central.

For snow/ice activities, the East North Central region was highest in added participants followed by the South Atlantic, Pacific, Middle Atlantic and New England. The East South Central region added the fewest new participants. Percentage growth, however, was wildly different among regions reflecting

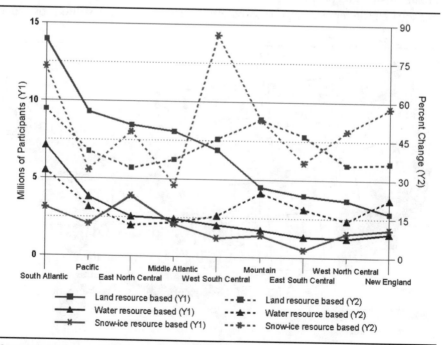

Figure 3.2 Change in millions of participants and percentage change in 3 categories of outdoor activities by region of the United States, 1994–1995 to 2000–2001

the large differences in the base participant population of these regions. The pattern of percentages did not follow any previously noted regional growth patterns. The West South Central region experienced a nearly 90% increase in snow/ice participation, while the Middle Atlantic had less than a 30% increase. Second highest percentage growth was in the South Atlantic, followed by New England, Mountain, West North Central and East North Central regions.

Growth by Population Density

Figure 3.4 shows growth in millions of participants and percentage increases for the same three types of resource-based activities by population density across the country. Population density for the year 2001 is differentiated by the widely accepted measure of persons per square mile at county scale.

As might be expected, because they represent the smallest proportion of the nation's population, the number of added participants in land, water, and snow/ice activities is lowest by far in counties with less than 10 persons per square mile at around 1 million added participants. Highest numbers of new participants, also reflecting to a large extent the proportion of the population living there, are found in counties with between 1,000 and 4,999 people per square mile. For all 3 categories of activities, the 2nd lowest number of new participants was in counties with the greatest density of population—those with greater than 5,000 people per square mile. (Population density of 5,000 persons per square mile represents approximately 8 persons per acre.) Millions of added

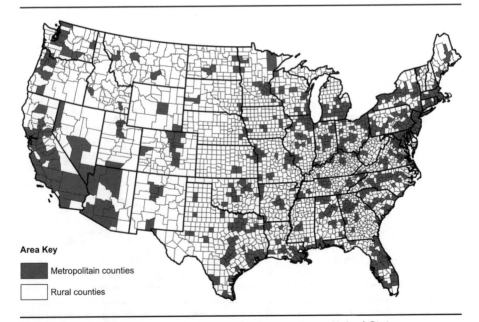

Area Key

■ Metropolitain counties

☐ Rural counties

Figure 3.3 Metropolitan area counties in the conterminous United States

participants between 1994 and 2001 followed a consistent upward pattern with
increasing population density for all other levels of population density (from less
than 10 up to 4,999 persons per square mile) in all 3 categories of activities.

Differences in percentage change in number of participants was less pronounced across counties with different levels of population density. For land
activities, highest percentage growth at around 52% was found among counties
with between 400 and 999 persons per square mile. Next highest was among
counties with 5,000 or more persons per square mile, followed by counties with
between 1,000 and 4,999 persons per square mile. Lowest percentage growth,
at around 33%, was in counties with less than 10 persons per square mile.

Like land-based activities, growth percentages for water activities was
highest in counties with 400 to 999 persons per square mile where the growth
percentage was about 30%. Next highest were counties with 1,000 to 4,999
persons at just under 20% followed closely by counties with 150 to 399 persons. All other counties had very close to the same percentage growth between
1994 and 2001, around 15%.

Percentage growth in snow/ice activity participants was less associated with
population density. Highest growth was in counties with 400–999 persons per
square mile at around 70%. But this growth was followed by counties with
less than 10 persons at around 60%. Next at around 58% were counties with

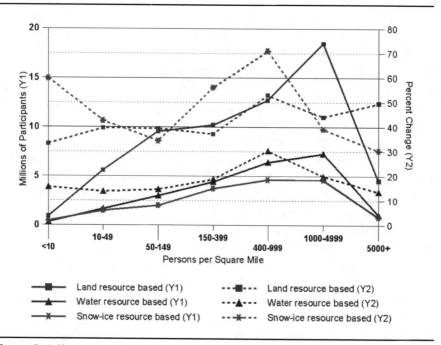

Figure 3.4 Change in millions of participants and percentage change in 3 categories
of outdoor activities by population density of residence county in the United States,
1994–1995 and 2000–2001

150 to 399 persons per square mile. Lowest growth percentage, about 30%, for snow/ice activities was in counties with over 5,000 persons, and next lowest at about 35% were counties with between 50 and 149 persons.

Participation Trends by Activity

Nationwide

Table 3.11 (pp. 71–73) lists 61 outdoor activities included in both the 1994–1995 and the 2000–2001 NSRE. This table represents growth in number and percentage of people who participate in each of the listed activities, ordered by percentage growth in number of participants (i.e., the last column).

The story in this table is nothing short of remarkable. Most of the 20 activities at the top of the list, starting with kayaking, are physically demanding, with the notable exceptions of viewing/photographing fish, ice fishing, viewing/photographing wildlife, and coldwater fishing. They reflect a continuing shift in the mix of activities occurring in many outdoor areas across this country. In all likelihood, this shift also represents a change in the composition of the people using the outdoor areas. Physically challenging sports such as kayaking, snowboarding, backpacking, and mountain climbing typically require specialized equipment, skills for using that equipment, and navigating terrain and water courses. Together with larger numbers of people participating in outdoor activities, this means very noticeable differences between what one would have photographed at a "typical" outdoor area in 1980 versus now. While many of the activities at or near the top of this list do not represent large numbers of people, for example kayaking participation has increased by just 4.8 million between 1994 and 2001, others not much further down the list have increased more substantially in numbers. Numbers reporting viewing/photographing wildlife has risen by over 34 million, viewing/photographing fish has risen by over 26 million, and viewing/photographing birds has increased by around 16 million.

All but 6 of the activities listed in Table 3.11 grew in number of participants since 1994–1995. Pool swimming, anadromous fishing, and caving each increased by fewer than a million people; nonetheless, they grew. Waterskiing, being replaced by jetskiing, was one of the activities that did not grow and actually decreased in both percentage and number participating. Other activities losing percentage and number of participants included sightseeing, orienteering, softball, volleyball, and windsurfing (once a fast growing new activity, windsurfing is probably being replaced by jetskiing as well).

Among those 13 activities that grew more than 50%, 5 are water oriented, 3 are snow/ice oriented, 5 occur mostly on trails, and 6 require expensive equipment. Two emphasize viewing and learning, a growth trend that has been unfolding since the 1980s. The 3 activities growing fastest, at over 100%, are physically demanding and are mostly the domain of younger participants. (Each

Table 3.11 Participation percentages and number of participants in the United States by activity, 1994–1995 to 2000–2001

Activity	% Participating 1994–1995	Millions of Participants 1994–1995	% Participating 2000–2001	Millions of Participants 2000–2001	% Change 1994–1995 to 2000–2001
Kayaking	1.3	2.6	3.5	7.4	185.7
Snowboarding	2.3	4.4	4.9	10.4	134.8
Jetskiing	4.7	9.3	9.5	20.3	119.3
Viewing/photographing fish	13.7	26.8	24.8	52.8	96.8
Soccer outdoors	4.7	9.3	8.1	17.3	87.2
Snowmobiling	3.6	7.0	5.6	11.8	70.2
Ice fishing	2.0	3.9	2.9	6.2	59.5
Sledding	10.2	20.0	14.7	31.2	56.2
Viewing/photographing wildlife	31.2	61.1	44.7	95.2	55.8
Backpacking	7.6	14.8	10.7	22.8	53.8
Day hiking	23.8	46.7	33.3	70.9	51.8
Canoeing	7.0	13.8	9.7	20.7	50.7
Bicycling	28.7	56.1	39.5	84.2	50.0
Horseback riding	7.1	13.9	9.7	20.6	48.0
Mountain climbing	4.5	8.8	6.0	12.9	46.5
Running or jogging	26.2	51.3	34.5	73.6	43.5
Coldwater fishing	10.4	20.3	13.6	28.9	42.8
Ice skating outdoors	5.2	10.3	6.9	14.6	42.7
Surfing	1.3	2.6	1.7	3.6	40.4
Developed camping	20.7	40.5	26.4	56.2	38.7
Handball/racquetball outdoors	5.6	11.0	7.1	15.1	36.8
Rafting	7.6	14.9	9.5	20.3	36.6
Driving off-road	13.9	27.3	17.5	37.2	36.5
Walking for pleasure	66.7	130.7	83.0	176.8	35.3
Visiting archeological sites	17.4	34.1	20.9	44.6	30.7
Viewing/photographing birds	27.0	52.8	32.4	69.0	30.6
Football	6.8	13.3	8.1	17.2	29.9
Family gatherings	61.8	121.0	73.5	156.6	29.4

Table 3.11 Participation percentages and number of participants in the United States by activity, 1994–1995 to 2000–2001 *continued*

Activity	% Participating 1994–1995	Millions of Participants 1994–1995	% Participating 2000–2001	Millions of Participants 2000–2001	% Change 1994–1995 to 2000–2001
Big game hunting	7.1	13.9	8.4	17.9	28.9
Cross-country skiing	3.3	6.4	3.8	8.1	27.6
Rock climbing	3.7	7.3	4.3	9.2	26.9
Attending outdoor concerts	34.2	66.9	39.8	84.8	26.7
Basketball outdoors	12.8	25.0	14.7	31.3	25.3
Primitive camping	14.0	27.4	16.0	34.1	24.8
Golfing	14.8	29.0	16.9	35.9	23.7
Small game hunting	6.5	12.7	7.2	15.4	21.4
Picnicking	49.1	96.0	54.5	116.1	20.9
Warmwater fishing	20.4	39.9	22.6	48.2	20.9
Migratory bird hunting	2.1	4.2	2.4	5.0	20.1
Saltwater fishing	9.5	18.5	10.4	22.1	19.0
Tennis outdoors	10.6	20.7	11.5	24.6	18.8
Yard games (e.g., croquet)	36.7	71.9	39.4	83.9	16.7
Sailing	4.8	9.3	5.1	10.9	16.6
Swimming in lakes, streams	39.0	76.3	41.7	89.0	16.6
Visiting nature centers	53.5	104.7	57.1	121.7	16.3
Attending outdoor sports events	47.5	93.0	49.9	106.3	14.2
Visiting historic sites	44.1	86.4	46.2	98.5	13.9
Rowing	4.2	8.2	4.4	9.4	13.6
Motorboating	23.5	45.9	24.4	52.0	13.2
Downhill skiing	8.4	16.5	8.5	18.2	10.5
Baseball	6.7	13.2	6.8	14.5	9.8
Snorkeling or scuba diving	7.2	14.2	7.3	15.5	9.3
Anadromous fishing	4.5	8.9	4.4	9.4	6.2
Pool swimming	44.2	86.5	41.0	87.3	0.9
Caving	4.7	9.2	4.3	9.3	0.3
Sightseeing	56.6	110.9	51.8	110.3	-0.5

Table 3.11 Participation percentages and number of participants in the United States by activity, 1994–1995 to 2000–2001 *continued*

Activity	% Participating 1994–1995	Millions of Participants 1994–1995	% Participating 2000–2001	Millions of Participants 2000–2001	% Change 11994–1995 to 2000–2001
Waterskiing	8.9	17.5	8.2	17.4	–0.6
Orienteering	2.4	4.7	2.0	4.3	–9.4
Softball	13.0	25.5	10.5	22.5	–12.0
Windsurfing	1.1	2.2	0.8	1.8	–19.5
Volleyball outdoors	14.3	28.0	10.6	22.6	–19.5

of these activities, it should be pointed out, began with relatively very low numbers of base participants in 1994–1995; this produces somewhat inflated growth rates.)

Of the activities growing between 25% and 50%, 3 are water oriented, just 2 are consumptive (fishing/hunting), 3 are viewing/learning oriented, and 5 are developed site activities. Among the top activities in this group, many are physically demanding (e.g., mountain climbing, running/jogging, ice skating, surfing). The 2 most popular activities across America, walking for pleasure (about 35% growth) and going to outdoor family gatherings (29%), appear in the middle tier of growth rates.

Region by Region

Table 3.12 (pp. 76–77) and Table 3.13 (pp. 78–79) show the fastest growing 13 activities countrywide in the United States (those having grown by over 50%) and percentage growth for each of these 13 activities across the 9 census divisions of the country. Regions (i.e., divisions) are arranged roughly from east to west (i.e., from New England to the Pacific Coast). Highlights by region are provided here.

New England

Highlighting growth of 100% or more, 4 activities top the growth list for the New England region: kayaking, soccer, snowboarding, and jetskiing, in that order. Kayaking experienced a phenomenal increase in this region, but this is mostly a function of a very small number of kayakers in the base year, 1994–1995 (see footnote 2, p. 77). All 13 activities are growing rapidly, but the slowest in New England is ice fishing. Growth rates for kayaking, soccer and canoeing in this region are highest in all 9 regions.

Middle Atlantic

Kayaking and jetskiing top the 100% growth list for the Middle Atlantic region. Both of these activities are considered slightly risky and exciting, and much of their growth is due to people wanting to try more exciting activities. Sledding, with just a 22% growth rate, is the slowest growing activity in this region and it's growing more slowly here than in the other 9 regions.

South Atlantic

Kayaking, snowboarding, and jetskiing all experienced over 100% growth in the South Atlantic region. These activities may attribute some of their rapid growth rate to the fact that they are considered fun, exciting, and slightly risky. The slowest growing activity in this region and all other regions, by far, is ice fishing, which has experienced a significant decline in popularity (–69%).

East North Central

Four activities for the East North Central region have experienced over 100% growth: kayaking, soccer, jetskiing, and snowboarding. The activity with the slowest growth in this region is ice fishing, followed by bicycling.

East South Central

Surprisingly ice fishing has the highest growth rate, mainly a function of a very small number of participants in the base year 1994–1995. It was followed by viewing/photographing fish and kayaking in the East South Central region. In fact, ice fishing and viewing/photographing fish along with viewing/photographing wildlife have the highest growth rates in this region and for all 9 regions. Not surprisingly, for the East South Central Region, the activity with the lowest percentage change is snowboarding (–25%). But wide swings in growth or decline are very much a function of a very small base of participants where a small addition or subtraction results in appreciable percentage changes.

West North Central

All activities listed for the West North Central region show growth. However, 5 activities in particular experienced over 100% growth: jetskiing, soccer, snowboarding, viewing/photographing fish, and sledding. Similar to most other regions, ice fishing is the slowest growing activity in this region, followed by day hiking.

West South Central

Highlighting growth of 100% or more, 3 activities top the growth list for the West South Central region: ice fishing, snowboarding, and viewing/photographing fish, in that order. With just a 23.5% growth rate, canoeing is the slowest growing activity in this region as well as among all 9 regions.

Mountain

The activities of kayaking, viewing/photographing fish, jetskiing, snowboarding, and snowmobiling all experienced 100% or more growth in the Mountain region. In fact, growth rates for snowboarding and jetskiing are highest in this region of all 9 regions. Bicycling is essentially tied with the South Atlantic as the fastest growing region or this activity. The slowest growing activity in the Mountain region is sledding, with a 27.3% growth rate.

Pacific

All activities listed for the Pacific region show a very good growth rate. However, 5 activities in particular experienced over 100% growth: ice fishing, snowboarding, kayaking, snowmobiling, and soccer. The growth rate for snowmobiling in the Pacific region is the highest among all 9 regions. Like the Mountain region, sledding is the slowest growing activity in the Pacific.

Table 3.12 Percentage change in number of participants in Eastern census regions, 1995–2001 and number of participants in millions for fastest growing U.S. activities by region, 2001 (1995 in parentheses)

Activity	Percentage Change and Millions of Participants 2001 (1995)[1]					
	United States	New England	Middle Atlantic	South Atlantic	East North Central	East South Central
Kayaking	185.7 7.4 (2.6)	1385.7[2] 1.0 (0.1)	128.6 1.0 (0.4)	164.4 1.2 (0.5)	159.0 1.0 (0.4)	137.5 0.2 (0.08)
Snowboarding	134.8 10.4 (4.4)	150.0 0.8 (0.3)	69.3 1.5 (0.9)	157.5 1.2 (0.5)	114.7 1.6 (0.8)	-25.0 0.18 (0.24)
Jetskiing	119.3 20.3 (9.3)	125.0 0.7 (0.3)	105.9 2.1 (1.0)	123.1 3.9 (1.7)	125.64 3.5 (1.6)	63.2 1.2 (0.8)
Viewing/photographing fish	96.8 52.8 (26.8)	73.8 2.9 (1.6)	91.6 6.8 (3.6)	98.9 10.4 (5.2)	87.6 8.1 (4.3)	142.6 3.1 (1.3)
Soccer outdoors	87.2 17.3 (9.3)	185.4 1.2 (0.4)	55.8 3.0 (1.9)	64.7 2.9 (1.7)	136.5 3.0 (1.3)	23.5 0.4 (0.3)
Snowmobiling	70.2 11.8 (7.0)	66.7 1.2 (0.7)	37.9 1.7 (1.2)	53.7 0.8 (0.5)	71.0 3.4 (2.0)	54.6 0.2 (0.1)
Ice fishing	59.5 6.2 (3.9)	35.5 0.4 (0.3)	34.3 0.5 (0.4)	-69.23 0.04 (0.1)	31.5 2.1 (1.6)	600.0 0.14 (0.02)
Sledding	56.2 31.2 (20.0)	69.8 2.9 (1.7)	22.4 5.4 (4.4)	74.9 3.9 (2.2)	71.9 8.2 (4.8)	49.3 1.0 (0.7)

Table 3.12 Percentage change in number of participants in Eastern census regions, 1995–2001 and number of participants in millions for fastest growing U.S. activities by region, 2001 (1995 in parentheses) *continued*

Activity	Percentage Change and Millions of Participants 2001 (1995)[1]					
	United States	New England	Middle Atlantic	South Atlantic	East North Central	East South Central
Viewing/photographing wildlife	55.8 95.2 (61.1)	56.4 5.2 (3.4)	43.4 12.8 (8.9)	73.2 17.3 (10.0)	40.9 16.0 (11.4)	77.2 5.6 (3.2)
Backpacking	53.8 22.8 (14.8)	68.3 1.8 (1.0)	41.5 2.8 (2.0)	43.6 3.2 (2.2)	72.6 3.0 (1.8)	16.5 0.9 (0.8)
Day hiking	51.8 70.9 (46.7)	61.5 4.2 (2.6)	44.9 8.9 (6.1)	67.0 10.4 (6.3)	38.7 10.5 (7.6)	31.4 3.4 (2.6)
Canoeing	50.7 20.7 (13.8)	79.3 2.1 (1.2)	30.6 2.9 (2.2)	45.3 3.5 (2.4)	55.5 4.7 (3.0)	34.8 0.9 (0.7)
Bicycling	50.0 84.2 (56.1)	53.0 4.8 (3.1)	53.3 12.4 (8.1)	62.3 15.1 (9.3)	37.7 15.3 (11.1)	55.6 3.8 (2.4)

[1] Percent change based on the nonrounded number of participants.

[2] This number is not a misprint. Very few New England residents (0.6%) said they went kayaking in 1994–1995. Conversely, about 9.6% said they kayaked in 2000–2001, much higher than the national rate of 1.3%. This resulted in an almost 14-fold increase in participants. Therefore, the very large growth rate results from the very small base year number of participants (1994–1995) and the larger than expected participation rate in 2000–2001.

Source: NSRE 1994–1995 data (1995 number of participants based on estimate of 195.8 million civilian, noninstitutionalized population 16 and older.) and NSRE 2000–2001, Versions 1–9 (2000–2001 number based on estimate of 213.1 million civilian, noninstitutionalized people 16 and older).

Table 3.13 Percentage change in number of participants in Western census regions, 1995–2001 and number in millions of participants for fastest growing U.S. activities by region, 2001 (1995 in parentheses)

Activity	Percentage Change and Millions of Participants 2001 (1995)[1]				
	United States	West North Central	West South Central	Mountain	Pacific
Kayaking	185.7 / 7.4 (2.6)	70.6 / 0.3 (0.2)	88.9 / 0.3 (0.2)	330.0 / 0.4 (0.1)	145.8 / 1.8 (0.7)
Snowboarding	134.8 / 10.4 (4.4)	110.3 / 0.6 (0.3)	133.3 / 0.4 (0.2)	223.3 / 1.0 (0.3)	196.0 / 2.9 (1.0)
Jetskiing	119.3 / 20.3 (9.3)	175.0 / 1.8 (0.6)	98.3 / 2.3 (1.2)	226.1 / 1.5 (0.5)	94.3 / 3.1 (1.6)
Viewing/photographing fish	96.8 / 52.8 (26.8)	106.9 / 3.6 (1.7)	118.6 / 5.6 (2.6)	131.2 / 3.3 (1.4)	78.1 / 8.8 (4.9)
Soccer outdoors	87.2 / 17.3 (9.3)	175.0 / 1.2 (0.4)	45.9 / 1.2 (0.9)	75.0 / 0.8 (0.5)	104.8 / 3.8 (1.9)
Snowmobiling	70.2 / 11.8 (7.0)	64.4 / 1.4 (0.9)	31.0 / 0.4 (0.3)	100.0 / 1.1 (0.6)	109.4 / 1.3 (0.6)
Ice fishing	59.5 / 6.2 (3.9)	32.2 / 1.2 (0.9)	183.3 / 0.17 (0.06)	53.7 / 0.6 (0.4)	518.2 / 0.7 (0.1)
Sledding	56.2 / 31.2 (20.0)	104.8 / 3.9 (1.9)	71.4 / 0.8 (0.5)	27.3 / 1.5 (1.2)	28.4 / 3.2 (2.5)

Table 3.13 Percentage change in number of participants in Western census regions, 1995–2001 and number in millions of participants for fastest growing U.S. activities by region, 2001 (1995 in parentheses) *continued*

Activity	Percentage Change and Millions of Participants 2001 (1995)[1]				
	United States	West North Central	West South Central	Mountain	Pacific
Viewing/photographibg wildlife	55.8 95.2 (61.1)	54.9 7.1 (4.6)	52.8 9.6 (6.3)	65.0 7.0 (4.3)	46.7 13.6 (9.3)
Backpacking	53.8 22.8 (14.8)	60.3 1.3 (0.8)	69.9 1.6 (0.9)	50.6 2.4 (1.6)	36.4 5.1 (3.7)
Day hiking	51.8 70.9 (46.7)	41.8 4.2 (3.0)	79.6 6.5 (3.6)	45.0 6.3 (4.3)	41.7 15.2 (10.7)
Canoeing	50.7 20.7 (13.8)	56.1 1.9 (1.2)	23.5 1.6 (1.3)	75.5 0.9 (0.5)	78.2 2.1 (1.2)
Bicycling	50.0 84.2 (56.1)	44.0 5.9 (4.1)	58.1 7.6 (4.8)	62.2 5.5 (3.4)	44.6 13.9 (9.6)

[1] Percent change based on the nonrounded number of participants.

Source: NSRE 1994–1995 data (1995 number of participants based on estimate of 195.8 million civilian, noninstitutionalized population 16 and older.) and NSRE 2000–2001, Versions 1–9 (2000–2001 number based on estimate of 213.1 million civilian, noninstitutionalized people 16 and older).

Chapter 4
Trends Before and After
September 11, 2001

On Monday, September 10, 2001, the media in the United States seemed unusually quiet. The top stories early that day focused on Notre Dame, which for the 3rd consecutive year, was ranked in the top 20 of the nation's schools. Across the country waves of freshman were patiently waiting to enter their new dorms, while families in Disneyland were eagerly anticipating the start of the new Buzz Lightyear Parade. The evening news discussed how the CBS show Survivor received an Emmy for best reality show, and crowds cheered the USA's 4–1 defeat of Germany in the Women's World Soccer Cup. In tennis, an epic battle between Pete Sampras and Lleyton Hewitt in the U.S. Open, interspersed with highlights of the previous night's battle between the Williams sisters, dominated sports news. Coverage ended that night showing crowds laughing and enjoying themselves outside the U.S. Open on the streets of Flushing Meadows, New York.

Unlike years earlier when Walter Cronkite, struggling to contain his emotions, somberly announced, "We interrupt this broadcast..." to inform us that President Kennedy had be shot, there was no moment of delay or grace. On September 11, 2001, television, the Internet, and mobile phones almost instantaneously gave us the news and live coverage of the horrors unfolding in New York, the District of Columbia, and Pennsylvania. But, for many, despite technology's ability to speed news to our doorsteps, in real-time, everything seemed to stand still.

It is unlikely that any of us will soon, if ever, forget what happened at the World Trade Center, the Pentagon, or Shanksville on September 11, 2001. Nor will we forget where we were when those tragic and evil acts took place. Never before had civilian aircraft of that size with so many on board been used as missiles. Never before had civilian aircraft been grounded for days all across the skies of the United States as they were. Never before had the safety of flying been so much a question in people's minds. For weeks after that terrible day, even after air traffic resumed, conferences, vacations, visits to family, business travel, and many other flying trips were canceled. Airline ticket sales plummeted. Would those forgone trips be rescheduled for another time? Would there be a lasting downturn in air and other commercial travel? What would happen to outdoor recreation participation and tourism travel?

Many of my colleagues in recreation management with federal and state agencies speculated about the effects of 9/11. Some predicted that visits to national forests, national parks, and other destinations would fall off—but for how long, no one was sure. Many more speculated that recreational travel involving mass transit, especially flying, would be curtailed, but that visits to areas close to home where mass transit was not needed would accelerate. After all, what could be safer than driving from Athens, Georgia, to camp at the Davidson River Campground on the Pisgah National Forest in western North Carolina? Speculation was, folks looking for recreation will increase visits to such places because they can safely drive and avoid flying.

Almost immediately following the Trade Center and Pentagon attacks, a short series of questions were developed, tested, and implemented through the NSRE to ask the American public how 9/11 would affect their outdoor recreation travel. This chapter presents the results of those questions and, in comparison, show short-term trends in participation among activities before, just after, and one year after September 11, 2001.

Highlights

Some interesting insights were gained from surveying a modest sample of Americans 16 or older regarding short-term travel changes resulting from the attacks of September 11, 2001. Revealed was a possible, very modest decrease in recreation and vacation travel. Results indicated that just over 48% of the U.S. population 16 or older took 1 to 3 trips during the 12 months prior to the tragedies of 9/11 (Figure 4.1). However, when asked about numbers of trips planned in the upcoming 12 months post-9/11, little decrease in trips planned relative to trips taken prior to 9/11 was evident. Just slightly less than before 9/11, 46% of respondents reported that they intended to take 1 to 3 trips over the next 12 months and percentages reporting higher numbers of planned trips were much the same as reported trips taken prior to 9/11. Apparently the terrorist attacks had little affect on travel plans, other than in the immediate postevent period when fears were running highest, airport check-in lines were long and slow, and air travel was restricted.

If planned travel were to be curtailed in modest amounts, we would expect to see this reflected in lower reported activity participation. Indeed, reported participation rates for post-9/11 periods seemed to be a bit lower than prior to 9/11. Participation in land-based activities for the immediate post-9/11 period (September 11, 2001, through February 28, 2002) was less than pre-9/11 periods. With interest, but without understanding why, we note that participation for most of the viewing/photographing activities (e.g., birding) was less than pre-9/11 periods. Participation in these and other activities in more recent times, however, has rebounded for the most part. Some modest decreases in post-9/11 periods may have resulted from the cool seasonal weather.

As with land-based activities, participation percentages for a few water activities fell following September 11, 2001. Notable were swimming, fishing, canoeing, and waterskiing. Participation in only a very few water activities rose, including boat tours and excursions, rafting, kayaking, and surfing. After February 28, 2002, participation resumed at former pre-9/11 rates for most of the water activities, which had decreased immediately following 9/11, indicating a weak and nonpersistent downward effect of the tragedy. For a few activities, participation percentages increased—for example, visiting beaches, boat tours and excursions, rafting, kayaking, and surfing. Participation in all snow/ice activities remained virtually the same as pre-9/11 periods.

Participation trends in pre- and post-9/11 periods were examined for men and women. Unexpectedly, there are a number of activities for which participation percentages for men decreased, while for women these percentages either rose or remained stable. Included were viewing/photographing natural scenery, visiting nature centers, bicycling, boating (of any type), snow/ice activities (of any type), visiting archeological or prehistoric sites, backpacking, downhill skiing, canoeing, horseback riding, and waterskiing. For a few activities participation increased for both men and women—indicating market resiliency. These activities included visiting a beach (fresh or saltwater), day hiking, snorkeling, snowboarding, and kayaking. Interesting to observe that for some activities, there was a downward trend in male participation that was opposite an upward trend in female participation. In come cases this difference was sufficient to put females at or above participation rates of males—for example, windsurfing, kayaking, and cross-country skiing.

Participation trends in pre- and post 9/11 were also examined for different ages. Among people age 16 to 24, percentages participating decreased between 2% and 6% for many activities. Modest increases occurred only for visiting a beach, snowboarding, sailing, kayaking, and surfing, and stable percentages

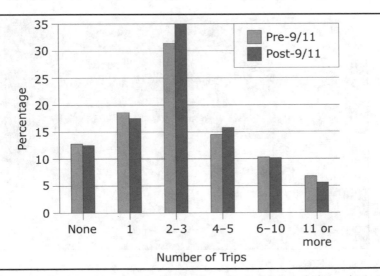

Figure 4.1 Recreation trips taken in 12 months prior to 9/11 and planned trips in 12 months after 9/11, people 16 or older in the United States, 2000–2002

were observed for bicycling, boating, camping, snorkeling, and scuba diving. For people age 25 to 45, there were considerably fewer activities where participation decreased compared with 16- to 24-year-olds. For this age group, activities losing the most in percentages participating were the more passive ones, such as walking, swimming, and sightseeing. Gains were seen only for driving for pleasure and visiting a beach. However, participation percentages remained the same for almost all of the more specialized active and skill activities. For people age 45 to 60, participation rates between pre- and post-9/11 time periods fell for still fewer activities (compared with the younger age groups). Increases were seen for driving for pleasure, visiting a beach, visiting a wilderness or other primitive areas, day hiking, and interestingly (for this more mature age group) rafting and kayaking. For people age 61 or older, the trend was still fewer activities where participation percentages fell and more activities where participation increased from pre- to post-9/11 periods. The bottom line of these age-group observations is that after 9/11 younger people became a bit less active while older people became a bit more active. For all activities and social strata, however, changes in participation rates were modest.

Americans' Anticipated Recreation Travel Just After 9/11

Beginning about October 15, 2001, a short set of questions was added to the NSRE asking respondents whether their travel plans had been affected by the 9/11 terrorist attacks. Running these questions within planned sampling for just

Cross-country skiing has long been a favored winter time activity. Photo courtesy of NHDTTD/Bob Grant

a few days, a total of 1,347 NSRE respondents were asked the 9/11 "drop-in" questions. A larger sample was not pursued so that results could be provided promptly to recreation providers for use in planning the coming year's management. Results from these questions are provided next. Following this section, we review short-term trends (i.e., actualized participation).

Introduction statement to respondents. To conclude this interview, we would like to ask you just a couple of questions about your travel plans for this year.

How many vacation or recreation trips away from home did you take in the last 12 months? The average number of trips taken in the past 12 months for vacationing or other recreation activity was 3.9, with a median of 2.0. Of the 1,347 interviewees reporting, 4.1% said they did not know or refused to answer the question. Percentage distribution of respondents by number of trips follows:

None	18.4%	4–5	13.1%
1	17.9%	6–10	10.1%
2–3	30.2%	11+	6.2%

How many vacation or recreation trips away from home do you plan to take in the next 12 months? From the previous question we estimate that just over 48% of the U.S. population 16 or older take 1 to 3 trips per year. This estimate is consistent with other data we have developed and with other surveys. If the terrorist attacks were to have an affect on travel plans, respondents would indicate that they intended to take fewer trips in the coming 12 months. On this question, 10.4% refused to respond or were not sure. The percentage distribution of responses from those giving us anticipated number of trips follows (does not sum to 100% due to rounding):

None	17.0%	4–5	12.3%
1	16.2%	6–10	9.1%
2–3	29.3%	11+	5.8%

Roughly 46% of respondents (and thus we estimate 46% of the population) reported that they intended to take 1 to 3 trips over the next 12 months. This is slightly less than the 48% who reported taking 1 to 3 trips in the past year, but the difference is modest. The profile of percentages across the number of trips planned is for all practical purposes the same as trips reported over the last 12 months. Apparently the terrorist attacks were to have little affect on travel plans, other than in the immediate postevent period.

The plane highjackings of September 11 may have caused some people to postpone or cancel travel plans. Have you postponed or canceled any vacation, recreation trip, or outing plans as a result of September 11? Of the 1,347 asked this question, 3.0% either refused or weren't sure. Almost 86% responded, however, that they had not and did not intend to postpone or cancel trips. About 11% said they had changed their trip itinerary. Of those 11% who had changed their plans, the percentages by travel plan response is shown in the next question.

As a result of September 11, is your recreation or vacation travel in the next 12 months likely to be

The same amount as planned	36.8%
Less than originally planned	42.6%
Won't travel, but had planned to	8.9%
More than originally planned	5.9%
Not sure	5.8%

Based on these percentages, apparently well over one third of those intending to change travel plans had intended to change something other than the number of trips they would take, since they indicated the number of trips would remain the same. Almost 43% of the 11% who changed their plans, however, were planning to take fewer trips for vacations or other recreation. Almost 9% of those changing their plans were going to cancel travel they had planned. Overall, less than 6% of all vacationing and recreation travelers made some change to reduce their travel after 9/11—not a dramatic shift in the recreation travel market.

Which statement best describes your recreation or vacation travel destinations for the next 12 months? All of the 1,347 respondents were asked about upcoming travel destinations. The following responses were offered:

Same destination as planned before September 11	74.4%
Different destination, one that's closer to home than originally planned	8.9%
Different destination farther from home, but one I consider safer than where I planned to go before September 11	6.6%
Don't know or refused	10.1%

Are any of these destinations likely to be national forests, state parks, or similar areas? This question was asked to help public land and other recreation providers anticipate how travel plan changes might affect their visitation in the coming year. Asked only of the 16% whose destinations were likely to be different than originally planned, 38% indicated the change destination would likely be a national forest, state park or other public land. Thus, about 6% of vacation or other recreation trips were likely to shift to federal or state public lands.

Reported Recreation Participation for Periods Before and After 9/11

Based on survey questions asking about travel plans, it appeared that some (but not much) change in vacation or recreation travel would likely result from the 9/11 terrorist attacks. We reported this prediction to the "field" (i.e., public land managers) by e-mail in December 2001 with more detail in January 2002. At this time there was a great deal of speculation that there was very likely to be substantial increases in visitation at national forests and state parks in the coming months. The increase, it was assumed, would come from local people trying to stay closer to home in more secure and familiar situations. This anticipated increase, however, did not materialize, just as responses to these questions predicted. Tables 4.1 (pp. 90–91), Table 4.2 (p. 92), and Table 4.3 (p. 93) show reported participation percentages for land, water and snow/ice activities in different periods relative to September 11, 2001. The time periods reported are September 1999 to August 2000; September 2000 to September 10, 2001; September 11, 2001 to the end of February 2002; and March 2002 through August 2002. The percentages reported are for participation occurring over the 12 months just prior to being interviewed. Thus, differences in length of the periods is immaterial. Since responses to participation questions disproportionately reflect current participation patterns (i.e., activity fresh in people's minds), we expected to see September 11, 2001, participation effects to show up promptly, if they existed at all.

Land-Based Activities

Across most of the activities in Table 4.1, there is a high degree of consistency in percentages of the population 16 or older participating for both of the two pre-9/11 periods. So similar, in fact, that with minor exceptions, there are no discernible trends. Generally however, reported participation, and thus percentages, for the immediate post-9/11 period (i.e., September 11, 2001, to February 28, 2002) are somewhat less than those in the two pre-9/11 periods. This is evident in walking for pleasure, gardening, viewing/photographing natural scenery, sightseeing, viewing/photographing wildlife, viewing/photographing wildflowers and trees, and playing yard games (which typically involves no travel). Some or most of this mild downturn may be seasonal. Immediate post-9/11 participation percentages for viewing/photographing birds and fish are also notably less than for other activities, as is participation for most of the viewing/photographing activities in the immediate post-9/11 period. Participation in the final period (i.e., after February 28, 2002) shows a slight rebound for almost all activities for which reported participation fell just after September 11. Assuming the cooler season up to February 28 is only a part of the explanation, the relatively small magnitude of the drop in participation percentages in the immediate post-9/11 period is consistent with results from the questions about changes in travel plans we reported earlier. These results showed a very modest decrease in travel caused by September 11, 2001.

Water-Based Activities

As with land-based activities, participation percentages for the 2 periods prior to September 11 were very similar across water-based activities. This pattern of similarity can be seen in Table 4.2, as it was in Table 4.1. Participation for a few water activities fell following September 11, 2001, notably swimming, fishing, warmwater fishing, canoeing, and waterskiing. But these activities are warm season activities, expected to drop off in cooler weather. Participation for still fewer activities rose. These included boat tours and excursions, rafting, kayaking, and surfing. Again, after February 28, participation for most of these activities resumed their former, pre-9/11 rates, with few exceptions. But the main point, as for land-based activities, is that there are far more similarities than differences from period to period, indicating a weak downward trend after the 9/11 tragedy. For a few activities, in fact, participation increased somewhat. Examples include visiting beaches, boat tours and excursions, rafting, kayaking, and surfing.

Snow/Ice Activities

Participation in all snow/ice activities (top row in Table 4.3), remained virtually the same as in pre-9/11 periods. Thus, notwithstanding the unprecedented nature of the September 11, 2001 events, recreation activity participation from fall 1999 to present time has remained highly constant. Not much else can be said of the data in Table 4.3, nor of the data in Tables 4.1 and 4.2.

Pre- and Post-9/11 Participation Differences Between Men and Women

Table 4.4 (pp. 94–95) shows participation differences before and after 9/11 for both men and women. As with the preceding 3 tables, there are many more similarities than differences between the 2 time periods, for both men and women (within 1.0 percentage point). However, there are some pattern differences worthy of mention. First, there are a number of activities for which participation percentages decreased somewhat for men, but for which the percentages either rose or remained stable for women. Activities with this short-term participation trend included viewing/photographing natural scenery, visiting nature centers, bicycling, boating (of any type), snow/ice activities (of any type), visiting archeological or historic sites, backpacking, downhill skiing, canoeing, horseback riding, and waterskiing. Activities which for both men and women reported participation percentages went down after 9/11 included walking for pleasure, picnicking, sightseeing, visiting historic sites, viewing/photographing wildlife, swimming, fishing, viewing or photographing wildflowers, viewing or photographing birds, visiting a farm for recreation, and mountain biking.

Not all of the aftermath of September 11 showed up as decreases. For several activities, participation remained virtually the same. These activities included attending family gatherings, driving for pleasure, visiting a wilderness or other primitive area, gathering natural products (e.g., mushrooms, berries, wood), motorboating, developed camping, driving motor vehicles off-road, primitive camping, hunting, and saltwater fishing. Also remaining the same were rafting, jetskiing, snowmobiling, and sailing. For a few activities, participation increased, for both men and women. Table 4.4 shows those activities for which participation increased for both men and women to be visiting a beach (fresh or saltwater), day hiking, snorkeling, snowboarding, and kayaking. Interesting to observe that for some activities, the downward trend in male participation opposite an upward trend in female participation was sufficient to put females right at (within 0.5%) or above participation rates of males. For example, participation rates for windsurfing, kayaking, and cross-country skiing show female participation essentially the same or above participation levels for males.

Pre- and Post-9/11 Participation Differences Between Age Groups

Noteworthy differences exist between pre- and post-9/11 participation rates among 4 age groups in Table 4.5 (pp. 97–99).

Age 16 to 24

As a general observation, the percentage of people in this age group participating in most of the activities listed in Table 4.5 decreased. Modest increases in percentage participating occurred for the activities of visiting a beach, snowboarding, sailing, kayaking, and scuba diving. Percentages remained more or less the same for a few activities, including boating, developed camping, snorkeling, and surfing. Percentages for all other activities decreased by 2 to 6 percentage points.

Age 25 to 45

The number of activities for which participation decreased for this age group was slightly fewer than for 16- to 24-year-olds. As with this younger age group, activities losing the most in percentages participating tended to be slightly more passive, widely popular activities, such as walking, swimming, bicycling, sightseeing, and boating. Gains were seen only for driving for pleasure and visiting a beach. Participation percentages remained the same for most activities in

Table 4.1 Percent participating in land-based outdoor activities in 4 periods relative to September 11, 2001, by persons 16 or older (95% confidence interval ±%)

Activity	Full NSRE Sample	9/1/99 to 8/31/00	9/1/00 to 9/10/01	9/11/01 to 2/28/02	After 2/28/02
Walking for pleasure	82.3 (0.3)	84.3 (0.5)	82.0 (0.5)	78.1 (1.1)	80.6 (1.3)
Family gathering	73.8 (0.4)	73.8 (0.6)	74.2 (0.5)	73.7 (1.2)	73.8 (1.4)
Gardening or landscaping for pleasure	65.1 (1.2)	(.)[1]	69.2 (1.5)	58.9 (2.2)	(.)
Viewing/photographing natural scenery	59.5 (0.4)	61.0 (0.7)	59.4 (0.6)	55.3 (1.3)	58.7 (1.6)
Visiting nature centers/museums	56.6 (0.4)	57.4 (0.7)	56.7 (0.6)	55.7 (1.3)	55.4 (1.6)
Picnicking	54.6 (0.4)	55.2 (0.7)	54.7 (0.6)	53.7 (1.0)	53.0 (1.4)
Driving for pleasure	52.2 (0.4)	53.9 (0.7)	48.3 (0.7)	56.5 (1.0)	55.0 (1.4)
Attending outdoor sports events	50.8 (1.1)	(.)	51.4 (1.3)	49.1 (2.2)	(.)
Sightseeing	50.6 (0.4)	54.3 (0.7)	49.1 (0.7)	46.5 (1.3)	47.9 (1.6)
Visiting historic sites	45.3 (0.4)	47.3 (0.7)	44.9 (0.7)	42.4 (1.3)	43 (1.6)
Viewing/photographing other wildlife	44.1 (0.4)	45.8 (0.7)	43.9 (0.6)	39.6 (1.3)	41.5 (1.6)
Viewing/photographing wildflowers/trees	43.9 (0.4)	45.8 (0.7)	43.6 (0.6)	39.8 (1.3)	42.3 (1.6)
Attending outdoor concerts/plays	40.9 (1.1)	(.)	41.3 (1.3)	40.3 (2.2)	(.)
Bicycling	39.4 (0.4)	39.4 (0.7)	40.2 (0.6)	38.1 (1.3)	37.3 (1.5)
Yard games (e.g., horseshoes)	38.9 (1.0)	(.)	40.0 (1.1)	34.9 (2.1)	(.)
Day hiking	33.0 (0.4)	33.8 (0.6)	31.8 (0.6)	34.1 (1.0)	35.9 (1.3)
Running or jogging	32.9 (0.9)	(.)	33.4 (1.0)	31.5 (2.0)	(.)
Visiting a wilderness or primitive area	32.6 (0.4)	33.9 (0.6)	31.4 (0.6)	33.1 (1.0)	33.6 (1.3)
Viewing/photographing birds	31.8 (0.4)	33.5 (0.6)	31.3 (0.6)	27.3 (1.2)	31.4 (1.5)
Gathering mushrooms/berries	28.4 (0.4)	27.5 (0.6)	29.7 (0.6)	27.7 (0.9)	26.1 (1.2)
Visiting a farm or agricultural setting	27.4 (0.5)	28.1 (1.4)	27.9 (0.6)	26.4 (1.2)	25.1 (1.4)
Developed camping	26.3 (0.3)	25.4 (0.6)	27.4 (0.5)	25.7 (0.9)	25.4 (1.2)
Viewing/photographing fish	24.3 (0.3)	25.3 (0.6)	24.3 (0.5)	22.5 (1.1)	22.2 (1.3)
Mountain biking	20.8 (0.3)	21.1 (0.6)	21.8 (0.5)	18.5 (0.8)	19.0 (1.1)
Visiting prehistoric/archeological sites	20.5 (0.3)	20.8 (0.6)	20.7 (0.5)	19.6 (1.1)	18.9 (1.3)
Driving off-road	18.0 (0.3)	17.6 (0.6)	17.6 (0.5)	19.9 (0.8)	18.0 (1.1)
Inline skating or rollerblading	17.5 (1.0)	(.)	21.3 (1.3)	11.4 (1.4)	(.)
Golfing	16.7 (0.7)	(.)	16.8 (0.8)	16.0 (1.6)	(.)

Table 4.1 Percent participating in land-based outdoor activities in 4 periods relative to September 11, 2001, by persons 16 or older (95% confidence interval ±%) *continued*

Activity	Full NSRE Sample	9/1/99 to 8/31/00	9/1/00 to 9/10/01	9/11/01 to 2/28/02	After 2/28/02
Primitive camping	16.0 (0.3)	15.7 (0.5)	16.5 (0.4)	16.4 (0.8)	15.6 (1.0)
Basketball outdoors	14.0 (0.7)	(.)	14.7 (0.8)	11.7 (1.4)	(.)
Hunting	11.4 (0.2)	11.2 (0.4)	11.4 (0.4)	11.8 (0.7)	10.9 (0.9)
Tennis outdoors	10.5 (0.6)	(.)	10.7 (0.7)	9.8 (1.3)	(.)
Volleyball outdoors	10.4 (0.6)	(.)	10.8 (0.7)	9.1 (1.3)	(.)
Backpacking	10.3 (0.2)	10.9 (0.4)	10.2 (0.4)	9.3 (0.6)	10.7 (0.9)
Softball	10.0 (0.6)	(.)	10.4 (0.7)	8.6 (1.2)	(.)
Horseback riding (general)	9.6 (0.2)	9.8 (0.4)	9.6 (0.4)	9.1 (0.8)	8.3 (0.9)
Big game hunting	8.7 (0.2)	8.3 (0.4)	8.7 (0.4)	9.4 (0.6)	8.6 (0.8)
Football	8.1 (0.5)	(.)	7.9 (0.6)	8.7 (1.2)	(.)
Horseback riding on trails	7.8 (0.2)	7.9 (0.4)	7.7 (0.3)	8.5 (0.6)	7.3 (0.7)
Handball or racquetball outdoors	7.6 (0.5)	(.)	7.4 (0.6)	8.3 (1.2)	(.)
Soccer outdoors	7.5 (0.5)	(.)	7.2 (0.6)	8.3 (1.2)	(.)
Small game hunting	7.1 (0.2)	7.2 (0.4)	7.2 (0.3)	5.9 (0.6)	7.4 (0.8)
Baseball	6.4 (0.5)	(.)	6.6 (0.5)	6.0 (1.0)	(.)
Mountain climbing	6.3 (0.5)	(.)	6.2 (0.5)	6.6 (1.1)	(.)
Rock climbing	4.3 (0.4)	(.)	4.3 (0.4)	4.2 (0.9)	(.)
Caving	4.2 (0.4)	(.)	4.1 (0.4)	4.3 (0.9)	(.)
Migratory bird hunting	2.3 (0.1)	2.4 (0.2)	2.4 (0.2)	1.9 (0.4)	2.3 (0.5)
Orienteering	1.8 (0.3)	(.)	1.8 (0.3)	1.6 (0.6)	(.)

Missing data indicates that the activity was not asked during this interview season.
Source: NSRE 2000–2001 Versions 1–13, N = 63,090, Interview dates: 7/99 to 8/02.
Season sample sizes in chronological order: 20,624; 26,348; 9,254; 4,977.

Table 4.2 Percent participating in water-based outdoor activities in 4 periods relative to September 11, 2001, by persons 16 or older (95% confidence interval ±%)

Activity	Full NSRE Sample	9/1/99 to 8/31/00	9/1/00 to 9/10/01	9/11/01 to 2/28/02	After 2/28/02
Swimming in an outdoor pool	41.6 (0.6)	(.)[1]	41.5 (0.6)	42.4 (1.5)	(.)
Visiting a beach	40.9 (0.4)	39.8 (0.7)	41.7 (0.6)	41.1 (1.3)	43.9 (1.6)
Swimming in lakes, streams	39.6 (0.4)	44.0 (0.7)	38.2 (0.6)	33.1 (1.0)	39.6 (1.4)
Fishing	33.9 (0.4)	34.3 (0.6)	34.2 (0.6)	32.8 (1.3)	31.1 (1.5)
Freshwater fishing	29.5 (0.4)	29.7 (0.6)	29.2 (0.5)	30.4 (0.9)	28.0 (1.2)
Visiting other waterside (besides beach)	25.6 (0.4)	27.5 (0.6)	24.8 (0.5)	23.0 (1.1)	25.9 (1.4)
Motorboating	24.3 (0.3)	24.6 (0.6)	24.5 (0.5)	22.9 (1.1)	24.4 (1.4)
Warmwater fishing	22.4 (0.3)	23.1 (0.6)	22.3 (0.5)	20.9 (1.1)	20.9 (1.3)
Boat tours or excursions	19.2 (0.8)	(.)	18.9 (0.9)	20.2 (1.8)	(.)
Coldwater fishing	13.2 (0.3)	13.4 (0.5)	13.8 (0.4)	12.5 (0.9)	10.6 (1.0)
Saltwater fishing	10.4 (0.2)	10.0 (0.4)	10.7 (0.4)	10.8 (0.8)	10.0 (1.0)
Rafting	10.2 (0.2)	9.7 (0.4)	9.7 (0.4)	12.2 (0.7)	11.9 (0.9)
Canoeing	9.6 (0.2)	9.6 (0.4)	10.0 (0.4)	8.2 (0.7)	9.3 (0.9)
Jetskiing	9.5 (0.2)	9.3 (0.4)	9.7 (0.4)	9.2 (0.8)	9.4 (0.9)
Waterskiing	8.0 (0.2)	8.2 (0.4)	8.0 (0.3)	7.3 (0.7)	8.3 (0.9)
Snorkeling	6.7 (0.2)	6.6 (0.3)	6.9 (0.3)	6.3 (0.7)	7.4 (0.8)
Sailing	5.2 (0.2)	5.1 (0.3)	5.2 (0.3)	5.5 (0.6)	5.4 (0.7)
Anadromous fishing	4.2 (0.2)	4.3 (0.3)	4.4 (0.2)	3.8 (0.5)	3.0 (0.6)
Rowing	4.2 (0.2)	4.5 (0.3)	4.3 (0.2)	4.0 (0.5)	3.6 (0.6)
Kayaking	3.7 (0.2)	3.2 (0.2)	3.9 (0.2)	4.2 (0.5)	4.4 (0.7)
Ice fishing	2.7 (0.3)	(.)	2.8 (0.4)	2.2 (0.6)	(.)
Scuba diving	1.9 (0.1)	1.9 (0.2)	1.9 (0.2)	2.0 (0.4)	2.2 (0.5)
Surfing	1.7 (0.1)	1.5 (0.2)	1.9 (0.2)	2.1 (0.4)	1.5 (0.4)
Windsurfing	0.8 (0.1)	0.9 (0.1)	0.8 (0.1)	0.7 (0.2)	0.6 (0.2)

[1] Missing data indicates that the activity was not asked during this interview season.
Source: NSRE 2000–2001 Versions 1–13, N = 63,090, Interview dates: 7/99 to 8/02.
Season sample sizes in chronological order: 20,624; 26,348; 9,254; 4,977.

Table 4.3 Percent participating in snow/ice-based outdoor activities in 4 periods relative to September 11, 2001, by persons 16 or older (95% confidence interval ±%)

Activity	Full NSRE Sample	9/1/99 to 8/31/00	9/1/00 to 9/10/01	9/11/01 to 2/28/02	After 2/28/02
Snow/ice activities	26.4 (0.4)	25.9 (0.6)	27.5 (0.6)	24.9 (1.2)	25.0 (1.4)
Sledding	15.1 (0.7)	. (.)[1]	15.1 (0.8)	14.6 (1.6)	. (.)
Downhill skiing	8.5 (0.2)	8.4 (0.4)	8.9 (0.4)	8.2 (0.7)	7.5 (0.8)
Ice skating outdoors	6.7 (0.5)	. (.)	6.7 (0.6)	6.5 (1.1)	. (.)
Snowmobiling	5.5 (0.2)	5.4 (0.3)	5.7 (0.3)	5.3 (0.6)	4.6 (0.7)
Snowboarding	4.9 (0.2)	4.5 (0.3)	5.2 (0.3)	5.0 (0.6)	5.1 (0.7)
Cross-country skiing	3.8 (0.2)	3.9 (0.3)	3.8 (0.3)	3.6 (0.5)	3.3 (0.6)
Snowshoeing	2.1 (0.3)	. (.)	2.0 (0.3)	2.5 (0.7)	. (.)

[1]Missing data indicates that the activity was not asked during this interview season.
Source: NSRE 2000–2001 Versions 1–13, N = 63,090, Interview dates: 7/99 to 8/02.
Season sample sizes in chronological order: 20,624; 26,348; 9,254; 4,977.

Table 4.4 Percent participating in outdoor activities by gender for survey periods before and after September 11, 2001 (95% confidence interval ±%)

Activity	Male, 9/1/99 to 8/31/00	Male, After 2/28/02	Female, 9/1/99 to 8/31/00	Female, After 2/28/02
Walking for pleasure	82.0 (0.8)	77.5 (2.0)	86.3 (0.6)	84.1 (1.6)
Family gathering	73.4 (0.9)	73.1 (2.2)	74.2 (0.8)	74.7 (1.9)
Viewing/photographing scenery	60.6 (1.0)	57.0 (2.4)	61.3 (0.9)	60.9 (2.1)
Visiting nature centers/museums	59.0 (1.0)	55.0 (2.4)	55.9 (0.9)	55.6 (2.1)
Driving for pleasure	54.2 (1.0)	55.6 (2.1)	53.6 (0.9)	55.2 (1.9)
Picnicking	53.1 (1.0)	51.0 (2.1)	57.1 (0.9)	54.9 (1.9)
Sightseeing	52.8 (1.0)	46.0 (2.4)	55.5 (0.9)	50.3 (2.2)
Visiting historic sites	49.8 (1.0)	44.8 (2.4)	44.9 (0.9)	42.0 (2.1)
Viewing/photographing other wildlife	47.7 (1.0)	42.3 (2.4)	44.2 (0.9)	41.1 (2.1)
Swimming in lakes, streams	47.3 (1.0)	41.7 (2.1)	41.2 (0.9)	38.1 (1.8)
Fishing	44.6 (1.0)	40.8 (2.4)	25.1 (0.8)	22.4 (1.8)
Bicycling	44.2 (1.0)	39.7 (2.4)	35.1 (0.9)	35.6 (2.1)
Viewing/photographing flowers/trees	42.9 (1.0)	38.7 (2.4)	48.2 (0.9)	46.1 (2.2)
Boating	42.5 (1.0)	39.7 (2.4)	31.8 (0.9)	32.1 (2.0)
Visiting a wilderness or primitive area	41.7 (1.0)	41.5 (2.1)	26.9 (0.8)	26.9 (1.7)
Visiting a beach	41.5 (1.0)	42.9 (2.4)	38.4 (0.9)	45.0 (2.1)
Freshwater fishing	39.0 (1.0)	37.5 (2.1)	21.6 (0.8)	19.6 (1.5)
Day hiking	38.4 (1.0)	39.4 (2.1)	29.9 (0.8)	32.7 (1.8)
Gathering mushrooms, berries	31.3 (1.0)	30.6 (2.0)	24.1 (0.8)	22.3 (1.6)
Viewing/photographing birds	31.3 (1.0)	28.9 (2.2)	35.4 (0.9)	33.7 (2.0)
Warmwater fishing	31.2 (1.0)	28.9 (2.2)	16.0 (0.7)	13.9 (1.5)
Snow/ice activities	30.0 (1.0)	28.1 (2.2)	22.5 (0.8)	23.0 (1.8)
Visiting a farm or agricultural setting	29.7 (2.2)	27.2 (2.2)	26.7 (1.9)	23.3 (1.8)
Motorboating	29.5 (1.0)	29.5 (2.2)	20.4 (0.7)	20.1 (1.7)
Visiting waterside (besides beach)	29.5 (1.0)	27.8 (2.2)	25.7 (0.8)	24.5 (1.9)
Viewing/photographing fish	27.9 (0.9)	24.6 (2.1)	22.9 (0.8)	20.0 (1.7)
Developed camping	27.6 (0.9)	28.6 (1.9)	23.6 (0.8)	22.7 (1.6)
Mountain biking	25.6 (1.0)	22.3 (1.8)	17.1 (0.7)	16.3 (1.4)
Driving off-road	22.5 (0.9)	22.2 (1.8)	13.4 (0.7)	14.5 (1.3)

Table 4.4 Percent participating in outdoor activities by gender for survey periods before and after September 11, 2001 (95% confidence interval ±%) *continued*

Activity	Male, 9/1/99 to 8/31/00	Male, After 2/28/02	Female, 9/1/99 to 8/31/00	Female, After 2/28/02
Visiting prehistoric/archeological sites	21.9 (0.9)	18.5 (1.9)	19.6 (0.7)	19.4 (1.7)
Primitive camping	21.0 (0.8)	20.5 (1.7)	11.2 (0.6)	11.2 (1.2)
Hunting	19.5 (0.8)	19.8 (1.7)	3.8 (0.4)	2.9 (0.6)
Coldwater fishing	18.1 (0.9)	15.0 (1.7)	9.1 (0.6)	6.5 (1.1)
Big game hunting	14.8 (0.8)	15.9 (1.6)	2.7 (0.3)	2.0 (0.5)
Backpacking	14.6 (0.7)	13.2 (1.4)	7.7 (0.5)	8.1 (1.0)
Saltwater fishing	13.9 (0.7)	13.6 (1.7)	6.5 (0.5)	6.8 (1.1)
Small game hunting	13.1 (0.8)	13.5 (1.7)	1.9 (0.3)	1.8 (0.6)
Canoeing	11.6 (0.7)	9.9 (1.5)	7.7 (0.5)	8.8 (1.2)
Downhill skiing	10.9 (0.7)	8.6 (1.4)	6.2 (0.5)	6.7 (1.1)
Rafting	10.7 (0.6)	12.9 (1.4)	8.8 (0.5)	11.1 (1.2)
Jetskiing	10.6 (0.6)	10.5 (1.5)	8.1 (0.5)	8.8 (1.2)
Horseback riding (general)	10.5 (0.6)	7.3 (1.3)	9.3 (0.5)	9.4 (1.3)
Waterskiing	10.3 (0.6)	9.2 (1.4)	6.4 (0.5)	7.8 (1.2)
Horseback riding on trails	8.5 (0.6)	7.0 (1.1)	7.5 (0.5)	7.5 (1.0)
Snorkeling	8.2 (0.6)	8.7 (1.4)	5.2 (0.4)	6.4 (1.1)
Snowmobiling	7.0 (0.6)	6.2 (1.2)	4.0 (0.4)	3.2 (0.8)
Snowboarding	6.6 (0.6)	6.8 (1.2)	2.7 (0.3)	3.7 (0.8)
Anadromous fishing	6.3 (0.5)	4.5 (1.0)	2.6 (0.3)	1.7 (0.6)
Rowing	5.7 (0.5)	4.1 (1.0)	3.5 (0.3)	3.1 (0.7)
Sailing	5.6 (0.5)	5.2 (1.1)	4.6 (0.4)	5.7 (1.0)
Cross-country skiing	4.5 (0.5)	3.4 (0.9)	3.5 (0.4)	3.3 (0.8)
Migratory bird hunting	4.3 (0.4)	4.2 (1.0)	0.6 (0.1)	0.4 (0.3)
Kayaking	3.7 (0.4)	4.6 (1.0)	2.7 (0.3)	4.3 (0.9)
Scuba diving	3.0 (0.4)	2.8 (0.8)	0.9 (0.2)	1.8 (0.6)
Surfing	2.0 (0.3)	2.0 (0.7)	0.9 (0.2)	1.2 (0.5)
Windsurfing	1.2 (0.2)	0.4 (0.3)	0.6 (0.1)	0.8 (0.4)

Source: NSRE 2000–2001 Versions 1–13, N = 63,090, Interview dates: 7/99 to 8/02.
Season sample sizes in chronological order: 20,624; 26,348; 9,254; 4,977.

the lower half of the list in Table 4.5—that is, activities that tend to be more specialized, active, and requiring skill. These are also activities in which this age group is less active than is the younger group, 16 to 24 years.

Age 46 to 60

In keeping with the trend observed of the previous 2 younger age groups, participation rates between pre- and post-9/11 periods fell for significantly fewer activities (compared with the younger age groups). Decreases were observed for only 33 of the 56 activities listed. As with the other age groups, these included the more widely popular activities, for example, walking, swimming, and sightseeing. Increases were seen for driving for pleasure, visiting a beach, visiting a wilderness or other primitive area, day hiking, and interestingly, rafting, and kayaking.

Age 61 or Over

Participation patterns for this oldest age group was very similar to that of the 46–60 year olds. Well over half—32 of 56— of the activities showed declining participation. There were many more where participation increased. Decreases were observed for many of the same activities noted earlier for younger age groups. Increases were observed for 20 of the 56 activities listed in Table 4.5. These included family gatherings out-of-doors, driving for pleasure, visiting a beach, snow/ice activities, driving off-road, hunting, and saltwater fishing. In essence, younger persons became a bit less active while older persons became a bit more active.

Table 4.5 Percent participating in outdoor activities by age for survey periods before and after September 11, 2001 (95% confidence interval ±%)

Activity	Ages 16–24 9/1/99 to 8/31/00	Ages 16–24 After 2/28/02	Ages 25–45 9/1/99 to 8/31/00	Ages 25–45 After 2/28/02	Ages 46–60 9/1/99 to 8/31/00	Ages 46–60 After 2/28/02	Ages 61+ 9/1/99 to 8/31/00	Ages 61+ After 2/28/02
Walking for pleasure	85.8 (1.3)	84.0 (3.1)	85.4 (0.8)	82.5 (1.9)	85.4 (1.0)	79.8 (2.6)	79.4 (1.3)	75.5 (3.2)
Family gathering	79.4 (1.5)	76.2 (3.6)	77.3 (0.9)	77.9 (2.1)	71.7 (1.2)	71.7 (2.9)	64.1 (1.6)	66.1 (3.6)
Swimming in lakes, streams	60.7 (1.8)	54.1 (3.7)	51.9 (1.1)	46.3 (2.2)	39.5 (1.3)	36.4 (2.6)	18.3 (1.2)	15.7 (2.4)
Visiting nature centers	58.9 (1.8)	55.4 (4.1)	66.1 (1.0)	65.2 (2.4)	58.2 (1.3)	52.8 (3.2)	38.4 (1.6)	37.6 (3.6)
Viewing/photographing scenery	58.4 (1.8)	54.2 (4.2)	64.6 (1.0)	63.9 (2.4)	66.4 (1.3)	65.0 (3.0)	50.2 (1.6)	47.3 (3.8)
Bicycling	55.5 (1.8)	53.2 (4.2)	46.4 (1.1)	43.4 (2.5)	31.9 (1.3)	29.7 (2.9)	18.3 (1.2)	17.5 (2.9)
Driving for pleasure	53.5 (1.8)	49.3 (3.7)	56.6 (1.1)	58.9 (2.2)	57.7 (1.3)	60.4 (2.7)	45.3 (1.6)	49.0 (3.2)
Sightseeing	50.2 (1.8)	41.6 (4.1)	56.5 (1.1)	51.7 (2.5)	58.5 (1.3)	54.5 (3.2)	49.2 (1.6)	41.1 (3.7)
Boating	50.1 (1.8)	50.2 (4.2)	41.4 (1.0)	37.9 (2.5)	34.0 (1.3)	34.9 (3.0)	18.5 (1.3)	16.6 (2.8)
Visiting a beach	49.3 (1.8)	52.3 (4.2)	46.1 (1.1)	49.2 (2.5)	37.2 (1.3)	42.9 (3.2)	21.6 (1.3)	25.3 (3.3)
Visiting historic sites	48.3 (1.8)	45.5 (4.2)	50.3 (1.1)	45.0 (2.5)	51.7 (1.4)	46.8 (3.2)	35.6 (1.6)	33.6 (3.6)
Picnicking	47.7 (1.8)	45.0 (3.7)	62.4 (1.0)	59.4 (2.2)	58.8 (1.3)	56.5 (2.7)	44.8 (1.6)	44.5 (3.2)
Snow/ice activities	46.8 (1.8)	42.3 (4.1)	31.2 (1.0)	29.7 (2.3)	17.7 (1.0)	17.5 (2.4)	5.0 (0.7)	7.0 (1.9)
Viewing/photographing wildlife	45.9 (1.8)	38.9 (4.1)	49.5 (1.1)	45.2 (2.5)	48.8 (1.4)	46.1 (3.2)	35.6 (1.5)	32.4 (3.5)
Visiting a wilderness/primitive area	44.7 (1.8)	39.0 (3.7)	38.0 (1.0)	38.9 (2.2)	30.9 (1.3)	32.2 (2.6)	19.0 (1.3)	20.4 (2.6)
Fishing	44.0 (1.8)	37.2 (4.0)	37.6 (1.0)	34.2 (2.4)	31.8 (1.3)	30.5 (2.9)	21.9 (1.3)	19.9 (3.0)
Viewing/photographing flowers/trees	41.3 (1.8)	36.3 (4.0)	47.3 (1.1)	43.9 (2.5)	50.9 (1.4)	47.4 (3.2)	41.3 (1.6)	40.6 (3.7)
Freshwater fishing	38.4 (1.8)	30.5 (3.5)	32.8 (1.0)	32.2 (2.1)	27.5 (1.2)	28.7 (2.5)	18.9 (1.3)	17.2 (2.4)
Day hiking	37.9 (1.8)	35.3 (3.6)	40.4 (1.0)	42.2 (2.2)	32.1 (1.3)	37.5 (2.7)	19.7 (1.3)	22.1 (2.7)
Visiting waterside (besides beach)	36.9 (1.8)	33.7 (3.9)	31.7 (1.0)	29.4 (2.3)	24.5 (1.2)	25.0 (2.8)	13.8 (1.1)	12.2 (2.5)
Mountain biking	33.6 (1.9)	27.9 (3.4)	26.4 (1.0)	23.7 (1.9)	14.9 (1.0)	15.5 (2.0)	5.5 (0.8)	5.2 (1.4)
Gather mushrooms, berries	32.9 (1.7)	28.8 (3.4)	29.5 (1.0)	29.1 (2.0)	26.9 (1.2)	25.7 (2.4)	19.4 (1.3)	18.8 (2.5)
Developed camping	31.5 (1.7)	32.0 (3.5)	30.7 (1.0)	31.1 (2.0)	22.8 (1.1)	21.5 (2.2)	12.7 (1.1)	12.3 (2.1)
Motorboating	31.2 (1.7)	31.7 (3.9)	27.8 (1.0)	26.4 (2.2)	23.7 (1.2)	25.0 (2.8)	13.8 (1.1)	13.0 (2.5)
Warmwater fishing	31.0 (1.8)	24.6 (3.6)	25.6 (1.0)	22.9 (2.1)	21.0 (1.2)	22.6 (2.7)	13.9 (1.2)	12.3 (2.5)
Visiting a farm/agricultural setting	29.8 (4.1)	24.6 (3.6)	32.8 (2.3)	29.5 (2.3)	26.7 (2.7)	25.0 (2.8)	19.3 (2.8)	17.1 (2.8)

Table 4.5 Percent participating in outdoor activities by age for survey periods before and after September 11, 2001 (95% confidence interval ±%) *continued*

Activity	Ages 16–24 9/1/99 to 8/31/00	Ages 16–24 After 2/28/02	Ages 25–45 9/1/99 to 8/31/00	Ages 25–45 After 2/28/02	Ages 46–60 9/1/99 to 8/31/00	Ages 46–60 After 2/28/02	Ages 61+ 9/1/99 to 8/31/00	Ages 61+ After 2/28/02
Driving off-road	28.9 (1.8)	27.3 (3.3)	20.5 (0.9)	21.3 (1.8)	13.9 (1.0)	13.0 (1.8)	5.8 (0.8)	8.4 (1.8)
Primitive camping	25.7 (1.6)	22.1 (3.1)	18.2 (0.8)	19.1 (1.7)	12.6 (0.9)	12.2 (1.8)	5.3 (0.7)	5.9 (1.5)
Viewing/photographing birds	23.3 (1.6)	17.3 (3.2)	33.6 (1.0)	30.6 (2.3)	38.9 (1.3)	41.0 (3.1)	37.1 (1.6)	37.3 (3.6)
Viewing/photographing fish	23.2 (1.6)	18.9 (3.3)	30.3 (1.0)	25.9 (2.2)	25.8 (1.2)	25.7 (2.8)	17.3 (1.2)	14.3 (2.6)
Visiting prehistoric/archaeological sites	22.1 (1.5)	19.4 (3.3)	22.6 (0.9)	20.9 (2.1)	22.6 (1.1)	21.4 (2.6)	13.8 (1.1)	11.8 (2.4)
Jetskiing	21.5 (1.5)	20.9 (3.4)	10.1 (0.6)	10.0 (1.5)	4.5 (0.6)	5.1 (1.4)	1.2 (0.4)	1.5 (0.9)
Rafting	20.1 (1.5)	21.4 (3.1)	10.6 (0.7)	13.2 (1.5)	6.5 (0.7)	9.3 (1.6)	1.6 (0.4)	2.5 (1.0)
Backpacking	18.1 (1.4)	16.8 (2.8)	13.3 (0.7)	12.6 (1.5)	8.4 (0.8)	8.9 (1.6)	2.3 (0.5)	1.7 (0.8)
Coldwater fishing	18.1 (1.5)	15.4 (3.0)	14.8 (0.8)	11.1 (1.6)	13.1 (1.0)	10.1 (1.9)	6.8 (0.9)	5.1 (1.7)
Waterskiing	17.9 (1.4)	18.5 (3.2)	9.4 (0.6)	8.5 (1.4)	4.2 (0.5)	5.6 (1.5)	1.0 (0.3)	0.8 (0.7)
Canoeing	16.0 (1.3)	15.3 (3.0)	10.8 (0.7)	10.4 (1.5)	8.0 (0.7)	8.5 (1.8)	2.9 (0.5)	1.4 (0.9)
Horseback riding (general)	15.9 (1.3)	11.5 (2.7)	11.3 (0.7)	9.1 (1.5)	8.4 (0.8)	8.2 (1.8)	2.9 (0.5)	3.5 (1.4)
Downhill skiing	15.8 (1.4)	12.9 (2.8)	10.1 (0.7)	8.6 (1.4)	5.5 (0.7)	5.6 (1.5)	1.1 (0.4)	2.1 (1.1)
Hunting	15.1 (1.3)	11.8 (2.4)	12.1 (0.7)	12.2 (1.4)	10.4 (0.8)	11.3 (1.7)	7.1 (0.8)	7.5 (1.7)
Snowboarding	13.4 (1.3)	15.8 (3.0)	4.3 (0.5)	4.2 (1.0)	1.1 (0.3)	1.2 (0.7)	0.2 (0.2)	(.)[1]
Horseback riding on trails	12.8 (1.3)	9.4 (2.2)	9.0 (0.7)	9.3 (1.3)	7.0 (0.7)	6.5 (1.3)	2.3 (0.5)	1.8 (0.9)
Saltwater fishing	12.7 (1.2)	11.6 (2.7)	11.3 (0.7)	11.0 (1.6)	9.4 (0.8)	9.5 (1.9)	5.7 (0.7)	7.0 (1.9)
Small game hunting	10.2 (1.2)	9.2 (2.4)	7.7 (0.6)	7.8 (1.4)	7.0 (0.7)	7.4 (1.7)	3.7 (0.7)	4.9 (1.6)
Big game hunting	10.1 (1.2)	8.9 (2.1)	9.7 (0.7)	10.2 (1.3)	8.1 (0.8)	8.7 (1.5)	4.8 (0.7)	5.5 (1.5)
Snowmobiling	10.0 (1.2)	7.5 (2.2)	6.4 (0.6)	5.6 (1.2)	3.2 (0.5)	2.9 (1.1)	1.2 (0.4)	1.7 (1.0)
Snorkeling	9.4 (1.1)	10.0 (2.5)	8.1 (0.6)	8.5 (1.4)	6.2 (0.7)	6.8 (1.6)	1.6 (0.4)	3.2 (1.3)
Rowing	7.7 (1.0)	5.6 (1.9)	4.4 (0.4)	4.0 (1.0)	4.6 (0.6)	3.0 (1.1)	1.7 (0.4)	1.1 (0.8)
Anadromous fishing	7.0 (0.9)	3.8 (1.6)	4.6 (0.4)	3.3 (0.9)	4.1 (0.5)	3.7 (1.2)	1.8 (0.4)	0.9 (0.7)
Sailing	6.9 (0.9)	9.0 (2.4)	5.3 (0.5)	5.0 (1.1)	5.0 (0.6)	5.4 (1.4)	3.0 (0.6)	2.7 (1.2)
Kayaking	5.9 (0.9)	9.4 (2.4)	3.5 (0.4)	3.2 (0.9)	2.3 (0.4)	4.4 (1.3)	0.6 (0.2)	1.6 (0.9)

Table 4.5 Percent participating in outdoor activities by age for survey periods before and after September 11, 2001 (95% confidence interval ±%) *continued*

Activity	Ages 16–24 9/1/99 to 8/31/00	Ages 16–24 After 2/28/02	Ages 25–45 9/1/99 to 8/31/00	Ages 25–45 After 2/28/02	Ages 46–60 9/1/99 to 8/31/00	Ages 46–60 After 2/28/02	Ages 61+ 9/1/99 to 8/31/00	Ages 61+ After 2/28/02
Cross-country skiing	5.3 (0.9)	4.5 (1.7)	4.5 (0.5)	3.5 (0.9)	4.6 (0.6)	3.5 (1.2)	1.0 (0.3)	1.4 (0.9)
Migratory bird hunting	4.2 (0.7)	3.6 (1.6)	2.4 (0.3)	2.0 (0.7)	1.8 (0.4)	2.5 (1.0)	1.1 (0.3)	0.9 (0.7)
Surfing	3.7 (0.7)	4.7 (1.8)	1.3 (0.2)	1.2 (0.6)	0.8 (0.2)	0.6 (0.5)	0.2 (0.1)	. (.)
Scuba diving	3.1 (0.6)	4.8 (1.8)	2.3 (0.3)	2.5 (0.8)	1.5 (0.3)	1.1 (0.7)	0.5 (0.2)	0.3 (0.4)
Windsurfing	2.0 (0.5)	1.8 (1.1)	0.8 (0.2)	0.4 (0.3)	0.7 (0.2)	0.4 (0.4)	0.1 (0.1)	. (.)

[1]Missing data indicate that the activity was not asked during that interview season.
Source: NSRE 2000–2001 Versions 1–13, N = 63,090, Interview dates: 7/99 to 8/02. Season sample sizes: 20,624—9/1/99 to 8/31/00; 4,977—after 2/28/02

Section III

Outdoor Recreation Participation by Activity Groups

The 3 chapters in this section (Chapters 5–7) examine outdoor recreation participation across different types of outdoor activities. In Chapter 5, estimates of the numbers and percentages of Americans participating are provided for land, water, or snow/ice-based activities. Of all 70+ activities examined, the most popular in 2000–2001, in terms of the number of Americans 16 years old or older who participated, was walking for pleasure. Almost 177 million (about 83%) did some walking outdoors within the last 12 months. For Chapter 6, estimates of the numbers and percentages of people who participate in viewing/learning/gathering activities were the focus. Included are activities such as wildlife viewing, viewing flowers and trees, gathering natural products (e.g., mushrooms), visiting historic sites, and other similar activities. When viewed from the perspective of total numbers of times or occasions in which people participate in them, viewing/learning/gathering activities as a group are found at the top of the list of general types of outdoor recreation by a substantial margin. Chapter 7 is devoted to outdoor sports. The term "outdoor sports," as used in this chapter, includes any activities undertaken out-of-doors that require physical exertion, some level of skill and, typically, specialized equipment and/or facilities. Sports come in many forms and entice many millions to participate in them as individuals or as teams. Over 84 million persons 16 or older participated in the sport of bicycling during the 12 months just prior to their being interviewed. Among the many forms of outdoor sports, a number are individual sports, including inline skating or rollerblading. We found that over 47 million Americans 16 or older participated in rollerblading in 2000–2001.

Chapter 5
Participation in Land, Water, and Snow/Ice-Based Outdoor Activities

Since 1960 the length and richness of the list of activities of interest to people as they sought and participated in outdoor recreation has grown. In 1960 people were asked about their participation in only 33 activities. For that time, 33 activities seemed to pretty well cover the many ways people sought to enjoy the out-of-doors. Now, a "short" list can exceed 100 activities. This short list would include only the more widely known forms of outdoor participation.

This chapter provides estimates of the numbers and percentages of Americans ages 16 and older who participate in activities generally dependent on the physical natural resources of land, water, and snow/ice in the "great outdoors" or in the more domesticated outdoors of backyards and city parks. We generally do not include in this chapter viewing/learning-oriented activities (e.g., birding) or individual or team sports (e.g., tennis or soccer). These types of activities are not included here because a chapter is devoted to each of them immediately following this chapter. In addition to percentages and numbers of participants, the number of different days during which participants engaged in the activities is listed. The interest here is to attach some measure of intensity or frequency to participation reporting. An activity such as walking, in which participants engage often, will assume a much different profile from an activity, such as backpacking, which is infrequently engaged. Knowledge of these different profiles is important when planning access, facilities, or information to accommodate the activities they describe.

Highlights

Of all activities, the most popular in 2000–2001 in terms of number of Americans participating was walking for pleasure. Among people 16 or older, 83%, almost 177 million, did some walking for pleasure in the last 12 months. In addition, around 71 million people chose to day hike and/or visit a wilderness or primitive area. For many people, day hiking or visiting a wilderness area are ways of escaping from the routine and pressures of daily life to enjoy the peace and tranquility of nature. The least popular land-based activities in terms of numbers participating are rock climbing (9.2 million), migratory bird hunting (5.1 million), and orienteering (4.3 million). These activities require specialization and knowledge that excludes many people.

At the top of the list for water-based activities was swimming in a pond, lake, stream, ocean, or other natural water. Over 89 million people ages 16 or older reported in the 2000–2001 survey period that they swam in natural waters over the previous 12 months. The number who visited a beach (86.5 million), either freshwater or saltwater, was a close 2nd in popularity. Fishing in any kind of water was 3rd at nearly 73 million. About 63 million stated that they had fished in freshwater and 22 million said they went saltwater angling, and about 12 million fished in both freshwater and saltwater. More than 55 million visited a waterside (other than a beach) for recreation activities. In 5th place among water-based activities was motorboating with almost 52 million people having participated at least once in the 12 months preceding their interview. Generally, fewer Americans participate in snow/ice-based outdoor activities and also spend far fewer days per year than they do in land or water activities. Much of this is due, of course, to climate, but also to the need for specialized skills such as those required for downhill skiing. In most snow/ice based activities, 80% or more of participants put in just 10 or fewer days per person per year.

Figure 5.1 illustrates the different levels of popularity of the 10 most popular land, water or snow/ice based activities among people living in the United States. It shows percentages of persons 16 or older participating and average days of participation per person per year.

As with number and percentage of the population participating, days of participation in walking topped the list, indicating that more Americans walk

Visiting beaches and other water activities are a growing activity in the United States. Photo courtesy of USDA Photography Center, Ken Hammond

on more days throughout the year than they participate in any other activity. The mean for the 83% of Americans who walk is almost 102 days per person per year, more by a substantial margin than for any other activity. Except for visiting a farm or other agricultural setting for recreation, all the top activities in terms of days of participation per year are road/trail based. With a few exceptions, even with the booming economy of the mid- to late-1990s, the number of days that participants in the various land, water and snow/ice activities put in over the course of a 12-month period was relatively stable. Exceptions were modest increases in days of big game hunting, coldwater fishing and anadromous fishing, and a decrease in days of visiting a beach.

Percentages and Numbers Participating in Land-Based Activities

We and others using the participation estimates reported in this book and in previous publications have found it useful to distinguish activities based on the primary type of resource on which the activities depend and occur. Presented first in this chapter are the land-based activities. These are activities that occur mostly along trails, roads, or cross-country, or they occur in or at developed or undeveloped recreation sites. Activities that are mostly urban based, such as running/jogging or swimming in pools, are not included in this chapter; they appear in chapter 7. Table 5.1 (p. 106) reports the percentages and numbers of people ages 16 or older who participated at least once in the past 12 months

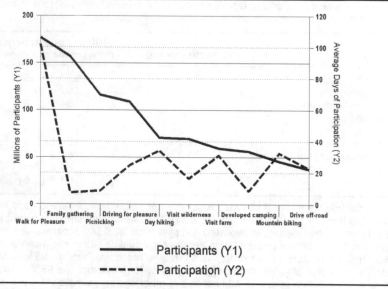

Figure 5.1 Millions of participants ages 16 or older and average days of participation per person per year for 10 most popular activities, 2000–2001

in the top third of land-based outdoor activities. This group of activities includes walking or driving for pleasure, family gatherings, gardening, picnicking, attending outdoor concerts/plays, bicycling, and yard games. Among these more popular activities, the most popular is walking, with almost 177 million participants of age 16 or older. It is not surprising that walking for pleasure is the most popular activity as people often find local areas in which to walk daily either before, during, or after work. The vast majority of walking undoubtedly occurs where people live, primarily in developed areas. It is probably the most accessible of all activities, which is a primary reason for its continued popularity. Family gatherings is the 2nd most popular activity with over 156 million participants. Family gatherings out-of-doors is a traditional activity that continues to be popular across the years as people come together to drink, eat, and socialize with family and friends. Gardening or landscaping for pleasure is also highly popular with nearly 3 out of 4 Americans participating (155 million). This is predominantly a home-based activity but other opportunities exist at community gardens, churches, and other neighborhood centers. Picnicking, with just over 116 million participants each year, also continues to be a popular activity for many of the same reasons as family gatherings (e.g., socializing, eating, and drinking with friends). More than one half of Americans age 16 and older (109 million) also enjoyed taking a drive for pleasure at least once in the past year. The last 3 activities in the top third of land-based nature activities (i.e., attending outdoor concerts, bicycling, and yard games) are participated in fairly equally by about 39% of the population, or between 83 and 85 million participants a year.

Table 5.1 Percentages and numbers of people 16 or older participating in the most popular third of land-based outdoor activities, 2000–2001

Activity	% Participating	Millions of Participants (95% Confidence Interval ±%)
Walking for pleasure	83.0	176.8 (0.5)
Family gathering	73.5	156.6 (0.5)
Gardening/landscaping for pleasure	72.6	154.7 (2.8)
Picnicking	54.5	116.1 (0.9)
Driving for pleasure	51.2	109.1 (0.9)
Attending an outdoor concert	39.8	84.8 (3.8)
Bicycling	39.5	84.2 (1.3)
Yard games	39.4	83.9 (3.6)

Note: A confidence interval is a statistical estimate based on sample data. At some designated level of confidence (usually 95%), the interval is believed to contain the true estimate of participants in repeated samples. That is, if 100 separate samples were drawn, the true estimate or population parameter would lie within the interval in 95 of those samples, or 95% of the time." It is *not* interpreted as "we are 95% confident the true parameter is in the range." For example, for bicycling, the 95% confidence interval is 84.2 million people ±1.3% of this number or approximately 1.1 million, resulting in an interval of 83.1 to 85.3 million. The confidence intervals for most activities are very small because of the large sample size of more than 40,000 people.

Table 5.2 shows the percentages and numbers of people 16 or older who participated in the middle third of land-based outdoor activities at least once during the last year. Among these activities, around 70 million people chose to hike and/or visit a wilderness or other primitive area within the last 12 months. For many people hiking or visiting a wilderness area are ways of escaping from the hustle and bustle of cities, towns, work, or daily life to enjoy the more peaceful atmosphere a natural setting can offer. Contrary to popular images of the "great outdoors," however, these activities do not occur only in backcountry areas. Many local and state parks and recreation areas, as well as private land, also provide opportunities for people to visit, enjoy, and hike in natural areas.

Almost 60 million people said they visited a farm or other agricultural setting for recreation. While not a new activity, it is new to the national recreation survey series in 2000–2001. Frequently called "agritourism" when it involves travel, this is actually a series of activities that share some type of agricultural theme. Examples include viewing rural scenery, watching farmyard and livestock activities, picking or buying fresh fruit or vegetables, hayrides, cutting Christmas trees, and any other leisure-time educational activity related to agriculture. Suppliers are frequently private landowners, but university experiment stations and other public agencies provide these types of recreation opportunities as well.

More than 56 million people camped at developed sites last year, while just over 34 million decided to camp in primitive areas. Primitive camping requires greater skill and knowledge than developed camping, and it embodies fewer conveniences and comforts, hence these are likely reasons for its lower participation relative to developed camping. People who hunt (24 million) and those who backpack (23 million) also need certain basic skills, such as the ability to read a map, and need a sizeable amount of specialized equipment. These too are likely reasons why fewer people participate in these particular activities than participate in mountain biking (46 million) or driving off-road (37 million). Though both backpacking and mountain biking require a significant amount of

Table 5.2 Percentages and numbers of people 16 or older participating in the middle third of land-based outdoor activities, 2000–2001

Activity	% Participating	Millions of Participants (95% Confidence Interval ±%)
Day hiking	33.3	70.9 (1.2)
Visiting a wilderness/primitive area	32.7	69.7 (1.2)
Visiting a farm/agricultural setting	27.9	59.5 (2.2)
Developed camping	26.4	56.2 (1.5)
Mountain biking	21.4	45.6 (1.9)
Driving off-road	17.5	37.2 (2.3)
Primitive camping	16.0	34.1 (1.9)
Hunting	11.3	24.1 (2.7)
Backpacking	10.7	22.8 (2.8)

physical stamina that may limit participation by older persons, more opportunities for mountain biking exist close-to-home than for backpacking, in or around the communities where cyclists live.

The least popular of land-based activities (not including viewing/learning and sports) are shown in Table 5.3. None of these activities draws more than 10% of people age 16 or older. At the top are nearly 21 million who participated 1 or more times in horseback riding during the 12 months just previous to their being interviewed for the NSRE. Of these riders, an estimated 16.6 million rode horses on trails. Horseback riding, whether in a ring or on a trail, is more readily available today as many facilities now lease horses and offer reasonably priced riding lessons. The least popular land-based activities in terms of total number of participants are rock climbing (9.2 million), migratory bird hunting (5.0 million), and orienteering (4.3 million). For the most part, these activities require a high degree of specialization and knowledge. All of the hunting activities inventoried by the NSRE are in this bottom third of activities. Some of the more risky activities, such as mountain and rock climbing, are also in this bottom third.

Percentages and Numbers Participating in Water-Based Activities

Water has always been a major attractant for outdoor recreation. That was one of the basic findings of the Outdoor Recreation Resources Review Commission in 1960. It remains true today. Table 5.4 provides the percentages and numbers of Americans age 16 or older who participated in the top third of water-based activities at least once during the last year. This group of activities includes swimming, visiting a beach, fishing (generally, any type of water or species), freshwater fishing, visiting watersides, and motorboating.

At the top of this list is swimming in a lake, pond, stream, or the ocean (i.e., any kind of outdoor swimming that does not occur in a pool). It was the most popular water-based nature activity with 89 million people reporting they partici-

Table 5.3 Percentages and numbers of Americans 16 or older participating in the bottom third of land-based outdoor activities, 2000–2001

Activity	% Participating	Millions of Participants (95% Confidence Interval ±%)
Horseback riding (general)	9.7	20.6 (3.1)
Big game hunting	8.4	17.9 (3.6)
Horseback riding on trails	7.8	16.6 (3.9)
Small game hunting	7.2	15.4 (4.2)
Mountain climbing	6.0	12.9 (11.7)
Rock climbing	4.3	9.2 (13.9)
Migratory bird hunting	2.4	5.0 (4.2)
Orienteering	2.0	4.3 (19.9)

Table 5.4 Percentages and numbers participating in the top third of water-based outdoor activities for 2000–2001

Activity	% Participating	Millions of Participants (95% Confidence Interval ±%)
Swimming (lakes, streams, ponds, oceans)	41.7	89.0 (1.2)
Visiting a beach	40.6	86.5 (1.2)
Fishing (all types)	34.1	72.7 (1.2)
Visiting a waterside (other than beaches)	26.0	55.4 (1.5)
Motorboating	24.4	52.0 (1.6)

pated in outdoor swimming activities over the previous 12 months. The number who visited a beach (86.5 million) came in a close 2nd in popularity. Though beach visits are closely associated with swimming, not all who visited a beach were assumed to have also gone swimming there so those activities were asked separately. Nearly 73 million people reported that they fished last year in freshwater, saltwater, or both. The 4th most popular water-based activity was simply visiting a waterside—other than a beach—for recreation activities (about 55 million). These visits are no doubt closely related to family gatherings, picnicking, and other passive leisure activities and demonstrate the popularity and attraction of water resources as a recreation setting. Almost 52 million people went motorboating at least once last year. Since the first of the United States' National Recreation Surveys, the technology of motorboats has changed nothing short of miraculously. Very powerful engines, development of new and stronger materials, and a host of other technological advances have changed motorboating dramatically.

Table 5.5 includes the percentages and numbers of Americans ages 16 or older who participated in the middle third of water-based activities at least once during the last 12 months. In regard to fishing, the number of Americans (48.2 million) who fished in warmwater at least once in the last year were only slightly less than the combined totals of people who fished in coldwater (29 million) and saltwater (22 million). Warmwater is typically defined to include inland

Table 5.5 Percentages and numbers participating in the middle third of water-based outdoor activities, 2000–2001

Activity	% Participating	Millions of Participants (95% Confidence Interval ±%)
Warm freshwater fishing	22.6	48.2 (1.8)
Cold freshwater fishing	13.6	28.9 (2.2)
Saltwater fishing	10.4	22.1 (2.9)
Canoeing	9.7	20.7 (3.1)
Jet skiing	9.5	20.3 (3.2)
Rafting	9.5	20.3 (3.2)

lakes, rivers, streams, and other flowing or still water where temperatures are too warm for trout or other coldwater species to live and breed. Coldwater usually is limited to high elevation or northerly streams and lakes where trout of various species are found. As for other activities, roughly the same percentage (about 9.5%) and number of people (about 20 million) participated in canoeing, jetskiing, or rafting at least once last year. Jetskiing is use of a personal watercraft, an activity that exploded in recent years, largely replacing waterskiing.

Table 5.6 presents the percentages and numbers of people age 16 or older who participated in 1 or more of the bottom third of water-based activities at least once during the last 12 months. The activity of sailing requires the development of several skills (e.g., navigating, tacking, docking) that often take considerable time to master. Nevertheless, almost 11 million Americans went sailing in the last year. Over 9 million people went rowing last year, which by coincidence was also the same number of people that went fishing for salmon, shad, or trout (i.e., anadromous species that live in saltwater but migrate back to freshwater for spawning). Only 3.5% of Americans went kayaking last year, but that percentage represents nearly 7.5 million people. Plus, kayaking since 1995 is the fastest growing activity in the United States (a 185.7% increase). Ice fishing was the least popular water-based nature activity inventoried with the NSRE, with just 2.9% of Americans or 6.2 million people having participated during the last year. The fact that ice fishing is a seasonal activity only possible in certain northern states and high elevation places helps explain why it receives lower participation.

Percentages and Numbers Participating in Snow/Ice-Based Activities

Winter activities have been growing in popularity over the last few decades. Much of this is driven by new technology and by the growth of snowboarding. Table 5.7 shows the percentages and numbers of people age 16 or older who have participated in snow/ice-based activities at least once within the last year. This group of activities includes sledding, downhill skiing, snowmobiling, snowboarding, cross-country skiing, and snowshoeing. More than one fourth of

Table 5.6 Percentages and numbers participating in the bottom third of water-based outdoor activities, 2000–2001

Activity	% Participating	Millions of Participants (95% Confidence Interval ±%)
Sailing	5.1	10.9 (3.9)
Anadromous fishing	4.4	9.4 (4.6)
Rowing	4.4	9.4 (4.6)
Kayaking	3.5	7.4 (5.7)
Ice fishing	2.9	6.2 (17.2)

Snowboarding has become highly popular in only a few short years. Photo courtesy of snowboard.com website

the population, about 56 million, said they participated in at least 1 snow/ice activity. Just over 31 million Americans reported they went sledding last year, while 18 million went downhill skiing and almost 12 million went snowmobiling. Sledding is a traditional activity that continues to be popular with people of all ages. Downhill skiing is another traditional activity that requires considerably more skill than sledding as well as expensive equipment. Obviously, downhill skiers tend to be concentrated in the West and Northeast—as is true of all snow and ice activities—but avid skiers are present throughout the United States. Snowmobiling, by contrast, is a relatively new activity with beginnings of popularity in the 1960s. It can be a risk activity depending on how the person chooses to participate. Unlike snowmobiling or sledding, cross-country skiing and snowshoeing are both very physically challenging activities. Over 8 million Americans went cross-country skiing and 3.8 million went snowshoeing at least once during the last year.

Table 5.7 Percentages and numbers participating in snow/ice-based outdoor activities, 2000–2001

Activity	% Participating	Millions of Participants (95% Confidence Interval ±%)
Any snow or ice activity	26.4	56.3 (1.5)
Sledding	14.7	31.2 (6.8)
Downhill skiing	8.5	18.2 (3.5)
Snowmobiling	5.6	11.8 (3.6)
Snowboarding	4.9	10.4 (4.1)
Cross-country skiing	3.8	8.1 (5.3)
Snowshoeing	1.8	3.8 (22.2)

Frequency of Participation in Land, Water, and Snow/Ice-Based Outdoor Activities

This section reports frequency of participation across a number of groupings of outdoor recreation activities. As reported here, days of participation per year (the 12 months just preceding the participation interview) is the adopted measure. A day, or activity day, or participation day, is the occurrence of participation in an activity for any length of time during a single day. It is not meant to imply spending an entire 12- or 24-hour day participating in an activity. Participation by the same person in a single activity on 5 different days for 5 minutes per day or for 5 hours per day are each 5 activity days. Participation by 5 persons in a single activity each during a single day is also 5 activity days.

Days of participation is viewed as an index to overall level or intensity of participation. Because a person can participate in any number of activities during a single day, the measure is not additive over activities to derive a measure of overall, population-wide days of participation. It can, however, be viewed as an overall index to volume of activity participation across persons, activities and time, and thus be monitored over time to detect changes in participation patterns.

The first few tables report current means and percentages by ranges of days of participation for groups of related activities. The tables that follow report trends in days of participation per person per year from 1994–1995 to 2000–2001, a 6-year trend period.

Days of Land-Based Participation

Table 5.8 presents the mean days per person per year and percentages of participants by number of days per year among the top third of land-based activities ranked by average days per year. As with number and percentage of the population participating, days of participation in walking for pleasure topped the list indicating that more Americans walk on more days throughout the year than they participate in any other activity. The mean for the 83% of Americans who walk is almost 102 days per person per year, more by a substantial margin than for any other activity. Walking neighborhood streets or sidewalks; around a park, section of town, monument, lakeside, or sea front; or on trails in forested or other areas is obviously highly popular. No other activity had nearly as high a percentage of participants putting in more than 50 days per year. For most activities, the greatest percentages were in the 1-to-2 or 3-to-10 day ranges. Except for visiting a farm or other agricultural area, all the top third activities are road or trail based.

The next or middle third of activities ranked by days of participation per person per year is covered in Table 5.9. Across all the activities in this table, except for orienteering, the greatest percentage of people participated 3 to 10 days per year. The 3 hunting activities had the highest proportions of people who

Table 5.8 Mean days per year and percentages of participants by number of days per year in the top third of land-based activities, 2000–2001

Activity	Mean Days (95% CI ±%)	1–2 Days	3–10 Days	11–25 Days	26–50 Days	51+ Days
Walking for pleasure	101.8 (3.7)	4.2	17.2	15.2	16.3	47.0
Day hiking	34.3 (10.2)	19.4	39.3	16.7	8.7	15.8
Mountain biking	32.6 (10.1)	14.6	35.5	19.7	14.2	16.0
Visiting a farm/ agricultural setting	31.3 (13.1)	46.4	30.9	9.2	3.3	10.3
Driving for pleasure	25.0 (8.4)	15.7	43.3	20.5	10.6	10.0
Horseback riding	24.1 (20.3)	45.3	30.1	8.5	4.9	11.1
Driving off-road	23.0 (13.5)	23.6	38.2	17.9	10.2	10.1

participated 11 to 25 days per year. Those who participated in orienteering did so less frequently than days of participation in other activities, which is not surprising since participation in orienteering is usually done as part of an organized 1-day or 2-day event or competition.

Table 5.10 (p. 114) shows the mean days per year and percentages of participants by number of days per year in the bottom third of land-based activities during the last year. All of the bottom third land-based activities received an average of 6 to 9 days of participation per year, with rock climbing receiving the fewest days.

Days of Water-Based Participation

Table 5.11 (p. 114) shows the mean days per year and percentages of participants by number of days per year in the top half of water-based outdoor activities during the last year. On average, Americans fished on more days per person in warmwater than they devoted days to visiting a waterside or swimming in a lake or stream or doing any other water-based activity. Across all water-based activities the greatest percentages (60.6% to 76.3%) participated for 10 or fewer days per year during the previous year. Activities such as warmwater fishing,

Table 5.9 Mean days per year and percentages of participants by number of days per year in the middle third of land-based activities, 2000–2001

Activity	Mean Days (95% CI ±%)	1–2 Days	3–10 Days	11–25 Days	26–50 Days	51+ Days
Small game hunting	17.1 (15.8)	19.5	41.1	19.9	13.8	5.7
Visiting a wilderness or primitive area	16.5 (15.2)	38.1	40.8	12.4	3.9	4.8
Big game hunting	14.5 (9.7)	13.1	43.3	30.9	8.3	4.4
Migratory bird hunting	12.7 (8.7)	18.0	48.6	22.2	8.0	3.1
Orienteering	11.9 (40.3)	43.2	28.8	18.7	4.2	5.1

Table 5.10 Mean days per year and percentages of participants by number of days per year in the bottom third of land-based activities for 2000–2001

Activity	Mean Days (95% CI ±%)	1–2 Days	3–10 Days	11–25 Days	26–50 Days	51+ Days
Backpacking	9.5 (18.9)	31.5	48.9	13.4	3.7	2.5
Picnicking	8.8 (6.8)	29.6	51.2	13.2	3.5	2.5
Primitive camping	8.7 (11.5)	31.0	49.5	13.1	4.9	1.5
Developed camping	8.6 (9.3)	27.6	53.6	13.2	4.1	1.5
Mountain climbing	7.6 (23.8)	52.1	37.1	6.6	1.9	2.4
Family gathering	7.5 (6.7)	36.1	48.3	10.9	2.6	2.1
Rock climbing	6.1 (44.3)	57.6	34.0	6.2	0.5	1.6

cold-water fishing, and swimming in lakes or streams had somewhat greater percentages of participants who put in 11 or more days per year.

As for the bottom half of water activities, Table 5.12 shows jetskiing as topping the list of mean days per year. Across all water-based activities in this table, the greatest percentage of people participated in their activities for 10 or fewer days. Rafting had both the lowest participation in terms of mean days per year (4.4) and the highest percentage (58.1%) of participants in the 1 to 2 days per year range. Anadromous fishing had the lowest percentage (34.2%) of participants in the 1 to 2 day range and the highest percentage (48.9%) in the 3 to 10 days per year range. People who participated in jetskiing had the highest percentages in days per year ranges beyond 10 days. Jetskiing is relatively new in popularity and is fast growing. It has substituted for water-skiing for many water recreationists.

Days of Snow/Ice-Based Participation

Table 5.13 shows the mean days per year and percentages of participants by number of days per year in snow/ice-based activities. On average, Americans

Table 5.11 Mean days per year and percentages of participants by number of days per year in top half of water-based activities for 2000–2001

Activity	Mean Days (95% CI ±%)	1–2 Days	3–10 Days	11–25 Days	26–50 Days	51+ Days
Warmwater fishing	18.9 (9.5)	18.4	42.2	19.7	11.8	7.9
Visiting other watersides	15.9 (5.0)	30.0	43.6	14.2	6.9	5.4
Swimming in lakes, streams	15.0 (2.0)	18.0	48.3	19.5	9.2	5.0
Visiting a beach	14.3 (3.5)	21.9	50.6	16.3	6.7	4.5
Coldwater fishing	14.0 (15.0)	24.2	43.8	19.2	8.9	3.8
Motorboating	13.5 (2.9)	27.5	42.9	16.5	8.4	4.7
Saltwater fishing	12.9 (7.8)	33.9	42.4	12.3	6.8	4.6

Table 5.12 Mean days per year and percentages of participants by number of days per year in bottom half of water-based activities for 2000–2001

Activity	Mean Days (95% CI ±%)	1–2 Days	3–10 Days	11–25 Days	26–50 Days	51+ Days
Jetskiing	9.6 (6.3)	38.7	39.6	12.9	6.3	2.6
Anadromous fishing	8.5 (28.2)	34.2	48.9	9.2	6.6	1.1
Sailing	8.4 (10.7)	46.8	38.1	9.0	4.0	2.2
Kayaking	7.7 (12.9)	50.4	35.6	7.7	3.9	2.3
Rowing	7.1 (12.7)	50.5	38.1	6.5	2.8	2.2
Canoeing	7.0 (8.6)	46.3	41.5	8.2	2.5	1.5
Rafting	4.4 (13.6)	58.1	32.7	7.1	1.7	0.4

snowmobiled for more days (10.4) per person than they downhill skied (8.1), snowboarded (7.4), cross-country skied (6.4), or snowshoed (6.2) in the previous 12 months. Snowmobiling is a growing activity presently attracting people looking to see and experience forests and other natural lands under snow conditions. For all the snow/ice activities, the greatest percentages of participants (77.8% to 87.6%) did so for 10 or fewer days per year. All these snow and ice activities had at least 10% of people who participated for 11–25 days last year.

Table 5.13 Mean days per year and percentages of participants by number of days per year in snow/ice-based activities for 2000–2001

Activity	Mean Days (95% CI ±%)	1–2 Days	3–10 Days	11–25 Days	26–50 Days	51+ Days
Snowmobiling	10.4 (19.2)	40.3	37.5	11.3	7.3	3.6
Downhill skiing	8.1 (16.1)	33.5	47.1	14.8	2.1	2.5
Snowboarding	7.4 (20.3)	35.5	47.2	11.5	4.8	1.1
Cross-country skiing	6.4 (15.6)	39.0	46.1	10.0	4.5	0.4
Snowshoeing	6.2 (24.2)	40.0	47.6	10.1	1.2	1.2

Trends in Days of Land, Water, and Snow/Ice-Based Participation

From the mid-1990s to the beginning of this century, there have been a number of trends worthy of note. Among them are several shifts in number of days on which people participate in various activities.

Site-Based Land Activities

In Table 5.14, very few shifts are evident in days of participation in activities such as camping, picnicking, or rock climbing, which take place at either developed or natural sites as opposed to across the landscape. Mostly the patterns of the past have held. An exception is family gatherings outdoors, which showed decreases in overall number of days per person on which participation, occurred based on the larger proportion of 1 to 2 days in 2000–2001. Generally, there have been slight shifts across the 5 site-based activities shown from greater to lesser days of participation per year.

Table 5.14 Trends in percentages of participants by number of days per year in site-based land activities, 2000–2001 and 1994–1995 (in parentheses)

Activity	1–2 Days	3–10 Days	11–25 Days	26–50 Days	51+ Days
Developed camping	27.6 (23.4)	53.6 (52.0)	13.2 (16.3)	4.1 (5.6)	1.5 (2.7)
Picnicking	29.6 (26.0)	51.2 (53.6)	13.2 (14.4)	3.5 (4.5)	2.5 (1.4)
Primitive camping	31.0 (29.8)	49.5 (48.1)	13.1 (15.2)	4.9 (4.9)	1.5 (2.0)
Family gathering	36.1 (28.8)	48.3 (52.0)	10.9 (13.2)	2.6 (4.3)	2.1 (1.7)
Rock climbing	57.6 (59.4)	34.0 (29.9)	6.2 (8.5)	0.5 (2.0)	1.6 (0.2)

Road and Trail Activities

Of the road- or trail-based activities in Table 5.15, roughly the same trends show up as for developed sites (i.e., little notable trending). Percentages of participants for each activity under the 5 ranges of days of participation per year are similar between 1994–1995 and 2000–2001. Percentages of participants across days of participation in 1994–1995 were much the same for driving motor vehicles off-road, horseback riding, walking for pleasure, and mountain climbing as they were more recently in 2000–2001. There were, however, shifts in days of participation in day hiking, orienteering, and backpacking. For each of these 3 activities, a smaller percentage of participants in 2000–2001 put in just 1 or 2 days for the year interviewed. For orienteering, there was also a smaller percentage putting in 3 to 10 days. Thus, the shift for this activity was from 1 to 10 days to 11 to 25 and 51 or more days. For day hiking, the shift was from 1 to 3 days to 51 or more days. For backpacking, the shift was not so dramatic, the increase was in participants putting in 3 to 10 and 11 to 25 days.

Biking days are not directly comparable because the NSRE 2000–2001 asked about mountain biking days only, while the 1994–1995 NSRE asked about bicycling days in general, which would include mountain biking and bicycling on streets.

Table 5.15 Trends in percentages of participants by days per year in activities largely road- or trail-based, 2000–2001 and 1994–1995 (in parentheses)

Activity	1–2 Days	3–10 Days	11–25 Days	26–50 Days	51+ Days
Driving off-road	23.6 (23.3)	38.2 (39.7)	17.9 (16.0)	10.2 (10.8)	10.1 (10.2)
Horseback riding	45.3 (47.3)	30.1 (26.0)	8.5 (8.2)	4.9 (7.3)	11.1 (11.3)
Bicycling[1]	14.6 (14.1)	35.5 (31.6)	19.7 (18.6)	14.2 (15.5)	16.0 (20.2)
Walking for pleasure	4.2 (2.9)	17.2 (14.4)	15.2 (14.8)	16.3 (16.5)	47.0 (51.4)
Day hiking	19.4 (28.7)	39.3 (40.5)	16.7 (15.9)	8.7 (8.2)	15.8 (6.8)
Orienteering	43.2 (51.3)	28.8 (35.4)	18.7 (7.6)	4.2 (4.6)	5.1 (1.1)
Backpacking	31.5 (40.8)	48.9 (41.0)	13.4 (10.9)	3.7 (4.8)	2.5 (2.5)
Mountain climbing	52.1 (55.6)	37.1 (36.3)	6.6 (5.9)	1.9 (1.7)	2.4 (0.6)

[1] NSRE 2000–2001 asked only about days of mountain biking participation, while the 1994–1995 NSRE asked about all bicycling days.

Hunting

Days of participation trends for 3 hunting activities are shown in Table 5.16. For big-game hunting, a slight shift is evident going from fewer hunting 1 to 10 days to more hunting 11 to 25 days. For small game hunting, the shift was in the same direction, going from fewer small game hunting on 3 to 10 days to more hunting on 26 to 50 days. The shift for migratory bird hunting was more dramatic with substantial decreases in person hunting just 1 to 2 days and increases in all other ranges of days of hunting, especially 11 to 25 days.

Table 5.16 Trends in percentages of participants by days per year in hunting activities, 2000–2001 and 1994–1995 (in parentheses)

Activity	1–2 Days	3–10 Days	11–25 Days	26–50 Days	51+ Days
Big game hunting	13.1 (14.5)	43.3 (48.9)	30.9 (23.6)	8.3 (8.5)	4.4 (4.5)
Small game hunting	19.5 (18.7)	41.1 (48.9)	19.9 (18.5)	13.8 (9.7)	5.7 (4.2)
Migratory bird hunting	18.0 (33.5)	48.6 (46.5)	22.2 (14.0)	8.0 (5.7)	3.1 (0.4)

Fishing

Table 5.17 (p. 118) shows trends in percentages of participants by days per year in fishing activities over the period 1994–1995 and 2000–2001. The percentage of people participating just 1 to 2 days per year in all fishing activities dropped between 1994–1995 and 2000–2001. For coldwater fishing (e.g., trout) the shift was generally across all higher levels of days of fishing by a few percentage points. The same shift pattern was true for warmwater fishing. For saltwater fishing, the shift was mostly from 1 to 2 days to 3 to 10 days. For anadromous fishing, the shift was dramatically from 1 to 2 days to 3 to 10 days and less so to 25 to 50 days. Overall, days of fishing per participant increased in the 6 years between surveys.

Table 5.17 Trends in percentages of participants by days per year in fishing activities, 2000–2001 and 1994–1995 (in parentheses)

Activity	1–2 Days	3–10 Days	11–25 Days	26–50 Days	51+ Days
Coldwater fishing	24.2 (33.2)	43.8 (40.4)	19.2 (15.6)	8.9 (7.7)	3.8 (3.0)
Warmwater fishing	18.4 (22.8)	42.2 (41.3)	19.7 (18.2)	11.8 (10.7)	7.9 (7.0)
Saltwater fishing	33.9 (39.4)	42.4 (35.9)	12.3 (12.8)	6.8 (6.9)	4.6 (5.0)
Anadromous fishing	34.2 (41.4)	48.9 (39.1)	9.2 (12.9)	6.6 (3.3)	1.1 (3.3)

Floating/Boating Activities

Table 5.18 shows trends in percentages of participants by days per year in water-based floating/boating activities. Some activities, such as sailing, canoeing, rowing, motorboating, and jetskiing, saw modest increases in percentages of American's participating more than 1 to 2 days per year. However, activities such as kayaking and rafting had slight decreases in the percentages participating 3 to 10 days and more than 25 days per year in the same period. Sailing, rowing, motorboating, and jetskiing had increases in percentages of participants for 3 to 10 days between 1994–1995 and 2000–2001. Decreases were evident for sailing and motorboating 11 to 50 days per year. Modest increases occurred for participating 11 to 50 days per year for canoeing and jetskiing. Only rowing showed significant increases for participants putting in more than 50 days per year in a floating/boating activity.

Table 5.18 Trends in percentages of participants by days per year in floating and boating water activities, 2000–2001 and 1994–1995 (in parentheses)

Activity	1–2 Days	3–10 Days	11–25 Days	26–50 Days	51+ Days
Sailing	46.8 (48.3)	38.1 (33.6)	9.0 (11.3)	4.0 (5.0)	2.2 (1.8)
Canoeing	46.3 (50.8)	41.5 (41.1)	8.2 (5.2)	2.5 (2.1)	1.5 (0.8)
Kayaking	50.4 (47.9)	35.6 (40.6)	7.7 (3.1)	3.9 (4.7)	2.3 (3.7)
Rowing	50.5 (56.8)	38.1 (34.2)	6.5 (5.6)	2.8 (2.8)	2.2 (0.7)
Motorboating	27.5 (29.1)	42.9 (39.2)	16.5 (17.6)	8.4 (8.9)	4.7 (5.2)
Jet Skiing	38.7 (47.2)	39.6 (37.6)	12.9 (9.0)	6.3 (4.1)	2.6 (2.1)
Rafting	58.1 (55.0)	32.7 (35.0)	7.1 (6.9)	1.7 (2.7)	0.4 (0.4)

Swimming or Beach Activities

Table 5.19 shows trends in percentages of participants by days per year in swimming and beach activities between 1994–1995 and 2000–2001. For swimming, the trend was basically flat. For visiting a beach, the trend was modestly down in number of days per year, especially in numbers of participants spending more than 50 days per year on the beach.

Table 5.19 Trends in percentages of participants by days per year in swimming and beach activities, 2000–2001 and 1994–1995 (in parentheses)

Activity	1–2 Days	3–10 Days	11–25 Days	26–50 Days	51+ Days
Swimming in oceans, lakes, streams	18.0 (18.5)	48.3 (45.6)	19.5 (19.8)	9.2 (10.5)	5.0 (5.7)
Visiting a beach	21.9 (16.4)	50.6 (41.3)	16.3 (21.0)	6.7 (11.7)	4.5 (9.6)
Visiting waterside (besides beach)	30.0 (.)[1]	43.6 (.)	14.2 (.)	6.9 (.)	5.4 (.)

[1] Data not available

Snow/Ice-Based Activities

With the booming economy of the mid-to-late 1990s, one would expect significant increases in days of participation in snow/ice activities. Table 5.20 shows trends in percentages of the population participating by days per year in snow-and-ice-based activities since 1994–1995. For snowmobiling the trend was a modest shift from 1 to 2 days up to 3 to 10 days per year. Downhill skiing showed a slight increase in the proportion of people who skied more than 50 days, and a commensurate decrease in the number who skied 25 to 50 days. The 1 to 2 and 3 to 10 days categories were essentially unchanged. For cross-country skiing, very little shifting in percentages among ranges of days of participation was evident. The economic boom had little effect on days of participation.

Table 5.20 Trends in percentages of participants by days per year in snow/ice-based activities, 2000–2001 and 1994–1995 (in parentheses)

Activity	1–2 Days	3–10 Days	11–25 Days	26–50 Days	51+ Days
Snowmobiling	40.3 (45.8)	37.5 (32.2)	11.3 (11.1)	7.3 (7.8)	3.6 (3.0)
Downhill skiing	33.5 (32.8)	47.0 (49.2)	14.8 (13.3)	2.1 (4.1)	2.5 (0.6)
Snowboarding	35.5 (.)[1]	47.2 (.)	11.5 (.)	4.8 (.)	1.1 (.)
Cross-country skiing	39.0 (37.0)	46.1 (47.0)	10.0 (10.9)	4.5 (3.1)	0.4 (2.1)
Snowshoeing	40.0 (.)	47.6 (.)	10.1 (.)	1.2 (.)	1.2 (.)

[1] Data not available

Chapter 6
Participation in Viewing/Learning/ Gathering Activities

Between 1982 and 1995, trends revealed by the National Recreation Surveys showed birding as the activity with the fastest growing percentage of the U.S. population (Cordell, Herbert & Pandolfi, 1999). At over 140%, the growth of birding was far greater than growth of population, indicating increasing per capita participation. The rapid, unexpected growth in birding (often referred to as birdwatching) from the 1980s through to the mid-1990s grabbed our attention and caused us to look more closely at other activities where the focus was on viewing, learning about, photographing, or gathering outdoor subjects in nature or history. Viewing/learning/gathering activities is defined as outdoor activities that focus on some aspect of nature, history, or prehistory through visits to developed or undeveloped outdoor recreation, wildland, or open space sites (publicly or privately owned, including around the home). The purpose of these visits would be to watch, study, identify, photograph, sample, observe, and learn about natural or cultural history, or to gather natural products. One might be tempted to summarize these activities with the passive term nature appreciation, but we prefer viewing/learning/gathering activities because they require an individual's active participation.

The list of viewing/learning/gathering activities can be endless, because of the many possible features of people's interest and attention. For example, attendant to the activity of birding, which different people approach in many different ways, there are now a number of birding organizations, tour businesses, identification books, websites, and magazines to help the participant see, learn about, and record sightings of birds in the wild. Birders range from the most novice of backyard viewers to the most avid enthusiasts who travel great distances to pursue their passion and also frequently participate in scientific bird counts. To a greater and lesser extent, the same range of interest and avidity can be said of other viewing/learning/gathering activities. Needless to say, people's interest in learning seems at least as high as their interest in just having fun through outdoor recreation activities. An activity such as mushroom taxonomy may sound purely educational to one person but may be a favorite leisure pursuit of someone else. In this chapter, statistics from the national survey describe participation in viewing/learning/gathering activities. The 2000–2001 National Survey on Recreation and the Environment (NSRE) was limited to a succinct set of 13 activities intended to capture the majority of this special form of outdoor recreation.

Highlights

The list of viewing/learning/gathering activities included in the National Survey on Recreation and the Environment is somewhat short, general, and focused on nature, history, and prehistory. Included are activities such as birding, wildlife viewing, viewing flowers and trees, gathering natural products (e.g., mushrooms), visiting historic sites, and similar, generally defined activities.

The magnitude of the growth in birding since the early 1980s indicated that other viewing/learning/gathering activities are growing rapidly in popularity. When examined from the perspective of total numbers of times or occasions in which people participate in these activities, viewing/learning/gathering activities as a group are at the top of the list of general categories of outdoor recreation by a substantial margin (Table 6.1). Summed across all the viewing/learning/gathering activities in the NSRE and averaged across all survey respondents indicating participation in one of more of these activities, the mean number of participation occasions of viewing/learning/gathering outdoor activity was just over 136 per person per year. (A person can participate in more than 1 activity per day, so 2 activities done by the same person on the same day is 2 activity occasions or days.) Next in magnitude was average number of occasions in developed site recreation (e.g., picnicking, family gatherings, camping) at just over 93 occasions per person per year.

Most popular of the viewing/learning/gathering activities is viewing/photographing natural scenery. Following close behind is sightseeing, which is followed by 95 million people who reported they participated one or more times in the last 12 months in both viewing/photographing wildflowers and viewing/photographing wildlife (other than birds) such as turtles, deer, or bears. Almost one third of Americans ages 16 and older (69 million people) chose to view or photograph birds. Of the activities involving visiting featured sites or areas, nearly 122 million people reported they had visited an outdoor nature center, nature trail, visitor center, or zoo at least once during the last 12 months.

Table 6.1 Percentage of population and mean number of occasions of participation by general type of outdoor activity, 2001

Activity Group	% of Population	Mean Number of Occasions
Viewing/learning/gathering activities	88.4	136.1
Developed site activities	94.9	93.3
Trail activities	40.4	40.3
Swimming/surfing/beach activities	62.8	36.6
Motorized activities	62.0	31.3
Hunting and fishing	38.1	26.9
Snow activities	19.3	13.3
Risk activities	35.2	12.0
Other nonmotorized activities	22.8	7.9

While visiting natural scenery, sightseeing, and viewing wildflowers and other plants are highest in number of participants, they are topped by viewing/photographing birds in total number of participant occasions. Next in days of participation is viewing or photographing wildflowers/trees, followed by viewing natural scenery and viewing wildlife. Compared with results for 1994–1995, percentages of participants across the different numbers of days remained very much the same between 1994–1995 and 2000–2001 for all activities.

Current Participation in Viewing/Learning/Gathering Activities
Percentages and Numbers Participating

Most popular of the viewing/learning/gathering activities—that is, the one with the greatest number of people participating—is viewing/photographing natural scenery (Table 6.2, p. 124). This activity is highly unstructured and can focus on anything from unspectacular rural vistas to the most spectacular of natural vistas or features, such as the Grand Canyon or Mount McKinley. Just over 60% of Americans 16 or older, almost 129 million people, chose to participate in this activity during 2000–2001. Following natural scenery is sightseeing. This activity is very generally defined as spending time outdoors touring, looking at, and enjoying sights, sounds, and features of places, but with no specific focus

Since the 1980s, birding has been among the fastest growth outdoor activities.
Photo courtesy of the National Park Service

such as a bird species or vista in mind. Over 110 million people enjoyed sight-seeing at some time during 2000–2001. Although closely related to viewing/photographing natural scenery, sightseeing refers mainly to the motorized activity of traveling in a vehicle to view scenery or any other attraction or opportunity of the moment. Viewing/photographing natural scenery, on the other hand, is not automobile dependent and may occur anywhere in a natural environment.

Ninety-five million people also reported that they participated 1 or more times in the last 12 months in viewing/photographing wildflowers, trees, and other natural vegetation. Approximately the same number viewed or photographed wildlife (other than birds) such as turtles, deer, or bears in the past year. These are not the same 95 million people who did each activity (the participation rates were nearly identical at about 45% each), although many people most likely participated in both. Approximately 69 million people chose to view or photograph birds last year, while almost 53 million people viewed or photographed fish. Of all the activities listed in Table 6.2, taking a boat tour or ocean excursion to see wildlife, birds, whales, or any other natural elements was the least popular. Still, nearly 40 million people participated in this activity.

Nature centers, visitor centers, historic sites, prehistoric sites, and other places are attractions to people interested in seeing, studying, or photographing them. Gathering natural products such as mushrooms, berries, minerals, and other natural materials is also of high interest. In recent years, a viable industry based on nontimber or "special" forest products has emerged, but much of the collecting and gathering that occurs—not just in forests but elsewhere—is of a recreational nature. Of the activities involving visiting featured sites or areas or gathering natural products, visiting a nature center, nature trail, visitor center, or zoo was the most popular with nearly 122 million people reporting they had visited one of these facilities at least once during the last 12 months (Table 6.3). In recent years, visitor centers and nature centers supported by local, state, and federal governments have expanded their facilities and coverage. This expansion is a likely reason for strong participation in this activity. People are also

Table 6.2 Estimated percentages and millions 16 or older viewing/photographing nature in 2000–2001

Activity	% Participating	Millions of Participants (95% Confidence Interval ±%)
Viewing/photographing natural scenery	60.3	128.5 (0.8)
Sightseeing	51.8	110.3 (0.9)
Viewing/photographing wildflowers/ trees	44.9	95.7 (1.1)
Viewing/photographing other wildlife	44.7	95.2 (1.1)
Viewing/photographing birds	32.4	69.0 (1.2)
Viewing/photographing fish	24.8	52.8 (1.6)
Viewing boat tours/excursions	18.7	39.9 (5.9)

very interested in history. In addition to reading books on history and viewing televised specials on history, many visit historic sites such as battlefields, historic homes, or remains of canals. In 2000–2001 over 98 million people took the time to visit historic sites at least once over the course of a 12-month period.

Seeking to escape the noise and stresses of their cities, towns, work, or daily life and to experience natural settings undisturbed by human development, almost 70 million people—just under a third of Americans ages 16 and older—visited a wilderness or primitive area. The NSRE survey question did not ask specifically about visits to federally designated wilderness, but rather to any primitive, roadless area. Nearly 61 people million participated in gathering natural products, such as mushrooms, berries, floral vegetation, pine cones, or stones. Participation in the last 2 activities listed in Table 6.3 was less than in many other activities, but still involved significant numbers. Over 44 million people visited prehistoric or archeological sites such as Indian mounds or ancient dwelling sites. State and federal agencies usually do a very good job of offering interpretation of such sites. Visiting caves or caverns was undertaken by only 4.3% of people ages 16 or older in 2000–2001, just over 9 million people. Government agencies and private businesses offer opportunities to visit caves of varying degrees of intact naturalness, in addition to spelunkers who explore caves on their own on both public and private lands.

Days of Participation

Oftentimes the order of activities from largest to smallest can shift dramatically when the criteria changes from number who participate to number of total days across all participants on which they engage in those activities. Contrasting Tables 6.2 and 6.4 (p. 126) illustrates this shift. While viewing natural scenery, visiting nature centers, and sightseeing are highest in number of participants, they are topped by viewing/photographing birds in total number of participant occasions. Table 6.4 shows the mean days per person per year and percentages of participants by number of days per year in viewing/photographing activities during the previous 12 months. On average, participants in these activities

Table 6.3 Estimated percentages and millions visiting featured sites or areas or gathering natural products in 2000–2001

Activity	% Participating	Millions of Participants (95% Confidence Interval ±%)
Visiting a nature center, nature trail, visitor center, or zoo	57.1	121.7 (0.9)
Visiting historic sites	46.2	98.5 (1.1)
Visiting a wilderness/primitive area	32.7	69.7 (1.2)
Gathering natural products	28.5	60.7 (1.4)
Visiting prehistoric/archeological sites	20.9	44.5 (1.9)
Visiting caves	4.3	9.3 (13.9)

viewed or photographed birds for 85.8 days per person per year, viewed or photographed wildflowers for 61.3 days, natural scenery for 58.1 days, and other wildlife for 38.5 days during the 12 months just prior to their being interviewed. However, most people who participated in these activities did so on fewer than 10 days during the year. The most dedicated of participants engaged their chosen activities more than 50 days per year, roughly 1 or more times per week. Of those who viewed or photographed birds, 29% participated on more than 50 days, as did 21% of wildflower viewers, and 18% of scenery viewers. Only a small percentage of participants went sightseeing on more than 50 days, averaging 19.7 days per person per year.

Birders are an interesting group of people. While more than one half of birders participate fewer than 10 days per year, nearly one third do some form of birding on 50 plus days annually. Further examination of the data reveals that 15%—more than half of the most active participants—participated in birding on a daily basis (i.e., on all 365 days during the year). This is the reason for the relatively large mean of 86 days annually. Such avid participation reflects not only the popularity of birding but also on its accessibility since people may view or study birds in their backyards, neighborhoods, and local communities as well as in isolated swamps miles from human habitation. In addition, more than one third (34.1%) of these daily birders are ages 65 and older, indicating the affinity for retirees of this activity. The same patterns emerge for viewing wildflowers and viewing natural scenery, but to a much lesser extent than for birding. Slightly more than 10% of wildflowers viewers did so on a daily basis, which, similar to birding, explains the relatively large annual mean days (61.3). About 17% of these individuals were age 65 and older, much lower than for birding but larger than the 12% nationally in this age group. Similar to birding, much of this avid activity no doubt occurs around people's homes and in their local communities. It also reflects on the popularity of gardening and landscaping as a leisure activity. More than 11% of natural scenery viewers participated daily, resulting in a mean number of annual days that also exceeds once per week. The same local influences apply to natural scenery viewing—which,

Table 6.4 Mean days per person per year and percentages of participants by number of days per year in viewing/photographing activities for 2000–2001

Activity	Mean Days (95% CI ±%)	1–2 Days	3–10 Days	11–25 Days	26–50 Days	51+ Days
Viewing/photographing birds	85.8 (2.6)	20.9	32.2	11.8	6.1	29.0
Viewing/photographing wildflowers	61.3 (2.6)	18.9	38.4	14.0	7.7	21.1
Viewing/photographing scenery	58.1 (7.1)	18.4	40.5	17.1	6.2	17.7
Viewing/photographing wildlife	38.5 (2.9)	22.8	41.2	14.2	7.6	14.2
Sightseeing	19.7 (9.1)	14.3	48.6	21.2	9.3	6.5

like wildflowers, viewing was defined very generally—but the effect of older and retired participants was smaller. Persons 65 and older comprised 13% of those who viewed natural scenery daily, about the same as their share of the U.S. population. The proportion of people who viewed other wildlife besides birds on a daily basis was much smaller than for the other 3 viewing activities, about 4.5%, although they still helped push the annual mean days up to almost 39 days.

Table 6.5 shows the mean days per person per year and percentages of participants by number of days per year in featured site or area visitation. On average, people visited wilderness or primitive areas on approximately 17 different days over the 12-month reporting period. Most, almost 80%, visited wild areas on fewer than 10 days per year. Similarly, over 70% of persons who participated in gathering natural products did so for 10 or fewer days per year. Further down the list by frequency of participation, the average days of participation for visiting historic sites was 7.2, for nature centers 7.1, and for prehistoric or archeological sites 5.5. The lowest participation in mean days for site visiting was for caving (2.3). Across all visit-related activities, the greatest percentage of people participated for 10 or fewer days per year.

Trends in Days of Participation

Table 6.6 (p. 128) shows trends in percentages of participants by days per year in viewing/learning/gathering activities in 2000–2001 compared with 1994–1995 (in parentheses). Shown only are the activities for which days of participation were collected in both the 1994–1995 and the 2000–2001 surveys. Compared with results for 1994–1995, percentages of participants in sightseeing across the different numbers of days in Table 6.6 remained very much the same in 2000–2001. Except for minor downward shifts in days of participation from 1994–1995 to 2000–2001 (with the exception of fewer 1–2 day nonbird wildlife viewers in 2000–2001), the same was true for birding, viewing wildlife,

Table 6.5 Mean days per person per year and percentages of participants by number of days per year in visits to featured sites or areas, or gathering natural products, 2000–2001

Activity	Mean Days (95% CI ±%)	1–2 Days	3–10 Days	11–25 Days	26–50 Days	51+ Days
Visiting a wilderness/primitive area	16.5 (15.2)	38.1	40.8	12.4	3.9	4.8
Gathering natural products	14.2 (7.8)	26.1	48.4	14.5	5.8	5.3
Visiting historic sites	7.2 (13.9)	48.7	42.4	5.9	1.7	1.3
Visiting a nature center, trail, zoo, or visitor center	7.1 (11.3)	45.0	43.4	7.7	2.0	1.9
Visiting a prehistoric or archeological site	5.5 (25.5)	63.7	27.9	6.3	1.1	1.0
Visiting caves	2.3 (34.8)	78.5	20.9	0.5	0.2	0.0

and all the other viewing/learning/gathering activities in Table 6.6. In the 6 years between the 2 surveys, the days on which people participate in the viewing/learning/gathering activities listed have changed little. In the years intervening between previous surveys, there had been more trending of days of participation, mostly toward fewer days per person per year as new people take on these activities (Cordell et al., 1999).

Table 6.6 Trends in percentages of participants by days per year in viewing/photographing activities, 2000–2001 and 1994–1995 (in parentheses)

Activity	1–2 Days	3–10 Days	11–25 Days	25–50 Days	51+ Days
Sightseeing	14.3 (14.6)	48.6 (48.6)	21.2 (22.3)	9.3 (9.3)	6.5 (5.3)
Viewing/photographing birds	20.9 (19.6)	32.2 (28.2)	11.8 (11.1)	6.1 (9.6)	29.0 (31.5)
Viewing/photographing wildlife	22.8 (27.4)	41.2 (39.1)	14.2 (13.1)	7.6 (6.6)	14.2 (13.6)
Visiting historic sites	48.7 (48.2)	42.4 (44.5)	5.9 (5.6)	1.7 (1.0)	1.3 (0.7)
Visiting prehistoric/ archeological sites	63.7 (62.7)	27.9 (31.3)	6.3 (4.4)	1.1 (0.8)	1.0 (0.9)
Visiting caves	78.5 (78.6)	20.9 (18.9)	0.5 (2.4)	0.2 (0.1)	0.0 (0.1)

Chapter 7
Participation in Outdoor Sports

Dating back to King Henry the VIII and well before, sports have been an integral part of people's lives—maybe more so for the well-off than for the rest of us. Over the centuries and millennia, different cultures have each had their unique sports and shared ones as well. Henry the VIII particularly liked and was exceptionally talented at jousting and tennis. He built tilting yards and tennis courts at most of his numerous castles and estates throughout England. Often the sports of past centuries tested some aspect of martial skills.

An outdoor sport is defined much as we think Henry would have. It is an activity undertaken out-of-doors that requires physical exertion, some level of skill, and typically specialized equipment and/or facilities. Often, for many sport activities, competition, individually or as a team, is also an objective. This chapter covers some 23 sports. By no means do we assert that these are the only, or even the primary sports (although some are). For the most part, the sports featured here are those included in the U.S. National Recreation Surveys over the years. From bicycling to snowboarding, people of all ages and backgrounds participate in and enjoy sports.

Highlights

Sports come in many forms and entice many millions to participate in them. Highlights of this chapter feature, among other things, the finding that over 84 million persons 16 or older participated in bicycling during the 12 months just prior to their being interviewed for the NSRE in 2000–2001. These statistics make bicycling one of the more popular sports and illustrates how people are taking advantage of the dramatic advancements in bicycle technology over the last 30 years. More than 45 million of those reporting biking rode mountain bikes, some in addition to street bikes. Other riding sports include horseback riding, in which over 20 million people participated in 2000–2001.

Among water sports, swimming in an outdoor pool was most popular with over 87 million people participating in 2000–2001. (Swimming in a stream, pond, lake, or ocean was included with the water-based activities in Chapter 5.) And even though waterskiing has been in decline in recent years, still more than 17 million people reported they went waterskiing at least once. Among snow/ice sports both downhill skiing and ice skating have been popular for many years, but snowboarding is fast taking its place among the more popular of snow/ice sports. In 2000–2001, over 10 million 16 or older reported snowboarding.

Among the many forms of outdoor sports (as we define them), there are a number of individual sports, one of which, inline skating (also known as "Rollerblading" after the original manufacturer of inline skates) assumed prominence in less than a decade. Over 47 million Americans 16 or older participated in rollerblading in 2000–2001. Of team sports, basketball outdoors is still popular with over 31 million reporting playing this sport outdoors in 2000–2001. Following basketball as a team sport is outdoor volleyball, with over 22 million participants. Similar in popularity to volleyball is softball in which also more than 22 million played one or more times over the course of a 12-month period.

Not only is knowing the number and percentage of people who participate important, but also is knowing how frequently people participate. Comparison of the sports for which days of participation were measured in both the 1994–1995 and 2000–2001 surveys found there has been a flat trend pattern in number of days of participation per 12-month period. From swimming in an outdoor pool to horseback riding to windsurfing, the percentages participating just 1 to 2 days per year were pretty much the same in 2000–2001 as in 1994–1995. Likewise, percentages putting in 51 or more days per year across the sports we studied were pretty much the same in 2000–2001 as they were in 1994–1995.

In Figure 7.1, two dimensions of participation in outdoor sports are shown, one relative to the other. First is the number of participants in millions (dashed line) and the other is average days of participation per participant per year. Outdoor pool swimming is highest in number of participants, but as the graph shows, the number of participants falls precipitously from that activity to windsurfing with the least participants. With the exceptions of surfing and mountain biking, average days per participant per year roughly follows the geometric pattern of number of participants. Surfing is included with outdoor

Children enjoy playing soccer. Photo courtesy of Athens YMCA, Athens, Georgia.

pool swimming, mountain biking, and horseback riding as highest in average days of participation. Downhill skiing, waterskiing, snorkeling, snowboarding, scuba diving, and windsurfing are lowest, but roughly equal in days of participation per participant. Millions of participants multiplied by days of participation per participant provides an estimate of total volume of demand for activities—that is, total population-wide days of activity participation. Outdoor pool swimming, mountain biking, and horseback riding are highest overall in total days of participation among the sports shown in Figure 7.1. Because average days of participation has remained somewhat stable over the last several years, growth in overall days across participants is mostly the result of growth in numbers of participants.

Participation in Riding, Water, and Snow/Ice Sports

Riding

The physically active sports featured in this section include bicycling and horseback riding. Bicycling is one of the more popular activities overall. The more specialized sport of mountain biking (mostly an off-road sport) is also popular, with about as many people participating compared to bicycling in general. Table 7.1 (p. 132) provides percentages and numbers of people 16 or older who reported participating in one of these riding sports at least once during

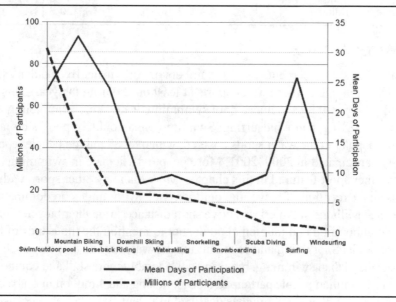

Figure 7.1 Participation in riding, water and snow/ice sports by millions of participants and mean days of participation (NSRE 2000–2001)

the 12 months prior to their being interviewed in 2000–2001. Over 84 million people participated in some form of bicycling, taking advantage of the very substantial advancements in bicycle technology that have occurred over the last 30 years. Most bikes today have lightweight frames, energy saving gear systems, on- and off-road tires, as well as a host of other features (e.g., greater safety, shocks, gel seats). Mountain biking notably takes advantage of the new technology in bicycles. Whether on- or off-road, more than 45.6 million Americans reported they had ridden mountain bikes in the last year. Bicycling is also one of the most accessible of all activities, as much of it—both on and off the street—occurs in the neighborhoods and communities where people live. Without a doubt, a great deal of bicycling also combines transportation with recreation (e.g., traveling to a destination such as to a shopping mall or coffee shop). As well, almost 10% of Americans, some 20.7 million people, reported that they went horseback riding during the last year. Until fairly recently horseback riding was considered a sport for the elite and too expensive for most. Now one can lease a horse, take riding lessons, and take advantage of private riding facilities at a more moderate cost than in the past.

Table 7.1 Percentages and numbers 16 or older participating in riding sports, 2000–2001

Activity	% Participating	Millions of Participants (95% Confidence Interval ±%)
Bicycling	39.5	84.2 (1.3)
Mountain biking	21.4	45.6 (1.9)
Horseback riding	9.7	20.7 (3.1)

Water Sports

Table 7.2 shows percentages and numbers of Americans 16 or older who participated in one or more water sports at least once during the year. This group of outdoor activities includes pool swimming, waterskiing, snorkeling, scuba diving, surfing, and windsurfing. Swimming in an outdoor pool is by far the most popular of the water sports covered, with over 87 million people reporting they participated in 2000–2001. More people participate in swimming than in any other sport featured in this chapter. More than any other sport, with the possible exception of bicycling, outdoor pool swimming is predominantly "local." Millions of Americans drive short distances, ride their bicycles, or walk to neighborhood and municipal pools, not to mention the thousands of backyard pools. Snorkeling and scuba diving are water sports that are much more specialized than swimming, requiring considerably more skill and equipment— about 14 million people participated in snorkeling and 4 million in scuba diving. Participation in waterskiing has declined in recent years largely because of substitution of independent jetskis for towed waterskis. Still over 17 million people reported they had gone waterskiing. Jetskiing participation has increased sharply, from just under 5% in 1994–1995 to 9.5% of Americans (20.3 million) in 2000–2001. Other water sports with much smaller numbers participating include surfing at 1.7% of Americans, 3.6 million people, and windsurfing at less than 1%, 1.8 million participating.

Table 7.2 Percentages and numbers 16 or older participating in water sports, 2000–2001

Activity	% Participating	Millions of Participants (95% Confidence Interval ±%)
Swimming in outdoor pool	41.0	87.4 (1.7)
Waterskiing	8.1	17.3 (3.7)
Snorkeling	6.7	14.3 (2.9)
Scuba diving	1.9	4.1 (5.3)
Surfing	1.7	3.6 (5.9)
Windsurfing	0.8	1.7 (12.5)

Snow/Ice Sports

Snow or ice sports usually require a relatively high level of practice and skill. From beginner to advanced ski slopes and from iced-over ponds to highly maintained ice rinks, snow and ice sports offer a wide variety of experience opportunities. Table 7.3 shows the percentages and numbers of people ages 16 or older who participated in a snow or ice-based sport at least once in the 12 months preceding their interview for the NSRE. Just over 18 million Americans reported they went downhill skiing in 2000–2001, and almost 15 million went ice skating outdoors. Both of these sports, downhill skiing and ice skating, have been popular for many years. However, snowboarding, still a relatively new sport, has shown enormous growth, particularly among younger downhill skiers. In the period 2000–2001, over 10 million people age 16 or older reported snowboarding on downhill slopes. As with skis, the technology of snowboards has advanced rapidly over the last few years. New materials and board designs for freestyle, Nordic, snow skating, and other styles and levels of skill continue to develop.

Table 7.3 Percentages and numbers 16 or older participating in snow/ice sports, 2000–2001

Activity	% Participating	Millions of Participants (95% Confidence Interval ±%)
Downhill skiing	8.5	18.1 (3.5)
Ice skating outdoors	6.9	14.7 (10.2)
Snowboarding	4.9	10.4 (4.1)

Participation in Competitive Sports

Individual Sports

Table 7.4 shows the percentages and numbers of Americans 16 or older who participated in one of the 5 individual sports listed. More than one third of the population did some running or jogging in 2000–2001, which is about 73 million people. Over the last 3 decades, advancements in running shoe technology has been a driver of growth in running and jogging participation. Lighter weight, more durable, more cushioned, and more specialized running shoes have made a big difference in participation and reduction of injuries. As well, the introduction of more comfortable soft boots and high-speed wheels for inline skating or rollerblading has been a driver of growth in this sport in which over 47 million Americans ages 16 or older participated in 2000–2001. Similarly, each year racquet manufacturers produce better, more powerful, and lighter racquets for people of all ages, which is reflected by the 24.5 million Americans who played outdoor tennis last year. Other court activities such as handball or racquetball were popular with 15.1 million people who participated in these sports in the last 12 months prior to being interviewed. The last 10 years have also witnessed a tremendous growth in the number of golf courses being developed, both publicly and privately owned, to meet the demand from 36 million Americans who reported that they golfed last year.

Table 7.4 Percentages and numbers 16 or older participating in individual sports, 2000–2001

Activity	% Participating	Millions of Participants (95% Confidence Interval ±%)
Running or jogging	34.5	73.5 (3.8)
Inline skating or rollerblading	22.1	47.1 (7.7)
Golfing	16.9	36.0 (5.9)
Tennis outdoors	11.5	24.5 (7.8)
Handball or racquetball outdoors	7.1	15.1 (9.8)

Team Sports

From basketball to baseball, team sports involve significant numbers of people ages 16 or older. Whether played informally as pickup games or more formally in organized leagues, team sports have continued over the years to engage sizeable numbers of players. Table 7.5 shows the percentages and numbers of people ages 16 or older who participated in 1 or more of the 6 team sports listed at least once during the last 12 months. Because many Americans have a basketball hoop in their driveway or nearby access to one in a community park or schoolyard, it is not surprising that basketball was found to be a popular team sport, with over 31 million reporting they played last year. Following basketball is volleyball with over 10% of Americans (22.6 million participants), reporting having played at least once during the year. Similar in popularity to volleyball, more than 10% of Americans, 22.5 million people played softball at least once last year. Within the last year, over 17 million also played football or soccer outdoors, while 14.5 million played baseball. While all the sports in Table 7.5 require a playing field or court, most do not require expensive equipment and are usually played close to home.

Table 7.5 Percentages and numbers 16 or older participating in team sports, 2000–2001

Activity	% Participating	Millions of Participants (95% Confidence Interval ±%)
Basketball outdoors	14.7	31.3 (6.8)
Volleyball outdoors	10.6	22.6 (8.5)
Softball	10.5	22.5 (7.6)
Football	8.1	17.3 (9.9)
Soccer outdoors	8.1	17.3 (9.9)
Baseball	6.8	14.5 (10.3)

Days of Participation in Sports

Riding

Days of participation were asked for only 2 of the riding activities discussed earlier: mountain biking and horseback riding. In Table 7.6 (p. 136), means and percentages by range of days per year are presented. Those who reported participating in mountain biking did so on average of almost 33 days in the previous 12 months prior to their interview in 2000–2001. Those who rode horses participated on fewer days per year, less than 10. This is quite a difference, but perhaps understandable when one compares the amount of effort needed to prepare and participate in each of these activities. Over one half of mountain bikers participated 3 to 25 days and just over 30% participated more than 25 days during the year. In contrast, just over 75% of persons who participated in horseback riding did so on 10 or fewer days. More than 10% of participants (with bikers again having a larger share) in the 2 respective sports participated 51 or more days, obviously being the more dedicated participants.

Table 7.6 Mean and percentages by days per person per year participating in riding sports, 2000–2001

Activity	Mean Days (95% CI ±%)	1–2 Days	3–10 Days	11–25 Days	26–50 Days	51+ Days
Mountain biking	32.6 (10.1)	14.6	35.5	19.7	14.2	16.0
Horseback riding	8.1 (16.1)	45.3	30.1	8.5	4.9	11.1

Water Sports

Days of participation were collected for 7 water sports. Surfing had the highest number of days per person per year of the activities listed. Table 7.7, shows the range of mean days of participation across the 7 activities—from almost 26 days for surfing to under 8 for snorkeling. Many more persons surfed waves or swam in an outdoor pool on more than 25 days during the year than participated at that level in the other 4 activities. Most scuba diving, waterskiing, windsurfing, and snorkeling participants put in less than 10 days per person per year. Less then 10% of participants in these 4 activities participated more than 25 days during the year.

Table 7.7 Mean and percentages by days per person per year participating in water sports, 2000–2001

Activity	Mean Days (95% CI ±%)	1–2 Days	3–10 Days	11–25 Days	26–50 Days	51+ Days
Surfing	25.8 (18.2)	25.4	40.2	12.5	8.8	13.1
Swimming (pools)	23.7 (3.4)	12.7	41.0	19.9	14.7	11.7
Scuba diving	9.6 (18.8)	43.0	40.5	9.6	4.4	2.5
Waterskiing	9.5 (5.3)	33.5	42.8	14.8	6.5	2.3
Windsurfing	8.0 (40.0)[1]	48.9	39.1	7.2	3.4	1.4
Snorkeling	7.6 (9.2)	48.3	40.0	7.1	2.4	2.2

[1] The 95% confidence interval for windsurfing, 4.7 to 11.2 mean days, is significantly larger than any other activity because it had the smallest sample size (328 persons).

Snow/Ice Sports

Days of participation were collected for 2 snow sports: downhill skiing and snowboarding. Table 7.8 shows the mean days per year and percentages of participants by number of days per year in these 2 sports. On average, downhill skiers and snowboarders participated in roughly the same number of annual days, about 7 to 8. Most participants in both sports, around 80%, participated on 10 or fewer days during the year. Very few participated on more than 50 days in either sport.

Table 7.8 Means and percentages by days per person per year participating in snow/ice sports, 2000–2001

Activity	Mean Days (95% CI ±%)	1–2 Days	3–10 Days	11–25 Days	26–50 Days	51+ Days
Downhill skiing	8.1 (16.1)	33.5	47.1	14.8	2.1	2.5
Snowboarding	7.4 (20.3)	35.5	47.2	11.5	4.8	1.1

Trends in Days of Participation

Days of sports participation were collected for 7 activities in the 1994–1995 and 2000–2001 surveys. They cover a variety of sports, including riding, water and snow activities. Table 7.9 (p. 138) shows trends in the percentages of participants by days of participation in each of these 7 sports with the 1994–1995 participation percentages in parentheses. Similar percentages between the 2 survey periods indicate a stable pattern of sports participation. For the most part, a stable pattern is seen in Table 7.9. From swimming in an outdoor pool to horseback riding, to waterskiing, the percentages participating just 1 to 2 days per year were basically the same in 2000–2001 as in 1994–1995. Likewise, percentages putting in 51 or more days per year across the 7 sports in 1994–1995 were much the same in 2000–2001. Noteworthy among the changes, Table 7.9 shows fewer surfers participating for 1 to 2 days, and more participating for 3 to 10 days in 2000–2001, when compared with 1994–1995. The percentage of downhill skiers who skied more than 50 days during the year increased from less than 1% to over 2%. This trend represents many thousands more high-participation skiers. Stability in number of days of participation in the 6 years between surveys represents a stable market for these sports, but not a strong growth market given the economic boom that occurred during that period.

Table 7.9 Trends in percentages by days per person per year participating in sports, 2000–2001 and 1994–1995 (in parentheses)

Activity	1–2 Days	3–10 Days	11–25 Days	25–50 Days	51+ Days
Swimming (pools)	12.7 (13.2)	41.0 (37.8)	19.9 (17.4)	14.7 (16.6)	11.7 (14.9)
Surfing	25.4 (33.4)	40.2 (28.9)	12.5 (15.0)	8.8 (9.1)	13.1 (13.6)
Downhill skiing	33.5 (32.8)	47.1 (49.2)	14.8 (13.3)	2.1 (4.1)	2.5 (0.6)
Waterskiing	33.5 (36.4)	42.8 (39.3)	14.8 (15.7)	6.5 (6.6)	2.3 (2.0)
Horseback riding	45.3 (47.3)	30.1 (26.0)	8.5 (8.2)	4.9 (7.3)	11.1 (11.3)
Windsurfing	48.9 (53.1)	39.1 (34.3)	7.2 (8.4)	3.4 (2.9)	1.4 (1.4)

Section IV

Outdoor Recreation Participation in Different Settings

The 5 chapters in this section (Chapters 8–12) examine participation in outdoor recreation activities by type of setting or natural resource on which those activities generally depend. For instance, Chapter 8 focuses on people's participation in activities that occurred in forest settings. The United States has approximately 747 million acres of forest land. Of this, almost 640 million acres, or about 86% of the total forest land area in this country, is available in some way for outdoor recreation. Estimates of recreation days occurring in forest settings show walking for pleasure, viewing natural scenery, viewing birds, viewing flowers, viewing wildlife, day hiking, sightseeing, driving for pleasure, mountain biking, and viewing a wilderness or primitive area in as the most actively engaged forest-based activities in 2000–2001.

The focus of Chapter 9 is on recreation activity at a farm or ranch. Examples of farm recreation activities include buying or picking fresh produce, seeing and petting farm animals, and viewing or photographing pastoral scenery. An estimated 62 million Americans visited farms 1 or more times in 2000–2001—almost 30% of the total population.

Recreation in marine or saltwater environments is also popular. Over 30% of Americans' visited one or more beaches in 2000–2001, while many others enjoyed swimming, fishing, viewing or photographing scenery, birdwatching, motorboating, and viewing wildlife in saltwater settings.

Chapter 11 examines participation in freshwater settings, such as lakes, rivers, and ponds. The most popular freshwater activities in 2000–2001 were viewing/photographing wildflowers, trees, and other flora; swimming; viewing/photographing fish; visiting watersides (other than beaches); viewing/photographing wildlife (other than birds and fish); warmwater fishing; and motorboating.

Finally, Chapter 12 examines how people living and working in urban areas choose to recreate. Not surprisingly, regardless of state or region, the most popular urban-related activities for the U.S. population at-large were walking, attending family gatherings, and gardening.

Chapter 8
Forest Recreation

The distribution of forestland across the United States varies greatly in area, species, and terrain. From the fast-growing forests of the Pacific Coast to the multispecies and coastal forests of the deep South, forestlands are a significant landscape feature in virtually every state. About two thirds (504 million acres) of the nation's unpreserved forests are classed as capable of producing significant quantities of commercial wood (Smith, Vissage, Darr & Sheffield, 2001). About 52 million additional acres of forests are preserved and managed by public agencies, such as for parks or wilderness areas. Another 191 million acres are important for watershed protection, wildlife habitat, livestock grazing, recreation, biodiversity maintenance and other uses, but are not used for timber production. The total forest acreage in the United States is approximately 747 million acres. Of this, almost 640 million acres, or about 86% of the total forestland area in this country, is available in some way for outdoor recreation. Almost all public forest is available to the public in general.

Of public forestland, about 78% is in federal ownership. The USDA Forest Service administers the largest amount of these federal forest lands (147 million acres). This is about 59% of the total federal forest. Other federal agencies administering smaller amounts of forestland include the Bureau of Land Management, the National Park Service, the Fish and Wildlife Service, and the Department of Defense. In total, 33% of all forestland is federally owned. This proportion of federal to other forest ownerships has remained relatively stable for the last 50 years.

To take care of this nation's forests, industry, state and federal governments, and private land owners employ professional foresters, as well as professionals trained in other natural resource disciplines. The profession of forestry is age-old and worldwide. In the United States it dates back to the late 1800s and came of age with Gifford Pinchot, a favored champion of conservation who was appointed Chief of the Division of Forestry (1898–1910) by Theodore Roosevelt. Recreation became recognized as one of the many management objectives and professional specializations in forestry as early as the 1940s and 1950s. While producing timber and other wood products continues to be the main focus of forestry today, forest recreation management has been rising in relative significance and interest, as have other specializations, such as wildlife biology and hydrology.

This chapter provides recent data on forest recreation participation in the United States. These data were originally developed for the 2003 National Report on Sustainable Forests (USDA Forest Service, 2002a). That report is the United States' response to an international agreement known among the participating countries as the Montreal Process (Natural Resources Canada, 1999). It began with an international seminar in Montreal, Canada, in 1993, where the focus was on sustaining vital forest ecosystem functions and attributes (i.e., biodiversity, productivity, forest health, the carbon cycle, and soil and water protection), socioeconomic benefits (i.e., timber, recreation, and cultural values) and the institutions through which forest management functions. The NSRE was responsible for reporting on forest recreation and social/cultural/spiritual benefits—5 of the 67 total indicators. One of these 5 indicators is meant to describe specific recreational use of forests as a measure of sustainable benefits from forests. Two measures of recreation use were employed and are reported here: percentage of the population participating in outdoor activities in forested settings, and visits by the public to national forests.

Highlights

Almost 750 million acres (33%) of the total land base of the United States is forested. Although not all of this forestland is available for recreational activities, depending on the access policies of various owners, almost 640 million acres, or about 86% of the total, is available. Outdoor recreation in forested settings is a fast-growing land use across the United States, continuing a steady trend since before the 1950s. Currently, well over 90% of Americans participate in at least 1 outdoor recreation activity. Estimates of recreation days occurring in forest settings show walking for pleasure, viewing natural scenery, viewing birds, viewing flowers, viewing wildlife, day hiking, sightseeing, driving for pleasure, mountain biking, and visiting a wilderness or primitive area as the most actively engaged activities in 2000–2001. On national forests alone, visitation estimates for the year 2000 show substantial use, most of which occurs in general, undeveloped forest areas (compared with use of developed sites). Use of national forests totals over 137 million visits per year. Most of this national forest use occurs on lands in the West. Generally, participation in outdoor activities continues to grow, with greatest growth occurring among nonconsumptive activities that have relatively low impact on forests. Rising demand and rising population, however, is leading to a decline in per capita acres of forest available for recreation—a trend likely to accelerate future conflicts over access and use by different interest groups.

Recreation Participation in Forested Settings

As a part of the NSRE, a sample of persons ages 16 or older across the United States were asked not only if they had participated in individual outdoor activities but also, if they had, whether some of their activity occurred in forested settings.

While numerous on-site surveys of visitors have been applied to people recreating at forested sites, no population-wide surveys that we know of have asked about participation specifically in forested settings.

Forestlands Available for Outdoor Recreation

There are an estimated 747 million acres of forest across the 50 states. This is about 33% of the total U.S. land area. Not all of this forestland is available for recreational uses, depending on who owns it. Of total forest area in the United States, 639 million acres, or about 86% of the total, is available for outdoor recreation by someone—inclusively or exclusively. Because so much of the forest in the South is nonindustrial private, it is important to acknowledge that this region has the lowest recreation availability at 72% of forest area open to some outdoor recreation. The public-land-rich Rocky Mountains and Great Plains have the highest percentage at almost 95%.

By region, forest area available for recreation varies considerably (Table 8.1, p. 144). In the North, a region ranging from Minnesota to Missouri to Delaware to Maine, over 144 million acres of forest is available for outdoor recreation (an area approaching the land area of Texas). In the South, a region stretching from Texas and Oklahoma to Virginia and south to Florida, over 154 million acres of forest are available. In the Rocky Mountain/Great Plains Region, including states from Idaho to Arizona and New Mexico to North Dakota, about 136 million acres are accessible (an area approximately the size of California plus Alabama). The Pacific Coast region has the greatest total area of forest available for outdoor recreation, almost 205 million acres. This regions stretches from

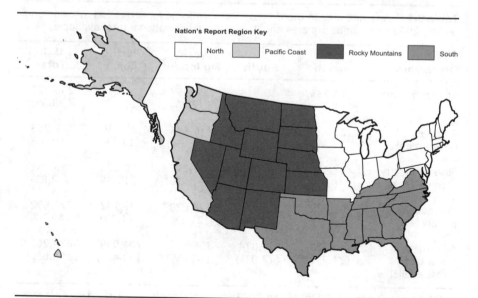

Figure 8.1 Forest Service Assessment Regions for the Nation's Report

California to Alaska, and includes Hawaii. This land area exceeds the land mass of Texas by nearly 10 million acres. Federal land makes up 56% of the Pacific region's total forest recreation land.

The distribution of forestlands across different categories of owners varies widely from region to region. The majority of forestland in the East is in private ownership while the majority in the West is in public ownership. This ownership pattern is significant because much greater proportions of public land than private forestland are available to the general public for recreation. For all regions, practically all forestland in public ownership is available to anyone wishing to use it for recreation. Access to most corporation-owned industrial forestlands is limited to persons with lease or other exclusive access privileges. Nonindustrial private forestland in the United States is vast, but recreational access to it is much more limited than for any other ownership category—usually available only to family, friends, others associated with the owners, or to people who lease access rights. Only a small portion is available to the public at-large—whether for free or for a fee. In recent years, only 15% to 20% has been open to the public (Cordell et al., 1999). This percentage, however, has been trending downward over the last several years. In 1985–1986, nearly 25% of owners permitted some public access. This percentage dropped nationally by 1995 to nearly 14.5% (Cordell et al., 1999). In 2000–2001, only 10.9% of owners permitted access. Thus, overall area of forest available to the general public for recreation has been declining over time—mainly because of reduced access to nonindustrial private forestland.

Table 8.1 Forest land area in the United States available for recreation by ownership region, 2002 (thousands of acres and % of regional or national total available)

Ownership	North	South	Rocky Mountains	Pacific Coast	U.S. Total
All federal land	13,933 9.7%	19,314 12.5%	98,697 72.7%	114,778 56.0%	246,722 38.6%
State and local government	27,225 18.9%	6,243 4.1%	6,146 4.5%	30,139 14.7%	69,753 10.9%
Forest industry corporations	11,962 8.3%	25,248 16.4%	2,372 1.7%	10,279 5.0%	49,861 7.8%
Nonindustrial private	91,239 63.2%	103,270 67.0%	28,620 21.1%	49,743 24.3%	272,872 42.7%
All owners (% of total forest available)	144,359 (84.7%)	154,074 (72.0%)	135,835 (94.8%)	204,939 (93.4%)	639,207 (85.6%)

USDA Forest Service. (2002a). Draft 2003 National Report on Sustainable Forests. Washington, DC. http://www.fs.fed.us/research/sustain/data.htm

Population-Wide Participation in Forest Recreation Activities

Outdoor recreation is a fast growing use of the available forestlands in the United States. This growth has been steady since before the 1950s as the U.S. population was transitioning from a rural, live-off-the-land society to an urban, detached one. Table 8.2 (pp. 146–147) shows estimates of forest recreation activity days (i.e., number of different days on which a forest recreation activity was undertaken). The data are organized by region and by recreation activity from the activity with the highest activity days at top to lowest at bottom. Except for walking, numbers of occasions in forest settings were generally greater in the more heavily populated North than in other regions. This reflects not only the high number of residents in this region but also the substantial amount of forest area that is available for recreation in this region. The next highest number of activity days is in the South except for snow/ice based activities. The 3rd highest is the Pacific Coast region, followed by the Rocky Mountain/Great Plains region. Across all regions, activities involving viewing/photographing natural attributes of forests are generally among the most actively engaged activities.

An activity occasion can be of any duration from a few minutes to many hours and more than one activity can be engaged more than once during an outing by the same person. For these reasons, the estimates provided in Table 8.2 should be treated as a nonadditive index. The trend in participation in the activities listed in the last column of Table 8.2 shows that growth has occurred in all but 1 activity for which estimates of the number of participants are

Fishing is one of the more traditional outdoor activities and it remains popular.
Photo courtesy of USDA Photography Center, Ken Hammond

Table 8.2 Millions of recreation activity days by persons ages 16 or older that occurred in forested settings by activity for the U.S. by region, 2000–2001

Activity	U.S. Total	North	South	Rocky Mountains	Pacific Coast	Trend 1994–1995 to 2000–2001 (Millions)
Walking for pleasure	5,922	1,281	2,131	880	1,194	46
Viewing/photographing scenery	5,148	2,549	1,137	537	831	—²
Viewing/photographing birds	3,876	2,288	1,374	189	709	16
Viewing/photographing flowers	3,295	2,236	591	335	752	—²
Viewing/photographing wildlife	2,391	960	978	278	141	34
Day hiking	1,946	749	874	124	423	24
Sightseeing	1,371	587	452	124	187	(1)
Driving for pleasure	1,146	473	622	72	65	—²
Mountain biking	1,121	445	385	103	125	—²
Visiting a wilderness	847	319	271	56	224	—²
Warmwater fishing	650	259	373	30	17	8
Driving off-road	610	239	229	79	36	10
Family gathering	592	263	173	50	98	36
Picnicking	566	282	125	48	107	20
Swimming	477	245	156	33	50	—²
Visit nature center	470	213	150	37	72	17
Developed camping	371	135	122	47	50	16
Horseback riding	351	74	159	44	37	7
Gathering mushrooms, berries	322	249	61	40	66	—²
Visiting historic sites	321	178	64	19	41	12
Coldwater fishing	288	122	55	38	52	9
Big game hunting	216	113	78	22	11	4
Backpacking	188	56	39	28	56	8
Primitive camping	181	42	46	29	66	7
Canoeing	122	64	30	2	33	7
Small game hunting	115	45	36	10	13	3
Downhill skiing	113	68	8	12	20	2
Snowmobiling	101	72	4	15	7	5

Table 8.2 Millions of recreation activity days by persons ages 16 or older that occurred in forested settings by activity for the U.S. by region, 2000–2001 *continued*

Activity	U.S. Total	North	South	Rocky Mountains	Pacific Coast	Trend 1994–1995 to 2000–2001 (Millions)
Mountain climbing	83	22	20	17	17	4
Rafting	72	32	18	9	10	5
Snowboarding	72	14	—[1]	15	18	6
Kayaking	59	25	10	3	21	5
Cross-country skiing	42	32	—[1]	6	12	2
Anadromous fishing	42	20	7	3	25	1
Orienteering	41	23	10	2	—[1]	0
Rock climbing	39	18	4	—[1]	—[1]	2
Visiting prehistoric sites	29	10	1	12	9	—[2]
Snowshoeing	27	20	—[1]	2	3	—[2]
Caving	14	5	4	1	6	0

Source: NSRE 2000–2001, Versions 1–11, July 1999 to November 2001. USDA Forest Service, Athens, GA. (Originally reported in USDA Forest Service, 2002 National Report on Sustainable Forest.)

Note: Regional numbers may not sum to U.S. total because of rounding and because they do not represent a weighted average. Regions are defined differently in this chapter than in other chapters because they are the ones used in the Nation's Report. See Figure 8.1 (p. 143) for regions.

[1] No estimate due to lack of NSRE data for this activity in this region.
[2] Participation data for these activities were not collected in 1995.

available from both the 1994–1995 and 2000–2001 national surveys. The activity that decreased was sightseeing, which in reality declined very little, almost negligibly so. In terms of numbers of added participants, ranking of activities put walking at the top, with an additional 46 million visits. Following walking in added participants were attending family gatherings outdoors (36), viewing/photographing wildlife (34), hiking (24), picnicking (20), visiting nature centers, museums (17), viewing/photographing birds (16), camping in developed campgrounds (16), visiting historic sites (12), and driving motor vehicles off-road (10). Generally, participation in outdoor activities in forested settings continues to grow as it has over the last several decades in the United States. Most of the activities with the greatest amount of growth in numbers of participants are nonconsumptive and of relatively low impact on the forest resources.

Table 8.3 reports visits for 2000–2001 based on nationwide on-site sampling of U.S. national forest use. The Forest Service has implemented a National Visitor Use Monitoring System (NVUM) that provides statistically valid estimates of recreation visitation (USDA Forest Service, 2002b). NVUM estimates in Table 8.3 show that National Forest use across the country is primarily in general, undeveloped areas. In 2000 there was a total of over 137 million estimated visits to general forest areas on national forests. A site visit is 1 occasion of any duration where 1 person enters into an area or site within a single national forest for recreation purposes. Because most of the land area in national forests is in the West, two thirds of all general forest use is in the 2 western regions. Likewise for developed-site day use, two thirds of national use is in the western national forests. Forty percent of overnight developed site use, on the other hand, occurs in eastern national forests, while only 13.6% of use of national forest areas in the National Wilderness Preservation System is in eastern wilderness. Comparable use statistics for state forests are generally not available.

Table 8.3 Estimated site visits in millions at national forests by region, calendar year 2000 and 2001

	Site Type			
Region	Day Use Developed 2000	Overnight Developed 2000	Designated Wilderness 2000	General Forest Area 2000
North	12.6	4.5	1.6	27.1
South	7.4	4.5	0.6	18.9
Rocky Mountains/ Great Plains	35.8	9.4	7.5	55.8
Pacific	31.2	3.7	6.5	35.4
U.S. Totals	87.0	22.2	16.2	137.2

Source: USDA Forest Service (2000b). National Visitor Use Monitoring Program.

Chapter 9
Farm Recreation

James J. Barry
Daniel Hellerstein[1]

Farms and ranches comprise about 40% of the total land base of the United States (just over 917 million acres). According to the 1999 Agricultural Economics and Land Ownership Survey (AELOS; USDA National Agricultural Statistics Service, 1999), there are nearly 2,134,000 farms in the United States. Almost one third is less than 50 acres in size, 15% are between 50 and 99 acres, and 15% are between 100 and 179 acres. Just under 9% are 1,000 or more acres in size. Over 90% of farms are family owned, either as sole proprietorships or as family held corporations. As seen in Figure 9.1, most of the income received by farm operators is from off-farm sources (i.e., other employment or investments).

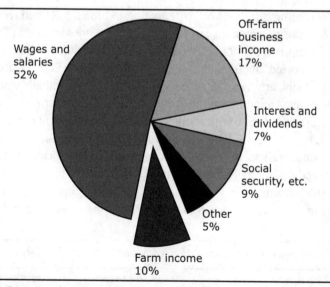

Figure 9.1 Sources of income for average farm operator household, 1999. Average operator household income = $64,347. Source: USDA Economic Research Service, 1999

[1] James Barry (james.j.barry@huskiemail.uconn.edu) is a graduate student at the University of Connecticut. Daniel Hellerstein (danielh@ers.usda.gov) is a natural resource economist with the Economics Research Service, USDA. The opinions and conclusions expressed in this chapter are not necessarily those of the Economic Research Service.

In addition to providing food and fiber to the American population and a livelihood to farm families, farms also provide rural amenities. These rural amenities range from wildlife habitat to scenic landscapes. One of these amenities is traveling to farms to enjoy on-farm recreation. Examples of on-farm recreation activities include buying or picking fresh produce, seeing and petting farm animals, and gazing at pastoral views.

This chapter looks at how Americans participate in recreation on farms. National and regional estimates of the rate of participation in recreation on farms are presented. This chapter examines what kinds of on-farm activities people enjoy, what types of scenery they value en route, and how they learned about the farm they visited. The terms on-farm recreation and on-farm activities in this chapter mean the same as agricultural tourism and agricultural experiences as used by other researchers.

To address these issues, data from 20,000 respondents drawn from the recent NSRE as described in earlier chapters is used. The NSRE is one of the few (if not the only) nationwide data sets that explicitly address the American public's participation in on-farm recreation. Analysis of the data is ongoing, and the results presented here intend to give the reader an overall picture. Hence, details such as measures of statistical significance between categorical differences are not reported.

Using screening questions on participation in broadly defined recreational activities, 2 sets of potential on-farm recreationists were identified (Table 9.1). The 1st set, comprising 6,399 individuals, are "farm visitors"—defined as individuals who reported visiting a farm in the prior year. The 2nd set, comprising 14,483 individuals, are "rural sightseers"—defined as individuals who reported taking a rural sightseeing trip in the last year. Of the 6,399 farm visitors, 1,329 were asked a detailed set of questions about their most recent trip to a farm. Similarly, 1,443 of the rural sightseers were asked detailed questions about their recent rural sightseeing trip. Of these 1,443, 277 reported visiting a farm and were asked questions identical to those given to the farm visitors.

Using this subsample of farm visitors and rural sightseers, the average respondent is in their early 40s with a median family size of 3. They typically

Table 9.1 NSRE respondents providing information about trips to farms

	Respondents Who Reported Visiting a Farm	Respondents Who Reported Going on Rural Sightseeing Trips
Total from 25,000 NSRE respondents	6,399	14,483
Interviewed about rural recreation	1,329	1,443
Visited a farm	1,329	277

Note: Even though a respondent can report both "visiting a farm" and "going on a rural sightseeing trip," in no case was a respondent asked both sets of questions.

work a 40-hour workweek, have at least some college-level education (one third have at least a bachelor's degree), and have an average family income of just over $50,000. When visiting a farm, the average distance traveled was about 80 miles with average trip costs of about $45 (including gasoline and other travel expenses).

Population-Wide Estimates of Numbers and Percentages Visiting Farms

This section presents population estimates of the numbers of people visiting farms and what they did there. These population estimates were computed by weighting NSRE sample percentages. The weights were derived from 2000 U.S. Census estimates of the persons ages 16 or older among the population, subdivided into age, race, and sex categories.

Overall, an estimated 62,400,000 Americans visited farms in 2000–2001, almost 30% of the total population. Most of these farm visitors (nearly two thirds) took between 1 and 5 trips to a farm in the year prior to their being interviewed for the NSRE. Table 9.2 gives a distribution of the estimated number of trips to farms by individuals over the last year.

Reasons for Visiting Farms

As summarized in Table 9.3 (p. 152) people visit farms for a number of reasons, and the importance of these reasons varies across farm visitors. Over 43 million Americans indicated that enjoying the rural scenery around the farm was important in their decision to go to a farm. An estimated 33 million indicated that visiting family or friends at their farms is important as a reason for visiting a farm. An estimated 33 million indicated that learning about or better appreciating that farms are where our food comes from is an important motivation for visiting. Also, an estimated 11 million indicated that hunting or fishing is an important aspect of their decision to visit farms.

Table 9.2 Estimated number of people (in thousands) and percentage of population taking trips to farms in the last 12 months, by number of trips

Number of Trips	Total Number Participating	Percent of Population
1 to 5	36,900	18
6 to 10	8,100	4
11 to 20	4,900	2
21 to 50	4,300	2
50 or more	3,300	2
Don't know/refused	4,900	2
Total	62,400	30

Note: Differences have not been tested for statistical significance.

Within the group of individuals who visited farms, about 85% rate "enjoying rural scenery" as important or somewhat important; about 40% felt it was important to "watch and participate in farm activities"; and about 55% reported that "visiting family and friends" was important. In contrast, about 70% did not rate hunting and fishing as important, and 51% did not rate purchasing agricultural products (or picking fruit) as important.

Table 9.3 Number (in thousands) and percentage of farm visitors by reason for visiting and importance of reason, 2000–2001

Reason for Visiting a Farm	Important	Somewhat Important	Not at all Important	Don't Know/ Refused
To enjoy the rural scenery around the farm	43,361 70%	9,899 16%	8,475 13%	401 1%
To visit family or friends	33,415 53%	6,697 10%	21,528 34%	1,510 3%
To learn about or to appreciate where our food comes from	32,506 53%	11,378 18%	17,736 29%	468 0.5%
To watch and to participate in farm activities	25,537 39%	15,593 25%	20,467 33%	1650 4%
To purchase agricultural products	19,126 28%	7,499 11%	34,895 51%	1620 10%
To pick fruit or produce	18,100 29%	8,863, 14%	34,392 55%	1,700 2%
To spend the night	13,897 6%	5,539 2%	30,396 15%	757 0.4%
To hunt or fish	10,904 18%	5,319 9%	45,250 72%	640 1%

Note: National estimates, in thousands. Percents are percent of the row. Because a separate question is used for each reason, each respondent could report that all, or none, of these reasons were "important." Due to rounding, row totals may not sum to 62.4 million. Differences have not been tested for statistical significance.

Importance of the Landscape En Route

As summarized in Table 9.4, a large number of people want to see less development along the roadside on their way to visit a farm. Our estimates show that they would like to see more woodlands, orchards/vines, and grazing animals along the way. Most indicated that there is about the right amount of some of the more common landscape characteristics associated with farms (e.g., farmsteads, croplands, pasture, or rangeland).

Table 9.4 Number (in thousands) and percentage of farm visitors by landscape feature along the way and desire to see more, same, or less, 2000–2001

Landscape Feature	Like to See More	About the Same	Like to See Less	Don't Know/ Refused
Woodlands	31,640 50%	23,440 38%	4,719 7%	2,843 5%
Grazing animals	30,605 49%	24,526 39%	4,188 7%	3,338 5%
Land in orchards and vines	30,540 48%	23,744 37%	4,835 8%	4,522 7%
Land in pasture or range	22,770 37%	32,185 51%	4,343 7%	3,351 5%
Farmsteads	21,945 35%	31,391 50%	6,006 10%	3,262 5%
Croplands	18,874 30%	33,777 54%	6,318 10%	3,638 6%
Nonfarm business and residential development	6,410 10%	15,839 25%	37,434 60%	2,925 5%

Note: National estimates, in thousands. Percents are percent of the row. Due to rounding, row totals may differ slightly. Because a separate question is used for each feature, each respondent could report that all, or none, of these features are in the "Like to See More" category. Due to rounding row totals may not sum to 62.4 million. Differences have not been tested for statistical significance.

On-Farm Activities

People participated in various activities while visiting a farm. An estimated 23 million people petted farm animals, over 9 million went on a hay ride or walked through a corn maze, 5 million went horseback riding, and over 3 million milked cows (Table 9.5).

Table 9.5 Number (in thousands) and percentage of farm visitors participating in selected recreational activity, in thousands, 2000–2001

Recreational Activity	Total	% of U.S. Population
Petting farm animals	23,515	11
Hay ride/corn maze	8,802	4
Horseback riding	5,366	2
Milking a cow	3,372	1

Note: Because a separate question is used for each activity, each respondent could report that he participated in all, or none, of these activities.

Sample Statistics About Farm Trips

The preceding text reported estimated numbers and percentages of the overall U.S. population ages 16 or older who visited farms for recreation in 2000–2001. In the following sections, this conversion is not performed to population estimate. Instead, it focuses on percentages of NSRE respondents who indicated they had either visited a farm or had taken a sightseeing trip to a rural area with farms in 2000–2001. Sample statistics are often used instead of population weighted statistics to identify differences between groups of survey respondents.

Farm Activities, Sources of Information, and Trip Spending

This section focuses on the activities people have participated in while visiting a farm, on sources of information for picking a farm to visit, and on the importance of certain aspects of the farm. Unless otherwise noted, the results are based on the 1,329 observations classified as farm visitors. (Similar questions were asked of the sample of 1,443 rural sightseers. This section, however, focuses only on farm visitors.)

As illustrated in Figure 9.2, regardless of age, most people who took a trip specifically to visit a farm petted farm animals. No age group was below 60% participation. Many farm visitors took hay rides or walked through corn mazes, ranging from about 16% for 45–55 year olds to over 30% for adults ages 35–44 (probably the parents of young children). Others went horseback riding or milked a cow although the youngest group exceeded 20% for horseback riding. Some people visited a farm as part of a rural sightseeing trip. For them, visiting a farm was not the main reason for their rural trip; they decided during the trip to visit a farm. Based on the sample of 1,443 rural sightseers, nearly 20% of sightseers decided to visit a rural farm while on their sightseeing trip.

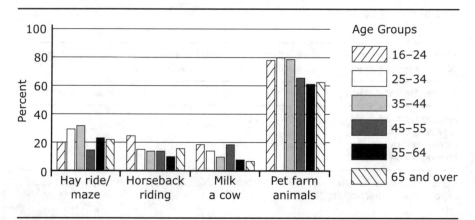

Figure 9.2 Percent participating in farm recreation activities by age group

Overall, word-of-mouth was the most common source of information used to find out about a farm to visit. About 58% of the people learned of the farm they visited through family or friends. Many others indicated they learned about the farm by means other than those listed for them in the survey. Table 9.6 lists individuals' answers to how they heard about the farm.

Over 21% of respondents who visited a farm indicated that the farm they visited was owned by either a family member or a friend. One might expect the kind and amount of expenses for visiting a farm to be different if the farm visited were owned by a family member or friend. One could also assume that people would usually travel further to see friends and family. However, in comparison, few differences were evident. A greater percentage of those visiting a family member or friend's farm were found to be in the highest categories of total spending (which includes expenditures on farm products) relative to those whose visit was not to a family member or friend's farm.

Table 9.6 Percent of sample of farm visitors by source of information about the farm they visited, 2000–2001

Source	% of Sample
Friends/family	58
Happened to pass by	7
Advertisements	6
Newspaper/magazine	3
Prior trip	3
TV/radio reports	1
Internet	1
Other	21

Landscape Characteristics En Route

Overall, the demographics and reasons for visiting farms for sightseers were very similar to those of farm visitors. However, as shown in Tables 9.7 and 9.8 (p. 156), sightseers' preferences for landscape characteristics differ somewhat from those who actually visited a farm. Considering farm visitors first, Table 9.7 shows that about 58% wanted to see less nonfarm business and residential development along the route they took to visit a farm. Many farm visitors would like to see instead more woodlands and orchards, with 49% saying they would like to see more woodlands and 48% wanting to see more orchards and vineyards. Farm visitors would also like to see more grazing animals en route (47%). Smaller percentages want to see more land in pasture (36%), farmsteads (34%), and croplands (29%). It is worth noting that while modest percentages indicated they wanted to see more pasture, farmsteads and croplands; an even lower percentage indicated they wanted to see less of these features.

Like farm visitors, sightseers were asked what characteristics of the landscape they would like to see more or less of while on sightseeing trips. In general,

Table 9.7 Farm visitor preferences (percent) for 7 en route rural landscape features, 2000–2001

Landscape Feature	More	About the Same	Less	Don't Know/ Refused
Woodlands	49	37	7	5
Land in orchards and vines	48	37	8	5
Grazing animals	47	40	6	5
Land in pasture or range	36	52	6	5
Farmsteads	34	51	9	5
Cropland	29	55	10	6
Nonfarm business and residential development	9	27	58	4

Note: Values are row percents. Due to rounding, row percents may not add up to 100%. Differences have not been tested for statistical significance.

Table 9.8 Rural sightseer preferences (percent) for 7 land landscape features, broken down by those who did and who did not visit a farm, 2000–2001

Landscape Characteristic	Farm visit?	More	About the Same	Less	Don't Know/ Refused
Grazing animals	No farm visit	53	33	9	2
	Farm visit	54	33	9	2
Woodlands	No farm visit	53	34	8	3
	Farm visit	49	38	8	4
Land in orchards and vines	No farm visit	50	35	8	5
	Farm visit	50	35	9	5
Land in pasture or range	No farm visit	37	44	12	4
	Farm visit	37	48	8	53
Farmsteads	No farm visit	38	43	14	4
	Farm visit	43	42	11	2
Cropland	No farm visit	31	47	16	4
	Farm visit	35	47	13	4
Nonfarm business and residential development	No farm visit	11	23	61	3
	Farm visit	15	21	60	3

Note: Values are row percents. Due to rounding, row percents may not add up to 100%. Differences have not been tested for statistical significance.

sightseers who included in their trip a visit to a farm had similar landscape preferences to those who did not visit a farm (on their sightseeing trip; Table 9.8). Higher percentages of those who visited a farm wanted to see more farmsteads and croplands (43% and 35%) compared to those who did not visit a farm (38% and 31%). Interestingly, sightseers who visited farms had slightly stronger preferences for more nonfarm business and development (15% compared to 11%).

Spending Profiles

Farm visitors were asked how much they had spent while visiting their chosen farm and what overall cost they incurred for their most recent trip to a farm (en route and on the farm). Table 9.9 shows the amount spent on the farm, which for most was $25 or less. Male respondents had higher percentages spending the greater amounts listed in Table 9.9 compared to women. By age, the 16–24 age group generally spent the least, with 45% spending less than $5 while visiting on the farm. The 35–44 age group was most likely to spend larger sums of money on the farm, more than 14% said they spent over $50.

Overall, about 35% of the surveyed farm visitors said the overall cost of their trip (en route and on the farm) was $10 or less, with almost 20% not spending anything. Almost 50% spent between $5 and $50, and about 20% spent over $50. The amount spent on the farm and the overall cost of the trip appear to be positively correlated (i.e., on the more expensive trips, people tended to spend more money while at the farm).

Table 9.9 Percent of farm recreation visitors by the amount of money spent on the farm and demographic characteristic, 2000–2001

| Demographic Characteristic | Amount Spent | | | | | |
	<$5	$5–25	$25–$50	$51–$100	$100>	Don't Know/ Refused
Gender						
Female	34%	38%	14%	3%	2%	6%
Male	37%	31%	13%	8%	5%	2%
Age Group						
16-24	45%	29%	14%	0%	1%	8%
25-34	39%	32%	11%	5%	4%	7%
35-44	27%	35%	18%	8%	6%	3%
45-54	38%	32%	18%	7%	2%	1%
55-64	31%	37%	9%	8%	6%	6%
65 and over	35%	47%	6%	2%	3%	3%
No age given	31%	26%	26%	0%	0%	5%

Note: Numbers may not add up due to missing values for the demographics variables. Differences have not been tested for statistical significance.

Regional Differences

As with other comparisons in this chapter, comparing percentages broken out by regions generally reveals more similarities than differences. This section will mostly leave it to the reader to identify regional differences and to attach significance to similarities. Table 9.10 (opposite) shows how much more or less of each identified landscape characteristic respondent farm visitors would like to see en route, region by region. Regions are defined using the U.S. Department of Agriculture Economic Research Service Farm Resource Regions (see Appendix Figure 9.3, p. 167). These regions are well-recognized by the agricultural community, likely the primary user of the results in the chapter.

Here are a few examples of some of the differences in Table 9.10. When asked about seeing animals grazing en route to a farm for a recreational visit, just over one half of the Northern Crescent, Northern Great Plains, and the Fruitful Rim region respondents said that they would like to see more. Nearly two thirds (65%) of individuals in the Northern Great Plains wanted to see more woodlands. Some respondents from the Northern Great Plains (23%), the Mississippi Portal (21%), and the Eastern Uplands (16%) wanted to see more nonfarm development.

Table 9.11 (below) shows percentages of farm visitors for each region by the activities in which they participated while visiting a farm. While individuals from all regions were likely to have petted farm animals, they were least likely to have milked a cow. However, for other activities there are some regional differences in the level of participation. The largest difference is found in the going for a hay ride and walking through a corn maze activities. Percentages participating range from 29% of respondents from the Northern Crescent having participated to only 10% from the Mississippi Portal. Table 9.12 (pp. 160–161) shows the importance of an array of reasons for visiting a farm by region. Visiting friends and family was much higher as a reason for Prairie Gateway farm visitors compared to any other region (72%) compared to the

Table 9.11 Percentages of farm visitors by activity on farm and by region, 2000–2001

Region	Milking a Cow	Horseback Riding	Hay Ride/ Corn Maze	Petting Farm Animals
Heartland	7	13	27	67
Northern Crescent	11	13	29	72
Northern Great Plains	12	18	18	63
Prairie Gateway	11	21	18	68
Eastern Uplands	10	16	15	65
Southern Seaboard	13	18	20	61
Fruitful Rim	8	11	23	64
Basin and Range	11	24	28	73
Mississippi Portal	3	16	10	56

Note: Differences have not been tested for statistical significance.

Table 9.10 Percentages of farm visitors indicating their preferences for more, same, or less of the listed landscape features en route to the farm they visited by region of the country, 2000–2001

Landscape Feature	Preference for Amount of Feature En Route	Heartland	Northern Crescent	Northern Great Plains	Prairie Gateway	Eastern Upland	Southern Seaboard	Fruitful Rim	Basin and Range	Mississippi Portal
Woodlands	Less	9	8	11	12	2	5	6	4	15
	About the same	33	40	16	38	43	35	37	37	34
	More	50	47	65	43	52	50	51	54	42
Lands in orchards and vines	Less	8	6	6	13	5	4	7	9	15
	About the same	38	37	30	37	35	40	34	40	36
	More	46	50	48	43	24	44	53	43	39
Grazing animals	Less	6	5	4	4	7	4	6	7	2
	About the same	43	37	39	53	43	38	34	48	47
	More	43	51	51	39	45	46	53	36	39
Land in pasture	Less	6	8	6	4	3	6	5	9	10
	About the same	54	52	55	58	55	47	45	50	47
	More	31	34	25	36	37	36	43	31	34
Farmsteads	Less	8	8	9	10	8	9	7	18	7
	About the same	53	49	44	52	48	50	50	53	55
	More	31	35	44	35	38	31	36	25	28
Cropland	Less	12	9	6	12	10	6	10	10	7
	About the same	59	54	58	53	51	55	49	59	63
	More	21	30	23	30	33	26	34	24	21
Nonfarm development	Less	56	61	44	68	52	53	64	57	26
	About the same	27	27	30	23	25	25	22	33	47
	More	7	7	23	5	16	10	7	7	21

Note: Percentages of respondents indicating they did not know how to respond to the question or refused the question are not shown. Differences have not been tested for statistical significance.

Table 9.12 Percentage of farm visitors indicating different levels of importance for reasons for visiting farms for recreation by region of the country, 2000–2001

	Heartland	Northern Crescent	Northern Great Plains	Prairie Gateway	Eastern Upland	Southern Seaboard	Fruitful Rim	Basin and Range	Mississippi Portal
Enjoy the rural scenery									
Important	75	76	76	73	74	74	75	68	65
Somewhat important	13	13	16	20	18	17	14	15	21
Not at all important	9	8	4	6	5	5	7	13	10
Visit family or friends									
Important	56	47	29	72	60	56	53	50	57
Somewhat important	15	9	5	4	10	12	10	16	13
Not at all important	25	41	62	22	27	29	33	30	26
Learn about farming									
Important	45	50	39	53	47	48	46	45	50
Somewhat important	21	19	20	9	13	15	19	15	13
Not at all important	30	28	37	37	37	31	31	36	34
Watch/participate in farm activities									
Important	44	44	44	37	36	35	43	45	50
Somewhat important	28	25	32	26	24	22	24	22	28
Not at all important	24	28	20	35	37	37	30	28	15
Pick fruit or produce									
Important	24	32	16	26	29	34	32	22	34
Somewhat important	20	15	11	12	13	11	10	10	18
Not at all important	52	50	69	60	56	50	55	63	42
Purchase agricultural products									
Important	25	35	18	25	29	32	34	21	31
Somewhat important	12	14	9	13	5	10	10	15	15
Not at all important	59	48	69	60	63	53	52	60	50

Table 9.12 Percentage of farm visitors indicating different levels of importance for reasons for visiting farms for recreation by region of the country, 2000–2001 *continued*

	Heartland	Northern Crescent	Northern Great Plains	Prairie Gateway	Eastern Upland	Southern Seaboard	Fruitful Rim	Basin and Range	Mississippi Portal
Spend the night									
Important	24	20	27	36	32	27	33	21	23
Somewhat important	10	8	9	15	7	16	10	13	18
Not at all important	62	68	58	47	58	50	54	60	55
Hunt or fish									
Important	16	16	25	25	24	24	14	22	31
Somewhat important	12	6	18	11	11	10	7	12	15
Not at all important	69	74	53	63	62	61	74	62	50

Note: Percentages of respondents indicating they did not know how to respond to the question or refusing the question are not shown. Differences have not been tested for statistical significance.

2nd highest region, Eastern Uplands (60%). The Northern Crescent had the highest percentage of respondents who rated visiting friends and family as not at all important (41%).

In general, hunting and fishing was not important across all regions. About one quarter of the respondents in the Northern Great Plains (25%), Prairie Gateway (25%), Eastern Uplands (24%), and the Southern Seaboard (24%) indicated that hunting or fishing was an important reason for their farm visit. The Northern Crescent (74%) and the Fruitful Rim (74%) had the highest percentage say that hunting and fishing was not at all important. Another reason for visiting farms that show relatively large differences is in the importance of staying the night. Nearly one third of the individuals from the Prairie Gateway (36%), Eastern Uplands (32%), and the Fruitful Rim (33%) said staying the night was important. Staying the night was least important in the Northern Crescent, where 68% rated it as not at all important. There was little correlation shown between staying the night and visiting a family or friend's farm across the regions shown.

Finally, to lend perspective to the importance of farm recreation to farm owners economically, Table 9.13 reports estimates of total and average annual income generated by recreation on farms as reported by farmers for each region (USDA 2002a, 2002b). In total, recreational income provides farmers with approximately $800 million per annum. Over two thirds of this income is generated in the Northern Crescent region (including New England, Wisconsin, Michigan, and New York) and Fruitful Rim (including California, Oregon, Washington, and the Gulf Coast). In contrast, for farms in the Eastern Uplands (West Virginia, Northwestern Arkansas, Southern Missouri, Eastern Tennessee, Eastern Kentucky, and Northeastern Alabama), total income from recreation is less than $5 million per year. It is also noteworthy that approximately 2% of

---

Table 9.13 Total annual and average farm income (in thousands) generated by recreation by region of the country (before expenses)

Region	Average Total Income Across All Farms per Year	Average Income per Farm per Year	% of Farms With Income From On-Farm Recreation
Heartland	$38,500	$90	7
Northern Crescent	$298,000	$963	2
Northern Great Plains	$14,000	$138	5
Prairie Gateway	$79,000	$267	4
Eastern Uplands	$5,000	$14	1
Southern Seaboard	$37,800	$161	3
Fruitful Rim	$278,600	$1,127	3
Basin & Range	$36,700	$437	6
Mississippi Portal	$8,000	$69	1
Total	$796,000	$368	2

Note: Differences have not been tested for statistical significance.
Source: USDA, 2002

U.S. farms obtain income from on-farm recreation, suggesting that income from on-farm recreation may be substantial for the few farmers receiving it.

Urban/Rural Differences

On the farm individuals tended to participate in the same activities whether they were from urban or rural communities (Table 9.14). Across metro and nonmetro counties, petting farm animals was the most popular activity, followed by hay rides/corn maze, horseback riding, and milking cows.

Table 9.15 (p. 164) compares percentages of urban and rural respondents by landscape characteristics they would like to see more or less of while en route to visit a farm. In general, few differences existed between respondents from metro counties compared to those from nonmetro counties. However, when more finely defined using a continuum between metro and nonmetro counties (see Urban-Rural Beale Codes, Appendix, p. 166), a few differences are evident. For example, small metro counties had nearly 20% of respondents reporting that they would like to see more nonfarm development en route to the farm. This is much different from moderately large near-metro counties where only 4% of farm visiting respondents indicated that they would like to see more nonfarm development. Another characteristic of note is croplands. Large metro counties had only 18% of respondents saying they would like to see more cropland, compared with one quarter to one third of farm visiting respondents who live in less populated counties wanting to see more cropland.

Between metro and nonmetro residents who visited farms, the importance of various reasons for visiting varied only a little (Table 9.16, p. 165). More respondents from smaller, nonmetro counties felt that visiting family and friends was important than did others from larger and fully metro counties. Individuals from most counties felt that visiting farms to purchase agricultural products was important. But respondents from large fringe counties, and those from very small nonmetro counties, did not feel that purchasing products was as important. Only about 20% from large metro fringe counties and 21% from rural counties rated visiting family or friends as important, compared to the range of 24% to 33% from the remaining counties. Hunting and fishing seems to have been more

Table 9.14 Percentages of farm visitors participating in 4 activities by metro and nonmetro residence, 2000–2001

Area of Residence	Milking a Cow	Horseback Riding	Hay Ride/ Corn Maze	Petting Farm Animals
Metro counties	9	15	27	45
Nonmetro counties	11	14	18	65

Note: Differences have not been tested for statistical significance.
Source: USDA, 2002

important to farm visitors from nonmetro as compared with metro counties. Over one third of respondents from nonmetro counties rated hunting and fishing as either an important or somewhat important reason for their visit.

Conclusions

This chapter took a broad look at American participation in on-farm recreation. While further analysis is in order, it does seem that visiting farms, either as a primary purpose of a trip or as part of a rural sightseeing outing, is a popular activity. It is estimated that over 60 million Americans (over 30% of the population) made 1 or more recreational visits to farms during the past year. While many of these visits were to see family and friends, a majority were not.

People valued a number of different attributes of their farm trips. Purchasing agricultural products and picking fruit and vegetables was important, but enjoying the rural scenery around the farm and learning where our food comes from was more important. Interestingly, petting farm animals was the most frequent on-farm activity mentioned. In general, en route to a farm people would like to see more woodlands and grazing animals, about the same amount of farmland, and less development.

Table 9.15 Percentages of farm visitors indicating they would like to see more, same, see less of landscape characteristics by urban or rural residence, 2000–2001

		Metro Counties	Rural Counties
Woodlands	More	51	48
	About the same	36	39
	Less	8	8
Lands in orchards and vines	More	49	48
	About the same	38	36
	Less	7	9
Grazing animals	More	49	44
	About the same	38	45
	Less	6	6
Land in pasture	More	36	35
	About the same	51	53
	Less	7	7
Farmsteads	More	34	35
	About the same	50	52
	Less	9	8
Cropland	More	31	26
	About the same	53	57
	Less	10	10
Nonfarm development	More	10	8
	About the same	25	30
	Less	59	57

Note: Differences have not been tested for statistical significance.

When broken down across regions, and along socioeconomic lines, the data do not reveal any striking patterns. Although there are a few noticeable differences (e.g., hunting was more important in the Northern Great Plains than in the Northern Crescent), the overall impression is that visiting farms is an activity enjoyed by people all across America.

Table 9.16 Percentage of farm visiting respondents indicating the importance of various reasons for visiting a farm by metro and nonmetro residence, 2000–2001

Reason	Importance	Metro Counties	Rural Counties
To enjoy the rural scenery	Important	75	75
	Somewhat important	16	16
	Not at all important	8	8
To visit family or friends	Important	52	61
	Somewhat important	11	13
	Not at all important	36	25
To learn about or to appreciate where food comes from	Important	47	51
	Somewhat important	18	17
	Not at all important	33	30
To watch/participate in farm activities	Important	42	44
	Somewhat important	25	27
	Not at all important	32	26
To purchase agricultural products	Important	32	29
	Somewhat important	13	11
	Not at all important	53	58
To pick fruit or produce	Important	29	30
	Somewhat important	14	15
	Not at all important	55	53
To spend the night	Important	28	25
	Somewhat important	11	12
	Not at all important	59	60
To hunt or fish	Important	15	28
	Somewhat important	8	12
	Not at all important	74	58

Note: Differences have not been tested for statistical significance.

Appendix

Urban-Rural Beale Codes

Metro Counties

0   Central counties of metro areas of 1 million population or more

1   Fringe counties of metro areas of 1 million population or more

2   Counties in metro areas of 250,000 to 1 million population

3   Counties in metro areas of fewer than 250,000 population

Nonmetro Counties

4   Urban population of 20,000 or more, adjacent to a metro area

5   Urban population of 20,000 or more, not adjacent to a metro area

6   Urban population of 2,500 to 19,999, adjacent to a metro area

7   Urban population of 2,500 to 19,999, not adjacent to a metro area

8   Completely rural or fewer than 2,500 urban population, adjacent to a metro area

9   Completely rural or fewer than 2,500 urban population, not adjacent to a metro area

For further details on Urban-Rural Beale Codes, please see
http://www.ers.usda.gov/briefing/rurality/RuralUrbCon

Figure 9.3 Nine USDA Economic Research Service Regions

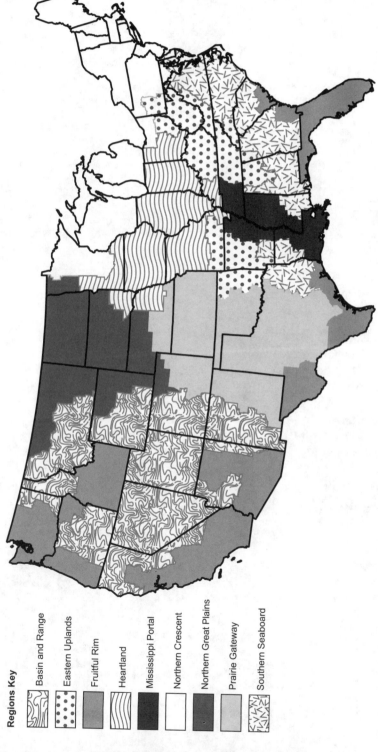

Regions Key

- Basin and Range
- Eastern Uplands
- Fruitful Rim
- Heartland
- Mississippi Portal
- Northern Crescent
- Northern Great Plains
- Prairie Gateway
- Southern Seaboard

For a more detailed color map, please refer to http://www.ers.usda.gov/publications/aib760/aib-760.pdf

Chapter 10
Marine Recreation

Vernon R. Leeworthy
Peter C. Wiley[1]

The United States enjoys beautiful and abundant coastlines bordered by the Atlantic, Pacific, and Arctic Oceans; the Great Lakes; and the Gulf of Mexico. Along these 95,000 miles of shoreline, vital and sometimes competing activities occur including transportation, trade, fishing, energy production, research, education, protection of historical and cultural sites, marine wildlife habitats, recreation, and tourism.

Almost half of the U.S. population lives and works within coastline states and counties. Yet this coastline covers only 11% of the country's total surface area. Within this 11% there are over 190 seaports and some of the largest cities in the United States. The U.S. coastal area also is the home, nursery, and spawning grounds for huge numbers of species of marine life. The health of the oceans and coastlines is critical to these species and to human populations as well.

To help protect the health of marine ecosystems, the United States has now established a National Marine Sanctuaries system. It includes over 18,000 square miles of ocean and coastal waters from the North Atlantic to the South Pacific. A new sanctuary still in the designation process is located in the Great Lakes. Sanctuaries aid in the recovery of endangered marine animals like the gray whale and lessen the threat of oil spills and ship groundings. They are used extensively for ocean research and education. They are also used for recreation and serve to draw tourism, as do the beaches and marshes of the East, Gulf, and West coasts.

The abundance and diversity of marine resources in the United States make recreational opportunities in coastal waters a popular choice of the American public. The United States boasts over 12,000 miles of ocean coastline, or shoreline, with the state of Florida alone containing over 1,300 miles (Harrington, 1975). Marine-related recreational opportunities abound in a variety of places, from those adjacent to major cities to rural areas to areas that are still wild. Depending on the particular location, recreationists can engage in surfing, fishing, scuba diving, or hunting waterfowl in a tidal marsh. This chapter explores the patterns of recreation usage as they relate to saltwater or marine environments.

---

[1] Vernon R. Leeworthy is Chief Economist, National Oceanic and Atmospheric Administration (NOAA), National Ocean Service, Special Projects and coleader of the NSRE 2000. Peter C. Wiley is a staff economist in NOAA's National Ocean Service, Special Projects.

The NSRE is the 1st National Survey to include a broad assessment of the nation's participation in marine recreation. About every 5 years since 1955, the U.S. Fish and Wildlife Service has conducted a National Survey of Fishing, Hunting, and Wildlife Associated Recreation. However, the marine component of recreation was only broken out for saltwater fishing. In 1979 the National Marine Fisheries Service (NMFS) initiated the Marine Recreational Fisheries Statistics Survey (MRFSS). This is an annual survey only of catch and effort. Prior to the NSRE, national surveys of marine recreation have been limited to saltwater fishing.

Measuring Marine Recreation Participation for the NSRE

Marine recreation is defined as participation in at least 1 of 19 ocean or ocean coastal activities or settings. To implement this definition through the NSRE, survey respondents were asked if they had participated in an activity "in fresh-water, saltwater, or both" or in a setting that was "in freshwater or saltwater surroundings or both." Examples include visiting beaches, visiting watersides besides beaches, viewing nature, and hunting for waterfowl. The respondent was asked to consider mixed fresh/salt water mixes in tidal portions of rivers and bays as saltwater or saltwater surroundings, in addition to saltwater oceans and sounds. Since the Great Lakes are freshwater, the NSRE did not break out participation in these water bodies.

If a respondent had participated in 1 or more marine recreation activities, they were next asked in which states that saltwater participation took place (up to 5 states for each activity/setting). For 16 of the activity settings, the number of days in each state was also asked. (The number of days by state was asked for all marine recreation activities/settings except canoeing, kayaking, and rowing. Given that national participation rates would not yield enough obser-vations to reliably estimate the number of days by state, the days question was eliminated to save survey time.) Participation estimates by state may be found in Leeworthy (2001) and Leeworthy and Wiley (2001).

This chapter presents marine recreation participation rates in a format similar to previous chapters. Participation rates are the percentages of the civilian, noninstitutionalized population ages 16 years or older in the United States who participated in an activity or visited a saltwater setting over a 12-month period. This chapter also presents data on numbers of participants in marine activities. As well, respondents were asked for the number of days in which they partici-pated in an activity or visited a setting over the past 12 months in each state. Any amount of time and any number of times by 1 person participating in an activity in a single day was counted as a day of participation in that activity. Thus counted, participation days are not additive across activities since a person can and typically does participate in multiple activities or visit multiple settings in a given day. It is also not appropriate to add the number of participants across activities/settings. Again, the reason is that people can participate in multiple activities/settings. For estimating days of participation, all sample observations with reported number of days that exceeded 200 were deleted. For estimating participation rates, number of participants and days of participation, a sample of nearly 43,000 respondents reporting marine recreation participation in 1 or more activities were utilized. More extensive tabular summaries of participation can be found in Leeworthy (2001), while a more detailed picture of activity-by-activity participation and days by state may be found in Leeworthy and Wiley (2001). Future reports will also be available on tabular summaries of days and forecasts of participation and days of activity to year 2005.

Highlights

The most popular marine activities are visiting beaches, swimming, fishing, viewing or photographing scenery, birdwatching, motorboating, and viewing other wildlife in saltwater settings (Figure 10.1). Three of the top 7 activities involve viewing or photographing the marine environment. The 2 most popular activities involve being in the water or at the water's edge. The boating and floating and consumptive (i.e., fishing and hunting) categories each had 1 activity in the top 7. It is interesting to note that the majority of the top 7 activities are nonconsumptive in nature. It is also interesting to note that participation in the viewing/learning activities involved many more days of participation per participant per year. As is discussed in the next chapter, recreation management is often focused on consumptive activities while many of the most popular activities are nonconsumptive. Growing recognition of this paradox may have future implications on the way scarce resources are allocated for management of resources used for consumptive and nonconsumptive activities.

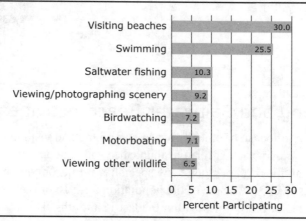

Figure 10.1 Most popular marine recreation activities based on percent of people ages 16 and older participating

Participation in Saltwater Recreation

Boating and Floating Activities

The variety of marine-related boating settings include open-water boating, which may require specialized skills in navigation and techniques for the more adventurous, but provide ample opportunities for the novice. In the marine environment, boating and floating activities vary from a luxurious cabin cruiser to activities which require a more hands-on approach such as sailing and wind-surfing. In the United States the most popular boating activity was motorboating in which over 7% of the population participated, which translates to over 15 million participants (Table 10.1).

Other saltwater floating and boating activities include sailing with just under 3% of the population participating. This translates to over 6 million participants. Following sailing in popularity was personal watercraft use (i.e., jetskiing) with about 2.5% participation, kayaking with 1.3% participation, waterskiing and canoeing with about 1% participation each and rowing and windsurfing, each with less than 1% participation.

It is important to bear in mind the significance of activities with relatively low participation rates. Even the boating and floating activity with the least participation, windsurfing, represents over 800,000 participants across the United States.

Table 10.1 Percentages and numbers of people ages 16 or older participating in boating and floating activities in saltwater, 2000–2001

Activity	% Participating	Number of Participants (in thousands)
Motorboating	7.11	15,153
Sailing	2.98	6,342
Personal watercraft use	2.57	5,483
Kayaking	1.33	2,839
Waterskiing	1.15	2,456
Canoeing	1.05	2,245
Rowing	0.53	1,136
Windsurfing	0.39	827

Swimming and Saltwater Beach Activities

The popularity of ocean or other saltwater swimming and visiting beaches can be attributed, in part, to their relative abundance and generally free access. As well, these activities do not require any specialized skills or equipment. In the United States over 30% of the of the population ages 16 or older visited 1 or more beaches 1 or more times within the last 12 months. This translates into just over 64 million beach-going participants (Table 10.2). Visiting beaches was the most popular activity of the entire set of saltwater based activities/settings in the NSRE survey. Another significant activity was swimming in saltwater. Over 25% of the population participated in such swimming, which translates into over 54 million participants. Other activities listed in Table 10.2, while not as popular as swimming and visiting a beach, still have significant participation. These activities include snorkeling, with over 5% of the population participating, amounting to over 10.8 million participants. Following snorkeling was visiting saltwater watersides other than beaches, with about 4.5% participation, and scuba diving and surfing, each with under 2% participation.

Table 10.2 Percentages and numbers of people 16 or older participating in swimming and beach activities in saltwater, 2000–2001

Activity	% Participating	Number of Participants (in thousands)
Visiting beaches	30.03	64,003
Swimming	25.53	54,406
Snorkeling	5.07	10,811
Visiting watersides (other than beaches)	4.50	9,581
Surfing	1.59	3,396
Scuba diving	1.35	2,880

Saltwater-Based Viewing and Learning Activities

While not as popular in the marine environment as in the freshwater environment, participation in saltwater-based viewing and learning activities is substantial. There are a wide variety of settings to which participants may be drawn where they may observe scenery or any of a great variety of fauna and flora. The dynamic nature of the meeting of ocean, sea, and sky often results in a unique viewing experience enjoyed by millions of Americans. The 3 activities in this category were fairly close in terms of participation rate. The most popular activity was viewing or photographing scenery in saltwater surroundings, in which over 9% of the of the population participated, about 19.5 million participants (Table 10.3, p. 174). Other saltwater viewing and learning activities include birdwatching, with over 7% of the population participating, around 15.3 million participants. Following birdwatching was viewing other wildlife

Table 10.3 Percentages and numbers of people 16 or older participating in saltwater-based viewing and learning activities, 2000–2001

Activity	% Participating	Number of Participants (in thousands)
Viewing/photographing scenery	9.19	19,580
Birdwatching	7.17	15,282
Viewing other wildlife	6.45	13,750

in saltwater surroundings with about 6.5% participation and about 13.8 million participants.

Saltwater-Based Fishing and Hunting

Saltwater-based hunting has been a traditional activity in many coastal communities in the United States. However, increasing pressure due to development along high-value coastlines has resulted in a decrease in habitat for waterfowl and a dearth of accessible hunting sites. In the United States about one third of 1% of the population participates in hunting waterfowl in saltwater surroundings. This translates to about 703,000 participants (Table 10.4). Saltwater fishing, on the other hand, attracts many more participants, many of whom tend to be extremely devoted to the sport. Recent advances in navigation technology has allowed saltwater fishers to pinpoint historically productive fishing sites with remarkable accuracy. Advances in prediction of dangerous offshore weather has also had a positive effect on the activity. Saltwater fishing is engaged in by 10.3% of the population, or about 22 million people.

Table 10.4 Percentages and numbers of people 16 or older participating in saltwater-based fishing and hunting activities, 2000–2001

Activity	% Participating	Number of Participants (in thousands)
Saltwater fishing	10.32	21,999
Hunting waterfowl in saltwater surroundings	0.33	703

Saltwater Activity Participation by Region

Participation in saltwater outdoor activities varies substantially across the 4 regions of the country. Total population by census region (see Figure 13.2, p. 203 for regions) from the 2000 Census of Population and Housing was:

Northeast	53.6 million
Midwest	64.4 million
South	100.2 million
West	63.2 million
U.S. Total	281.4 million

In terms of number of participants, however, the estimates do not follow these patterns. The Midwest generally contains a disproportionately low per capita number of participants. This is likely since this region's most northern population is not adjacent to any marine environment, houses an older population, and is near a close substitute, the Great Lakes (Table 10.5). It is also interesting to note that with the exception of kayaking and canoeing the

Table 10.5 Percentages and numbers of Americans ages 16 and older participating in saltwater-based activities by region, 2000–2001

Activity	Northeast % Participating	Northeast Number of Participants (Millions)	South % Participating	South Number of Participants (Millions)	Midwest % Participating	Midwest Number of Participants (Millions)	West % Participating	West Number of Participants (Millions)
Swimming and Beach								
Visiting beaches	34.3	13.90	31.4	23.80	14.3	7.00	35.9	17.20
Swimming	34.1	13.80	27.5	20.90	13.1	6.40	24.2	11.60
Visiting watersides (besides beaches)	5.4	2.20	4.9	3.70	2.3	1.10	4.8	2.30
Snorkeling	5.2	2.10	4.6	3.50	3.7	1.80	6.5	3.10
Scuba diving	1.2	0.50	1.3	1.00	0.8	0.40	1.9	0.90
Surfing	1.1	0.43	1.4	1.03	0.6	0.31	3.1	1.48
Boating and Floating								
Motorboating	9.9	4.00	8.3	6.30	2.7	1.30	6.5	3.10
Sailing	4.9	1.98	2.5	1.92	1.2	0.60	3.4	1.65
Personal watercraft use	3.0	1.20	3.4	2.60	1.0	0.50	2.1	1.00
Kayaking	2.2	0.89	0.8	0.64	0.5	0.23	2.2	1.03
Canoeing	1.3	0.52	1.2	0.91	0.2	0.12	1.3	0.60
Waterskiing	1.3	0.54	1.6	1.24	0.3	0.16	0.9	0.43
Rowing	1.0	0.39	0.4	0.31	0.1	0.04	0.7	0.35
Windsurfing	0.6	0.23	0.4	0.31	0.2	0.08	0.4	0.19
Viewing and Learning								
Viewing/photographing scenery	10.6	4.30	8.4	6.40	4.9	2.40	12.1	5.80
Birdwatching	9.6	3.90	7.2	5.50	3.3	1.60	7.9	3.80
Viewing other wildlife	7.2	2.90	6.6	5.00	3.3	1.60	7.9	3.80
Fishing and Hunting								
Saltwater fishing	11.4	4.60	13.8	10.50	2.9	1.40	10.0	4.80
Hunting waterfowl	0.1	0.03	0.5	0.41	0.1	0.03	0.4	0.19

Based on November 2000 estimate of 213.1 million civilian, noninstitutionalized U.S. population ages 16 and older.
Region populations (ages 16 and older): Northeast 40.5 million, Midwest 48.8 million, South 75.9 million, and West 47.9 million.

number of participants in boating and floating activities in the West is lower than it is in the Northeast, even though the population in the West is greater. The South has the largest population of the 4 regions and the number of participants in saltwater-based activities follows suit with the exceptions of surfing, sailing, kayaking, and rowing in a saltwater environment. In terms of participation rate, the northeast had the highest participation rate in 7 of the 19 activity settings. The West followed with the next highest number of activities with the highest participation rates (6 of 19), followed by the South (4 of 19). For 2 activities, canoeing and kayaking, the northeastern and western regions had about the same participation rate (1.3% and 2.2%, respectively).

Days of Participation

The previous section reported percentages and numbers of the population participating in outdoor saltwater activities. The tables that follow report current means and percentages by ranges of days of participation for groups of related activities.

Boating and Floating Activities

As mentioned earlier, one of the data elements collected in the survey was the number of days a respondent participated in an activity during the past 12 months. Averages in days per participant per year and percentages by ranges of days per year are shown in Table 10.6 for boating and floating activities. These averages ranged from over 7 for windsurfing to almost 12 for personal watercraft use (i.e., jetskiing) and waterskiing. No activity had more than 6% of participants engaged in the activity for 51 days or more. With the exception of waterskiing, slightly higher proportions participated 26 to 50 days. The majority participated under 10 days or less. For windsurfing and sailing, about half participated just 1 to 2 days. For many, travel to water sites, trip preparation and short warm-weather seasons made participating large numbers of days during the year prohibitive.

Table 10.6 Mean days per year and percentages of participants by number of days per year in boating and floating saltwater activities, 2000–2001

Activity	Mean Days	1–2 Days	3–10 Days	11–25 Days	26–50 Days	51+ Days
Personal watercraft use	11.9	43.4	40.0	9.2	5.3	2.1
Waterskiing	11.9	33.5	38.7	17.3	5.0	5.5
Sailing	8.3	47.3	36.9	9.5	4.1	2.3
Motorboating	7.9	30.7	42.3	13.8	7.2	6.0
Windsurfing	7.3	50.2	40.2	5.8	2.2	1.6

Note: The number of days by state was asked for all marine recreation activities/ settings except canoeing, kayaking, and rowing. Given that national participation rates would not yield enough observations to reliably estimate the number of days by state, those days questions were eliminated to save survey time.

Swimming and Beach Activities

Because beach and swimming activities are pursuits in which almost anyone can participate and do not require any specialized equipment, they have higher mean number of days than most other activities shown in Table 10.7, such as marine snorkeling and scuba diving. Visiting beaches, visiting watersides other than beaches, and marine swimming all had mean number of days between 10 and 20. Surfing had the highest mean number of days, as well as the highest proportion of respondents participating in the activity for 51 or more days indicating that the relatively low percentage of people who surf tend to be quite avid. Scuba diving had the lowest mean annual days and the lowest proportion of respondents engaging in the activity for more than 25 days. Snorkeling participation patterns closely mirrored those of scuba diving. More than 40% of scuba divers and snorkelers participated just 1 to 2 days per year.

Table 10.7 Mean days per year and percentages of participants by number of days per year in saltwater-based swimming and beach activities, 2000–2001

Activity	Mean Days	1–2 Days	3–10 Days	11–25 Days	26–50 Days	51+ Days
Surfing	23.3	24.7	43.3	10.7	7.7	13.7
Visiting watersides (besides beaches)	17.1	27.0	45.2	13.3	7.2	7.3
Swimming	14.3	18.3	51.2	18.4	7.2	4.9
Visiting beaches	13.8	22.5	50.8	15.9	5.9	5.0
Snorkeling	8.8	47.3	39.5	7.2	2.8	3.3
Scuba diving	8.2	41.4	43.1	9.6	4.0	2.0

Viewing/Learning Activities

Participants in these activities had the highest average number of days by a substantial margin. The activities with the greatest mean number of days are birdwatching and viewing/photographing scenery in saltwater surroundings with over 40 days per year. Those engaged in birding and viewing/photographing scenery and putting in 51 or more days per year make up more than 20% of the participant population. There is also a large percentage for all 3 activities engaging in the activity for 3 to 10 days per year (40% or greater; Table 10.8).

Table 10.8 Mean days per year and percentages of participants by number of days per year in saltwater-based viewing/learning activities, 2000–2001

Activity	Mean Days	1–2 Days	3–10 Days	11–25 Days	26–50 Days	51+ Days
Viewing/photographing scenery	43.6	13.0	40.6	17.3	8.0	21.1
Birdwatching	42.6	18.1	39.6	14.8	7.1	20.4
Viewing other wildlife	25.6	20.3	43.6	16.5	7.2	12.4

Fishing and Hunting

The mean number of days per year and the proportions within ranges of days are comparable between fishing and hunting waterfowl. Both had about a third of the participants engaging in one or two days and about 43% engaging between 3 and 10 days per year. Fewer participants in hunting waterfowl engaged in the activity for 51 days or greater (1.5%) than participate that much in fishing (4.5%; Table 10.9).

Table 10.9 Mean days per year and percentages of participants by number of days per year in saltwater-based fishing and hunting, 2000–2001

Activity	Mean Days	1–2 Days	3–10 Days	11–25 Days	26–50 Days	51+ Days
Saltwater fishing	12.2	33.9	42.8	11.2	7.6	4.5
Hunting waterfowl in saltwater surroundings	9.3	33.0	42.9	14.0	8.5	1.5

Chapter 11
Freshwater Recreation

Across the United States about 161 million acres, 7% of the country's total land area, is covered by water, mostly freshwater. Streams, rivers, natural lakes, ponds, reservoirs, and other forms of water cover are not only essential for aquatic microbiota, aquatic and terrestrial wildlife, household consumption, agriculture, and manufacturing but also important and highly valued as recreation resources.

Water resources occur on federal, state, and local government and private properties alike. On national forests, for example, there are 128,000 miles of rivers and streams, 2.2 million acres of lakes, ponds, and reservoirs, and 12,500 miles of shoreline. Among federal properties, the National Parks, National Wildlife Refuges, and Bureau of Land Management lands also have extensive water resources amounting to almost five million acres of water area. The Army Corps of Engineers, Tennessee Valley Authority, and Bureau of Reclamation manage extensive areas of water projects throughout the country, totaling around 10 million acres. Federal and state agencies combined protect and manage almost 11,000 miles of designated wild and scenic rivers. And there are over 30,000 miles of whitewater in the country for rafting, canoeing, kayaking or other means of floating.

Federal, state and local government resources, together with the water resources on private lands, constitute an enormous resource for the recreation-seeking American public. This chapter focuses on activity participation in freshwater streams and water bodies.

Highlights

The most popular activities occurring in freshwater venues include the following (see Figure 11.1, p. 180):
- Viewing/photographing wildflowers, trees, and other flora
- Swimming
- Viewing/photographing fish
- Visiting watersides (other than beaches)
- Viewing/photographing wildlife (other than birds and fish)
- Warmwater fishing
- Motorboating

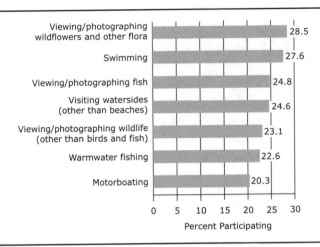

Figure 11.1 Percentages participating in the most popular freshwater outdoor activities, 2000–2001

Three of these 7 activities focus on viewing/photographing. Two involve human contact with the water or waterside. Two, with the lowest percentages, are motor or consumptive focused. Recreation management of freshwater resources in the country have usually focused on the latter 2 activities—not on improvement of opportunities for viewing, photographing and learning about freshwater ecosystems and their inhabitants, or on improving access to watersides and the water for swimming. The data presented in this chapter provide a useful insight into a possible need to shift management priorities a bit more toward nonconsumptive freshwater recreation opportunities. By far the greatest numbers of days of participation per year occur in the viewing and photographing activities.

Participation in Freshwater Recreation

Boating and Floating Activities

The options and advanced technology of the equipment now available for boating and floating are numerous and highly varied. Chapter 1 noted some of the technological advances in canoes and kayaks. Motorboats, too, have evolved. From the modest 12-foot fishing flat with a five-horse "kicker" to elaborate cabin cruisers with over 500 horsepower and all the luxuries one could imagine, motorboats offer a wide array of opportunities. In the United States, just over 20% of the population 16 or older participated in some form of freshwater motorboating in 2000–2001 (Table 11.1). Power reservoirs, flood control projects, natural rivers and lakes, and a number of other freshwater resources accommodate motorboating in all its varieties. Given that there are over 213 million people ages 16 or older in this country, this 20% translates into more than 42 million motorboating participants.

Table 11.1 Percent and number of people age 16 and older participating in boating and floating activities in freshwater, 2000–2001

Activity	% Participating	Number of Participants (in thousands)
Motorboating	20.3	43,259
Rafting	9.5	20,245
Canoeing	9.1	19,392
Jetskiing	7.8	16,622
Waterskiing	7.3	15,556
Rowing	4.0	8,524
Sailing	2.6	5,541
Kayaking	2.4	5,114
Windsurfing	0.4	852

Based on November 2000 estimate of 213.1 million civilian, noninstitutionalized U.S. population ages 16 and older.

In addition to motorboating, the NSRE inventories 8 other boating or floating activities in freshwater venues. Just over 9% of persons 16 or older participated in rafting and likewise in canoeing. Most rafting is in whitewater, using either rented or guided commercial rafts. Most canoeing is in still water, but a sizeable portion is in whitewater. Following canoeing, almost 8% participated in jetskiing, also known as personal watercraft use. Jetskiing, like most other motorized activities is fast growing and in some venues, controversial. Being a close substitute for waterskiing, the percentage of people who jetski has been growing while the percentage for boat-towed waterskiing has been declining. Nonetheless, over 15 million persons 16 or older waterskied in freshwater bodies in 2000–2001.

Rowing in freshwater bodies, including dinghies, shells, and other rowboats, is an activity of 4%, sailing is an activity of 2.6%, and kayaking is an activity of 2.4% of the population. Windsurfing, the least participated activity, includes 0.4% of the population, between 800,000 and 900,000 participants. The numbers across all boating and floating activities in freshwater are sizeable. They represent substantial markets for equipment manufacturers, rental businesses, guides and outfitters, and retailers. They also represent sizeable markets for use of freshwater resources in the various regions of the United States.

Swimming and Freshwater Beach Activities

Swimming and related activities are generally more popular than boating and floating activities. In freshwater bodies such as lakes, rivers and ponds, swimming has long been a summer activity of Americans. Close behind swimming is visiting watersides (other than a beach). These would include river walks, lake shorelines, waterside play areas, and many other such venues. Third in the list (Table 11.2, p. 182) is visiting a freshwater beach for sunbathing, and other purposes. A beach differs from other watersides in that the main focus of a beach is the sandy interface between land and water. Snorkeling and scuba diving have not been growing nearly as fast as other activities recently, especially in freshwater. But there are still large numbers of Americans 16 or older who participate in these activities in freshwater venues—a little over 5 million. Freshwater springs, such as Ginnie Springs in northern Florida, offer a unique opportunity to see and experience underwater environments in crystal clear freshwater.

Table 11.2 Percent and number of people ages 16 and older participating in freshwater-based swimming and beach activities, 2000–2001

Activity	% Participating	Number of Participants (in thousands)
Swimming in lakes, streams	27.6	58,816
Visiting other watersides (besides beaches)	24.6	52,423
Visiting beaches	17.1	36,440
Snorkeling	1.8	3,836
Scuba diving	0.7	1,492

Based on November 2000 estimate of 213.1 million civilian, noninstitutionalized U.S. population age 16 and older.

Freshwater-Based Viewing and Learning Activities

Across the United States in terrestrial and aquatic environments alike, activities that focus on viewing, photographing, and learning about natural subjects is growing fast and increasingly involving sizeable percentages of the population. Generally more popular than either boating or swimming activities, viewing/photographing flowers, trees, fish, wildlife, birds, and aquatic animals in freshwater environments is recreation for many millions of Americans 16 and older (Table 11.3). Viewing/photographing flowers, trees, and other freshwater or adjacent terrestrial flora is enjoyed by nearly 61 million people. Next is viewing/photographing fish, followed closely by viewing/photographing wildlife—both at around 50 million. A fast-rising activity is viewing/photographing birds (as seen in Chapter 2). In freshwater venues, birdwatching is an activity of almost 41 million persons—just over 19% of the population. Following is taking boat tours or open water excursions for the purpose of seeing wildlife or scenery of any type, almost 19% of the population—nearly 40 million people.

Freshwater-Based Fishing and Hunting

Fishing and hunting are among the more traditional outdoor activities in the United States, as they are worldwide (Table 11.4). As with almost all other outdoor activities, technology has advanced for both forms of outdoor participation. "Bass boats" with fish finders and many new reel, bait, and rod innovations

Table 11.3 Percent and number of people ages 16 and older participating in freshwater-based viewing and learning activities, 2000–2001

Activity	% Participating	Number of Participants (in thousands)
Viewing/photographing wildflowers, trees	28.5	60,734
Viewing/photographing fish	24.8	52,849
Viewing/photographing other wildlife	23.1	49,226
Viewing/photographing birds	19.1	40,702
Boating tours or excursions	18.7	39,850

Based on November 2000 estimate of 213.1 million civilian, noninstitutionalized U.S. population age 16 and older.

have expanded modes of participation. Warmwater fishing in freshwater is an activity of nearly 50 million in this country. This is almost 23% of the population of persons 16 or older. Species such as bass, bream, catfish, perch, and many others are the focus in warmwater fishing. Coldwater fishing focuses on trout, salmon, and other species that live in cold river or lake environments, often at high elevations. Almost all trout spend part of their lives in rivers and streams. Even trout that migrate to sea—the steelhead and sea-run cutthroat of North America and the Atlantic sea trout of Europe—are born in rivers. But then they make their journey down river to saltwater where they spend most of their lives. When fully grown, the urge to reproduce drives them back to their natal rivers. Both trout that migrate and those which spend their entire lives in rivers and streams are the focus of coldwater and anadromous species anglers, 13.6% and 4.4%, respectively.

Migratory bird hunting in freshwater areas is an activity of 2.3% of the population—nearly 5 million people. Hunting in general has been either stable or trending downward in the past 2 decades, with some short-term resurgence in the late 1990s. Freshwater swamps, rivers, lakes, and ponds are favored habitats of both freshwater fowl and their hunters.

Table 11.4 Percent and number of people ages 16 and older participating in freshwater-based fishing and hunting activities, 2000–2001

Activity	% Participating	Number of Participants (in thousands)
Warmwater fishing	22.6	48,161
Coldwater fishing	13.6	28,982
Anadromous fishing	4.4	9,376
Ice fishing	2.9	6,180
Migratory bird hunting	2.3	4,901

Based on November 2000 estimate of 213.1 million civilian, noninstitutionalized U.S. population age 16 and older.

Freshwater Activity Participation by Region

Across the four regions of the country participation in freshwater outdoor activities varies considerably. The 2000 Census of Population and Housing indicated that there were the following numbers of people ages 16 or older in each of the 4 census regions at the time of NSRE surveying:

Northeast	40.5 million
Midwest	48.8 million
South	75.9 million
West	47.9 million
U.S. Total	213.1 million

These numbers are somewhat reflected in the estimates of numbers of participants in the freshwater activities listed in Table 11.5. Generally the South shows larger numbers of person 16 or older participating in the listed activities, followed by the Midwest, West, and Northeast. However, percentages of population participating tend to be highest in the Midwest, relative to the South or to other regions. Thus, for some activities, numbers participating in the Midwest approach or in a few instances exceed number participating in the South, even though the population of the South is larger. Percentage participating in the Midwest exceeds that of any other region for 11 of the 19 activities listed in Table 11.5. Percentages for the Midwest's population exceed those of other regions by a wide margin for the activities of motorboating, swimming, and visiting a beach, and to a lesser extent for jetskiing, rafting, waterskiing and warmwater fishing. The South has the largest participation percentage in just one activity—scuba diving—but has the most participants overall in nearly every activity because of its relatively large population base. Coldwater and anadromous fishing are especially prominent in the West, which has more abundant coldwater resources.

Days of Participation

The first few tables reported percentages and numbers of the population participating in freshwater outdoor activities without regard to the number of times they participated. The tables that follow report current means and percentages by ranges of days of participation for groups of related activities.

Boating and Floating Activities

Part of the questioning of respondents to the NSRE asked how many days in the past 12 months survey respondents had participated in each activity. The averages and percentages by ranges of days per year are shown in Table 11.6 (p. 186) for boating and floating activities. These averages ranged from over 4 days per person per year for rafting to almost 14 for motorboating. The median

Table 11.5 Percent and number of people ages 16 and older participating in freshwater-based activities by region, 2000–2001

Activity	Northeast		Midwest		South		West	
	% Participating	Number of Participants (Thousands)	% Participating	Number of Participants (Thousands)	% Participating	Number of Participants (Thousands)	% Participating	Number of Participants (Thousands)
Boating and Floating								
Motorboating	14.9	6,015	28.8	13,970	19.6	14,800	17.8	8,474
Rafting	8.6	3,477	11.2	5,441	8.8	6,654	9.8	4,672
Canoeing	12.2	4,854	13.4	6,405	7.4	5,506	5.6	2,627
Jetskiing	4.2	1,708	10.2	4,983	7.7	5,856	8.5	4,075
Waterskiing	4.3	1,747	10.2	4,978	6.8	5,166	8.1	3,880
Rowing	5.6	2,218	5.6	2,664	2.9	2,148	3.2	1,494
Windsurfing	0.5	180	0.5	216	0.3	202	0.6	255
Swimming and Beach								
Swimming in lakes, streams	29.1	11,814	35.4	17,267	23.4	17,767	25.0	11,968
Visiting other watersides (besides beach)	24.0	9,753	24.6	12,011	24.2	18,392	25.6	12,267
Scuba diving	0.6	249	0.5	250	0.9	699	0.6	294
Visiting beach	17.5	7,051	28.7	13,893	11.8	8,892	13.9	6,604
Snorkeling	2.0	839	2.0	1,008	1.8	1,412	1.6	791
Viewing and Learning								
Viewing/photographing birds	20.1	8,151	22.4	10,914	16.8	12,742	18.6	8,895
Viewing/photographing wildflowers/trees	28.1	11,422	30.2	14,750	25.6	19,463	31.5	15,099
Viewing/photographing other wildlife	21.4	8,701	26.6	12,994	21.2	16,121	23.8	11,410
Fishing and Hunting								
Warmwater fishing	15.5	6,219	31.7	15,283	27.2	20,413	13.2	6,246
Coldwater fishing	13.8	5,682	10.3	5,095	10.4	8,009	21.0	10,196
Migratory bird hunting	1.0	409	3.3	1,622	2.3	1,760	2.3	1,110
Anadromous fishing	4.5	1,855	3.2	1,585	3.1	2,390	7.3	3,548

Based on November 2000 estimate of 213.1 million civilian, noninstitutionalized U.S. population ages 16 and older. Regional populations: Northeast—40.5 million, Midwest—48.8 million, South—75.9 million, and West—47.9 million.

for these activities was around 9. Few participated in any of the boating or floating activities 51 or more days per year. A few more participated 26 to 50 days. Most participated under 11 days. For kayaking, rowing, canoeing, and rafting approximately half participated just 1 to 2 days. For many, travel to water sites, preparation and short warm weather seasons for the activity prohibit participating large numbers of days during the year.

Table 11.6 Mean days of participation per year and percentage of participants by number of days per year in boating and floating freshwater activities, 2000–2001

Activity	Mean Days	1–2 Days	3–10 Days	11–25 Days	26–50 Days	51+ Days
Motorboating	13.8	24.7	44.1	17.6	8.8	4.9
Jetskiing	10.4	34.5	41.4	14.4	6.9	2.8
Sailing	9.8	40.7	41.9	10.8	4.3	2.4
Waterskiing	9.5	32.4	43.7	15.2	6.7	2.1
Kayaking	8.8	44.6	39.2	9.1	4.2	2.8
Rowing	7.1	50.1	38.5	6.5	2.7	2.1
Windsurfing	6.8	41.7	44.5	9.9	2.8	1.1
Canoeing	6.2	45.4	42.7	8.3	2.4	1.2
Rafting	4.4	58.1	32.7	7.1	1.7	0.4

Freshwater-Based Swimming and Beach Activities

Typically requiring less travel and preparation, swimming and related activities show somewhat higher average number of days of annual participation (Table 11.7). Means for swimming in lakes and streams, visiting freshwater watersides, scuba diving, and visiting a freshwater beach are all in the teens. Much smaller percentages of swimming and the other activity participants spend just 1 to 2 days in these activities. The largest percentages among the ranges shown are for 3 to 10 days.

Table 11.7 Mean days of participation per year and percentage of participants by number of days per year in freshwater-based swimming and beach activities, 2000–2001

Activity	Mean Days	1–2 Days	3–10 Days	11–25 Days	26–50 Days	51+ Days
Swimming (lakes, streams)	16.4	15.0	46.4	21.8	11.2	5.5
Visiting other watersides (besides beach)	16.2	29.0	43.8	14.7	7.1	5.4
Scuba diving	13.5	35.4	44.7	11.6	4.2	3.9
Visiting a beach	13.4	19.8	49.7	18.4	8.5	3.6
Snorkeling	8.6	39.3	45.4	9.3	3.6	2.4

Viewing/Learning Activities

By far the greatest number of days per year are put in by viewing, photographing, and learning activity participants (Table 11.8). Highest is birding with almost 86 days per year. Birding enthusiasts putting in 51 or more days per year make up almost 30% of the birding participant population. Viewers and photographers of flora, including wildflowers, average over 71 days of participation per year, and wildlife viewers just over 45 days per year. Much of this participation undoubtedly occurs around the home and in the communities where people live. Percentages spending 11 to 25 and 26 to 50 days per year are roughly the same for all the viewing/photographing activities. A difference is the larger percentage of wildlife viewers putting in 3 to 10 days and a smaller percentage putting in 51 or more days.

Table 11.8 Mean days of participation per year and percentage of participants by number of days per year in freshwater-based viewing and learning activities for 2000–2001

Activity	Mean Days	1–2 Days	3–10 Days	11–25 Days	26–50 Days	51+ Days
Viewing/photographing birds	85.9	15.7	33.6	14.2	7.3	29.2
Viewing/photographing wildflowers/flora	71.2	12.2	37.3	16.3	9.5	24.8
Viewing/photographing other wildlife	45.1	14.7	40.9	17.8	9.5	17.1

Freshwater-Based Fishing and Hunting

Mean number of days per year ranges very significantly between the fishing and migratory bird hunting activities in Table 11.9 (p. 188). From almost 19 days per year for warmwater fishing to around 8 for anadromous fishing, a difference of over 10 days per year is evident. Higher percentages of warmwater anglers spend 26 or more days fishing, while over 80% of anadromous anglers fish 10 or fewer days per year.

Table 11.9 Mean days of participation per year and percentage of participants by number of days per year in freshwater-based fishing and hunting activities for 2000–2001

Activity	Mean Days	1–2 Days	3–10 Days	11–25 Days	26–50 Days	51+ Days
Warmwater fishing	18.9	18.4	42.2	19.7	11.8	7.9
Coldwater fishing	14.0	24.2	43.8	19.2	8.9	3.8
Migratory bird hunting	13.2	16.6	48.7	22.7	8.6	3.4
Anadromous fishing	8.5	34.2	48.9	9.2	6.6	1.1

Chapter 12
Urban Outdoor Recreation

Today in the United States, most of the country's population growth occurs in urban areas. In 1790, when the first U.S. Census of population was done, a mere 5% of the country's population lived in urban areas. By 1920, the population balance between rural and urban had shifted and the population became predominantly urban. By 1990, 75% of the people in the United States lived in urban areas. Since 1990, metropolitan growth has accounted for an estimated 82% of total U.S. population growth, even though metropolitan counties account for only 18% of the total U.S. land base (Cordell & Overdevest, 2001). Today over 80% of the U.S. population lives in urban communities and that percentage continues to grow. This growth in urban or metropolitan population represents an addition of well over 2 million persons per year, every year. Metropolitan population was predicted to grow 18.8% between 2000 and 2020, compared to a predicted 12.4% growth in rural counties for this same period. Growth in metropolitan areas was expected to total about 41.3 million people in this 20-year period, while nonmetropolitan areas will grow by just roughly 6.8 million persons. Eighty percent of the American urban population lives in just 315 metropolitan areas of the country.

Defining What Is Urban

This chapter examines participation by people living, working, and recreating in urban areas. Our definition of urban people is based on the Bureau of Census definition of a Metropolitan Area (MA). That definition states that an MA is a cluster of counties that includes at least 1 city with 50,000 or more inhabitants and a total metropolitan population of at least 100,000 (75,000 in New England). The county (or counties) that contains the largest city becomes the "central county." Outlying counties are included in the MA if they are "feeder" counties for commuters traveling to and from the central city. Figure 12.1 (p. 190) shows the counties across the United States that make up the country's MAs.

Urban population growth and its spread on the land, fueled by economic growth and the location of natural amenities, is the leading social trend of the 20th century. Urban population growth and the demands that go with it lead to conversion of land from primarily rural uses to primarily urban and highly developed uses. Between 1992 and 1997, nearly 16 million acres of farm, forest, and other open rural land were converted for developed and urban uses. This development includes rural transportation in addition to urban expansion. At this rate, over 3 million acres are being converted from rural to urban developed uses annually across the country.

By 1997, when the most recent land use survey was done by the U.S. Department of Agriculture, the rate of urban development per year had doubled. This doubling occurred in just 5 years. Total acreage of rural land converted to urban uses between 1992 and 1997 was greatest in the following 10 states, all with more than a half-million acres converted in those 5 years:

1. Texas   (1.2 million)
2. Pennsylvania   (1.1 million)
3. Georgia   (1 million)
4. Florida   (945,000)
5. North Carolina   (782,000)
6. California   (694,000)
7. Tennessee   (612,000)
8. Michigan   (551,000)
9. South Carolina   (540,000)
10. Ohio   (521,000)

Of these 10 states that had the highest levels of rural-to-urban land use conversion, 6 are in the South. Hawaii had the least conversion (8,700 acres), but Hawaii is also very small in total land area.

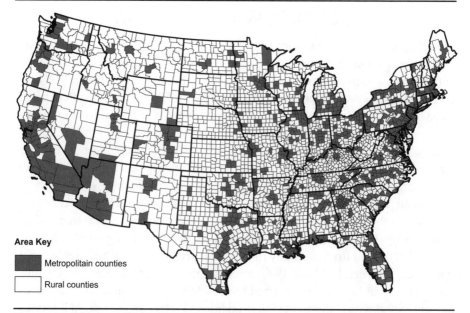

Area Key

■ Metropolitain counties

☐ Rural counties

Figure 12.1 Metropolitan area counties in the conterminous United States

Defining Urban Recreation

The definition of urban recreation for the National Survey on Recreation and the Environment (NSRE) is a simple one. Eight major MAs were chosen on which to focus in this chapter. These are listed and their populations described in Table 12.1. Within the list of outdoor activities administered through the NSRE, a number of activities can occur almost anywhere, including urban settings, and do not depend on the great out-of-doors or natural areas. Table 12.2 (p. 193) lists 27 such activities. This chapter reports outdoor recreation participation in these 27 activities by the people who live in MAs—rural residents excluded.

The density of population in these 8 MAs varies widely, from a low of 304 persons per square mile for Denver to a high of 2,171 persons per square mile greater New York. Population makeup by ethnicity also varies, widely with non-Hispanic Whites being over 70% of the make up in Denver and Seattle to being less than 40% in Los Angles and Miami. Hispanics make up 40% of the population in Los Angeles and Miami. Blacks are most prevalent in Atlanta, Chicago, Miami, New York, and Houston. As a percentage of the population, persons over 45 are in higher proportions in Miami, New York, Seattle, and Chicago. Houston and Atlanta have the lowest percentages in this age group. Outdoor recreation is also a defining characteristic of populations, and the last column in Table 12.1 shows a considerable range in participation. The note at the bottom of the table explains what an active outdoor sport is, mainly being physically demanding. Lowest percentage participating in one or more of the active sports of kayaking, mountain biking, downhill skiing, snowboarding, jetskiing, swimming, and backpacking are in Houston, Los Angeles, and New York. Highest participation percentages are in Seattle, Denver, and Atlanta. There is a moderately strong correlation between percent of population that is non-Hispanic White and percentage of population participating in physically active sports.

Participation in Urban Outdoor Recreation by Urban People

Table 12.2 (p. 193) and Table 12.3 (p. 194) provide participation percentages for the populations ages 16 and older in western and eastern metro areas across 27 urban outdoor activities. Table 12.4 (p. 196) compares the western and eastern metro participation rates.

Western Metropolitan Areas

Four of the largest metropolitan areas in the western half of the country are listed in Table 12.2: Denver, Houston, Los Angeles, and Seattle. Twenty-seven activities are listed in this table and ordered by popularity in the 4 cities combined (same as the West in Table 12.4). Some interesting differences can be seen.

Table 12.1 Population characteristics for 8 of the largest metropolitan areas of the United States, 2002

Metropolitan Area	Population Density (Persons per Square Mile)	% White non-Hispanic	% Hispanic	% Black non-Hispanic	% Over 45	% Participating in 7 Active Outdoor Sports
New York/Northern New Jersey/Long Island/Connecticut/Pennsylvania	2,171	55	19	17	35	65
Chicago, IL/Gary, IN/Kenosha, WI	1,321	59	16	18	32	67
Miami/Fort Lauderdale, FL	1,230	36	40	19	36	66
Atlanta, GA	671	60	7	29	28	71
Houston/Galveston/Brazoria, TX	645	48	29	17	28	59
Seattle/Tacoma/Bremerton, WA	492	77	5	5	33	73
Los Angeles/Riverside/Orange County, CA	482	39	40	7	30	60
Denver/Boulder/Greeley, CO	304	72	19	5	31	72

Note: Active outdoor sports include participation in one or more of the following: kayaking, mountain biking, downhill skiing, snowboarding, jetskiing, swimming in natural water, or backpacking.
Source: NSRE 2000–2001. Versions 1–9, N = 5,716, 8 metropolitan areas. Interview dates: 7/99 to 7/01.

As with the population of the United States at large, walking for pleasure is at the top of the list of activities in which western metropolitan residents participate. Including people living in both urban and rural areas and large and small cities, walking is an activity done by 83%, just at the Denver percentage. Attending family gatherings outdoors is an activity done by almost 74% of the U.S. population, close to the percentages for Houston and Seattle. Gardening is an activity of 72.6% of the U.S. population, closest to the Denver population. Beyond these 3 activities, the order of most popular activities for the U.S. population at large diverges somewhat. For the metro areas in Table 12.2, bicycling ranges from 41% to 50% and averages around 46%; for the United States as a whole bicycling is 39%. In general, participation in the activities in this table—which are easily engaged in urban settings and do not require expansive stretches of land, water, or trails—are participated in by larger percentages of the people living in Denver, Seattle, Los Angeles, and Houston.

Participation differences between metro areas are clearly evident in Table 12.2. Generally, participation percentages are higher in Denver and Seattle and lower in Houston and Los Angeles, with some exceptions. Between Houston

Table 12.2 Percentages of population participating in urban-based outdoor recreation activities for 4 major metropolitan areas in the western United States, 2000–2001

Activity	Denver	Houston	Los Angeles	Seattle
Walking for pleasure	83	77	77	88
Family gathering	77	75	70	76
Visiting nature centers, zoos	70	56	52	67
Picnicking	67	48	50	66
Gardening/landscaping for pleasure	72	44	47	46
Bicycling	48	44	41	50
Attending outdoor sports events	60	30	34	53
Attending outdoor concerts, plays	48	40	38	34
Swimming (outdoor pools)	40	44	38	30
Swimming (lakes, streams)	36	37	35	45
Running/jogging	37	32	35	41
Yard games (e.g., horseshoes)	42	32	20	41
Viewing/photographing birds	24	24	25	32
Inline skating/Rollerblading	18	20	21	12
Golfing	19	10	12	18
Basketball outdoors	16	7	11	16
Warmwater fishing	18	17	9	11
Tennis outdoors	16	8	11	12
Horseback riding (general)	13	12	9	9
Handball/racquetball outdoors	15	2	11	5
Soccer outdoors	12	5	10	7
Softball	14	5	8	11
Sledding	20	2	4	20
Volleyball outdoors	15	7	6	10
Baseball	12	4	5	5
Football	13	4	6	4
Ice skating outdoors	5	0	4	3

and Los Angeles, participation is about the same, but varies from activity to activity.

For Denver, activities higher than any of the other 3 metro areas include family gatherings outdoors, gardening or landscaping, visiting nature centers/zoos, picnicking, attending outdoor sports events, attending concerts/plays, yard games, golfing, warmwater fishing, basketball, tennis, volleyball, handball/racquetball, softball, horseback riding, football, baseball, soccer, and ice skating. For Houston, only pool swimming has higher participation percentages than the other 3 metro areas. For Los Angeles only inline skating/rollerblading is highest. For Seattle, walking for pleasure, bicycling, swimming in natural waters, running/jogging, and viewing/photographing birds are the activities with participation percentages higher than for the other 3 metro areas. Denver participation rates are especially higher for most sports, such as tennis, football, and soccer.

Eastern Metropolitan Areas

Table 12.3 shows participation in the 27 activities already discussed for the 4 western metros: Atlanta, Chicago, Miami, and New York. (Although a mid-

Table 12.3 Percentages of population participating in urban-based outdoor recreation activities for 4 major metropolitan areas in the eastern United States, 2000–2001

Activity	Atlanta	Chicago	Miami	New York
Walking for pleasure	83	83	80	85
Family gathering	76	74	73	69
Gardening/landscaping for pleasure	52	65	49	61
Visiting nature centers/zoos	60	62	50	55
Picnicking	56	56	44	48
Attending outdoor sports events	66	58	54	40
Bicycling	39	48	52	41
Swimming (outdoor pool)	55	40	51	40
Swimming (lakes, streams)	54	39	47	40
Attending outdoor concerts, plays	47	46	47	39
Running/jogging	44	33	63	29
Yard games (e.g., horseshoes)	36	36	30	30
Viewing/photographing birds	32	31	25	29
Inline skating/Rollerblading	27	20	23	15
Basketball outdoors	15	16	29	16
Sledding	3	22	3	15
Warmwater fishing	23	22	15	9
Golfing	12	22	16	10
Tennis outdoors	15	12	18	15
Volleyball outdoors	17	15	11	8
Handball/racquetball outdoors	5	9	10	13
Softball	6	12	10	10
Ice skating outdoors	5	13	4	10
Soccer outdoors	9	7	20	9
Horseback riding (general)	13	9	7	7
Football	8	9	9	7
Baseball	7	8	4	8

western city, Chicago is a part of the Forest Service's Eastern Region.) Generally, Atlanta has the highest participation percentages across the largest number of activities. The activities for which Atlanta is highest or tied include family gatherings, attending outdoor sports events, picnicking, swimming in both pools and natural waters, attending outdoor concerts/plays, yard games, birding, inline skating, warmwater fishing, volleyball, and horseback riding. Chicago has the next highest number of activities with the highest participation percentages. Activities highest (or tied for highest) for Chicago include visiting nature centers/ zoos, picnicking, gardening/landscaping, golfing, football, baseball, softball, ice skating, and sledding (a very high percentage compared with the national percentage or 14.7). Following Atlanta and Chicago in number of activities for which participation percentages are highest or tied for highest is Miami—a retirement destination. Activities for which participation percentages in Miami are highest include attending outdoor concerts/ plays, running or jogging, bicycling, basketball, tennis, soccer, and football (equal with Chicago). Only walking, handball/racquetball, and baseball are highest or tied for highest for New York. Many of New York's metro area participation percentages are substantially lower than those of the other 3 metro areas, especially for attending outdoor sports events, attending outdoor concerts/plays, running/jogging, inline skating, warmwater fishing, and volleyball.

Comparison of West and East

Table 12.4 (p. 196) shows combined participation percentages for the 4 western metro areas compared with the 4 eastern areas. The activities are ordered by percentage participation in the western metro areas. Generally, participation percentages across the 4 eastern metro areas are higher than those for the 4 western areas. Percentages are virtually the same between west and east for visiting nature centers/zoos, bicycling, soccer, and golfing. Percentages are higher in the west only for family gatherings, picnicking, running/jogging, inline skating/ rollerblading, and horseback riding. Percentages of metro population ages 16 and older participating are higher for all the other 18 activities in the east. Especially higher than the west are gardening/landscaping, attending outdoor sports events, basketball, warmwater fishing, tennis, volleyball, sledding, and ice skating.

Comparison of Days of Participation Among Metro Areas

Average number of days per participant per year are shown in Table 12.5 (p. 197). They range from a low of 3.5 per participant for visiting nature centers/ zoos in Houston to a high of 112.6 for walking in New York. Walking in these 4 metro areas and for the United States as a whole enjoys the highest percentages

Table 12.4 Comparison of percentages of western and eastern metro population participating in outdoor activities, 2000–2001

Activity	West	East
Walking for pleasure	79	84
Family gathering	73	71
Visiting nature centers, zoos	57	57
Picnicking	55	51
Gardening/landscaping for pleasure	50	60
Bicycling	43	43
Attending outdoor sports events	40	48
Attending outdoor concerts, plays	39	42
Swimming in an outdoor pool	38	42
Swimming in lakes, streams	37	42
Running or jogging	36	33
Yard games (e.g., horseshoes)	28	32
Viewing/photographing birds	26	30
Inline skating or rollerblading	19	18
Golfing	14	14
Basketball outdoors	12	17
Warmwater fishing	11	14
Tennis outdoors	11	14
Horseback riding (general)	10	8
Handball or racquetball outdoors	10	11
Soccer outdoors	9	9
Softball	9	10
Sledding	9	15
Volleyball outdoors	8	11
Baseball	6	8
Football	6	8
Ice skating outdoors	4	10

of the population and as well the highest number of activity days per participant per year. Viewing/photographing birds is 2nd to walking in number of days.

Across the activities, New York has the highest number of days for picnicking, family gatherings, and walking. Atlanta has the highest average number of days for warmwater fishing. Miami has the highest average number of activity days for swimming in natural water and pool swimming by far. New York, Seattle, Miami, and Chicago's annual days of birding participation per participant are about equal and are higher than for the other 4 metro areas. Denver has the highest average days for visiting nature centers and zoos.

Table 12.5 Average days of participation per participant for urban-based recreation activities by metropolitan area, 2000–2001

Metro Area	Picnic	Family Gatherings	Walking for Pleasure	Warmwater Fishing
New York	10.9	8.2	112.6	15.8
Seattle	7.0	6.9	82.2	11.0
Los Angeles	6.9	7.4	91.0	5.8
Denver	6.5	6.1	94.9	10.0
Miami	6.4	6.2	97.3	5.7
Houston	5.9	6.6	105.0	16.3
Chicago	5.8	8.1	92.1	11.8
Atlanta	4.5	7.0	78.5	17.6

Metro Area	Swimming (Outdoor Pool)	Swimming (Lakes, Ponds)	Viewing/ Photographing Birds	Visiting Nature Centers
New York	13.6	22.4	61.3	7.6
Seattle	12.0	14.2	63.7	5.3
Los Angeles	16.0	26.2	54.8	4.9
Denver	8.9	30.7	50.8	9.8
Miami	36.6	46.1	63.4	3.7
Houston	10.6	27.3	47.9	3.5
Chicago	13.4	17.7	64.7	6.5
Atlanta	11.1	21.0	47.8	8.1

Comparison of Established Urban, New Urban, and Rural Area Participation

This chapter concludes with examining participation rates between communities downtown, communities a little out but near downtown, newer and further out residential communities (suburbs for the most part), and rural areas. Eastern and western communities are separated for comparison as well (Table 12.6). Generally, participation rates are highest in the suburbs, next highest in established urban communities, and lowest in rural areas. Participation rates for individual sports are higher across all communities in the West compared with the East.

Table 12.6 Comparison of percent participating in individual and team sports by place of urban residence by eastern and western regions of the country, 2000–2001

Region of Metropolitan Areas	Established Area in or Near Downtown	Newer Residential or Developing Area	Rural Homes/Farms or Undeveloped Areas
East	78.2/25.8	84.1/32.9	75.3/20.5
West	84.7/19.7	94.9/29.3	78.5/23.7

Note: The 1st number is percentage participating in individual sports (e.g., tennis, golf) and the 2nd is percentage participating in team sports (e.g., baseball, soccer).

Section V

Participation Comparisons

When we think of the modern geography of the United States, most people think of regions and states. When we think of the make up of the people living in these regions and states, lifestyles, types of employment, and demographic composition come to mind. Chapter 13 focuses on participation differences across the regions and states of the country. In doing so, the authors found far more similarities than differences in what people chose for outdoor recreation activities across regions and states in the United States.

In Chapter 14 the theme of comparing to identify similarities and differences in outdoor recreation participation continues, but in relation to outdoor personality types. An outdoor personality describes the dominant theme of the activities people chose. The analysis revealed 8 such outdoor personalities. These outdoor personalities included the Inactives, the Passives, the Nonconsumptive Moderates, the Nature Lovers, the Water Bugs, the Backcountry Actives, the Outdoor Avids, and the Motorized Consumptives. Participation in activities by the people who make up these 8 outdoor recreation personalities differ in many ways as does their demographic composition.

In concluding this section, Chapter 15 takes a closer look at those people among us who are the most active third of all outdoor recreation participants, activity by activity, across the activities included in the NSRE. This most active third of participants is referred to as the Enthusiasts. For any single activity, the Enthusiasts typically represent less than 5% of the overall U.S. population of persons ages 16 or older. They truly are a minority of the population, yet they account for most of the nation's activity days of recreation participation by a wide margin. For almost all activities, Enthusiasts account for 70% to almost 90% of recreation participation days summed across all participants. A comparison of participation by the Enthusiasts with participation by the general population concludes this book.

Chapter 13
Comparisons by Region and State

From a world history perspective, the United States is relatively young. In other parts of the Old World, such as Asia, the Middle East and Europe, nations have come and gone for many centuries. World recognition of nation status for the United States, however, is very recent. The maps in Figure 13.1 (p. 202) illustrate some of the stages of nation evolution that occurred in the area known as the United States—from early European settlement and possessions to territories and 13 states and then to 50 states.

We can only imagine what it was like before European settlement across the 50 states. Native populations then lived pretty much in harmony with the land. There were vast populations of water fowl, bison, and other species in the East and West. Then, nature dominated. Humans, in such numbers as they were then, lived within the endemic natural systems.

As population grew in the East and expanded westward, many social, economic, and environmental changes took place. The maps in Figure 13.1 depict in a way the growth of the nation of the United States from a few states in the East and territories in the West to coast to coast states. As documented earlier in this book, population, economic growth, and land development now dominate the landscape. Nature has been relegated to enclaves of public land and a few isolated, protected private parcels.

When we characterize different parts of the United States, we usually think first of the human populations who reside there—their cities, and their cultures. Natural land and water isn't the first thought any more. When we think of the modern geography of the United States, we think of regions and states. And we usually think about differences in human cultures, lifestyles, economies, and makeup of regions and states. Differences between regions in these dimensions are real. California has a large contingent of Hispanics, Maine does not. Mississippi has a large contingent of Blacks, Utah does not. Minnesota has strong Scandinavian roots, Louisiana does not.

This chapter explores one aspect of cultural difference between regions and states—outdoor recreation participation. Let us say right up front that far more similarities than differences exist when participation is compared among regions and states. In fact, for some activities, participation from region-to-region and state-to-state is surprisingly similar. But because the lifestyles and cultures and the types of outdoor opportunities available vary naturally from state to state, there are differences. In planning for public lands and public recreation programs and in private investment decisions for providing recreation services and products, success lies in large part in knowing not only about the overall patterns of population behavior and preferences but also about differences and acknowledging them in budgeting, management, and production.

The first section of this chapter describes briefly, in narrative and tabular forms, recreation participation percentages by Census region (see Figure 13.2). The latter section provides only the tabulations for participation, but does so state-by-state. The purpose of these state tables is to make available to planners, researchers and industry up-to-date recreation participation estimates specific to their own particular state. In deciding which table has participation data for a particular state refer to the map in Figure 13.2. This will aid in identifying which Census division table contains the data of interest.

Participation Comparisons Across Regions
Land-Based Activities

Across many of the land-based activities in Table 13.1 (pp. 204–205), participation percentages for people living in the Midwest is somewhat higher (not higher in all activities, but in many). Higher participation percentages for the Midwest are especially noticeable for the more popular land activities, such as

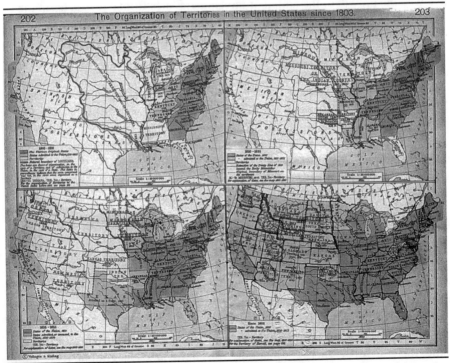

Figure 13.1 Different periods in the U.S. history of territories and states, from colonies to 50 states (University of Texas at Austin, 2003)

family gatherings, visiting nature centers/zoos/museums, driving for pleasure, attending outdoor sports events, and viewing/photographing wildlife. The Midwest also has the highest participation percentages for bicycling, yard games, gathering natural products, visiting a farm or other agriculture setting, mountain biking, golfing, volleyball, softball, and hunting. Highest participation percentages for the Northeast are for walking, attending outdoor concerts/plays, birding, tennis, soccer, and handball. The South had higher participation percentages only for basketball and football. Relative to the other 3 regions, higher participation percentages for the West were for the most part nature-based activities. Highest for the West were viewing/photographing natural scenery, viewing/photographing wildflowers and other plants, day hiking, visiting wildness, camping, visiting archeological sites, driving off-road, backpacking, horseback riding, mountain climbing, rock climbing, caving, and orienteering.

One good way to use Table 13.1 is to compare data for a particular region to the participation estimates for the U.S. population as a whole. Comparing a region with the nation in this manner makes important differences stand out. For example, gardening, attending outdoor sports events, and golfing stand out for the Midwest. Day hiking, developed and primitive camping, backpacking, and mountain climbing stand out for the West.

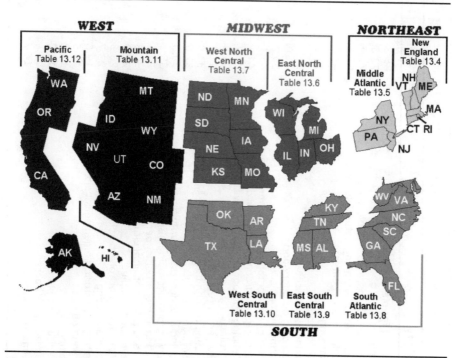

Figure 13.2 United States census regions and divisions

Table 13.1 Comparisons of percentages of persons 16 or older participating in land-based outdoor activities by census region, 2000–2001

Activity	Northeast	Midwest	South	West	U.S. Total
Walking for pleasure	86.3	84.4	81.4	81.4	83.0
Family gathering	72.6	75.2	72.4	74.0	73.5
Gardening/landscaping for pleasure	73.9	77.7	73.2	65.3	72.6
Viewing/photographing natural scenery	61.5	61.9	55.4	65.0	60.3
Visiting nature centers	57.2	61.2	53.4	58.8	57.1
Picnicking	55.1	57.0	50.1	58.0	54.5
Sightseeing	52.1	52.7	51.0	51.8	51.8
Driving for pleasure	51.4	53.6	50.3	50.2	51.2
Attending outdoor sports events	47.0	57.8	48.4	47.4	49.9
Visiting historic sites	50.2	46.2	44.9	45.0	46.2
Viewing/photographing wildflowers/trees	45.1	45.4	42.3	48.0	44.9
Viewing/photographing other wildlife	44.1	47.8	42.8	45.0	44.7
Attending outdoor concerts, plays	44.7	42.5	36.0	38.7	39.8
Bicycling	41.9	43.1	34.6	41.5	39.5
Yard games (e.g., horseshoes)	41.4	46.3	37.1	35.1	39.4
Running or jogging	33.0	34.0	34.7	35.9	34.5
Day hiking	32.6	30.2	26.8	45.8	33.3
Visiting a wilderness or primitive area	30.3	33.3	29.2	39.3	32.7
Viewing/photographing birds	35.1	34.9	30.5	30.7	32.4
Gathering mushrooms, berries	29.1	32.1	26.7	27.3	28.5
Visiting a farm or agricultural setting	30.8	32.8	26.3	23.7	27.9
Developed camping	22.9	29.5	21.7	32.9	26.4
Inline skating or rollerblading	23.3	24.8	20.6	20.5	22.1
Mountain biking	23.7	24.6	17.1	23.1	21.4
Visiting prehistoric/archeological sites	19.0	19.9	20.0	24.6	20.9
Driving off-road	14.5	17.0	17.2	20.5	17.5
Golfing	15.2	23.3	14.0	16.5	16.9
Primitive camping	12.7	15.6	13.1	23.1	16.0
Basketball outdoors	14.4	15.2	17.0	11.4	14.7
Tennis outdoors	14.7	11.3	10.4	10.8	11.5

Table 13.1 Comparisons of percentages of persons 16 or older participating in land-based outdoor activities by census region, 2000–2001 *continued*

Activity	Northeast	Midwest	South	West	U.S. Total
Backpacking	11.8	8.7	7.4	16.3	10.7
Volleyball outdoors	10.4	12.6	11.1	8.4	10.6
Softball	10.2	12.0	10.2	10.0	10.5
Horseback riding (general)	7.4	10.1	9.8	10.9	9.7
Big game hunting	6.5	9.8	9.3	7.3	8.4
Football	8.2	8.3	8.5	7.2	8.1
Soccer outdoors	10.1	8.6	5.8	9.3	8.1
Horseback riding on trails	5.9	7.9	8.1	8.6	7.8
Small game hunting	4.9	9.6	8.2	5.5	7.2
Handball or racquetball outdoors	9.5	6.4	6.6	6.4	7.1
Baseball	7.4	7.7	6.8	5.6	6.8
Mountain climbing	7.3	3.7	4.0	9.8	6.0
Rock climbing	4.8	3.9	3.7	5.1	4.3
Caving	2.5	4.8	3.8	6.0	4.3
Migratory bird hunting	1.1	3.3	2.4	2.4	2.4
Orienteering	2.4	2.1	1.1	2.8	2.0

Source: NSRE 2000–2001. Versions 1–9, N = 42,868. Interview dates: 7/99 to 7/01.

Water-Based Activities

A pattern between regions similar to that for land activities is evident for water activities in Table 13.2. But instead of the Midwest having higher participation percentages across more activities than the other 3 regions, it is the Northeast having higher percentages for 8 of the 22 water activities listed. The Northeast leads in percentages participating for swimming, visiting beaches, boat tours and excursions, sailing, rowing, kayaking, and windsurfing. Next highest number of activities with highest participation percentages is the West with 7 of the 22 activities. Visiting watersides, viewing/photographing fish, coldwater fishing, snorkeling, anadromous fishing, scuba diving, and surfing are highest in the West compared with other regions. The South was highest only in saltwater fishing.

Compared with the national participation percentages, the Northeast stands out for swimming in natural waters, visiting beaches, and sailing. The Midwest stands out for motorboating, warmwater fishing, and canoeing. The West stands out for coldwater and anadromous fishing and for surfing.

Table 13.2 Comparisons of percentages of persons ages 16 or older participating in water-based outdoor activities by census region, 2000–2001

Activity	Northeast	Midwest	South	West	U.S. Total
Swimming (lakes, streams)	49.3	41.6	39.6	39.1	41.7
Swimming (outdoor pools)	44.9	40.2	42.2	37.1	41.0
Visiting a beach	46.1	38.2	38.2	42.0	40.6
Visiting other watersides (other than beaches)	26.1	25.4	25.7	26.9	26.0
Viewing/photographing fish	23.8	24.2	25.2	25.5	24.8
Motorboating	22.2	30.0	24.2	21.4	24.4
Warmwater fishing	15.5	31.7	27.2	13.2	22.6
Boat tours/excursions	23.4	16.3	17.0	19.2	18.7
Coldwater fishing	13.8	10.3	10.4	21.0	13.6
Saltwater fishing	12.3	3.2	14.0	10.1	10.4
Canoeing	13.0	13.5	8.0	6.4	9.7
Jetskiing	6.8	11.0	9.8	9.9	9.5
Rafting	8.6	11.2	8.8	9.8	9.5
Waterskiing	5.4	10.4	7.9	8.6	8.1
Snorkeling	7.2	5.6	5.9	8.2	6.7
Sailing	7.8	4.5	4.3	4.8	5.1
Anadromous fishing	4.5	3.2	3.1	7.3	4.4
Rowing	6.2	5.6	3.2	3.7	4.4
Kayaking	5.5	2.6	2.2	4.5	3.5
Scuba diving	1.8	1.3	2.0	2.3	1.9
Surfing	1.2	0.7	1.4	3.4	1.7
Windsurfing	1.1	0.6	0.7	1.0	0.8

Snow/Ice Based Activities

The Northeast and Midwest generally stand out as having higher participation percentages across many of the snow/ice activities listed in Table 13.3. Especially notable are sledding, downhill skiing, ice skating, snowmobiling, and cross-country skiing. Because of the climate and lack of high elevation areas for snow, the South lags far behind other regions in participation in snow/ice activities—below the national percentages for all activities. Except for sledding and ice skating, snow/ice activity participation in the West is higher than the national participation percentages. Sledding participation is especially high in the Midwest.

Table 13.3 Comparisons of percentages of persons ages 16 or older participating in snow/ice-based outdoor activities by census region, 2000–2001

Activity	Northeast	Midwest	South	West	U.S. Total
Sledding	21.4	25.0	7.5	10.4	14.7
Downhill skiing	11.3	9.0	5.2	10.9	8.5
Ice skating outdoors	11.6	9.7	3.8	5.0	6.9
Snowmobiling	7.4	10.0	1.8	5.6	5.5
Snowboarding	5.7	4.5	2.3	8.2	4.9
Cross-country skiing	6.0	5.4	1.3	4.4	3.8
Ice fishing	2.5	7.0	0.5	3.1	2.9
Snowshoeing	3.4	2.2	0.3	2.4	1.8

State Participation Tables by Census Division

No further text accompanies Tables 13.4 through 13.12 (pp. 208–231). These tables are offered for planning and investment professionals.

Table 13.4 Comparisons of percentages participating 1 or more times in the previous 12 months by states in the New England census division, 2000–2001

Activity	CT	ME	MA	NH	RI	VT	New England Census Division Total
Walking for pleasure	84.9	89.5	91.3	90.7	81.7	91.1	88.0
Gardening/landscaping for pleasure	72.2	68.9	71.3	83.7	85.9	79.3	76.1
Family gathering	72.7	79.2	73.5	78.8	68.2	78.6	74.2
Viewing/photographing natural scenery	62.0	73.7	68.1	78.4	57.4	70.1	67.0
Visiting nature centers	57.6	62.3	60.3	66.3	60.3	52.0	59.8
Swimming in lakes, streams	50.3	65.9	60.3	70.9	54.0	63.6	59.0
Picnicking	57.5	63.9	54.3	60.7	50.9	58.8	56.7
Driving for pleasure	48.7	65.7	53.5	67.2	47.9	67.3	55.5
Sightseeing	49.1	63.0	56.7	64.0	47.4	59.4	55.2
Visiting historic sites	48.4	55.8	60.4	57.3	46.8	45.4	53.3
Visiting a beach	49.2	56.0	53.9	56.7	45.3	47.1	51.4
Attending outdoor sports events	62.5	62.0	42.6	45.1	42.6	45.6	50.0
Viewing/photographing other wildlife	41.3	61.3	44.3	59.7	39.0	63.0	48.0
Viewing/photographing wildflowers, trees	40.7	54.8	48.7	56.9	45.2	50.6	48.0
Attending outdoor concerts, plays	51.7	41.5	43.5	50.2	44.2	52.1	46.8
Yard games (e.g., horseshoes)	38.7	57.1	36.0	63.9	49.0	62.1	46.4
Swimming in an outdoor pool	46.1	43.4	45.9	54.5	39.1	47.8	45.7
Bicycling	41.7	46.5	44.4	46.7	39.9	48.9	44.0
Viewing/photographing birds	33.9	45.5	37.8	47.3	40.4	46.4	39.9
Day hiking	35.8	44.5	40.0	43.4	27.7	46.5	38.5
Visiting a wilderness or primitive area	29.2	49.4	35.4	44.7	28.4	47.8	36.5
Gathering mushrooms, berries	28.3	52.8	31.8	42.3	27.5	47.3	35.2
Visiting a farm or agricultural setting	30.4	43.0	33.8	49.0	28.5	34.6	34.8
Running or jogging	46.9	34.2	27.0	26.7	36.5	35.0	34.8
Visiting other waterside (besides beach)	26.4	36.4	30.1	34.2	21.4	29.1	28.9
Mountain biking	23.3	35.3	27.9	33.8	22.3	34.4	27.9

Table 13.4 Comparisons of percentages participating 1 or more times in the previous 12 months by states in the New England census division, 2000–2001 *continued*

Activity	CT	ME	MA	NH	RI	VT	New England Census Division Total
Motorboating	24.1	40.4	25.2	37.9	21.1	31.0	27.9
Sledding	26.0	31.0	20.1	28.3	34.2	29.0	26.8
Developed camping	22.4	38.9	23.6	33.3	21.4	31.3	26.4
Boat tours or excursions	29.8	32.1	24.1	31.8	23.8	17.2	26.4
Viewing/photographing fish	23.6	30.5	25.4	33.6	24.6	23.5	26.1
Inline skating or rollerblading	32.5	19.9	22.8	31.8	20.2	14.2	24.7
Visiting prehistoric/archeological sites	19.5	23.2	19.4	22.2	22.1	16.9	20.3
Canoeing	13.1	34.1	15.8	28.0	14.6	23.4	19.0
Golfing	22.3	16.7	16.1	22.7	15.2	15.9	18.2
Coldwater fishing	13.4	31.4	10.8	25.1	9.7	27.5	16.5
Ice skating outdoors	18.6	16.6	10.9	10.0	20.9	26.3	16.3
Basketball outdoors	26.3	8.4	14.6	4.7	15.8	17.5	16.1
Backpacking	12.8	22.9	17.3	20.4	8.3	20.1	16.0
Primitive camping	11.9	28.4	13.0	23.9	9.6	22.0	15.9
Warmwater fishing	11.9	24.5	13.3	23.5	11.9	22.1	15.8
Driving off-road	13.8	25.9	11.7	20.8	10.8	18.6	15.2
Downhill skiing	11.6	16.0	18.1	19.9	8.6	18.2	15.0
Saltwater fishing	15.3	18.8	14.1	17.9	13.0	4.7	14.3
Tennis outdoors	21.9	14.4	7.3	7.4	21.1	6.4	13.9
Volleyball outdoors	17.8	6.4	13.2	5.1	14.0	9.1	12.5
Mountain climbing	14.3	23.8	11.3	14.8	2.4	9.4	11.9
Softball	13.8	11.0	10.6	0.6	18.0	9.7	11.6
Soccer outdoors	16.5	4.6	8.0	9.0	9.0	17.0	10.7
Snowmobiling	5.0	28.5	6.6	16.8	4.8	19.3	10.5
Sailing	10.6	9.8	11.8	10.5	9.2	8.4	10.5
Cross-country skiing	6.1	17.2	10.0	13.3	3.8	23.0	10.2
Rafting	9.5	13.1	10.2	11.4	7.3	8.3	9.9

Table 13.4 Comparisons of percentages participating 1 or more times in the previous 12 months by states in the New England census division *continued*

Activity	CT	ME	MA	NH	RI	VT	New England Census Division Total
Football	16.4	1.0	8.6	7.1	12.5	1.7	9.7
Kayaking	8.2	14.9	9.2	13.4	6.8	7.6	9.5
Snorkeling	8.5	6.4	10.8	12.6	8.1	8.3	9.3
Handball or racquetball outdoors	9.7	9.2	5.6	9.5	12.5	5.9	8.6
Rowing	5.4	11.8	8.5	8.3	3.4	9.8	7.4
Snowboarding	6.3	10.2	7.1	10.3	5.5	6.7	7.3
Horseback riding (general)	6.6	8.0	7.3	8.4	4.9	7.8	7.0
Snowshoeing	1.7	25.1	3.6	5.9	1.8	22.8	6.8
Jetskiing	5.9	6.5	7.7	9.4	4.7	4.8	6.6
Waterskiing	5.8	7.7	6.1	11.5	3.9	8.0	6.6
Big game hunting	1.9	19.0	4.7	5.2	2.5	18.5	6.4
Baseball	6.3	8.1	6.3	2.0	8.0	6.3	6.3
Horseback riding on trails	5.0	6.9	5.7	8.3	2.7	6.1	5.5
Anadromous fishing	5.0	8.9	3.3	5.4	4.1	5.7	4.9
Small game hunting	2.9	11.7	3.1	3.1	2.7	8.1	4.4
Rock climbing	6.4	7.2	3.8	1.0	3.8	0.0	4.1
Ice fishing	1.7	17.2	2.9	3.1	1.5	4.5	3.9
Orienteering	2.5	0.0	5.0	1.5	0.0	2.1	2.4
Caving	2.6	0.9	1.0	8.4	0.0	3.0	2.2
Scuba diving	1.9	1.0	1.4	2.9	1.9	1.8	1.8
Surfing	2.1	0.6	1.0	2.4	2.2	0.1	1.5
Windsurfing	1.3	1.5	1.8	0.7	1.2	1.2	1.4
Migratory bird hunting	0.2	0.9	1.3	2.1	0.8	3.3	1.2

Table 13.5 Comparisons of percentages participating 1 or more times in the previous 12 months by states in the Middle Atlantic census division

Activity	NJ	NY	PA	Middle Atlantic Census Division Total
Walking for pleasure	85.9	85.2	85.3	85.4
Gardening/landscaping for pleasure	71.3	74.7	69.0	72.0
Family gathering	69.2	71.9	73.5	71.8
Viewing/photographing natural scenery	59.8	56.2	60.8	58.4
Visiting nature centers	55.0	56.8	54.5	55.7
Picnicking	51.1	52.0	59.6	54.1
Sightseeing	50.3	46.8	55.5	50.3
Driving for pleasure	47.8	45.8	54.8	49.0
Visiting historic sites	52.1	46.8	48.2	48.5
Attending outdoor sports events	59.1	36.8	48.4	45.0
Swimming in an outdoor pool	49.6	40.7	46.4	44.5
Swimming in lakes, streams	49.8	41.3	42.7	43.7
Viewing/photographing wildflowers, trees	40.8	42.5	46.9	43.4
Attending outdoor concerts, plays	42.9	41.2	47.4	43.3
Visiting a beach	50.2	42.4	38.8	43.1
Viewing/photographing other wildlife	40.7	38.6	47.5	41.8
Bicycling	42.7	42.3	36.5	40.6
Yard games (e.g., horseshoes)	41.7	31.7	46.1	38.0
Viewing/photographing birds	32.1	31.5	34.0	32.4
Running or jogging	35.3	31.3	29.2	31.7
Day hiking	31.8	27.8	29.1	29.1
Visiting a farm or agricultural setting	26.4	28.4	29.4	28.2
Visiting a wilderness or primitive area	24.1	25.5	30.3	26.6
Gathering mushrooms, berries	21.8	23.7	31.5	25.6
Visiting other waterside (besides beach)	23.2	23.5	27.3	24.6
Viewing/photographing fish	23.0	21.1	24.0	22.4
Inline skating or rollerblading	13.3	24.2	27.9	22.2
Mountain biking	20.0	21.5	22.3	21.4
Boat tours or excursions	21.5	18.9	25.5	21.3
Developed camping	18.0	20.7	23.5	20.9
Motorboating	18.7	18.8	19.1	18.9
Visiting prehistoric/archeological sites	16.2	19.7	17.5	18.3
Sledding	19.3	14.4	22.5	17.8
Warmwater fishing	14.5	12.8	19.9	15.4
Tennis outdoors	20.7	14.7	11.5	15.3
Driving off-road	11.5	12.7	18.1	14.1
Basketball outdoors	13.6	14.9	9.9	13.3
Golfing	12.9	11.6	16.5	13.2
Coldwater fishing	11.0	9.6	17.2	12.3
Saltwater fishing	18.4	9.5	8.1	11.1
Primitive camping	7.0	11.5	12.9	10.9
Handball or racquetball outdoors	9.3	12.6	6.3	10.1
Soccer outdoors	13.0	10.2	5.9	9.7
Canoeing	9.1	9.5	9.9	9.5
Softball	5.8	9.6	12.2	9.4
Backpacking	7.8	10.5	8.5	9.3
Downhill skiing	9.5	9.4	8.7	9.2
Volleyball outdoors	8.0	8.8	9.9	8.9
Ice skating outdoors	11.7	8.0	6.3	8.4

Table 13.5 Comparisons of percentages participating 1 or more times in the previous 12 months by states in the Middle Atlantic census division *continued*

Activity	NJ	NY	PA	Middle Atlantic Census Division Total
Baseball	6.1	9.4	7.5	8.1
Rafting	7.6	7.4	8.8	7.9
Horseback riding (general)	6.0	7.5	8.8	7.6
Football	7.9	8.0	5.2	7.2
Jetskiing	7.0	6.9	6.8	6.9
Big game hunting	2.7	4.2	13.1	6.6
Sailing	6.5	7.0	4.7	6.2
Horseback riding on trails	5.3	5.5	7.6	6.1
Snorkeling	7.5	6.3	4.5	6.0
Snowmobiling	3.2	6.5	6.0	5.6
Rowing	5.5	6.6	4.0	5.5
Rock climbing	4.2	5.7	5.2	5.2
Small game hunting	3.4	3.7	8.9	5.2
Snowboarding	4.5	4.4	5.9	4.9
Waterskiing	2.9	5.1	5.1	4.6
Anadromous fishing	4.8	4.1	3.9	4.2
Mountain climbing	3.4	4.6	3.8	4.1
Cross-country skiing	1.7	4.9	3.2	3.6
Kayaking	3.5	3.4	2.5	3.2
Caving	2.2	2.5	3.6	2.7
Orienteering	0.3	2.5	4.2	2.4
Scuba diving	2.1	1.9	1.4	1.8
Ice fishing	1.1	2.0	1.0	1.5
Snowshoeing	1.6	1.4	0.1	1.1
Surfing	2.0	0.7	0.9	1.1
Migratory bird hunting	1.2	0.6	1.6	1.0
Windsurfing	1.1	1.1	0.5	0.9

Table 13.6 Comparisons of percentages participating 1 or more times in the previous 12 months by states in the East North Central census division

Activity	IL	IN	MI	OH	WI	East North Central Census Division Total
Walking for pleasure	83.7	83.2	84.7	86.3	87.2	84.9
Gardening/landscaping for pleasure	71.1	80.8	82.8	80.8	76.7	78.6
Family gathering	75.3	75.5	76.9	75.6	76.0	75.9
Visiting nature centers	63.1	63.0	59.3	61.0	66.3	62.2
Viewing/photographing natural scenery	61.2	59.9	63.0	60.5	65.8	61.9
Picnicking	55.3	57.7	57.7	62.7	56.4	58.1
Attending outdoor sports events	58.4	54.1	53.3	52.3	59.2	55.6
Driving for pleasure	48.3	53.8	53.6	56.6	57.7	53.5
Sightseeing	49.2	53.5	52.2	56.7	51.6	52.6
Viewing/photographing other wildlife	40.6	47.7	49.4	46.6	54.4	46.9
Yard games (e.g., horseshoes)	39.7	38.6	53.9	53.2	41.2	45.8
Visiting historic sites	48.0	43.4	45.1	44.4	44.2	45.3
Viewing/photographing wildflowers, trees	44.6	43.0	46.6	44.7	46.4	45.1
Bicycling	47.3	41.9	48.2	40.1	45.4	44.8
Attending outdoor concerts, plays	44.1	37.8	49.6	43.4	39.0	43.4
Swimming in lakes, streams	37.6	40.5	49.1	42.0	45.8	42.7
Swimming in an outdoor pool	40.8	44.8	40.5	48.1	38.5	42.6
Visiting a beach	38.9	38.0	49.3	39.0	43.2	41.7
Running or jogging	38.2	39.3	33.6	27.2	34.4	34.4
Viewing/photographing birds	32.7	34.6	36.7	31.5	37.0	34.2
Visiting a wilderness or primitive area	33.1	33.9	32.9	29.4	40.0	33.2
Gathering mushrooms, berries	27.5	34.0	35.2	29.8	37.2	32.0
Visiting a farm or agricultural setting	32.4	28.2	33.4	29.7	31.7	31.3
Day hiking	31.1	32.1	25.5	31.3	36.7	30.8
Warmwater fishing	25.5	30.8	27.8	28.3	36.2	28.9
Developed camping	26.4	26.5	31.9	26.5	34.0	28.7
Motorboating	26.3	26.4	35.1	22.6	36.1	28.7

Table 13.6 Comparisons of percentages participating 1 or more times in the previous 12 months by states in the East North Central census division *continued*

Activity	IL	IN	MI	OH	WI	East North Central Census Division Total
Mountain biking	26.6	24.4	26.6	23.7	28.9	25.9
Visiting other watersides (besides beach)	24.1	24.3	26.0	26.4	28.6	25.7
Inline skating or rollerblading	26.7	21.3	31.9	22.6	20.6	25.5
Sledding	22.4	32.4	25.0	17.1	27.8	24.0
Viewing/photographing fish	23.7	23.8	24.2	22.7	25.8	23.9
Golfing	21.1	33.4	21.0	19.6	27.2	23.4
Visiting prehistoric/archeological sites	21.6	19.9	19.0	19.2	19.3	19.9
Boat tours or excursions	14.2	13.4	21.6	18.3	11.1	16.1
Driving off-road	13.6	15.7	19.8	12.8	19.6	15.9
Basketball outdoors	18.8	22.3	13.4	12.9	12.5	15.9
Primitive camping	12.7	15.3	14.7	14.8	15.5	14.4
Canoeing	10.4	12.5	16.7	11.2	20.3	13.6
Volleyball outdoors	14.5	12.8	9.9	14.0	13.7	13.0
Tennis outdoors	12.9	11.8	10.8	9.5	17.5	12.2
Softball	12.7	12.7	13.4	8.0	10.6	11.5
Rafting	9.5	10.8	14.4	8.8	12.3	11.0
Jetskiing	8.1	11.2	13.5	9.2	10.3	10.3
Coldwater fishing	8.4	9.4	12.9	8.2	13.9	10.2
Snowmobiling	7.9	7.1	15.6	5.0	17.0	10.0
Ice skating outdoors	10.8	11.7	12.3	3.8	11.0	9.8
Horseback riding (general)	10.4	9.5	9.9	8.1	9.4	9.5
Downhill skiing	10.2	8.0	10.8	6.2	11.6	9.3
Waterskiing	8.6	9.8	9.7	6.8	12.0	9.1
Backpacking	8.5	9.4	8.5	8.9	9.5	8.9
Soccer outdoors	7.4	5.7	9.2	7.8	15.1	8.7
Baseball	7.1	15.2	9.0	5.6	8.5	8.5
Football	9.8	13.6	9.3	3.8	5.8	8.3

Chapter 13: Comparisons by Region and State   215

Table 13.6 Comparisons of percentages participating 1 or more times in the previous 12 months by states in the East North Central census division *continued*

Activity	IL	IN	MI	OH	WI	East North Central Census Division Total
Big game hunting	3.5	5.4	12.6	5.6	16.7	8.1
Horseback riding on trails	7.8	7.4	7.9	6.6	7.9	7.5
Small game hunting	5.2	5.3	8.3	6.1	11.7	7.0
Handball or racquetball outdoors	6.7	7.7	6.6	10.7	1.5	6.9
Snorkeling	7.0	4.1	7.8	5.2	6.2	6.2
Ice fishing	5.0	8.6	8.9	1.9	8.0	6.1
Rowing	5.8	5.6	7.6	4.2	8.4	6.1
Cross-country skiing	4.5	3.3	7.7	2.7	12.8	5.7
Sailing	5.5	3.6	6.2	4.5	5.4	5.1
Snowboarding	4.8	6.0	5.0	4.1	3.9	4.7
Caving	4.1	7.5	4.9	4.3	0.9	4.3
Rock climbing	4.1	3.3	2.9	3.4	8.4	4.2
Anadromous fishing	1.6	5.0	8.2	2.5	4.1	4.1
Saltwater fishing	2.9	3.7	3.9	4.6	1.4	3.5
Mountain climbing	3.2	3.1	2.5	3.8	4.6	3.4
Kayaking	2.8	2.6	3.7	2.3	3.5	3.0
Snowshoeing	0.5	1.8	2.7	1.2	7.8	2.4
Migratory bird hunting	1.9	1.5	2.3	1.3	4.0	2.1
Orienteering	0.4	2.2	2.2	2.4	3.4	1.9
Scuba diving	1.7	0.9	1.6	1.0	0.9	1.3
Windsurfing	0.5	1.0	0.9	0.7	0.7	0.7
Surfing	0.9	0.7	0.8	0.4	0.4	0.7

Table 13.7 Comparisons of percentages participating 1 or more times in the previous 12 months by states in the West North Central census division

Activity	IA	KS	MN	MO	NE	ND	SD	West North Central Census Division Total
Walking for pleasure	82.8	78.9	85.9	83.7	83.1	85.9	84.2	83.5
Gardening/landscaping for pleasure	72.9	68.9	90.3	81.9	62.4	74.3	66.2	76.3
Family gathering	72.1	73.8	75.4	74.1	74.9	74.7	74.7	74.2
Viewing/photographing natural scenery	61.6	61.0	69.3	56.2	59.4	63.4	63.9	61.9
Attending outdoor sports events	66.6	55.2	54.5	55.8	87.2	63.4	59.9	61.5
Visiting nature centers	62.1	61.8	62.3	58.8	57.8	56.5	53.4	59.6
Picnicking	59.0	50.5	59.7	52.6	54.5	53.2	58.5	55.3
Driving for pleasure	52.4	52.0	54.4	52.4	55.4	55.7	55.8	53.7
Sightseeing	52.0	52.6	56.6	51.2	54.7	51.6	50.0	52.9
Viewing/photographing other wildlife	49.0	46.6	55.2	45.5	45.7	54.9	49.3	49.2
Visiting historic sites	44.0	48.1	46.1	49.2	49.8	48.2	48.8	47.6
Yard games (e.g., horseshoes)	52.4	36.4	51.5	41.3	62.1	39.8	49.8	47.2
Viewing/photographing wildflowers, trees	45.0	45.6	53.7	42.6	43.7	44.9	44.0	46.0
Attending outdoor concerts, plays	45.9	45.2	33.4	39.3	41.1	39.3	48.1	40.8
Bicycling	42.1	36.3	47.4	33.0	43.3	45.2	39.9	40.4
Swimming in lakes, streams	33.7	35.6	48.2	39.2	37.9	43.0	40.2	39.9
Swimming in an outdoor pool	32.5	44.0	31.7	45.6	37.3	31.1	23.3	36.4
Warmwater fishing	36.5	32.3	38.9	35.1	33.4	43.6	36.5	36.3
Viewing/photographing birds	36.1	32.4	44.9	34.6	33.1	31.4	33.2	35.9
Visiting a farm or agricultural setting	37.1	31.0	34.9	30.2	38.4	36.8	42.1	35.0
Visiting a wilderness or primitive area	32.6	30.5	37.4	30.3	36.9	33.3	34.1	33.4
Running or jogging	40.4	29.7	31.3	34.4	39.8	30.2	24.9	33.4
Visiting a beach	33.2	26.7	43.0	26.7	30.1	35.2	37.2	32.8
Gathering mushrooms, berries	34.8	31.7	31.8	35.9	26.1	32.4	27.0	32.2
Motorboating	29.8	26.2	42.6	26.3	26.7	40.3	36.1	32.0
Developed camping	29.8	28.9	32.1	26.7	33.5	38.2	33.6	30.9
Day hiking	27.5	23.9	38.2	26.7	31.9	23.9	29.7	29.2

Table 13.7 Comparisons of percentages participating 1 or more times in the previous 12 months by states in the West North Central census division *continued*

Activity	IA	KS	MN	MO	NE	ND	SD	West North Central Census Division Total
Sledding	33.2	16.4	27.0	29.2	25.2	28.3	25.8	26.7
Visiting other watersides (besides beach)	20.1	25.6	29.1	26.9	23.6	20.6	23.8	24.9
Viewing/photographing fish	21.4	22.2	30.0	24.4	19.9	29.0	24.6	24.7
Inline skating or rollerblading	18.8	18.0	28.8	23.3	29.3	14.4	31.3	23.6
Golfing	35.3	19.5	28.6	12.7	26.1	24.8	19.1	23.2
Mountain biking	26.0	17.6	29.1	17.3	23.9	24.0	19.2	22.4
Visiting prehistoric/archeological sites	17.8	16.3	18.7	21.4	19.9	22.8	25.0	19.9
Driving off-road	16.0	17.9	19.7	17.4	15.9	24.4	24.3	18.7
Primitive camping	17.0	18.3	19.9	14.3	17.8	21.3	16.1	17.5
Boat tours or excursions	17.3	14.2	13.5	13.8	16.0	17.9	30.8	16.6
Basketball outdoors	23.0	16.6	5.8	17.4	14.3	6.6	11.9	14.2
Small game hunting	12.3	12.7	12.8	12.5	10.1	20.3	23.5	13.8
Canoeing	13.6	8.5	22.1	13.3	9.1	12.5	7.2	13.3
Big game hunting	8.6	8.3	15.1	12.5	8.4	23.8	16.4	12.7
Softball	20.4	13.6	11.1	6.8	18.6	13.4	6.8	12.6
Waterskiing	10.0	12.8	14.7	9.4	13.8	15.8	13.7	12.4
Jetskiing	10.4	13.1	10.4	11.2	11.5	18.6	14.3	12.2
Volleyball outdoors	12.5	9.3	14.3	9.6	11.5	19.4	9.9	12.0
Rafting	8.8	8.9	11.9	12.4	11.1	13.8	13.6	11.4
Horseback riding (general)	9.1	13.2	8.7	8.0	14.9	12.6	16.6	11.0
Coldwater fishing	8.9	8.2	10.1	13.8	7.5	8.0	14.7	10.4
Snowmobiling	9.6	3.0	19.4	2.1	5.2	20.9	17.9	9.9
Tennis outdoors	6.4	9.9	11.1	9.5	17.2	7.1	7.4	9.9
Ice skating outdoors	7.3	3.4	17.2	9.4	14.6	5.8	6.2	9.5
Horseback riding on trails	6.4	11.6	7.2	6.5	11.6	10.3	10.9	8.6
Backpacking	5.9	9.1	11.8	6.6	8.4	9.2	10.3	8.6
Downhill skiing	8.6	8.0	13.0	5.1	6.4	10.5	11.0	8.6

Table 13.7 Comparisons of percentages participating 1 or more times in the previous 12 months by states in the West North Central census division *continued*

Activity	IA	KS	MN	MO	NE	ND	SD	West North Central Census Division Total
Soccer outdoors	17.8	8.3	2.2	15.0	1.6	0.0	6.2	8.4
Ice fishing	5.2	0.5	21.2	0.0	8.7	12.3	16.1	8.2
Football	14.5	2.7	6.9	8.8	7.8	5.0	11.4	8.2
Baseball	7.8	4.1	6.8	9.3	0.0	2.4	11.4	6.3
Caving	6.1	7.2	2.7	7.0	6.1	6.0	2.5	5.5
Handball or racquetball outdoors	5.1	2.5	3.8	8.7	10.3	1.4	4.4	5.5
Migratory bird hunting	2.5	2.5	6.5	2.0	6.2	13.2	11.6	5.3
Cross-country skiing	4.4	1.6	14.4	1.0	2.0	5.9	3.2	4.9
Rowing	5.3	4.5	6.9	4.3	4.6	3.3	1.3	4.7
Snorkeling	4.1	4.8	6.5	4.3	3.1	6.3	3.0	4.7
Snowboarding	4.9	2.8	5.2	3.6	3.7	4.6	4.7	4.2
Mountain climbing	1.7	7.4	4.4	1.2	3.8	2.5	11.0	4.1
Sailing	4.2	3.8	5.0	3.3	1.6	2.2	3.8	3.5
Rock climbing	1.4	7.1	4.3	2.8	2.3	0.0	5.7	3.4
Saltwater fishing	2.0	2.3	4.0	3.3	1.4	3.7	2.4	2.9
Orienteering	0.0	5.4	1.2	2.1	0.7	5.9	2.2	2.3
Kayaking	2.3	2.3	3.0	1.6	1.0	2.3	0.8	2.0
Snowshoeing	0.5	2.3	6.1	0.0	0.0	3.2	0.7	1.8
Anadromous fishing	2.7	1.0	2.1	1.3	0.9	3.5	0.8	1.7
Scuba diving	1.4	1.4	1.5	1.4	0.7	1.5	0.9	1.3
Surfing	0.4	0.5	0.3	1.3	0.5	0.7	0.2	0.6
Windsurfing	0.8	0.1	0.1	0.7	0.1	1.0	0.7	0.5

Table 13.8 Comparisons of percentages participating 1 or more times in the previous 12 months by states in the South Atlantic census division

Activity	DC	DE	FL	GA	MD	NC	SC	VA	WV	South Atlantic Census Division Total
Walking for pleasure	79.2	83.6	80.3	83.4	86.0	83.4	84.6	84.5	86.1	83.2
Gardening/landscaping for pleasure	70.7	39.6	85.6	74.1	96.3	68.7	82.1	85.3	75.6	77.5
Family gathering	67.9	70.9	71.1	74.5	76.2	72.9	72.0	78.2	74.6	73.3
Viewing/photographing natural scenery	55.5	47.7	58.2	58.0	58.6	55.4	56.8	61.5	63.8	57.5
Visiting nature centers	55.6	59.1	56.1	54.4	57.2	52.2	55.1	57.2	56.1	55.7
Picnicking	51.9	51.1	46.4	50.4	59.4	47.6	50.8	59.6	62.4	51.9
Sightseeing	45.4	44.1	49.2	53.5	54.1	53.7	51.0	56.7	57.2	51.9
Driving for pleasure	44.2	40.2	44.4	52.9	51.2	51.9	51.1	57.6	64.2	50.2
Visiting historic sites	48.2	60.5	40.8	50.5	61.7	44.0	50.1	56.2	48.4	49.7
Attending outdoor sports events	50.1	50.4	45.4	56.0	45.9	41.8	51.4	56.8	65.5	49.6
Visiting a beach	49.3	41.5	53.5	45.1	44.0	42.1	43.3	39.9	25.9	44.7
Swimming in an outdoor pool	45.5	35.8	51.6	47.8	43.6	39.3	45.2	40.3	39.6	44.5
Swimming in lakes, streams	42.3	29.6	50.8	47.5	42.4	40.8	45.3	44.0	40.3	44.2
Viewing/photographing other wildlife	39.7	29.7	42.7	45.5	45.7	41.5	42.0	47.4	58.7	43.6
Viewing/photographing wildflowers, trees	41.0	36.8	45.3	43.3	43.4	39.2	40.4	45.3	48.1	42.9
Attending outdoor concerts, plays	33.8	50.8	40.4	40.7	37.5	38.8	49.3	33.4	37.0	40.6
Yard games (e.g., horseshoes)	58.7	32.6	34.6	41.0	36.4	38.4	38.0	46.1	60.2	40.1
Bicycling	37.5	37.3	44.2	34.5	39.6	30.3	37.2	37.5	38.4	37.9
Running or jogging	35.2	37.2	44.2	36.1	39.3	28.3	22.4	27.7	34.3	35.4
Viewing/photographing birds	31.5	23.8	33.4	29.6	32.5	35.5	29.9	33.8	33.0	32.0
Visiting a wilderness or primitive area	20.6	23.5	30.5	31.8	29.8	26.0	26.5	30.0	39.4	29.0
Visiting other waterside (besides beach)	26.4	23.4	30.4	27.2	24.4	24.2	29.3	27.9	26.5	27.1
Day hiking	25.1	28.1	23.7	28.6	29.4	23.1	19.9	28.1	35.9	26.2
Viewing/photographing fish	25.1	21.6	30.4	26.9	22.5	24.8	28.2	24.3	24.1	26.1
Visiting a farm or agricultural setting	26.1	18.1	21.3	26.3	28.6	27.2	28.2	27.9	36.3	25.7
Gathering mushrooms, berries	20.5	13.9	20.9	27.7	24.8	26.8	25.9	29.9	48.5	25.5

Table 13.8 Comparisons of percentages participating 1 or more times in the previous 12 months by states in the South Atlantic census division *continued*

Activity	DC	DE	FL	GA	MD	NC	SC	VA	WV	South Atlantic Census Division Total
Motorboating	23.1	12.8	26.8	28.6	22.0	24.1	27.4	21.3	23.5	24.2
Warmwater fishing	16.2	10.2	22.5	29.9	16.6	27.7	29.6	25.8	34.0	24.0
Boat tours or excursions	20.1	27.1	25.5	16.0	22.9	21.1	26.4	25.2	14.2	22.6
Visiting prehistoric/archeological sites	18.3	23.5	20.9	21.8	23.0	18.4	17.4	22.8	20.6	20.9
Inline skating or rollerblading	24.7	32.0	21.4	27.1	16.9	13.7	12.5	16.1	9.0	20.0
Developed camping	20.2	13.9	20.0	22.3	19.0	18.1	17.7	21.9	23.9	19.7
Mountain biking	18.9	22.0	18.3	17.3	23.7	14.1	19.1	20.4	26.6	19.3
Saltwater fishing	21.4	8.3	27.0	15.3	16.0	17.7	15.3	17.3	4.6	17.9
Driving off-road	12.7	4.9	12.3	17.4	14.8	21.2	16.1	17.8	33.5	16.2
Golfing	11.6	20.7	18.8	10.3	15.7	15.7	16.2	15.4	20.6	16.1
Basketball outdoors	13.2	16.3	18.8	16.0	14.0	9.7	17.2	17.0	17.5	15.6
Tennis outdoors	12.3	22.5	14.0	12.1	11.1	13.4	7.3	6.9	10.2	12.6
Primitive camping	9.7	6.7	9.8	15.6	11.9	12.2	10.3	13.9	18.2	11.9
Coldwater fishing	7.9	5.9	6.3	13.2	10.0	12.7	10.8	14.0	26.2	10.9
Sledding	28.3	9.5	1.5	5.0	18.8	6.1	2.2	18.5	19.9	9.8
Jetskiing	7.0	3.8	11.6	12.4	9.2	9.3	9.1	9.7	8.1	9.7
Volleyball outdoors	17.5	3.5	12.0	11.9	10.2	5.4	4.9	8.0	12.7	9.6
Softball	6.0	1.2	11.9	6.6	10.8	8.2	14.3	13.5	9.3	9.4
Rafting	8.7	7.7	8.7	12.8	7.1	8.0	10.3	10.2	9.8	9.3
Canoeing	10.6	7.7	11.3	8.4	8.6	6.5	5.7	9.5	10.0	8.9
Horseback riding (general)	5.4	6.9	8.3	10.5	8.9	6.8	6.7	9.1	10.3	8.3
Football	10.6	2.0	12.8	7.9	11.9	6.1	3.8	5.0	3.7	8.2
Backpacking	5.9	8.2	6.9	10.3	7.8	7.1	7.3	9.5	8.6	7.9
Big game hunting	6.9	1.6	4.8	10.0	4.5	7.4	9.9	10.9	19.2	7.7
Handball or racquetball outdoors	5.3	5.5	11.8	8.8	9.4	1.5	7.5	4.9	4.5	7.5
Waterskiing	4.7	2.8	6.8	12.1	5.9	7.5	9.0	7.9	5.5	7.4
Snorkeling	4.8	7.4	14.6	8.4	4.5	3.9	3.4	4.6	3.2	7.4

Table 13.8 Comparisons of percentages participating 1 or more times in the previous 12 months by states in the South Atlantic census division *continued*

Activity	DC	DE	FL	GA	MD	NC	SC	VA	WV	South Atlantic Census Division Total
Soccer outdoors	16.5	13.9	9.2	5.9	7.7	1.8	3.9	3.2	0.6	7.1
Horseback riding on trails	4.4	5.1	6.8	8.0	8.3	5.8	6.2	7.5	9.5	6.9
Baseball	6.9	0.7	9.4	2.0	14.0	4.4	6.5	3.1	4.1	6.4
Small game hunting	4.8	1.2	3.7	8.0	1.8	7.6	9.5	8.3	17.2	6.3
Downhill skiing	9.1	7.3	2.8	5.7	12.5	6.3	4.6	7.1	7.9	6.3
Sailing	6.3	8.2	6.0	3.8	8.7	3.3	4.2	4.4	2.7	5.3
Ice skating outdoors	14.8	7.4	1.6	2.7	11.3	0.8	0.8	0.7	4.5	4.4
Mountain climbing	6.2	3.5	4.2	1.6	5.8	2.1	2.7	7.4	4.3	4.0
Anadromous fishing	4.7	1.6	4.2	4.1	4.5	3.7	3.6	4.7	3.4	3.9
Rowing	4.1	5.4	4.0	3.9	3.9	3.1	2.7	3.3	5.2	3.8
Rock climbing	8.1	6.6	3.2	0.6	4.2	2.5	2.2	2.6	5.9	3.5
Snowboarding	4.0	4.3	1.2	1.7	5.2	3.8	1.4	4.6	4.8	3.1
Kayaking	2.4	2.7	3.3	2.6	4.3	1.3	3.5	3.8	2.3	3.0
Caving	7.1	0.7	0.4	2.4	1.4	2.4	2.0	5.2	11.5	2.6
Scuba diving	1.4	1.5	4.5	2.4	2.1	1.2	1.6	1.5	1.1	2.3
Snowmobiling	3.8	2.3	1.7	0.9	4.2	2.2	0.6	2.1	2.5	2.1
Surfing	0.8	1.7	3.7	1.5	1.2	2.1	1.5	1.8	0.5	2.0
Cross-country skiing	1.7	3.4	1.0	1.2	3.1	1.2	0.0	1.6	2.8	1.6
Migratory bird hunting	1.4	0.6	1.3	2.2	0.6	1.8	2.1	1.3	2.6	1.5
Orienteering	0.0	0.0	0.0	1.0	0.0	2.7	1.7	2.0	0.9	0.8
Windsurfing	1.1	1.3	0.8	0.5	0.6	0.4	1.0	0.3	0.1	0.6
Snowshoeing	0.3	1.2	0.0	0.4	0.0	0.0	0.0	0.7	0.0	0.2
Ice fishing	0.0	1.1	0.0	0.0	0.0	0.0	0.0	0.0	0.0	0.1

Table 13.9 Comparisons of percentages participating 1 or more times in the previous 12 months by states in the East South Central census division

Activity	AL	KY	MS	TN	East South Central Census Division Total
Walking for pleasure	83.2	82.8	83.0	81.1	82.4
Gardening/landscaping for pleasure	89.4	65.3	67.2	88.4	76.4
Family gathering	74.0	76.3	75.4	71.6	74.1
Driving for pleasure	55.5	59.3	56.7	53.1	55.9
Sightseeing	55.8	57.2	51.3	51.4	53.9
Viewing/photographing natural scenery	53.2	56.4	43.4	59.0	53.8
Visiting nature centers	50.8	51.6	46.8	53.8	51.1
Picnicking	49.1	55.1	45.2	52.6	50.8
Attending outdoor sports events	47.3	51.0	58.0	50.0	50.8
Viewing/photographing other wildlife	40.8	45.5	39.0	45.7	43.0
Visiting historic sites	44.9	45.4	37.0	41.1	42.3
Viewing/photographing wildflowers, trees	41.7	41.5	40.5	40.9	41.2
Swimming in an outdoor pool	37.5	43.6	42.3	40.9	40.9
Yard games (e.g., horseshoes)	26.2	45.2	29.1	45.4	36.4
Swimming in lakes, streams	38.3	38.8	32.7	34.9	36.3
Attending outdoor concerts, plays	34.3	33.4	35.0	35.3	34.5
Warmwater fishing	34.2	34.8	36.4	31.7	34.0
Running or jogging	35.6	30.0	28.6	37.8	33.5
Visiting a beach	34.5	30.1	36.7	27.9	31.9
Visiting a farm or agricultural setting	28.2	36.5	28.8	31.1	31.1
Viewing/photographing birds	27.6	32.3	27.3	31.8	29.9
Visiting a wilderness or primitive area	27.5	33.1	23.7	32.0	29.4
Bicycling	30.0	28.4	29.2	28.0	28.8
Gathering mushrooms, berries	25.4	32.8	29.3	27.3	28.5
Day hiking	26.7	30.5	15.7	28.8	26.1
Visiting other watersides (besides beach)	27.1	25.8	21.4	26.5	25.5
Motorboating	25.4	25.9	23.2	23.0	24.4
Viewing/photographing fish	26.8	24.0	24.7	21.4	24.1
Developed camping	20.8	25.1	21.8	22.7	22.6
Driving off-road	22.0	21.0	22.3	16.3	20.1
Visiting prehistoric/archeological sites	21.8	19.5	18.8	19.6	20.0
Basketball outdoors	22.2	13.4	16.9	23.0	19.3
Inline skating or rollerblading	9.3	14.8	6.4	26.9	15.9
Mountain biking	15.8	13.2	13.4	13.6	14.1
Primitive camping	12.3	19.0	12.3	13.2	14.1
Golfing	13.4	16.8	5.3	14.0	12.8
Big game hunting	13.6	8.9	16.7	8.7	11.6
Softball	11.1	14.1	7.7	12.7	11.6
Small game hunting	11.6	10.3	14.1	10.0	11.3
Coldwater fishing	10.6	10.8	7.5	13.0	10.8
Volleyball outdoors	8.1	9.7	9.1	15.4	10.6
Horseback riding (general)	10.3	12.5	9.0	10.0	10.5
Football	10.5	7.8	13.8	7.9	9.8
Jetskiing	11.4	7.1	9.7	9.5	9.5
Boat tours or excursions	11.3	9.8	7.1	8.7	9.4
Horseback riding on trails	9.1	11.7	6.3	9.2	9.2
Rafting	8.5	7.9	5.6	9.3	8.0
Saltwater fishing	11.2	3.7	11.7	5.7	7.9

Table 13.9 Comparisons of percentages participating 1 or more times in the previous 12 months by states in the East South Central census division *continued*

Activity	AL	KY	MS	TN	East South Central Census Division Total
Waterskiing	8.5	6.2	8.7	8.3	7.9
Sledding	3.9	14.6	0.0	11.5	7.7
Tennis outdoors	3.8	8.9	3.5	12.6	7.3
Baseball	7.9	3.9	1.8	13.3	7.2
Backpacking	7.8	5.9	3.3	9.9	7.1
Canoeing	7.6	5.7	7.4	7.7	7.1
Caving	6.1	6.2	1.3	10.9	6.5
Handball or racquetball outdoors	7.9	2.4	4.9	8.4	6.1
Snorkeling	5.6	4.9	3.6	4.4	4.7
Mountain climbing	3.6	0.4	0.9	9.1	3.8
Ice skating outdoors	4.6	1.6	2.6	4.9	3.6
Downhill skiing	2.5	5.5	1.6	4.4	3.6
Sailing	3.4	3.1	4.5	3.4	3.5
Soccer outdoors	1.6	5.3	2.8	3.6	3.2
Rock climbing	3.2	3.2	1.0	3.5	2.8
Migratory bird hunting	2.9	1.7	3.7	2.2	2.6
Rowing	2.3	3.5	2.6	2.0	2.5
Anadromous fishing	3.2	1.5	2.1	1.8	2.2
Kayaking	1.9	1.3	1.0	1.6	1.5
Orienteering	3.4	0.0	0.6	1.0	1.4
Snowboarding	1.4	1.5	0.8	1.8	1.4
Scuba diving	1.4	1.4	1.7	1.1	1.4
Snowmobiling	1.6	2.0	1.0	0.7	1.3
Cross-country skiing	1.2	1.6	1.1	0.9	1.2
Ice fishing	2.2	0.0	2.3	0.0	1.1
Snowshoeing	2.2	0.0	0.0	0.0	0.7
Surfing	1.3	0.4	0.7	0.3	0.7
Windsurfing	0.6	0.3	0.2	0.7	0.5

Table 13.10 Comparisons of percentages participating 1 or more times in the previous 12 months by states in the West South Central census division

Activity	AR	LA	OK	TX	West South Central Census Division Total
Walking for pleasure	79.1	77.9	80.8	77.1	78.0
Family gathering	67.9	69.8	73.2	69.8	70.0
Gardening/landscaping for pleasure	82.1	51.8	70.7	64.3	64.0
Viewing/photographing natural scenery	52.2	47.0	57.1	54.0	52.9
Visiting nature centers	44.8	45.2	57.3	53.0	51.1
Sightseeing	54.0	46.7	51.9	46.1	47.9
Driving for pleasure	47.2	46.7	52.4	45.8	47.0
Picnicking	43.7	39.9	52.9	48.4	46.8
Attending outdoor sports events	54.6	49.0	51.1	39.2	44.6
Viewing/photographing wildflowers, trees	41.2	35.7	47.4	43.2	42.2
Viewing/photographing other wildlife	44.6	36.8	50.0	40.0	41.3
Swimming (outdoor pools)	34.3	43.6	46.2	36.3	39.0
Visiting historic sites	33.1	35.2	43.4	40.4	39.0
Swimming (lakes, streams)	35.4	30.0	41.1	34.1	34.4
Running or jogging	20.7	46.3	32.0	33.5	34.4
Bicycling	24.4	32.0	34.2	34.6	32.8
Yard games (e.g., horseshoes)	40.0	39.2	41.2	25.7	32.6
Visiting a beach	21.3	32.0	30.8	33.9	31.6
Visiting a wilderness or primitive area	29.1	26.4	36.8	28.3	29.2
Attending outdoor concerts, plays	25.5	34.0	31.4	27.1	29.0
Viewing/photographing birds	30.5	25.8	31.3	28.5	28.6
Warmwater fishing	36.8	33.0	37.0	22.9	28.2
Day hiking	25.1	17.6	29.8	31.8	28.1
Gathering mushrooms, berries	28.6	28.4	33.7	25.4	27.4
Inline skating or rollerblading	12.9	27.0	32.4	23.8	25.1
Developed camping	24.8	22.9	32.7	22.7	24.3
Viewing/photographing fish	24.7	27.1	27.8	22.5	24.3
Visiting a farm or agricultural setting	23.4	25.2	26.7	23.3	24.2
Motorboating	28.6	27.6	27.6	20.9	24.0
Visiting other watersides (besides beach)	24.5	23.8	27.9	22.5	23.7
Visiting prehistoric/archeological sites	16.8	14.0	17.4	20.7	18.6
Basketball outdoors	6.9	26.5	18.9	16.0	17.5
Driving off-road	21.9	17.1	21.6	15.1	17.1
Mountain biking	11.6	11.8	18.3	16.8	15.5
Primitive camping	17.2	11.7	18.8	13.5	14.3
Volleyball outdoors	11.0	19.0	15.5	11.9	13.9
Boat tours or excursions	15.9	20.8	5.3	11.2	12.9
Horseback riding (general)	10.6	9.5	16.1	11.9	11.9
Saltwater fishing	3.1	20.5	3.9	12.1	11.5
Golfing	3.1	10.3	13.4	13.4	11.5
Softball	5.8	18.0	12.2	8.4	10.7
Big game hunting	15.5	13.1	11.6	8.2	10.4
Jetskiing	9.9	8.7	12.4	9.9	10.0
Small game hunting	13.5	12.4	11.5	7.1	9.4
Horseback riding on trails	7.8	6.3	12.7	9.7	9.2
Coldwater fishing	16.6	7.2	14.9	7.1	9.2
Tennis outdoors	2.9	10.0	10.2	9.4	8.9
Waterskiing	8.8	8.9	12.8	7.8	8.8

Table 13.10 Comparisons of percentages participating 1 or more times in the previous 12 months by states in the West South Central census division *continued*

Activity	AR	LA	OK	TX	West South Central Census Division Total
Rafting	8.0	7.4	12.6	8.4	8.7
Football	1.4	13.5	7.6	8.0	8.3
Baseball	2.9	17.4	5.0	4.5	7.1
Canoeing	11.3	6.5	7.1	6.3	7.0
Backpacking	7.7	5.4	7.6	6.9	6.8
Handball/racquetball outdoors	8.0	8.6	5.5	3.6	5.5
Soccer outdoors	0.6	4.0	8.8	6.0	5.3
Rock climbing	1.1	0.5	9.8	5.5	4.5
Snorkeling	5.6	2.6	4.8	4.7	4.4
Downhill skiing	3.3	2.2	5.3	4.8	4.2
Mountain climbing	1.4	1.0	4.3	5.9	4.1
Caving	6.5	4.0	2.9	4.0	4.1
Migratory bird hunting	4.9	6.0	4.6	2.4	3.7
Sledding	11.6	0.0	5.3	2.8	3.6
Sailing	3.4	2.2	3.6	3.4	3.2
Ice skating outdoors	3.9	3.3	1.0	3.1	2.9
Rowing	2.5	2.2	2.3	2.8	2.6
Anadromous fishing	0.8	2.4	3.6	2.5	2.4
Snowboarding	2.2	0.6	3.8	1.7	1.8
Scuba diving	2.5	0.7	2.3	1.9	1.8
Snowmobiling	2.0	0.8	2.6	1.6	1.6
Kayaking	2.8	0.8	1.0	1.5	1.5
Orienteering	0.0	0.0	6.5	0.6	1.3
Cross-country skiing	0.4	0.1	1.3	1.1	0.9
Windsurfing	0.0	0.8	1.2	0.9	0.8
Surfing	0.2	0.4	0.8	1.1	0.8
Ice fishing	1.2	0.0	3.8	0.0	0.7
Snowshoeing	0.0	0.0	0.0	0.4	0.2

Table 13.11 Comparisons of percentages participating 1 or more times in the previous 12 months by states in the Mountain census division

Activity	AZ	CO	ID	MT	NV	NM	UT	WY	Mountain Census Division Total
Walking for pleasure	80.0	82.8	85.2	86.4	78.9	77.3	82.0	86.9	81.6
Gardening/landscaping for pleasure	93.8	74.3	82.4	73.6	77.7	51.0	66.7	84.6	76.3
Family gathering	70.6	76.1	81.7	76.8	70.4	74.6	84.5	79.1	75.7
Viewing/photographing natural scenery	62.0	72.7	76.6	78.0	56.8	54.9	75.0	75.1	67.2
Picnicking	51.8	65.7	64.1	63.5	57.0	54.9	72.6	68.0	61.0
Visiting nature centers	59.7	67.6	56.0	56.0	51.9	60.8	64.6	54.9	59.9
Driving for pleasure	51.8	58.0	63.4	61.1	49.2	53.1	64.2	63.7	56.6
Sightseeing	52.7	58.5	57.9	58.6	48.4	48.3	61.8	65.0	55.3
Viewing/photographing other wildlife	42.3	55.7	64.0	74.0	41.6	42.8	56.8	70.2	52.5
Attending outdoor sports events	56.4	56.7	66.0	61.1	47.9	39.7	36.1	53.7	50.6
Viewing/photographing wildflowers, trees	43.9	50.3	54.9	55.2	42.8	41.4	55.8	51.5	48.3
Visiting historic sites	42.9	48.4	53.9	55.2	39.5	42.3	54.5	62.0	47.7
Day hiking	44.3	48.4	47.4	56.2	42.9	42.8	51.8	45.5	46.9
Visiting a wilderness or primitive area	39.5	42.6	50.8	59.7	37.4	39.3	48.1	54.3	44.1
Bicycling	36.9	44.4	47.3	47.1	37.7	35.3	45.3	42.7	41.2
Yard games (e.g., horseshoes)	33.5	41.5	57.0	52.2	33.1	31.3	40.0	33.4	38.3
Swimming in an outdoor pool	38.4	34.9	35.9	32.9	45.8	27.7	40.2	25.5	36.3
Swimming in lakes, streams	32.7	34.9	46.6	41.7	36.0	26.0	43.4	36.9	36.1
Attending outdoor concerts, plays	40.7	43.2	47.9	40.3	44.3	22.9	19.3	27.6	35.6
Developed camping	26.2	34.4	44.4	43.7	28.7	28.6	47.3	41.8	34.8
Viewing/photographing birds	31.4	27.8	36.4	43.0	27.1	28.5	33.0	34.7	31.4
Primitive camping	22.0	25.8	47.9	40.7	20.2	26.6	38.6	46.2	30.0
Visiting a beach	28.8	30.0	34.0	25.9	35.1	22.2	35.3	26.4	29.9
Gathering mushrooms, berries	22.8	24.7	49.5	48.1	21.6	24.3	35.6	40.6	29.9
Running or jogging	27.8	39.2	37.5	39.2	26.9	13.1	31.8	36.6	29.9
Visiting prehistoric/archeological sites	28.4	27.2	31.6	31.2	26.8	29.0	36.6	32.5	29.8
Coldwater fishing	15.4	30.5	46.0	49.7	21.2	20.3	31.5	47.4	28.7

Table 13.11 Comparisons of percentages participating 1 or more times in the previous 12 months by states in the Mountain census division *continued*

Activity	AZ	CO	ID	MT	NV	NM	UT	WY	Mountain Census Division Total
Visiting other watersides (besides beach)	23.6	25.5	36.5	31.5	22.7	24.3	33.9	26.1	27.0
Driving off-road	21.6	24.9	38.9	32.3	21.9	25.7	29.7	36.3	26.9
Mountain biking	17.4	28.3	29.2	31.8	20.8	24.2	26.1	26.2	24.5
Viewing/photographing fish	19.0	23.8	32.7	33.8	23.1	17.6	28.9	28.5	24.4
Motorboating	20.0	19.5	35.1	30.8	20.2	15.5	36.7	29.2	24.1
Visiting a farm or agricultural setting	20.2	26.1	36.7	33.5	21.4	15.7	25.1	23.8	24.0
Backpacking	14.3	19.8	23.2	26.0	12.6	16.7	21.5	18.6	18.2
Warmwater fishing	16.5	17.0	21.9	29.9	14.3	13.3	12.9	21.9	17.2
Inline skating or rollerblading	9.4	17.9	36.0	2.8	17.0	15.2	13.1	24.3	15.6
Golfing	8.5	15.2	25.6	17.8	18.7	13.3	17.5	14.9	15.3
Boat tours or excursions	14.3	21.1	20.3	14.1	12.6	6.0	12.4	16.0	14.1
Downhill skiing	7.7	19.1	14.7	21.6	9.1	8.8	19.5	15.0	13.7
Horseback riding (general)	9.2	12.9	16.9	20.6	8.2	11.8	16.8	25.3	13.4
Mountain climbing	14.8	7.4	16.2	15.5	8.6	12.7	13.4	19.2	12.6
Rafting	9.0	12.0	22.8	20.6	6.4	7.9	17.1	14.6	12.4
Big game hunting	5.4	7.0	25.5	32.9	5.2	11.4	8.9	27.8	11.9
Sledding	8.6	17.1	23.5	18.5	6.4	0.3	15.0	16.3	11.5
Waterskiing	8.1	8.6	16.0	14.5	9.0	7.8	21.4	14.5	11.5
Jetskiing	10.0	9.0	14.6	12.3	8.8	8.2	19.4	10.7	11.2
Horseback riding on trails	8.8	11.3	12.9	17.0	5.9	9.8	13.2	19.9	11.1
Softball	8.8	13.7	11.0	8.6	13.8	9.0	9.0	13.5	10.8
Basketball outdoors	6.7	12.0	4.6	8.4	11.3	6.9	10.6	13.9	9.2
Tennis outdoors	9.1	14.4	2.0	9.3	7.8	8.9	6.5	11.8	9.1
Snowmobiling	2.3	6.3	16.7	20.0	3.3	3.0	14.3	20.3	8.4
Small game hunting	6.1	5.9	11.8	19.9	4.4	6.4	8.0	14.0	8.1
Volleyball outdoors	5.1	10.9	8.8	1.8	7.0	7.8	12.6	3.9	7.7

Table 13.11 Comparisons of percentages participating 1 or more times in the previous 12 months by states in the Mountain census division *continued*

Activity	AZ	CO	ID	MT	NV	NM	UT	WY	Mountain Census Division Total
Rock climbing	4.1	5.7	7.1	10.1	6.4	11.6	5.0	15.2	7.3
Snowboarding	3.8	8.6	9.6	11.0	8.3	5.2	7.8	7.3	7.3
Baseball	3.0	12.0	3.5	4.7	8.0	5.7	7.6	12.8	7.0
Canoeing	4.5	5.1	8.9	13.8	5.3	2.4	9.2	9.0	6.4
Handball or racquetball outdoors	9.7	9.3	4.7	2.3	5.9	5.7	4.8	1.8	6.4
Soccer outdoors	4.6	12.4	6.5	9.5	4.2	1.2	5.2	11.5	6.3
Snorkeling	5.0	7.3	5.1	5.5	5.1	3.0	10.5	3.5	5.9
Cross-country skiing	2.4	5.8	8.4	12.8	1.6	4.4	5.9	10.5	5.4
Caving	4.1	1.5	14.7	6.7	7.1	2.2	9.7	0.9	5.3
Football	0.9	8.7	0.0	11.9	7.8	1.2	4.6	13.7	5.3
Ice skating outdoors	2.4	6.4	8.4	10.9	4.3	5.8	2.8	6.7	5.2
Anadromous fishing	2.8	4.0	10.2	9.2	4.0	3.3	5.7	4.3	4.8
Ice fishing	1.2	5.7	8.6	9.9	0.5	0.8	6.1	19.5	4.7
Snowshoeing	0.8	4.7	11.8	5.8	4.2	2.8	0.9	10.3	3.9
Migratory bird hunting	1.4	3.6	7.7	8.4	2.4	1.0	3.6	6.5	3.5
Saltwater fishing	4.7	3.3	3.0	4.4	3.9	1.9	2.6	2.6	3.4
Sailing	3.7	4.4	4.4	2.8	2.1	2.1	4.0	3.0	3.4
Rowing	4.1	2.3	3.5	6.1	2.0	1.7	5.4	3.5	3.4
Kayaking	2.3	3.3	3.7	5.3	2.2	2.6	4.6	3.1	3.2
Orienteering	1.4	0.9	10.2	0.8	4.6	3.1	1.2	4.9	2.8
Scuba diving	1.2	1.9	1.8	1.8	3.0	1.0	3.6	1.8	2.0
Surfing	1.1	1.3	0.4	1.4	2.2	0.4	1.6	0.8	1.2
Windsurfing	0.5	1.1	1.1	0.9	1.4	1.0	1.2	1.2	1.0

Table 13.12 Comparisons of percentages participating 1 or more times in the previous 12 months by states in the Pacific census division

Activity	AK	CA	HI	OR	WA	Pacific Census Division Total
Walking for pleasure	89.0	80.1	83.1	79.9	84.3	81.3
Family gathering	79.2	72.5	75.7	70.0	73.4	73.0
Viewing/photographing natural scenery	78.4	60.6	67.3	67.1	70.2	63.7
Visiting nature centers	70.0	56.2	58.4	61.2	61.2	58.1
Gardening/landscaping for pleasure	56.0	50.3	84.7	61.0	63.7	57.4
Picnicking	58.8	52.5	65.4	61.6	64.1	56.2
Sightseeing	58.2	46.1	53.4	56.9	57.2	49.7
Visiting a beach	39.4	46.2	70.5	47.5	54.5	49.2
Viewing/photographing wildflowers, trees	59.4	45.6	47.3	51.5	53.1	47.9
Driving for pleasure	60.5	42.9	43.3	53.5	55.8	46.3
Attending outdoor sports events	54.3	43.5	42.2	45.7	53.5	45.4
Day hiking	57.1	44.6	34.5	51.4	47.0	45.2
Visiting historic sites	45.1	41.0	49.0	47.8	47.6	43.3
Bicycling	48.6	41.0	33.8	42.7	47.0	41.6
Swimming in lakes, streams	28.6	37.9	62.9	39.2	45.9	40.8
Attending outdoor concerts, plays	33.5	42.5	34.0	43.7	40.5	40.8
Viewing/photographing other wildlife	74.1	36.5	30.1	47.7	51.2	40.5
Running or jogging	36.9	39.9	36.4	44.4	42.8	40.0
Swimming in an outdoor pool	19.0	41.8	35.2	31.8	33.2	37.6
Visiting a wilderness or primitive area	59.4	32.8	27.7	46.1	45.3	36.4
Yard games (e.g., horseshoes)	35.8	30.5	19.8	54.9	43.5	33.0
Developed camping	40.3	28.5	29.3	40.3	41.0	31.7
Viewing/photographing birds	47.5	28.3	26.9	33.8	33.1	30.2
Visiting other waterside (besides beach)	30.1	24.5	24.8	35.8	33.2	26.9
Viewing/photographing fish	45.2	22.1	43.0	24.0	29.3	26.2
Gathering mushrooms, berries	58.4	20.7	18.3	37.6	35.8	25.7
Inline skating or rollerblading	20.9	28.5	10.7	17.7	22.8	24.0

Table 13.12 Comparisons of percentages participating 1 or more times in the previous 12 months by states in the Pacific census division *continued*

Activity	AK	CA	HI	OR	WA	Pacific Census Division Total
Visiting a farm or agricultural setting	19.8	21.5	22.4	32.9	28.2	23.4
Boat tours or excursions	33.4	20.1	30.5	18.8	24.4	22.8
Mountain biking	33.9	21.1	14.7	25.1	28.2	22.4
Visiting prehistoric/archeological sites	22.9	21.3	28.6	18.6	18.8	21.5
Motorboating	35.1	17.6	12.3	21.3	29.4	19.7
Primitive camping	45.5	14.6	16.2	28.1	26.8	18.9
Golfing	17.1	15.2	25.1	16.8	19.3	17.3
Driving off-road	31.8	15.1	12.9	19.1	21.4	16.8
Coldwater fishing	41.8	13.8	2.2	28.4	22.4	16.4
Backpacking	30.8	12.9	11.7	16.3	22.1	15.1
Saltwater fishing	40.3	11.3	27.8	8.4	12.6	14.1
Basketball outdoors	16.0	12.4	12.1	13.8	14.3	13.0
Tennis outdoors	6.9	13.4	5.8	10.1	15.2	12.0
Soccer outdoors	9.1	13.4	8.5	6.2	8.9	11.4
Warmwater fishing	6.7	11.4	3.2	14.1	12.8	10.9
Sledding	26.1	6.2	0.0	14.6	24.0	9.6
Snorkeling	6.9	7.6	29.8	6.0	8.6	9.6
Softball	7.0	9.2	5.5	12.5	14.1	9.5
Horseback riding (general)	11.1	9.7	6.6	9.3	9.8	9.4
Jetskiing	7.9	10.2	5.9	5.5	9.7	9.2
Downhill skiing	16.0	8.6	1.9	10.6	14.2	9.2
Volleyball outdoors	0.8	8.9	8.6	12.5	11.2	9.0
Anadromous fishing	47.5	5.7	0.5	14.0	13.1	8.9
Snowboarding	13.5	9.2	2.0	8.3	9.8	8.7
Football	9.9	9.2	8.6	2.6	8.4	8.5
Rafting	11.9	7.0	2.2	15.5	12.2	8.2
Mountain climbing	31.1	6.9	3.2	2.0	9.4	7.8

Table 13.12 Comparisons of percentages participating 1 or more times in the previous 12 months by states in the Pacific census division *continued*

Activity	AK	CA	HI	OR	WA	Pacific Census Division Total
Horseback riding on trails	9.0	7.1	5.3	7.8	7.2	7.1
Waterskiing	5.1	6.8	3.4	7.9	10.5	6.9
Caving	4.2	6.3	1.4	18.4	6.8	6.5
Handball or racquetball outdoors	2.7	8.5	1.1	4.0	5.2	6.4
Canoeing	16.9	4.3	8.9	8.6	9.4	6.3
Sailing	4.5	5.4	7.7	4.0	6.5	5.6
Kayaking	5.9	4.4	12.0	5.1	5.1	5.3
Ice skating outdoors	20.7	5.0	0.0	0.8	4.6	4.9
Big game hunting	21.2	1.9	4.7	9.7	9.5	4.7
Baseball	3.1	4.5	4.8	2.0	7.5	4.7
Surfing	1.2	3.8	18.7	1.6	2.1	4.6
Snowmobiling	28.5	2.3	1.0	3.8	6.3	4.0
Small game hunting	11.9	2.6	2.4	6.1	7.6	3.9
Cross-country skiing	20.3	2.4	0.6	5.3	6.9	3.9
Rowing	7.2	3.6	0.7	4.5	5.8	3.8
Rock climbing	0.0	4.6	0.6	3.8	3.5	3.6
Orienteering	2.7	3.2	2.5	4.4	1.1	2.9
Scuba diving	2.8	1.9	6.1	2.1	3.2	2.5
Ice fishing	27.0	0.1	0.0	1.4	2.4	2.0
Migratory bird hunting	7.5	1.2	0.4	2.3	3.4	1.8
Snowshoeing	4.4	1.2	0.0	1.5	1.9	1.4
Windsurfing	0.0	0.7	2.0	2.0	1.1	0.9

Chapter 14
Outdoor Recreation Personalities

American society, segmented according to demographic characteristics, indeed presents a picture of diversity. Likewise, segmenting society according to outdoor recreation participation characteristics presents a picture just as diverse. The private sector has long sought to identify different segments of society with different tastes and interests, each theoretically representing a different potential market. Their purpose is to tailor their sales pitches to each market segment for improved sales of products or services. The public sector has not been so insightful in understanding and catering to diversity, but "market segmentation" of public sector markets is equally as important to this sector. Tailoring information programs, service delivery, or any other aspect of public service can serve well both the private and public sectors.

The reported results of the 1994–1995 NSRE presented 8 outdoor personalities, basing their identification on differences in activity choices. Each of these outdoor personalities represents a different market for sites, information, services, equipment, and tourism. These earlier NSRE results were reported for use by the Sporting Goods Manufacturing Association and the Outdoor Recreation Coalition of America in a report entitled Emerging Markets (Cordell, McDonald, Teasley & Bergstrom, 1998). The analysis done for the 1994–1995 NSRE was replicated for the 2000–2001 NSRE. This chapter reports the results of that data analysis to describe contemporary market segment or outdoor recreation personalities.

Highlights

Eight outdoor recreation personalities emerged from cluster analysis of the 2000–2001 NSRE. Each of the 8 identified clusters is distinguished by the number and type of activities they favor (Figure 14.1, p. 234). The Inactives, the largest of all the outdoor personality groups, makes up almost one quarter of the U.S. population of persons 16 or older. In terms of the percentage of people in the group who participate in outdoor recreation activities and the number of activities they choose (see Table 14.1, pp. 238–239, for list of activities), the Inactives are the least active of the 8 outdoor personalities. They participate in a bit of picnicking, hiking, visiting nature centers, birding and other viewing activities, and not much more. Even their participation in walking, the most popular activity, is way below the national rate. Unlike the Inactives, who have no favored activities, the Passives have a list of highly favored activities, although it is a short list. Most sightsee, drive for pleasure, walk for pleasure, attend family gatherings out-of-doors, and picnic. The Nonconsumptive Moderates participate in a much larger list of activities than either the Inactives or Passives, from going to the beach and outdoor swimming to sailing and visiting prehistoric sites. But, they do not participate in consumptive activities such as hunting. Activities favored by this group (i.e., those in which the percentage of the group participating is greater than that of the population generally) include visiting a beach, swimming in natural waters, downhill skiing, and snowboarding. The Nature Lovers, another outdoor personality, is characterized by quite large percentages of its members who participate in viewing/learning activities, especially birding and viewing and photographing wildflowers and other plants, wildlife, natural scenery and fish. Also included as favored activities are visiting nature centers and museums.

Four of the 8 personalities are among the more active of Americans. The Water Bugs chose participation in water-based activities as their single most distinguishing characteristic. Going to the beach or other watersides, swimming, snorkeling, sailing, boating, fishing, kayaking, and surfing are among their most favored activities. The Backcountry Actives differ from other groups by their high relative percentages who backpack, camp in primitive areas, visit wilderness, day hike, and cross-country ski. This group is also into developed camping, gathering natural products, motorized activities, viewing/learning activities, and fishing. A distinguishing characteristic is that most of these activities occur largely in undeveloped settings. The most active outdoor personality in American society is the Outdoor Avids. This group highly favors canoeing, scuba diving, windsurfing, cross-country skiing, rowing, rafting, kayaking, backpacking, snowmobiling, surfing, and snorkeling. Across all activities, the

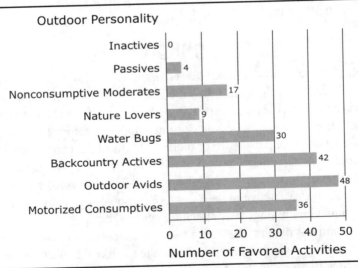

Figure 14.1 Number of favored activities for each of 8 outdoor personalities based on a cluster analysis of NSRE 2000–2001 activity participation data

Outdoor Avids' participation rates are higher by far than the rest of the U.S. population. The last personality, and one that stands out as far different than any of the other outdoor personalities, is the Motorized Consumptives personality. Members of this group list hunting, fishing, camping, motorized activities (on land, water, and snow), horseback riding, snowboarding, swimming, and driving for pleasure as their highly favored activities. As well, somewhat larger percentages than the national population participate in water activities and camping.

Not only do the 8 personalities differ in the number and type of outdoor activities they choose but also they differ in demographic makeup. In Figure 14.2 differences in makeup of the 8 outdoor personalities with regard to such characteristics, sex and age, are highlighted. The Inactives, Passives, Water Bugs, and Nature Lovers are older than the other 4 personalities; the Motorized Consumptives are the youngest. Five of the 8 recreation personalities are more than 50% female, especially Nature Lovers and Water Bugs, each over 60% female. Two of the personalities are clearly male-dominated: Motorized Consumptives (more than 70% male) and Outdoor Avids (about 62% male). A 3rd personality, Backcountry Actives, is also comprised of more males than females (55% male).

The Eight Outdoor Personalities in Detail

Participation data for over 42,000 respondents to the NSRE were analyzed using cluster analysis. The application of this statistical analysis technique examined recreation participation across all the NSRE nature-based outdoor activities to identify similar patterns of activity choices (profiles) among all respondents. (Activities that occur primarily in urban settings, such as most

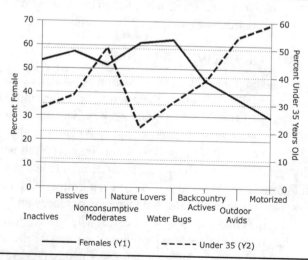

Figure 14.2 Percentage female and under 35 for 8 outdoor personalities representing favored outdoor activities, 2000–2001

individual and team sports, were not included in this analysis.) Those respondents with very similar activity profiles were statistically grouped (or clustered). As a result, individuals grouped within a cluster are very much alike in terms of their recreation participation patterns, but they are not like people in other clusters. Revealed were 8 outdoor activity profiles representing different recreation personalities ranging from people who had participated in very few or even no activities over the previous 12 months to those who had participated in quite a number of activities.

These 8 personalities are described in the following sections and a table is presented for each showing how each group relates to others and to the population in general. Shown in each table for each activity are the percentages of respondents in the personality group who participated in the activity, percentages of persons not in the personality group who participated (i.e., everyone else) and percentages of the population generally who participated. Shown also are the ratios of percentages of persons in the personality group relative to those not in the group and relative to the population generally. These ratios help direct the eye to activities in which the personality group is more or less active than everyone else. Especially telling is the ratio in the last column (i.e., the percentage of the group participating to the percentage of population generally participating in an activity). A ratio greater than 1.0 indicates an activity favored by the group relative to the population. These favored activities are the primary characteristic defining the personality. Also telling are activities not favored by a personality group (i.e., a ratio less than 1.0). Also shown in the tables are the percentages of a group participating in the listed activities. Any percentage over 50% is a defining participation characteristic. As each personality is described in terms of activity participation, shown also is its percentage of the population, defining that group's size or market share. In addition, the group's demographic characteristics, such as age, sex, race, and income, are described.

Comparison of Activity Profiles

The people who make up the 8 outdoor recreation personalities differ in many ways. They are especially different in their activity profiles and demographic composition. Table 14.1 (pp. 238–239) shows the activity participation profiles for each personality. Demographic compositions are compared at the end of this chapter. From these profiles it is clear that people who fall within each of the personality groupings have chosen quite different recreation activities to emphasize in their leisure. More than 75% of each group, with the exception of the Inactives, participate in walking and attending outdoor family gatherings. From there, similarities end and diversity begins. The Inactives are as their label suggests, inactive, and very few participate in many of the listed activities, certainly not the physically demanding ones. The Passives are participants in many more activities than the Inactives, but their activity choices are not physically demanding. The Nonconsumptive Moderates participate in yet a wider list of activities, but in moderate numbers. For the most part, they shun use of motor vehicles and hunting in their recreation. The Nature Lovers demonstrate their values and preferences by choosing to emphasize viewing, photographing and learning about natural things, and history. Together, these 4 outdoor personalities constitute nearly two thirds (63%) of the population of the people in this country ages 16 and older.

The remaining 4 personalities, making up 37% of the population, are much more active in outdoor recreation. The Water Bugs, obviously having an affinity for water-based outdoor activities, participate in a wide range of activities, but at the top are beach, swimming, and boating activities. The Backcountry Actives emphasize backcountry, wilderness, hiking, and cross-country skiing. Of all groups the Outdoor Avids are the most active across almost all activities. They are especially active in the muscle-powered, risky activities. Motorized Consumptives emphasize motor vehicle activities, hunting, and fishing.

The profiles in Table 14.1 can and should be used prodigiously by both public and private sector outdoor recreation opportunity providers. In selecting products or services to offer and then marketing those offerings, each of the outdoor personalities represents a market segment. In planning and managing public and private areas for outdoor recreation, the 8 personalities also represent market segments, each of which is looking for something different. Site and facility design, management objectives, promotion and information provision, and many other aspects of outdoor recreation management should consider the information in Table 14.1 and the other tables that follow.

Nonmotorized activities such as mountain biking have grown as has the technology of outdoor equipment. Photo courtesy of USDA Forest Service, J. Michael Bowker

Table 14.1 Percentages of members ages 16 or older of 8 outdoor personalities who participated in listed activities, 2000–2001

Activity	All Groups Combined	Inactives	Passives	Nonconsumptive Moderates	Nature Lovers	Water Bugs	Backcountry Actives	Outdoor Avids	Motorized Consumptives
Walking for pleasure	82.9	56.9	89.0	89.4	89.5	95.9	95.7	95.0	82.3
Family gathering	73.3	41.1	79.8	83.9	75.9	87.2	88.2	92.2	81.4
Visiting nature centers	57.0	14.3	51.2	73.9	62.0	84.8	88.7	90.4	50.0
Viewing/photographing natural scenery	56.6	11.1	34.4	51.8	89.8	94.1	92.0	94.0	50.7
Picnicking	54.4	16.2	56.8	63.7	57.3	78.8	82.9	82.2	47.8
Sightseeing	51.7	6.3	92.7	10.2	53.6	90.0	77.9	80.0	55.2
Driving for pleasure	51.1	5.4	90.0	6.7	51.0	88.6	78.7	81.1	66.0
Visiting historic sites	46.0	7.6	41.5	51.7	48.4	78.9	77.4	81.9	37.2
Viewing/photographing flowers	42.5	8.8	11.2	25.0	86.9	79.7	76.2	78.4	22.8
Viewing/photographing other wildlife	42.0	8.3	11.2	21.2	74.5	71.5	81.9	85.8	45.6
Swimming (lakes, ponds)	41.7	6.6	20.8	64.7	6.9	82.1	57.9	94.6	73.8
Visiting a beach	40.5	7.2	24.0	65.0	11.8	89.1	45.8	84.6	52.8
Day hiking	33.2	14.0	19.4	32.6	28.0	33.7	83.4	76.4	29.5
Visiting a wilderness	32.6	4.7	16.1	28.5	28.2	37.8	84.8	81.3	50.2
Viewing/photographing birds	30.6	8.2	10.8	14.5	64.6	55.4	52.7	55.3	14.3
Gathering mushrooms, berries	28.5	6.8	15.4	18.3	29.0	28.7	67.7	70.9	50.4
Developed camping	26.4	3.9	14.6	29.6	15.6	28.2	64.9	67.0	46.3
Visiting watersides (besides beach)	25.9	2.8	11.0	27.3	9.3	56.4	41.2	70.9	38.3
Motorboating	24.4	4.1	8.4	18.8	11.3	35.8	19.5	85.9	75.0
Viewing/photographing fish	23.4	4.0	7.9	14.1	25.8	40.8	39.7	65.1	33.5
Warmwater fishing	22.5	7.9	10.9	13.1	16.0	18.9	33.4	62.3	73.1
Mountain biking	21.4	6.0	12.6	25.7	11.6	22.7	42.5	63.6	29.7

Table 14.1 Percentages of members 16 or older of 8 outdoor personalities who participated in listed activities, 2000–2001 *continued*

Activity	All Groups Combined	Inactives	Passives	Nonconsumptive Moderates	Nature Lovers	Water Bugs	Backcountry Actives	Outdoor Avids	Motorized Consumptives
Visiting prehistoric sites	20.8	3.3	14.6	22.1	19.8	30.7	49.2	46.3	12.5
Driving off-road	17.5	2.8	13.7	4.7	9.6	14.7	35.6	56.1	53.4
Primitive camping	16.0	2.4	5.0	10.0	5.8	5.0	59.9	58.7	33.8
Coldwater fishing	13.5	3.7	5.6	7.3	7.5	8.1	30.1	48.1	37.2
Backpacking	10.7	1.6	2.9	9.1	3.7	5.0	40.7	44.0	10.8
Saltwater fishing	10.3	3.2	5.0	12.0	4.5	13.4	9.7	32.4	24.1
Canoeing	9.7	0.8	2.4	7.2	3.0	10.4	18.4	50.2	16.3
Jetskiing	9.5	1.3	2.5	9.3	2.1	9.5	4.4	43.3	34.6
Rafting	9.5	0.6	2.0	7.5	2.2	10.4	10.8	52.0	22.8
Downhill skiing	8.5	1.6	3.6	11.8	3.0	7.6	13.2	35.8	14.9
Big game hunting	8.4	2.8	2.7	3.2	5.0	2.2	13.0	26.9	40.1
Waterskiing	8.1	0.7	1.4	6.1	1.0	5.8	2.8	45.4	33.5
Horseback riding on trails	7.8	1.9	4.6	6.3	5.3	8.5	14.1	23.8	14.6
Small game hunting	7.2	2.6	2.1	2.2	3.7	2.6	9.8	25.2	34.6
Snorkeling	6.7	0.4	1.8	7.9	0.7	12.6	6.4	30.8	9.6
Snowmobiling	5.6	1.0	1.9	3.9	1.8	2.9	7.8	28.0	17.1
Sailing	5.1	0.6	2.4	5.4	1.7	9.6	6.2	21.3	4.8
Snowboarding	4.9	1.0	1.6	6.4	1.2	3.3	6.8	21.5	12.4
Anadromous fishing	4.4	1.0	1.2	3.4	1.8	3.4	7.4	18.2	11.9
Rowing	4.4	0.5	1.1	3.3	1.4	5.9	6.2	22.6	7.3
Cross-country skiing	3.8	0.4	1.2	3.4	1.3	4.0	9.5	19.1	3.4
Kayaking	3.5	0.3	0.9	3.2	0.7	4.5	6.9	17.6	3.8
Migratory bird hunting	2.4	0.6	0.5	0.6	0.9	0.7	2.6	10.1	11.9
Scuba diving	1.9	0.2	0.5	1.6	0.2	2.4	2.1	10.1	3.8
Surfing	1.7	0.2	0.2	2.5	0.1	2.0	1.7	8.3	3.5
Windsurfing	0.8	0.0	0.3	0.8	0.2	0.7	1.1	4.9	1.2

The Inactives (23.9%)

The Inactives are the largest of all the outdoor personality groups based on profiles of activity choices. This group makes up almost one quarter of the U.S. population of persons ages 16 and older. In terms of percentages of this group which participate in the activities listed in Table 14.2 (pp. 242–243), the Inactives are the least outdoor active segment of American society. This group also includes people who for whatever reason do not participate in outdoor recreation.

A few in this group participate in hunting and fishing; do a bit of picnicking, visiting nature centers, birding, and other viewing activities; and to a much lesser extent than other Americans walk and attend family gatherings out-of-doors. They do little else in any numbers. They are virtually absent in water sports, such as canoeing, rafting, or kayaking. All ratios in the final column are less than 1.0, and substantially so. Walking is the only activity in which more than half of this outdoor personality group participates (57%). The next closest activity is attending family gatherings. All other activities fall well under one half the national rate. The percentage of Inactives participating is less than 10% for 42 of the 48 activities shown.

The demographic composition of this group indicates in part why their participation percentages are relatively low. Relative to the population as a whole, this group is disproportionately more female (females participate generally at lower rates), more Black and Hispanic, older (especially in percentage over 65), have lower incomes, more of foreign-born origin, and more likely to be from the South Atlantic and Pacific subregions.

The Passives (15.0%)

Unlike the Inactives, who have no favored activities (i.e., ratio greater than 1.0), the Passives have a list of highly favored activities, although it is a short list (Table 14.3, pp. 244–245). Most sightsee, drive for pleasure, walk for pleasure, attend family gatherings out-of-doors, and picnic. But there the list of favored activities ends. Nearly 93% of this group reported sightseeing as an activity, compared with just slightly more than 50% of the population at large. Nearly 90% reported driving for pleasure, relative to about 50% of the population at large. But this group generally does little else and for the most part their percentages participating do not approach the national participation rate. They do not participate in muscle-powered activities, such as surfing, kayaking, rowing, and canoeing, nor in viewing/photographing activities (i.e., birding, photographing wildlife, flowers, fish). Only moderate percentages visit beaches, swim, view/photograph scenery, day hike, or camp in developed areas. Very few hunt, fish or participate in motorized outdoor activities.

The demographics of this group shows relatively high proportions of females, Blacks, Asian/Pacific Islanders, and people ages 65 and older. Otherwise, this group mostly mirrors the national population and is almost proportionately distributed across regions of the country.

The Nonconsumptive Moderates (11.7%)

This outdoor personality group is somewhat more expansive in activity choices than either the Inactives or the Passives. Moderate percentages of this group participate in a number of activities from going to the beach and outdoor swimming to sailing and visiting prehistoric sites (Table 14.4, pp. 246–247). Favored activities (i.e., those in which their percentages participating are greater than that of the population generally) include visiting a beach, swimming in natural waters, surfing, downhill skiing, snowboarding, visiting nature centers, mountain biking, snorkeling, picnicking, saltwater fishing, attending family gatherings, developed camping, visiting historic sites, walking, sailing, visiting prehistoric sites, and watersides. Outstanding as a mark of their identity is that this group favors only 1 consumptive activity: saltwater fishing.

Some of the members of this outdoor personality group participate in physically active activities, such as surfing, downhill skiing, snowboarding, mountain biking, and snorkeling. Moderate percentages are into picnicking, visiting historic sites and viewing/photographing scenery. Activities not favored include driving for pleasure, sightseeing, hunting (all types), driving off-road, viewing/ photographing nature, fishing (all types), primitive camping, gathering natural products, and snowmobiling. Most of these nonfavored activities are either consumptive or motorized and percentages participating in these activities are especially low relative to the population.

The demographics of the Nonconsumptive Moderates show that this group is about equally male and female, and includes disproportionately large percentages of Asian/Pacific Islanders and Hispanics. They are young relative to the overall population, have moderate incomes, are more likely to be foreign born relative to other groups, and are more urban than other personalities. Further, this group includes disproportionately large percentages of people who live in the New England, Middle Atlantic, South Atlantic, and Pacific states of the country, which is reflected in the popularity of beach- and water-oriented activities.

The Nature Lovers (12.5%)

The Nature Lovers are yet another distinct outdoor personality. This group is dominated by the relatively large percentages reporting participation in viewing/ learning activities, especially birding, wildflowers and other plants, wildlife, natural scenery, and fish (Table 14.5, pp. 250–251). Also included is visiting nature centers and museums. The top 5 activities for this group—6 including nature centers—are all viewing/learning activities. Also high on the participation list for the Nature Lovers are walking, picnicking, visiting historic sites, attending family gatherings outdoors, sightseeing, gathering natural products,

Table 14.2 Participation profile of the Inactives personality and ratios of cluster and population-wide participation percentages by activity, 2000–2001

Activity	% in Cluster Participating	% Participation if NOT in Cluster	Ratio of Column 1 to Column 2	% of U.S. Population Participating	Ratio of Column 1 to Column 4
Walking for pleasure	56.9	91.0	0.6	82.9	0.7
Family gathering	41.1	83.4	0.5	73.3	0.6
Day hiking	14.0	39.2	0.4	33.2	0.4
Small game hunting	2.6	8.7	0.3	7.2	0.4
Warmwater fishing	7.9	27.1	0.3	22.5	0.4
Big game hunting	2.8	10.2	0.3	8.4	0.3
Saltwater fishing	3.2	12.6	0.3	10.3	0.3
Picnicking	16.2	66.3	0.2	54.4	0.3
Mountain biking	6.0	26.3	0.2	21.4	0.3
Viewing/photographing birds	8.2	37.5	0.2	30.6	0.3
Coldwater fishing	3.7	16.6	0.2	13.5	0.3
Horseback riding on trails	1.9	9.6	0.2	7.8	0.2
Migratory bird hunting	0.6	2.9	0.2	2.4	0.2
Visiting nature centers	14.3	70.3	0.2	57.0	0.3
Anadromous fishing	1.0	5.4	0.2	4.4	0.2
Gathering mushrooms, berries	6.8	35.2	0.2	28.5	0.2
Viewing/photographing flowers	8.8	52.8	0.2	42.5	0.2
Viewing/photographing scenery	11.1	70.6	0.2	56.6	0.2
Snowboarding	1.0	6.2	0.2	4.9	0.2
Viewing/photographing other wildlife	8.3	52.4	0.2	42.0	0.2
Visiting a beach	7.2	50.9	0.1	40.5	0.2
Downhill skiing	1.6	10.8	0.1	8.5	0.2
Viewing/photographing fish	4.0	29.3	0.1	23.4	0.2
Snowmobiling	1.0	7.1	0.1	5.6	0.2
Motorboating	4.1	30.7	0.1	24.4	0.2
Visiting historic sites	7.6	58.3	0.1	46.0	0.2
Visiting prehistoric sites	3.3	26.2	0.1	20.8	0.2
Backpacking	1.6	13.5	0.1	10.7	0.2

Table 14.2 Participation profile of the Inactives personality and ratios of cluster and population-wide participation percentages by activity, 2000–2001 *continued*

Activity	% in Cluster Participating	% Participation if NOT in Cluster	Ratio of Column 1 to Column 2	% of U.S. Population Participating	Ratio of Column 1 to Column 4
Primitive camping	2.4	20.2	0.1	16.0	0.2
Developed camping	3.9	33.4	0.1	26.4	0.2
Driving off-road	2.8	22.3	0.1	17.5	0.2
Swimming in lakes, ponds	6.6	52.6	0.1	41.7	0.2
Visiting a wilderness	4.7	41.3	0.1	32.6	0.1
Jetskiing	1.3	12.1	0.1	9.5	0.1
Sailing	0.6	6.5	0.1	5.1	0.1
Sightseeing	6.3	66.4	0.1	51.7	0.1
Cross-country skiing	0.4	4.9	0.1	3.8	0.1
Surfing	0.2	2.1	0.1	1.7	0.1
Visiting watersides (other than beach)	2.8	33.1	0.1	25.9	0.1
Rowing	0.5	5.6	0.1	4.4	0.1
Driving for pleasure	5.4	65.9	0.1	51.1	0.1
Kayaking	0.3	4.4	0.1	3.5	0.1
Scuba diving	0.2	2.4	0.1	1.9	0.1
Waterskiing	0.7	10.5	0.1	8.1	0.1
Canoeing	0.8	12.5	0.1	9.7	0.1
Rafting	0.6	12.3	0.1	9.5	0.1
Snorkeling	0.4	8.6	0.1	6.7	0.1
Windsurfing	0.0	1.1	0.0	0.8	0.1

Source: NSRE 2000–2001. Versions 1–9, N = 42,868, Interview dates: 7/99 to 7/01.

Table 14.3 Participation profile of the Passives personality and ratios of cluster and population-wide participation percentages by activity, 2000–2001

Activity	% in Cluster Participating	% Participation if NOT in Cluster	Ratio of Column 1 to Column 2	% of U.S. Population Participating	Ratio of Column 1 to Column 4
Sightseeing	92.7	44.5	2.1	51.7	1.8
Driving for pleasure	90.0	44.3	2.0	51.1	1.8
Family gathering	79.8	72.2	1.1	73.3	1.1
Walking for pleasure	89.0	81.9	1.1	82.9	1.1
Picnicking	56.8	54.0	1.1	54.4	1.0
Visiting historic sites	41.5	46.7	0.9	46.0	0.9
Visiting nature centers	51.2	58.0	0.9	57.0	0.9
Driving off-road	13.7	18.1	0.8	17.5	0.8
Visiting prehistoric sites	14.6	21.9	0.7	20.8	0.7
Viewing/photographing natural scenery	34.4	60.5	0.6	56.6	0.6
Horseback riding on trails	4.6	8.3	0.6	7.8	0.6
Visiting a beach	24.0	43.5	0.6	40.5	0.6
Mountain biking	12.6	23.0	0.6	21.4	0.6
Day hiking	19.4	35.7	0.5	33.2	0.6
Developed camping	14.6	28.5	0.5	26.4	0.6
Gathering mushrooms, berries	15.4	30.8	0.5	28.5	0.5
Swimming in lakes, ponds	20.8	45.4	0.5	41.7	0.5
Saltwater fishing	5.0	11.3	0.5	10.3	0.5
Visiting a wilderness	16.1	35.6	0.5	32.6	0.5
Warmwater fishing	10.9	24.6	0.4	22.5	0.5
Sailing	2.4	5.6	0.4	5.1	0.5
Downhill skiing	3.6	9.4	0.4	8.5	0.4
Coldwater fishing	5.6	14.9	0.4	13.5	0.4
Visiting watersides (besides beach)	11.0	28.6	0.4	25.9	0.4
Viewing/photographing birds	10.8	34.1	0.3	30.6	0.4
Motorboating	8.4	27.2	0.3	24.4	0.3
Snowmobiling	1.9	6.2	0.3	5.6	0.3
Viewing/photographing fish	7.9	26.1	0.3	23.4	0.3

Table 14.3 Participation profile of the Passives personality and ratios of cluster and population-wide participation percentages by activity, 2000–2001 *continued*

Activity	% in Cluster Participating	% Participation if NOT in Cluster	Ratio of Column 1 to Column 2	% of U.S. Population Participating	Ratio of Column 1 to Column 4
Big game hunting	2.7	9.4	0.3	8.4	0.3
Snowboarding	1.6	5.5	0.3	4.9	0.3
Primitive camping	5.0	18.0	0.3	16.0	0.3
Cross-country skiing	1.2	4.3	0.3	3.8	0.3
Windsurfing	0.3	0.9	0.3	0.8	0.3
Small game hunting	2.1	8.2	0.3	7.2	0.3
Anadromous fishing	1.2	5.0	0.2	4.4	0.3
Backpacking	2.9	12.0	0.2	10.7	0.3
Snorkeling	1.8	7.5	0.2	6.7	0.3
Viewing/photographing other wildlife	11.2	47.5	0.2	42.0	0.3
Jetskiing	2.5	10.8	0.2	9.5	0.3
Rowing	1.1	5.0	0.2	4.4	0.3
Viewing/photographing flowers	11.2	48.0	0.2	42.5	0.3
Scuba diving	0.5	2.1	0.2	1.9	0.3
Canoeing	2.4	11.0	0.2	9.7	0.3
Kayaking	0.9	3.9	0.2	3.5	0.3
Rafting	2.0	10.9	0.2	9.5	0.2
Migratory bird hunting	0.5	2.7	0.2	2.4	0.2
Waterskiing	1.4	9.3	0.2	8.1	0.2
Surfing	0.2	1.9	0.1	1.7	0.1

Source: NSRE 2000–2001. Versions 1–9, N = 42,868, Interview dates: 7/99 to 7/01.

Table 14.4 Participation profile of the Nonconsumptive Moderates personality and ratios of cluster and population-wide participation percentages by activity, 2000–2001

Activity	% in Cluster Participating	% Participation if NOT in Cluster	Ratio of Column 1 to Column 2	% of U.S. Population Participating	Ratio of Column 1 to Column 4
Visiting a beach	65.0	37.3	1.7	40.5	1.6
Swimming in lakes, ponds	64.7	38.6	1.7	41.7	1.6
Surfing	2.5	1.6	1.6	1.7	1.5
Downhill skiing	11.8	8.1	1.5	8.5	1.4
Snowboarding	6.4	4.7	1.4	4.9	1.3
Visiting nature centers	73.9	54.7	1.4	57.0	1.3
Mountain biking	25.7	20.8	1.2	21.4	1.2
Snorkeling	7.9	6.5	1.2	6.7	1.2
Picnicking	63.7	53.2	1.2	54.4	1.2
Saltwater fishing	12.0	10.1	1.2	10.3	1.2
Family gathering	83.9	71.9	1.2	73.3	1.1
Developed camping	29.6	26.0	1.1	26.4	1.1
Visiting historic sites	51.7	45.2	1.1	46.0	1.1
Walking for pleasure	89.4	82.1	1.1	82.9	1.1
Sailing	5.4	5.1	1.1	5.1	1.1
Visiting prehistoric sites	22.1	20.6	1.1	20.8	1.1
Visiting watersides (other than beach)	27.3	25.7	1.1	25.9	1.1
Jetskiing	9.3	9.5	1.0	9.5	1.0
Day hiking	32.6	33.3	1.0	33.2	1.0
Kayaking	3.2	3.5	0.9	3.5	0.9
Windsurfing	0.8	0.8	0.9	0.8	0.9
Viewing/photographing scenery	51.8	57.2	0.9	56.6	0.9
Cross-country skiing	3.4	3.9	0.9	3.8	0.9
Visiting a wilderness	28.5	33.2	0.9	32.6	0.9
Backpacking	9.1	10.9	0.8	10.7	0.9
Scuba diving	1.6	1.9	0.8	1.9	0.9
Horseback riding on trails	6.3	8.0	0.8	7.8	0.8
Rafting	7.5	9.8	0.8	9.5	0.8

Table 14.4 Participation profile of the Nonconsumptive Moderates personality and ratios of cluster and population-wide participation percentages by activity, 2000–2001 *continued*

Activity	% in Cluster Participating	% Participation if NOT in Cluster	Ratio of Column 1 to Column 2	% of U.S. Population Participating	Ratio of Column 1 to Column 4
Motorboating	18.8	25.1	0.8	24.4	0.8
Anadromous fishing	3.4	4.5	0.7	4.4	0.8
Waterskiing	6.1	8.4	0.7	8.1	0.8
Rowing	3.3	4.6	0.7	4.4	0.7
Canoeing	7.2	10.1	0.7	9.7	0.7
Snowmobiling	3.9	5.8	0.7	5.6	0.7
Gathering mushrooms, berries	18.3	29.8	0.6	28.5	0.6
Primitive camping	10.0	16.8	0.6	16.0	0.6
Viewing/photographing fish	14.1	24.6	0.6	23.4	0.6
Viewing/photographing flowers	25.0	44.8	0.6	42.5	0.6
Warmwater fishing	13.1	23.8	0.6	22.5	0.6
Coldwater fishing	7.3	14.4	0.5	13.5	0.5
Viewing/photographing wildlife	21.2	44.8	0.5	42.0	0.5
Viewing/photographing birds	14.5	32.7	0.4	30.6	0.5
Big game hunting	3.2	9.1	0.4	8.4	0.4
Small game hunting	2.2	7.9	0.3	7.2	0.3
Driving off-road	4.7	19.2	0.3	17.5	0.3
Migratory bird hunting	0.6	2.6	0.2	2.4	0.2
Sightseeing	10.2	57.3	0.2	51.7	0.2
Driving for pleasure	6.7	57.1	0.1	51.1	0.1

Source: NSRE 2000–2001. Versions 1–9, N = 42,868, Interview dates: 7/99 to 7/01.

and driving for pleasure. The list of favored activities for this group is relatively short and focused.

Activities not favored by the nature lovers include surfing, snorkeling, scuba diving, waterskiing, swimming, kayaking, jetskiing, rafting, windsurfing, snowboarding, visiting a beach, canoeing, rowing, snowmobiling, sailing, and snow skiing. All of these not favored activities are either water-based or snow/ice-based, and most require some degree of physical exertion and skill. Hunting and fishing are also low relative to the general population for this outdoor personality.

The demographics of the Nature Lovers shows more than three fifths to be female, nearly the same proportion to be over 45, and shows more Hispanic participation than most other personalities. Compared to national proportions this group is slightly underrepresented in the lowest and two highest income groups. This group is also more rural than the population generally and disproportionately from the West North Central states, such as Minnesota and the Dakotas, and from the Mountain states, such as Colorado, Wyoming, and Utah.

The Water Bugs (13.3%)

Most people are drawn to water as an outdoor recreation venue. The Outdoor Recreation Resources Review Commission reported that as far back as the 1960s. However, some are obviously drawn more than others. Although the Water Bugs are generally very active, participation in more than two thirds is greater than the national rate. Participation in water-based activities is the single most distinguishing characteristic of this group (Table 14.6, pp. 252–253). Going to the beach or other watersides, swimming, snorkeling, sailing, motorboating, saltwater fishing, scuba diving, kayaking, and surfing are among the favored activities of this group, relative to the rest of the population. Other favored activities where participation is at least 1.5 times the national rate include viewing, photographing and learning about various aspects of nature, such as wildflowers and birds; sightseeing and driving for pleasure; visiting nature centers, historic and prehistoric sites; and picnicking.

Activities not especially favored by the Water Bugs include hunting, primitive camping, backpacking, snowmobiling, skiing (both water and snow), and (generally) motorized recreation. Other than motorboating, this outdoor personality is muscle-power oriented in water venues and into viewing and learning activities. As with the Nature Lovers, this group is nearly two thirds women and disproportionately White. Unlike the Nature Lovers, this group is more middle aged, has a higher proportion who are upper income, is much more U.S.-born (than foreign-born), more urban, and disproportionately from the New England, Middle Atlantic and South Atlantic or Southern coastal states (which helps to explain their affinity for beach and water-based activities).

The Backcountry Actives (8.6%)

This outdoor personality is a very active group, participating at a higher rate than the national average for all but four activities, It stands out from other groups by its high relative percentages who backpack, primitive camp, visit wilderness, day hike, cross-country ski, and camp in developed areas all at a rate at least 2.5 times that of the general population (Table 14.7, pp. 254–255). This group also is into gathering natural products, visiting prehistoric sites, fishing (especially in coldwater), driving off-road, horseback riding, and viewing/ learning activities. Kayaking, mountain biking, canoeing are also among the favored activities. Only motorized water activities and other marine recreation are off this group's list of favored activities.

The demographics of this group shows it to be more male than female, predominantly White (with greater than proportionate representation by Native Americans), U.S.-born, disproportionately rural, and disproportionately from the Mountain and Pacific states. This is logical given the relative abundance of backcountry recreation opportunities in the western United States. Participation is significantly higher among the younger age groups as expected, with persons ages 65 and older participating at just slightly more than one third their proportion of the population. Like Water Bugs, participants are centered around the middle income groups, with the lowest income earners the most underrepresented.

The Outdoor Avids (7.5%)

Higher than average participation across the entire spectrum of outdoor recreation activities is the most distinguishing characteristics of the Outdoor Avids. Canoeing, scuba diving, windsurfing, waterskiing, cross-country skiing, rowing, rafting, kayaking, and snowmobiling make this group stand out relative to the other 7 outdoor recreation personalities. The Outdoor Avids participate in these 9 activities at a rate 5 times or more than that of the general population (Table 14.8, pp. 256–257). Many of this group's most favored activities require a good deal of both skill and physical exertion. Not only is participation proportionately higher for all activities but also the degree to which nearly all activities surpass the national participation rate is what makes this group truly the "Avids." For all but 10 of the 48 activities listed, this group participates at more than double the national proportion. For 27 of the 48, this group's participation rate is three times the national population rate. Only surfing and windsurfing have less than 10% participation, but even this is 5 to 6 times the national population participation rate.

Visiting wilderness, swimming, viewing/photographing natural scenery, wildlife and birds, visiting beaches, visiting nature centers, and walking are others among this group's favored activities. Well over half of this group also participate in primitive camping, warmwater fishing, mountain biking, viewing/ photographing fish, gathering natural products, and motorboating. They are

Table 14.5 Participation profile of the Nature Lovers personality and ratios of cluster and population-wide participation percentages by activity, 2000–2001

Activity	% in Cluster Participating	% Participation if NOT in Cluster	Ratio of Column 1 to Column 2	% of U.S. Population Participating	Ratio of Column 1 to Column 4
Viewing/photographing birds	64.6	25.7	2.5	30.6	2.1
Viewing/photographing flowers	86.9	36.1	2.4	42.5	2.1
Viewing/photographing wildlife	74.5	37.3	2.0	42.0	1.8
Viewing/photographing scenery	89.8	51.8	1.7	56.6	1.6
Viewing/photographing fish	25.8	23.0	1.1	23.4	1.1
Visiting nature centers	62.0	56.3	1.1	57.0	1.1
Walking for pleasure	89.5	82.0	1.1	82.9	1.1
Visiting historic sites	48.4	45.6	1.1	46.0	1.1
Picnicking	57.3	54.0	1.1	54.4	1.1
Family gathering	75.9	73.0	1.0	73.3	1.0
Sightseeing	53.6	51.5	1.0	51.7	1.0
Gathering mushrooms, berries	29.0	28.4	1.0	28.5	1.0
Driving for pleasure	51.0	51.2	1.0	51.1	1.0
Visiting prehistoric sites	19.8	20.9	0.9	20.8	1.0
Visiting a wilderness	28.2	33.3	0.9	32.6	0.9
Day hiking	28.0	33.9	0.8	33.2	0.8
Warmwater fishing	16.0	23.4	0.7	22.5	0.7
Horseback riding on trails	5.3	8.1	0.7	7.8	0.7
Big game hunting	5.0	8.9	0.6	8.4	0.6
Developed camping	15.6	27.9	0.6	26.4	0.6
Coldwater fishing	7.5	14.4	0.5	13.5	0.6
Driving off-road	9.6	18.5	0.5	17.5	0.6
Mountain biking	11.6	22.8	0.5	21.4	0.5
Small game hunting	3.7	7.7	0.5	7.2	0.5
Motorboating	11.3	26.2	0.4	24.4	0.5
Saltwater fishing	4.5	11.2	0.4	10.3	0.4
Anadromous fishing	1.8	4.8	0.4	4.4	0.4
Migratory bird hunting	0.9	2.6	0.3	2.4	0.4

Table 14.5 Participation profile of the Nature Lovers personality and ratios of cluster and population-wide participation percentages by activity, 2000–2001 *continued*

Activity	% in Cluster Participating	% Participation if NOT in Cluster	Ratio of Column 1 to Column 2	% of U.S. Population Participating	Ratio of Column 1 to Column 4
Primitive camping	5.8	17.5	0.3	16.0	0.4
Visiting watersides besides beach	9.3	28.3	0.3	25.9	0.4
Backpacking	3.7	11.7	0.3	10.7	0.4
Cross-country skiing	1.3	4.2	0.3	3.8	0.4
Downhill skiing	3.0	9.3	0.3	8.5	0.4
Sailing	1.7	5.6	0.3	5.1	0.3
Snowmobiling	1.8	6.1	0.3	5.6	0.3
Rowing	1.4	4.8	0.3	4.4	0.3
Canoeing	3.0	10.7	0.3	9.7	0.3
Visiting a beach	11.8	44.6	0.3	40.5	0.3
Snowboarding	1.2	5.4	0.2	4.9	0.2
Windsurfing	0.2	0.9	0.2	0.8	0.2
Rafting	2.2	10.6	0.2	9.5	0.2
Jetskiing	2.1	10.6	0.2	9.5	0.2
Kayaking	0.7	3.9	0.2	3.5	0.2
Swimming in lakes, ponds	6.9	46.7	0.2	41.7	0.2
Waterskiing	1.0	9.2	0.1	8.1	0.1
Scuba diving	0.2	2.1	0.1	1.9	0.1
Snorkeling	0.7	7.5	0.1	6.7	0.1
Surfing	0.1	1.9	0.1	1.7	0.1

Source: NSRE 2000–2001. Versions 1–9, N = 42,868, Interview dates: 7/99 to 7/01.

Table 14.6 Participation profile of the Water Bugs personality and ratios of cluster and population-wide participation percentages by activity, 2000–2001

Activity	% in Cluster Participating	% Participation if NOT in Cluster	Ratio of Column 1 to Column 2	% of U.S. Population Participating	Ratio of Column 1 to Column 4
Visiting a beach	89.1	33.1	2.7	40.5	2.2
Visiting watersides (other than beach)	56.4	21.3	2.7	25.9	2.2
Swimming in lakes, ponds	82.1	35.5	2.3	41.7	2.0
Snorkeling	12.6	5.7	2.2	6.7	1.9
Sailing	9.6	4.4	2.2	5.1	1.9
Viewing/photographing flowers	79.7	36.4	2.2	42.5	1.9
Viewing/photographing birds	55.4	26.7	2.1	30.6	1.8
Viewing/photographing fish	40.8	20.7	2.0	23.4	1.8
Sightseeing	90.0	45.9	2.0	51.7	1.7
Driving for pleasure	88.6	45.4	2.0	51.1	1.7
Visiting historic sites	78.9	40.9	1.9	46.0	1.7
Viewing/photographing other wildlife	71.5	37.4	1.9	42.0	1.7
Viewing/photographing natural scenery	94.1	50.8	1.9	56.6	1.7
Visiting nature centers	84.8	52.7	1.6	57.0	1.5
Visiting prehistoric sites	30.7	19.3	1.6	20.8	1.5
Motorboating	35.8	22.6	1.6	24.4	1.5
Picnicking	78.8	50.7	1.6	54.4	1.5
Rowing	5.9	4.2	1.4	4.4	1.3
Scuba diving	2.4	1.8	1.4	1.9	1.3
Saltwater fishing	13.4	9.9	1.4	10.3	1.3
Kayaking	4.5	3.3	1.4	3.5	1.3
Surfing	2.0	1.6	1.2	1.7	1.2
Family gathering	87.2	71.2	1.2	73.3	1.2
Visiting a wilderness	37.8	31.8	1.2	32.6	1.2
Walking for pleasure	95.9	81.0	1.2	82.9	1.2
Horseback riding on trails	8.5	7.6	1.1	7.8	1.1
Rafting	10.4	9.4	1.1	9.5	1.1
Canoeing	10.4	9.6	1.1	9.7	1.1

Table 14.6 Participation profile of the Water Bugs personality and ratios of cluster and population-wide participation percentages by activity, 2000–2001 *continued*

Activity	% in Cluster Participating	% Participation if NOT in Cluster	Ratio of Column 1 to Column 2	% of U.S. Population Participating	Ratio of Column 1 to Column 4
Developed camping	28.2	26.1	1.1	26.4	1.1
Mountain biking	22.7	21.2	1.1	21.4	1.1
Cross-country skiing	4.0	3.8	1.0	3.8	1.0
Day hiking	33.7	33.1	1.0	33.2	1.0
Gathering mushrooms, berries	28.7	28.4	1.0	28.5	1.0
Jetskiing	9.5	9.5	1.0	9.5	1.0
Windsurfing	0.7	0.8	0.9	0.8	0.9
Downhill skiing	7.6	8.7	0.9	8.5	0.9
Driving off-road	14.7	17.9	0.8	17.5	0.8
Warmwater fishing	18.9	23.1	0.8	22.5	0.8
Anadromous fishing	3.4	4.5	0.7	4.4	0.8
Waterskiing	5.8	8.5	0.7	8.1	0.7
Snowboarding	3.3	5.1	0.7	4.9	0.7
Coldwater fishing	8.1	14.4	0.6	13.5	0.6
Snowmobiling	2.9	6.0	0.5	5.6	0.5
Backpacking	5.0	11.5	0.4	10.7	0.5
Small game hunting	2.6	7.9	0.3	7.2	0.4
Primitive camping	5.0	17.7	0.3	16.0	0.3
Migratory bird hunting	0.7	2.6	0.3	2.4	0.3
Big game hunting	2.2	9.4	0.2	8.4	0.3

Source: NSRE 2000–2001. Versions 1–9, N = 42,868, Interview dates: 7/99 to 7/01.

Table 14.7 Participation profile of the Backcountry Actives personality and ratios of cluster and population-wide participation percentages by activity, 2000–2001

Activity	% in Cluster Participating	% Participation if NOT in Cluster	Ratio of Column 1 to Column 2	% of U.S. Population Participating	Ratio of Column 1 to Column 4
Backpacking	40.7	7.8	5.2	10.7	3.8
Primitive camping	59.9	11.9	5.1	16.0	3.8
Visiting a wilderness	84.8	27.7	3.1	32.6	2.6
Day hiking	83.4	28.5	2.9	33.2	2.5
Cross-country skiing	9.5	3.3	2.9	3.8	2.5
Developed camping	64.9	22.7	2.9	26.4	2.5
Gathering mushrooms, berries	67.7	24.8	2.7	28.5	2.4
Visiting prehistoric sites	49.2	18.1	2.7	20.8	2.4
Coldwater fishing	30.1	12.0	2.5	13.5	2.2
Driving off-road	35.6	15.8	2.3	17.5	2.0
Kayaking	6.9	3.1	2.2	3.5	2.0
Mountain biking	42.5	19.4	2.2	21.4	2.0
Viewing/photographing other wildlife	81.9	38.2	2.1	42.0	2.0
Canoeing	18.4	8.9	2.1	9.7	1.9
Horseback riding on trails	14.1	7.2	2.0	7.8	1.8
Viewing/photographing flowers	76.2	39.3	1.9	42.5	1.8
Viewing/photographing birds	52.7	28.5	1.9	30.6	1.7
Viewing/photographing fish	39.7	21.8	1.8	23.4	1.7
Anadromous fishing	7.4	4.1	1.8	4.4	1.7
Visiting historic sites	77.4	43.0	1.8	46.0	1.7
Viewing/photographing natural scenery	92.0	53.2	1.7	56.6	1.6
Visiting watersides (other than beach)	41.2	24.5	1.7	25.9	1.6
Visiting nature centers	88.7	54.0	1.6	57.0	1.6
Downhill skiing	13.2	8.1	1.6	8.5	1.6
Big game hunting	13.0	8.0	1.6	8.4	1.6
Driving for pleasure	78.7	48.6	1.6	51.1	1.5
Picnicking	82.9	51.7	1.6	54.4	1.5
Sightseeing	77.9	49.3	1.6	51.7	1.5

Table 14.7 Participation profile of the Backcountry Actives personality and ratios of cluster and population-wide participation percentages by activity, 2000–2001 *continued*

Activity	% in Cluster Participating	% Participation if NOT in Cluster	Ratio of Column 1 to Column 2	% of U.S. Population Participating	Ratio of Column 1 to Column 4
Warmwater fishing	33.4	21.5	1.6	22.5	1.5
Rowing	6.2	4.2	1.5	4.4	1.4
Snowmobiling	7.8	5.4	1.5	5.6	1.4
Windsurfing	1.1	0.8	1.4	0.8	1.4
Swimming in lakes, ponds	57.9	40.2	1.4	41.7	1.4
Snowboarding	6.8	4.7	1.4	4.9	1.4
Small game hunting	9.8	7.0	1.4	7.2	1.4
Sailing	6.2	5.0	1.2	5.1	1.2
Family gathering	88.2	71.9	1.2	73.3	1.2
Walking for pleasure	95.7	81.7	1.2	82.9	1.2
Rafting	10.8	9.4	1.2	9.5	1.1
Visiting a beach	45.8	40.0	1.1	40.5	1.1
Migratory bird hunting	2.6	2.3	1.1	2.4	1.1
Scuba diving	2.1	1.9	1.1	1.9	1.1
Surfing	1.7	1.7	1.0	1.7	1.0
Snorkeling	6.4	6.7	1.0	6.7	1.0
Saltwater fishing	9.7	10.4	0.9	10.3	1.0
Motorboating	19.5	24.8	0.8	24.4	0.9
Jetskiing	4.4	10.0	0.4	9.5	0.8
Waterskiing	2.8	8.7	0.3	8.1	0.3

Source: NSRE 2000–2001. Versions 1–9, N = 42,868, Interview dates: 7/99 to 7/01.

Table 14.8 Participation profile of the Outdoor Avids personality and ratios of cluster and population-wide participation percentages by activity, 2000–2001

Activity	% in Cluster Participating	% Participation if NOT in Cluster	Ratio of Column 1 to Column 2	% of U.S. Population Participating	Ratio of Column 1 to Column 4
Windsurfing	4.9	0.5	10.3	0.8	6.0
Waterskiing	45.4	5.1	8.9	8.1	5.6
Rafting	52.0	6.1	8.6	9.5	5.5
Scuba diving	10.1	1.2	8.5	1.9	5.4
Canoeing	50.2	6.4	7.8	9.7	5.2
Rowing	22.6	2.9	7.8	4.4	5.1
Kayaking	17.6	2.3	7.6	3.5	5.1
Snowmobiling	28.0	3.8	7.4	5.6	5.0
Cross-country skiing	19.1	2.6	7.3	3.8	5.0
Surfing	8.3	1.1	7.3	1.7	4.9
Snorkeling	30.8	4.7	6.6	6.7	4.6
Jetskiing	43.3	6.8	6.4	9.5	4.6
Snowboarding	21.5	3.6	6.0	4.9	4.4
Migratory bird hunting	10.1	1.7	5.8	2.4	4.3
Downhill skiing	35.8	6.4	5.6	8.5	4.2
Sailing	21.3	3.8	5.6	5.1	4.2
Anadromous fishing	18.2	3.3	5.6	4.4	4.2
Backpacking	44.0	8.0	5.5	10.7	4.1
Primitive camping	58.7	12.5	4.7	16.0	3.7
Coldwater fishing	48.1	10.8	4.5	13.5	3.6
Motorboating	85.9	19.4	4.4	24.4	3.5
Small game hunting	25.2	5.8	4.3	7.2	3.5
Driving off-road	56.1	14.4	3.9	17.5	3.2
Big game hunting	26.9	7.0	3.9	8.4	3.2
Saltwater fishing	32.4	8.5	3.8	10.3	3.1
Horseback riding on trails	23.8	6.5	3.7	7.8	3.1
Mountain biking	63.6	18.0	3.5	21.4	3.0
Viewing/photographing fish	65.1	20.0	3.3	23.4	2.8

Table 14.8 Participation profile of the Outdoor Avids personality and ratios of cluster and population-wide participation percentages by activity, 2000–2001 *continued*

Activity	% in Cluster Participating	% Participation if NOT in Cluster	Ratio of Column 1 to Column 2	% of U.S. Population Participating	Ratio of Column 1 to Column 4
Warmwater fishing	62.3	19.3	3.2	22.5	2.8
Visiting watersides (other than beach)	70.9	22.3	3.2	25.9	2.7
Developed camping	67.0	23.1	2.9	26.4	2.5
Gathering mushrooms, berries	70.9	25.0	2.8	28.5	2.5
Visiting a wilderness	81.3	28.7	2.8	32.6	2.5
Day hiking	76.4	29.7	2.6	33.2	2.3
Swimming in lakes, ponds	94.6	37.4	2.5	41.7	2.3
Visiting prehistoric sites	46.3	18.7	2.5	20.8	2.2
Visiting a beach	84.6	36.9	2.3	40.5	2.1
Viewing/photographing other wildlife	85.8	38.4	2.2	42.0	2.0
Viewing/photographing flowers	78.4	39.5	2.0	42.5	1.9
Viewing/photographing birds	55.3	28.5	1.9	30.6	1.8
Visiting historic sites	81.9	43.1	1.9	46.0	1.8
Viewing/photographing natural scenery	94.0	53.5	1.8	56.6	1.7
Visiting nature centers	90.4	54.3	1.7	57.0	1.6
Driving for pleasure	81.1	48.7	1.7	51.1	1.6
Sightseeing	80.0	49.5	1.6	51.7	1.6
Picnicking	82.2	52.2	1.6	54.4	1.5
Family gathering	92.2	71.8	1.3	73.3	1.3
Walking for pleasure	95.0	82.0	1.2	82.9	1.1

Source: NSRE 2000–2001. Versions 1–9, N = 42,868, Interview dates: 7/99 to 7/01.

more active than Americans in general in every single activity, from backpacking to walking for pleasure.

This group is also quite different demographically with relatively high proportions of males (62%), Whites (87%), persons under 45 (80%), and persons under 25 (34%). Higher proportions than the population are in upper income brackets (34% in households earning $75,000 or more annually), born in the U.S. (98%), and from New England, West North Central, East North Central, and Mountain states.

The Motorized Consumptives (7.5%)

Hunting, fishing, and motorized activities (on land, water, and snow) are the activities that most distinguish this group (Table 14.9, pp. 260–261). Somewhat larger percentages than the national population participate in water activities and camping. Somewhat lower percentages participate in viewing, photographing, learning activities. Like the Outdoor Avids, this is a very active group, though not to the same extent nor in the same activities. The main difference is that this group seems to prefer hunting and fishing (the "consumptive" activities) and motorized the most, as opposed to muscle-powered activities. Outdoor Avids participate in motorized activities at about the same rates as the Motorized Consumptives, but the real difference is the substantially lower participation by the Motorized Consumptives in the physically demanding and challenging activities. For example, 17.6% of Avids went kayaking, compared to just 3.8% of Motorized Consumptives.

The demographics of this outdoor personality show it to have many more males than any other group, to be 85% White, to have almost 60% under age 35 (39% under 25), and almost all U.S.-born. They are primarily middle income earners (60% in households making between $25,000 and $75,000), they are much more rural than any other group, and they are disproportionately from the Midwest and South (i.e., East North Central, West North Central, East South Central, West South Central, and South Atlantic).

Comparison of Demographic Characteristics

The preceding sections described separately the demographic composition of each outdoor recreation personality. In Table 14.10 (pp. 262–263) full demographic profiles of all 8 groups are compared. The proportion of the U.S. population within each cluster is repeated in the table's 1st line. Nearly one fourth (23.9%) of the U.S. population are labelled Inactives. Individuals in this group are very limited in their recreation participation with only a few participating in any of the recreation activities listed in previous tables. A full 25% of Inactives are in the lowest income group (under $15,000 annually), more than twice that of any other cluster. Inactives also have the lowest proportion of Whites and the largest proportion of Hispanics by a wide margin, and together with the Passives, they have a much larger share of African Americans than the other 6 clusters.

Males and the youngest age group dominate the 2 most active segments, Outdoor Avids and Motorized Consumptives. Females comprise a noticeably larger proportion of both the Nature Lovers and Water Bugs. The largest segment of those age 65 and older are in the Inactives group (29%), but the Nature Lovers are close behind with more than 25% of their numbers in the oldest age group. The highest income group, earning $100,000 or more annually, is most visible in the Outdoor Avids (20%), by a fairly wide margin. The Water Bugs are 2nd with 15% of their members in the highest income group. The most notable information about place of birth is the very large proportion (both above 98%) of American-born in the Outdoor Avids and Motorized Consumptives segments.

Nonconsumptive Moderates have the greatest share of metropolitan residents. And as mentioned earlier, the Motorized Consumptives have by far the largest proportion of nonmetropolitan members. Regional trends are not that conspicuous, except for beach and water-oriented clusters. Water Bugs and Nonconsumptive Moderates, are understandably more prevalent in coastal regions, especially the South Atlantic and Pacific. The 2 western regions, Mountain and Pacific, predictably dominated the Backcountry Actives group, with about 36% of individuals with that outdoor personality living in those regions.

Table 14.9 Participation profile of the Motorized Consumptives personality and ratios of cluster and population-wide participation percentages by activity, 2000–2001

Activity	% in Cluster Participating	% Participation if NOT in Cluster	Ratio of Column 1 to Column 2	% of U.S. Population Participating	Ratio of Column 1 to Column 4
Migratory bird hunting	11.9	1.6	7.5	2.4	5.1
Small game hunting	34.6	5.1	6.9	7.2	4.8
Big game hunting	40.1	5.9	6.8	8.4	4.8
Waterskiing	33.5	6.1	5.5	8.1	4.1
Jetskiing	34.6	7.5	4.6	9.5	3.6
Warmwater fishing	73.1	18.4	4.0	22.5	3.3
Motorboating	75.0	20.3	3.7	24.4	3.1
Snowmobiling	17.1	4.6	3.7	5.6	3.1
Driving off-road	53.4	14.6	3.7	17.5	3.1
Coldwater fishing	37.2	11.6	3.2	13.5	2.8
Anadromous fishing	11.9	3.8	3.2	4.4	2.7
Snowboarding	12.4	4.3	2.9	4.9	2.5
Rafting	22.8	8.5	2.7	9.5	2.4
Saltwater fishing	24.1	9.2	2.6	10.3	2.3
Primitive camping	33.8	14.6	2.3	16.0	2.1
Surfing	3.5	1.5	2.3	1.7	2.1
Scuba diving	3.8	1.7	2.2	1.9	2.0
Horseback riding on trails	14.6	7.2	2.0	7.8	1.9
Gathering mushrooms, berries	50.4	26.7	1.9	28.5	1.8
Swimming in lakes, ponds	73.8	39.1	1.9	41.7	1.8
Developed camping	46.3	24.8	1.9	26.4	1.8
Downhill skiing	14.9	8.0	1.9	8.5	1.7
Canoeing	16.3	9.2	1.8	9.7	1.7
Rowing	7.3	4.2	1.8	4.4	1.7
Visiting a wilderness	50.2	31.2	1.6	32.6	1.5
Windsurfing	1.2	0.8	1.6	0.8	1.5
Visiting watersides besides beach	38.3	24.9	1.5	25.9	1.5
Viewing/photographing fish	33.5	22.5	1.5	23.4	1.4

Table 14.9 Participation profile of the Motorized Consumptives personality and ratios of cluster and population-wide participation percentages by activity, 2000–2001 *continued*

Activity	% in Cluster Participating	% Participation if NOT in Cluster	Ratio of Column 1 to Column 2	% of U.S. Population Participating	Ratio of Column 1 to Column 4
Snorkeling	9.6	6.4	1.5	6.7	1.4
Mountain biking	29.7	20.7	1.4	21.4	1.4
Visiting a beach	52.8	39.5	1.3	40.5	1.3
Driving for pleasure	66.0	49.9	1.3	51.1	1.3
Family gathering	81.4	72.7	1.1	73.3	1.1
Kayaking	3.8	3.4	1.1	3.5	1.1
Viewing/photographing other wildlife	45.6	41.7	1.1	42.0	1.1
Sightseeing	55.2	51.4	1.1	51.7	1.1
Backpacking	10.8	10.7	1.0	10.7	1.0
Walking for pleasure	82.3	83.0	1.0	82.9	1.0
Sailing	4.8	5.1	0.9	5.1	0.9
Cross-country skiing	3.4	3.9	0.9	3.8	0.9
Viewing/photographing natural scenery	50.7	57.1	0.9	56.6	0.9
Day hiking	29.5	33.5	0.9	33.2	0.9
Visiting nature centers	50.0	57.6	0.9	57.0	0.9
Picnicking	47.8	55.0	0.9	54.4	0.9
Visiting historic sites	37.2	46.7	0.8	46.0	0.8
Visiting prehistoric sites	12.5	21.5	0.6	20.8	0.6
Viewing/photographing flowers	22.8	44.1	0.5	42.5	0.5
Viewing/photographing birds	14.3	31.9	0.5	30.6	0.5

Source: NSRE 2000–2001. Versions 1–9, N = 42,868, Interview dates: 7/99 to 7/01.

Table 14.10 Comparison of demographic characteristics among 8 outdoor personalities, 2000–2001

Demographic Group	Inactives	Passives	Nonconsumptive Moderates	Nature Lovers	Water Bugs	Backcountry Actives	Outdoor Avids	Motorized Consumptives
% of NSRE Sample	23.9	15.0	11.7	12.5	13.3	8.6	7.5	7.5
Gender								
Male	46.3	42.4	48.2	38.4	37.2	54.8	62.2	70.2
Female	53.7	57.6	51.8	61.6	62.8	45.2	37.8	29.8
Race/Ethnicity								
White, non-Hispanic	49.5	62.3	62.0	71.2	79.3	81.5	87.2	85.4
Black, non-Hispanic	20.9	19.0	12.2	11.1	8.6	4.4	2.7	4.8
American Indian, non-Hispanic	0.5	0.7	0.5	0.6	0.5	1.1	1.1	0.9
Asian/Pacific Islander, non-Hispanic	3.9	3.8	6.2	2.8	3.7	2.3	2.2	1.3
Hispanic	25.2	14.3	19.1	14.3	7.9	10.7	6.7	7.7
Age								
16–24	15.8	17.0	29.6	10.5	14.1	19.5	33.9	39.0
25–34	12.7	16.4	20.9	11.2	16.7	19.1	20.7	20.2
35–44	15.0	17.7	21.6	17.4	25.0	26.8	25.6	19.4
45–54	14.7	16.2	12.6	19.5	20.4	18.9	13.1	11.1
55–64	12.5	12.5	7.6	16.0	11.6	9.4	4.4	5.6
65+	29.3	20.2	7.7	25.4	12.1	6.2	2.4	4.7
Household Income								
<$15,000	25.2	11.9	10.5	12.3	5.0	8.9	5.8	6.2
$15,000–$24,999	21.0	16.3	14.0	16.7	9.6	11.3	6.9	10.1
$25,000–$49,999	31.3	35.9	33.1	33.1	32.9	34.4	29.1	36.0
$50,000–$74,999	12.1	19.2	19.3	20.4	24.4	24.4	24.1	24.2
$75,000–$99,999	4.7	8.5	10.2	8.8	13.2	11.2	13.9	12.3
$100,000+	5.8	8.2	12.9	8.7	14.9	9.9	20.2	11.3

Table 14.10 Comparison of demographic characteristics among 8 outdoor personalities, 2000–2001 *continued*

Demographic Group	Inactives	Passives	Nonconsumptive Moderates	Nature Lovers	Water Bugs	Backcountry Actives	Outdoor Avids	Motorized Consumptives
Citizenship								
U.S. citizen	81.0	90.7	87.8	91.0	95.5	95.6	98.1	98.2
Foreign born	19.0	9.3	12.2	9.0	4.5	4.4	1.9	1.8
Metropolitan Status								
Nonmetro resident	20.0	19.2	12.6	24.3	15.1	23.6	22.5	30.2
Metro area resident	80.0	80.8	87.4	75.7	84.9	76.4	77.5	69.8
Region								
New England	5.1	6.2	7.9	5.2	10.0	7.4	10.0	5.1
Middle Atlantic	12.4	12.7	14.7	11.6	13.1	9.7	8.6	7.9
East North Central	11.8	14.4	13.6	14.2	14.0	11.6	15.3	14.9
West North Central	7.5	8.6	6.7	10.4	6.7	8.9	9.3	12.9
South Atlantic	18.2	17.7	19.0	14.9	21.2	12.1	15.2	16.6
East South Central	7.8	7.7	4.1	7.0	6.1	5.4	5.0	10.1
West South Central	13.7	11.0	8.4	12.5	8.1	8.6	8.1	13.2
Mountain	7.8	8.6	6.8	10.4	5.8	17.6	12.3	8.7
Pacific	15.7	13.0	18.8	13.6	15.0	18.7	16.2	10.7

Chapter 15
The Enthusiasts

Some Americans like a little outdoor recreation mixed in with an easy pace of life and a laid-back lifestyle. Others like an ongoing diet of a variety of activities but never in large portions or for extended times, because they are busy with many things. And then there are the outdoor Enthusiasts.

We all know someone who is an Enthusiast at something: obsessed with keeping up with sports, devoted to collecting antiques, driven to travel the world over, or genuinely loves the outdoors and experiencing it firsthand. This chapter looks at the most active outdoor recreation participants. Daily, if not more than once a day, these folks engage themselves in a variety of outdoor activities, seemingly as if there would be no such opportunities tomorrow. In earlier research Cordell and colleagues (1999) found that while for most activities, these most active of outdoor recreationists make up less than 10% of the population, yet they account for between 70% and 90% of the population-wide number of activity days of participation. These most active of outdoor recreation participants are called the Enthusiasts. As we have defined them, Enthusiasts are the most active one third of all participants in any given activity. Their level of activeness is measured in terms of the number of days during a year on which they participate in a chosen activity. For example, the definition of a day hiking Enthusiast would include the upper third of day hiking participants (i.e., those who put in the equivalent of the 67th percentile or more days of participation per year). As used in previous chapters, a day of participation is any amount of time or number of times spent in an activity on a single day. Participation in more than 1 activity counts as multiple "activity days," 1 counted for each activity in which a person participated.

In public land management or in marketing outdoor equipment or services, the Enthusiast is a primary target. Because Enthusiasts are, by far, putting in more days participating than the majority of Americans, the Enthusiasts are the people one most often sees using federal or state lands for outdoor recreation. Likewise, because they participate more and thus use more equipment and services, the Enthusiasts are also the people spending and consuming the most at private outdoor recreation businesses. For these reasons, public- and private-sector suppliers alike need to be fully informed about who the Enthusiasts are and what they do in the out-of-doors.

Highlights

Enthusiasts are the most active of participants in outdoor activities—the participants who put in the highest number of days per year. Table 15.1 (pp. 268–269) summarizes the participation characteristics of this highly important group of outdoor participants. The 1st characteristic of Enthusiasts that stands out is the low percentages of the overall U.S. population of persons 16 or older who participate at a level sufficient to qualify them as an Enthusiast. Across the activities listed in Table 15.1, percentages of the population who are Enthusiasts fall mostly under 5%. The Enthusiasts are truly a minority of the population. Yet, they account for most of the nation's activity days of participation by a wide margin. For almost all activities, Enthusiasts account for 70% up to almost 90% of participation days summed across all participants in any given activity.

While they represent the upper third of most active participants, within their ranks Enthusiasts themselves vary widely in number of days per year on which they pursue their chosen activities. Days per year for surfing Enthusiasts, for example, range from 13 to 365 per year. For snowboarding, the range is 7 to 60 days per year. But Enthusiast participants are not distributed evenly across these ranges of days of participation. When comparing percentages of Enthusiasts within each of 3 equal intervals of days, it is evident that most Enthusiasts participate at levels near the lower bound of their range for days of participation (i.e., the number of days found at the 67th percentile). In Table 15.1, for

Surfing has held its own as a water activity over the years. Photo courtesy of Jon Sullivan

example, over 91% of wilderness Enthusiasts participate in the lower ranges of 7 to 126 days. Nearly all kayaker, rock climber, mountain climber, backpacker, and caver Enthusiasts also participate at levels within the lower third of the range of days per year. Very small percentages of Enthusiasts typically participate at levels placing them in the upper third of the range of days for Enthusiasts.

Across activities for which participation has been tracked between the 1994–1995 and 2000–2001 surveys, there have been trends in the participation characteristics of Enthusiasts. Generally, the percentages of the population that Enthusiasts represent have risen slightly. For some activities, however, the number of days of participation per year that an individual had to participate to qualify as an Enthusiast fell. Consistent with this trend, for a number of activities the percentage of total participation days accounted for by Enthusiasts fell modestly. Across the activities, percentages of Enthusiasts under 25 years of age decreased somewhat, while the percentages of Enthusiasts ages 45 and older rose.

The most dedicated half of Enthusiasts—that is, the half putting in the highest number of days participating in outdoor activities—are defined as Ultra Enthusiasts. The 1st distinguishing trait of Ultra Enthusiasts is that the lower bound on the number of activity days on which they participate is much higher than for Enthusiasts in general. To be an Ultra Enthusiasts in day hiking and mountain biking, for example, a person must participate in these activities at least 50 days per year. To be an Ultra Enthusiast in horseback riding, driving motor vehicles off-road, or small game hunting, someone must participate at least 30 days per year. Generally, Ultra Enthusiasts are composed of much higher percentages who are male, White, and under 25 when compared with other Enthusiasts. For snow/ice participants, minimum days of participation to be classified an Ultra Enthusiast are lower than for most land and water activities. Also, except for downhill skiing, most snow/ice Ultras are male and White, and many are under 25 years old.

The Enthusiasts
Land-Based Activities

Table 15.2 (pp. 271) gives results of analysis of days of participation across three levels of participation. It also shows in Column 1 the percentage of the population that puts in zero days of participation per year in each of the activities listed (i.e., the nonparticipants). The 1st level of participation represents those who put in the least number of days per year and represent the least active third of participants. For example, for day hiking, the least active third puts in 1 to 4 days per year. The moderately active, or middle one third, puts in 5 to 15 days of hiking per year. The most active third, the Enthusiasts, put in 16 to 365 days per year. In recording days of participation from survey respondents, no effort was made to challenge high reported numbers of days, for example, 365

Table 15.1 Participation characteristics of Enthusiasts for 34 outdoor activities, 2000–2001

Activity	Percent of Population Who Are Enthusiasts	Minimum Days per Year to Qualify as Enthusiast	Percent of Total Participation Days by Enthusiasts	Lower One Third of Enthusiast Days	Percent of Enthusiasts in Lower One Third Group	Middle One Third of Enthusiast Days	Percent of Enthusiasts in Middle One Third Group	High One Third of Enthusiast Days	Percent of Enthusiasts in High One Third Group
Surfing	0.5	13	89.0	13–130	85.1	131–247	9.4	248–365	5.5
Visiting a wilderness or other primitive area	10.3	7	88.9	7–126	91.5	127–245	2.2	246–365	6.3
Day hiking	10.4	16	88.5	16–132	73.4	133–248	13.9	249–365	12.8
Orienteering	0.6	7	85.6	7–46	83.2	47–85	3.1	86–125	13.7
Kayaking	1.2	5	84.2	5–110	98.3	111–215	1.0	216–320	0.7
Mountain biking	6.8	25	83.6	25–138	80.2	139–251	15.1	252–365	4.7
Saltwater fishing	3.1	8	83.5	8–127	95.7	128–246	3.1	247–365	1.2
Gathering mushrooms, berries	9.3	9	83.4	9–128	94.8	129–247	3.6	248–365	1.6
Scuba diving	0.6	6	83.3	6–126	96.9	129–247	2.0	247–365	1.2
Snorkeling	2.2	5	82.5	5–125	97.8	126–245	1.7	246–365	0.5
Rock climbing	1.4	4	82.4	4–86	97.1	87–168	1.4	169–250	1.5
Jetskiing	3.1	7	82.0	7–111	98.7	112–215	0.8	216–320	0.5
Mountain climbing	1.8	5	82.0	5–125	96.6	126–245	1.7	246–365	1.7
Rowing	1.4	5	81.0	5–125	98.4	126–245	1.2	246–364	0.4
Warmwater fishing	7.5	15	80.6	15–78	85.0	79–141	8.0	142–203	7.0
Canoeing	3.2	5	80.5	5–125	98.8	126–245	0.6	246–365	0.6
Coldwater fishing	4.3	11	80.3	11–129	96.0	130–247	2.7	248–365	1.3
Sailing	1.4	6	80.2	6–126	97.5	127–246	1.4	247–365	1.1
Backpacking	3.5	7	79.8	7–126	97.7	127–245	2.0	246–365	0.3
Waterskiing	2.6	8	79.0	8–127	99.4	128–246	0.5	247–365	0.1
Windsurfing	0.2	6	78.9	6–126	97.8	127–246	0.0	247–365	2.2
Walking for pleasure	26.3	101	77.8	101–189	35.2	190–277	20.3	278–365	44.4
Small game hunting	2.2	16	76.8	16–132	97.6	133–248	1.2	249–365	1.3
Swimming (outdoor pools)	11.8	21	76.6	21–136	94.1	137–251	3.6	252–365	2.3
Swimming (lakes, streams)	12.7	13	76.5	13–130	97.0	131–247	2.1	248–365	0.9

Table 15.1 Participation characteristics of Enthusiasts for 34 outdoor activities, 2000–2001 *continued*

Activity	Percent of Population Who Are Enthusiasts	Minimum Days per Year to Qualify as Enthusiast	Percent of Total Participation Days by Enthusiasts	Lower One Third of Enthusiast Days	Percent of Enthusiasts in Lower One Third Group	Middle One Third of Enthusiast Days	Percent of Enthusiasts in Middle One Third Group	High One Third of Enthusiast Days	Percent of Enthusiasts in High One Third Group
Anadromous fishing	1.3	7	76.3	7–65	96.3	66–123	1.4	124–180	2.3
Downhill skiing	2.6	7	76.1	7–85	97.9	86–163	1.7	164–240	0.4
Migratory bird hunting	0.8	12	75.5	12–130	99.4	131–248	0.0	249–365	0.6
Snowboarding	1.5	7	74.0	7–25	80.7	26–43	10.0	44–60	9.3
Rafting	2.9	4	72.7	4–23	88.8	24–42	10.0	43–60	1.2
Snowshoeing	0.5	6	72.2	6–37	92.2	38–68	6.3	69–98	1.5
Cross-country skiing	1.2	6	72.2	6–24	83.6	25–42	13.7	43–60	2.7
Big game hunting	2.6	15	69.9	15–60	91.2	61–105	5.5	106–150	3.3
Caving	0.9	3	58.0	3–53	99.2	54–103	0.0	104–153	0.8

for day hiking. A few in the country may in fact hike every day of the year. Enthusiasts for one activity are not necessarily the same people who are Enthusiasts for another activity. However, previous research on Enthusiasts has shown considerable crossover such that many who are Enthusiasts for 1 activity are also the Enthusiasts for 1 or more other activities.

The most active Enthusiasts' participation profile is shown in the last 2 columns in Table 15.2. Across the activities, Enthusiasts account for percentages of the population ranging from less than 1 for orienteering to just over 10 for visiting wild areas and day hiking. Most of these activities are physically challenging, yet upper ranges of participation for some Enthusiasts exceed 200 to 300 days per year. Lower bounds on the ranges of days is much more modest, ranging from 3 to 5 or up to 15 to 25.

Segmenting participants by levels of participation is highly informative for decision makers. In public land management, the people most affected by changing the way hiking trails are managed would be the Enthusiasts. Even though they are only about 10% of the population, they devote considerably more days to hiking than does the rest of the population or even the other two thirds of people who hike. Likewise for hunting, less than 3% of the population are the more avid hunters, but this is the group most affected by season limits and other hunting regulations. The Enthusiasts are also more likely to be the ones challenging policy changes. In marketing private sector goods or services, the Enthusiasts represent the primary markets. Target marketing to these participants is likely to pay off most in revenue and profits.

Many more people participate in the more passive, less physically active land activities, such as those listed in Table 15.3 (p. 272). The ranges of days of participation from the least to the most active (the Enthusiasts) are greater than for the more physically demanding activities shown in Table 15.2. At the upper end of activity days of participation in the activities in Table 15.3, the ranges include walking at 101 to 365 days per year and visiting prehistoric or archeological sites at 4 to 365 days per year. As a percentage of the population of noninstitutionalized persons 16 or older, Enthusiasts range from just over 5% for prehistoric site visitors to over 26% for walkers.

To be categorized as an Enthusiast, a participant must have participated on at least the number of days representing the bottom of the range of number of days shown in the last column in Table 15.3. For walking, a participant must have participated on at least 101 days to be classified as an Enthusiast walker. For birding, a participant must have participated on at least 31 days to be called an Enthusiast birder. A person need only have visited prehistoric sites 4 days to join the ranks of Enthusiasts.

Table 15.2 Percentages of U.S. population 16 or older not participating and percent by range of days of participation per year for 3 levels of activity days per year in physically active, land-based outdoor activities, 2000–2001

Activity	Percent of Population Who Do Not Participate	Least Active Third		Moderately Active Third		Enthusiasts Most Active Third	
		Percent of Population	Days per Year	Percent of Population	Days per Year	Percent of Population	Days per Year
Day hiking	66.7	11.5	1–4	11.5	5–15	10.4	16–365
Visiting a wilderness or primitive area	67.3	12.5	1–2	9.9	3–6	10.3	7–365
Mountain biking	78.6	7.2	1–5	7.4	6–24	6.8	25–365
Driving off-road	82.5	6.3	1–4	5.9	5–15	5.3	16–365
Primitive camping	84.0	7.0	1–3	3.8	4–6	5.2	7–330
Backpacking	89.3	4.8	1–3	2.3	4–6	3.5	7–365
Horseback riding	90.3	4.4	1–2	2.4	3–6	2.9	7–365
Big game hunting	91.6	3.0	1–5	2.7	6–14	2.6	15–150
Small game hunting	92.8	2.4	1–4	2.6	5–15	2.2	16–365
Mountain climbing	94.0	3.1	1–2	1.1	3–4	1.8	5–365
Rock climbing	95.7	1.6	1–1	1.3	2–3	1.4	4–250
Caving	95.7	2.5	1–1	0.8	2–2	0.9	3–153
Migratory bird hunting	97.6	0.9	1–4	0.7	5–11	0.8	12–365
Orienteering	98.0	0.9	1–2	0.5	3–6	0.6	7–125

Note: Percentages for nonparticipants and the three activity days groups sum across to 100.
Source: NSRE 2000–2001. Versions 1–9, N = 42,868. Interview dates: 7/99 to 7/01.

Table 15.3 Percentages of U.S. population 16 or older not participating and percentages by range of days of participation per year for 3 levels of activity days per year in physically passive, land-based outdoor activities, 2000–2001

Activity	Percent of Population Who Do Not Participate	Least Active Third		Moderately Active Third		Enthusiasts Most Active Third	
		Percent of Population	Days per Year	Percent of Population	Days per Year	Percent of Population	Days per Year
Walking for pleasure	17.0	27.8	1–20	28.9	21–100	26.3	101–365
Family gathering	26.5	26.5	1–2	23.4	3–5	23.5	6–300
Viewing/photographing natural scenery	39.7	20.5	1–4	21.0	5–15	18.8	16–365
Visiting nature centers	42.9	25.7	1–2	13.7	3–4	17.7	5–365
Sightseeing	48.2	20.9	1–5	14.1	6–12	16.7	13–365
Driving for pleasure	48.8	20.6	1–5	14.8	6–15	15.8	16–365
Picnicking	45.5	23.7	1–3	15.2	4–6	15.6	7–365
Viewing/photographing other wildlife	55.3	17.5	1–4	12.6	5–12	14.5	13–365
Viewing/photographing wildflowers, trees	55.1	18.2	1–5	12.8	6–20	13.9	21–365
Visiting historic sites	53.8	22.5	1–2	10.5	3–4	13.2	5–365
Viewing/photographing birds	67.6	11.0	1–4	11.2	5–30	10.2	31–365
Gathering mushrooms, berries	71.5	11.1	1–3	8.1	4–8	9.3	9–365
Visiting a farm or agricultural setting	72.1	12.9	1–2	6.0	3–5	8.9	6–365
Developed camping	73.6	11.0	1–3	8.2	4–7	7.2	8–250
Visiting prehistoric or archeological sites	79.1	8.2	1–1	7.4	2–3	5.3	4–365

Water-Based Activities

Swimming is among the most popular of activities in the country and is at the top of the list in popularity of the water-based activities shown in Table 15.4 (p. 274). Lake, stream, and ocean swimming Enthusiasts make up almost 13% of the population 16 or older, pool swimming Enthusiasts are nearly 12%, beach-going Enthusiasts make up just over 11% and warmwater angler Enthusiasts make up over 7%. Windsurfing, surfing, scuba diving, kayaking, rowing, sailing, and snorkeling Enthusiasts, at the bottom of the list in Table 15.4, make up between 0.2% and 2.2% of the population. All of these percentages are relatively small, however, as can seen by the range of days of participation, the Enthu-siasts account for the bulk of activity days in all the water activities listed.

Snow/Ice Based Activities

The percentages shown in Column 1 of Table 15.5 (p. 275) in part reflect the relatively small proportion of the population living in northern or in high eleva-tion climates where snow is abundant in winter. In part also the high percent-ages not participating in snow/ice activities reflects, for some of the activities in Table 15.5, the expense of travel, equipment, and access to areas. Many of these activities are also highly physically demanding. Snow/ice activity Enthu-siasts are a very small percentage of the population, from a low of 0.5% for snowshoeing to a high of 2.6% for downhill skiing. Participation 6 to 8 days per year places a participant in the most active one third, thus defining them as Enthusiasts by our definition.

Table 15.4 Percentages of U.S. population 16 or older not participating and percent by range of days of participation per year for 3 levels of activity days per year in water–based outdoor activities, 2000–2001

Activity	Percent of Population Who Do Not Participate	Least Active Third		Moderately Active Third		Enthusiasts Most Active Third	
		Percent of Population	Days per Year	Percent of Population	Days per Year	Percent of Population	Days per Year
Swimming (lakes, streams)	58.2	14.3	1–4	14.8	5–12	12.7	13–365
Swimming (outdoor pools)	59.0	14.3	1–5	14.8	6–20	11.8	21–365
Visiting a beach	59.4	16.4	1–4	13.0	5–10	11.2	11–365
Warmwater fishing	77.4	9.1	1–5	6.1	6–14	7.5	15–203
Motorboating	75.6	9.4	1–3	7.8	4–10	7.2	11–365
Visiting other watersides (besides beach)	74.0	10.6	1–3	8.5	4–10	6.9	11–365
Coldwater fishing	86.4	4.9	1–3	4.4	4–10	4.3	11–365
Canoeing	90.3	4.5	1–2	2.0	3–4	3.2	5–365
Saltwater fishing	89.6	3.5	1–2	3.7	3–7	3.1	8–365
Jetskiing	90.5	3.7	1–2	2.7	3–6	3.1	7–320
Rafting	90.5	5.5	1–2	1.1	3–3	2.9	4–60
Waterskiing	91.9	2.7	1–2	2.7	3–7	2.6	8–365
Snorkeling	93.3	3.2	1–2	1.2	3–4	2.2	5–365
Sailing	94.9	2.4	1–2	1.3	3–5	1.4	6–365
Rowing	95.6	2.2	1–2	0.8	3–4	1.4	5–364
Anadromous fishing	95.6	1.5	1–2	1.6	3–6	1.3	7–180
Kayaking	96.5	1.8	1–2	0.6	3–4	1.2	5–320
Scuba diving	98.1	0.8	1–2	0.5	3–5	0.6	6–365
Surfing	98.3	0.6	1–3	0.6	4–12	0.5	13–365
Windsurfing	99.2	0.4	1–2	0.2	3–5	0.2	6–365

Table 15.5 Percentages of U.S. population 16 or older not participating and percent by range of days of participation per year for 3 levels of activity days per year in snow/ice-based outdoor activities, 2000–2001

Activity	Percent of Population Who Do Not Participate	Least Active Third		Moderately Active Third		Enthusiasts Most Active Third	
		Percent of Population	Days per Year	Percent of Population	Days per Year	Percent of Population	Days per Year
Downhill skiing	91.5	2.8	1–2	3.1	3–6	2.6	7–240
Snowmobiling	94.4	2.3	1–2	1.6	3–7	1.7	8–200
Snowboarding	95.1	1.7	1–2	1.7	3–6	1.5	7–60
Cross-country skiing	96.2	1.5	1–2	1.2	3–5	1.2	6–60
Snowshoeing	98.2	0.7	1–2	0.5	3–5	0.5	6–98

Demographics of the Enthusiasts
Land-Based Activities

The 1st column of data in Table 15.6 shows the minimum number of days for each activity that a participant would have to participate to be categorized as an Enthusiast. These range from a low of 3 for caving to a high of 25 for mountain biking. As the percentages clearly show, participants in the physically active land activities, for the most part, are male, non-Hispanic White, under 45 (with strong percentages under 25), and urban. Exceptions are majority percentages of women in day hiking and horseback riding and about the same percentage non-White as White for day hiking. For mountain biking, day hiking, small game hunting, big game hunting, horseback riding, orienteering, primitive camping, visiting a wilderness, rock climbing, and caving, the percentage earning less than $50,000 per year is larger than the percentage who earn more than this amount. Modest annual earnings for these activities reflect, in large part, high proportions of young participants, some of whom are still students in high school or college.

Compared with Enthusiasts in the physically active land activities, Enthusiasts in the more passive land activities are composed of substantially lower percentages who are male, somewhat lower percentages who are non-Hispanic White (with the exception of developed camping), much higher percentages who are 45 or older, lower percentages who earn $50,000 or more per year, and slightly higher percentages of urban residents (Table 15.7, p. 278). Exceptions are gathering natural products, such as mushrooms, where a relatively high percentage of the Enthusiasts for this activity are male and a lower percentage are 45 or older; attending family gatherings, where a somewhat lower percentage of the Enthusiasts are non-Hispanic White; viewing and photographing birds, where a very small percentage of Enthusiasts are under 25 and a large percentage are 45 or older; and visiting historic sites, where a higher percentage of the Enthusiasts earn $50,000 or more. Generally 70% to 80% of the Enthusiasts in passive land activities are urban residents.

Water-Based Activities

Except for swimming in a pool, visiting beaches, and rafting, the majority of water activity Enthusiasts are male (Table 15.8, p. 279). Roughly 74% to 90% are non-Hispanic White, two thirds are under 45, and one third are under 25. Water activity Enthusiasts are about evenly split between those who earn over $50,000 and those who earn less. Most live in metropolitan areas of the country. Especially high percentages of motorboating, sailing, canoeing, and rafting Enthusiasts are White, around 90%. Larger percentages of surfing, waterskiing, jetskiing, and rafting Enthusiasts are under 25. And, larger percentages of warmwater, anadromous and saltwater fishing and sailing Enthusiasts are over 45

Table 15.6 Percentages of Enthusiasts in physically active land activities by demographic characteristic, 2000–2001

Activity	Minimum Days per Year To Qualify as an Enthusiast	Percent Male	Percent White, Non-Hispanic	Percent Ages 25 and Under	Percent Ages 45 and Older	Percent Earning $50,000 or More	Percent Who Live in Metropolitan Areas
Mountain biking	25	62.0	74.7	24.9	20.6	49.0	79.4
Day hiking	16	46.4	50.5	19.4	32.0	41.7	80.3
Driving off-road	16	69.5	85.4	34.7	27.1	51.8	66.2
Small game hunting	16	93.2	87.3	31.2	28.4	36.2	53.1
Big game hunting	15	88.6	92.6	26.7	33.5	38.9	51.0
Migratory bird hunting	12	92.9	93.1	31.0	24.7	53.4	56.5
Backpacking	7	69.0	79.2	36.5	22.9	53.5	74.5
Horseback riding	7	49.4	85.0	26.7	30.9	42.2	64.7
Orienteering	7	76.9	92.2	56.2	17.0	38.5	79.6
Primitive camping	7	68.2	88.8	27.5	29.8	46.4	69.0
Visiting a wilderness or primitive area	7	63.4	87.9	28.7	31.6	47.5	73.9
Mountain climbing	5	64.4	79.7	32.7	25.8	56.5	78.8
Rock climbing	4	77.0	85.7	54.1	14.7	47.0	90.9
Caving	3	42.8	74.8	36.8	26.7	43.6	75.0

Table 15.7 Percentages of Enthusiasts in passive land activities by demographic characteristic, 2000–2001

Activity	Minimum Days per Year To Qualify as an Enthusiast	Percent Male	Percent White, Non-Hispanic	Percent Ages 25 and Under	Percent Ages 45 and Older	Percent Earning $50,000 or More	Percent Who Live in Metropolitan Areas
Walking for pleasure	101	40.7	72.3	17.7	50.3	45.2	80.1
Viewing/photographing birds	31	39.0	85.7	7.0	65.6	42.4	70.7
Viewing/photographing wildflowers, trees	21	44.5	82.4	14.0	48.7	46.2	73.5
Driving for pleasure	16	46.7	82.1	17.3	45.1	42.4	71.7
Viewing/photographing natural scenery	16	43.2	84.8	17.4	42.4	47.8	76.3
Viewing/photographing other wildlife	13	52.2	86.6	16.0	44.8	47.5	69.7
Sightseeing	13	42.0	80.4	10.5	51.4	48.3	76.8
Gathering mushrooms, berries	9	57.1	82.1	23.3	38.5	44.4	69.7
Developed camping	8	49.5	92.2	20.2	34.1	55.7	76.4
Picnicking	7	39.5	74.9	16.7	37.2	44.9	78.4
Visiting a farm or agricultural setting	6	50.3	88.2	21.8	41.8	49.6	69.6
Family gathering	6	43.9	66.3	18.7	36.9	47.7	81.4
Visiting historic sites	5	47.4	86.1	22.0	43.4	61.2	80.6
Visiting nature centers	5	47.8	80.3	18.7	33.9	54.3	84.2
Visiting prehistoric or archeological sites	4	44.2	84.3	23.9	40.4	52.8	83.0

Table 15.8 Percentages of Enthusiasts in water-based activities by demographic characteristic, 2000–2001

Activity	Minimum Days per Year To Qualify as an Enthusiast	Percent Male	Percent White, Non-Hispanic	Percent Ages 25 and Under	Percent Ages 45 and Older	Percent Earning $50,000 or More	Percent Who Live in Metropolitan Areas
Swimming in an outdoor pool	21	40.8	82.7	32.6	25.2	56.1	84.4
Warmwater fishing	15	71.9	86.9	25.2	35.5	42.7	72.4
Surfing	13	79.4	64.1	54.8	13.2	49.4	88.7
Swimming in lakes, streams, ponds	13	50.6	84.9	30.6	25.2	53.6	79.2
Visiting a beach	11	49.7	79.4	24.0	33.0	53.6	84.2
Coldwater fishing	11	76.2	82.8	23.6	35.4	45.6	72.6
Motorboating	11	63.2	90.3	22.3	34.2	57.5	73.5
Visiting other watersides (besides beaches)	11	54.9	85.6	24.7	30.8	52.1	76.3
Saltwater fishing	8	72.9	74.9	20.7	39.3	56.1	84.1
Waterskiing	8	62.1	87.9	42.9	13.9	61.2	77.0
Anadromous fishing	7	80.6	82.9	19.4	53.9	46.6	78.0
Jetskiing	7	57.1	83.2	45.8	15.0	60.6	77.8
Sailing	6	56.4	90.5	24.8	39.5	64.5	87.0
Scuba diving	6	77.6	84.3	26.2	22.0	65.5	86.6
Windsurfing	6	74.7	74.2	36.4	21.7	63.2	86.5
Canoeing	5	61.6	90.2	30.5	30.4	55.4	77.8
Kayaking	5	63.6	88.3	32.4	27.7	63.4	81.6
Rowing	5	58.3	89.3	28.3	35.2	53.1	79.0
Snorkeling	5	63.0	81.5	25.7	29.5	64.5	84.2
Rafting	4	40.6	90.3	44.8	12.6	39.2	78.7

Table **15.9** Percentages of Enthusiasts in snow/ice activities by demographic characteristic, 2000–2001

Activity	Minimum Days per Year To Qualify as an Enthusiast	Percent Male	Percent White, Non-Hispanic	Percent Ages 25 and Under	Percent Ages 45 and Older	Percent Earning $50,000 or More	Percent Who Live in Metropolitan Areas
Snowmobiling	8	69.3	92.1	40.5	19.9	53.5	63.6
Downhill skiing	7	58.7	88.9	42.3	14.5	68.2	87.6
Snowboarding	7	75.6	87.0	62.8	4.7	54.8	88.4
Snowshoeing	6	61.9	88.5	14.4	50.0	48.2	61.1
Cross-country skiing	6	51.0	97.1	17.6	40.4	43.7	60.9

than for other activities. As might be expected, the minimum number of days Enthusiasts put into pool swimming, warmwater fishing, surfing, natural water swimming, visiting beaches, coldwater fishing, motorboating, and visiting watersides is larger than for other, more costly and more physically demanding activities, such as canoeing or kayaking.

Snow/Ice Activities

Enthusiasts in snow/ice activities spend fewer days per activity than is spent in many of the land and water-based activities (Table 15.9, p. 280). While the percentages who are male are roughly the same as for water and active land activities, the percentages of snow/ice Enthusiasts are definitely more non-Hispanic White and people under 25 (except for showshoeing and cross-country skiing). Half of snowshoeing Enthusiasts are 45 or over. Over two thirds of downhill skiing Enthusiasts earn over $50,000 per year, while just about 44% of cross-country skiers do. Smaller percentages of snowmobiling, snow shoeing, and cross-country skiing Enthusiasts than for the other snow/ice activities live in metropolitan areas.

Ultra Enthusiasts

Earlier Enthusiasts in any given activity were defined as one of the most active third of participants, when measured on the basis of number of days during a 12-month period on which they participated in an activity. Within this group we call Enthusiasts, there are differing levels of participation and thus differing levels of enthusiasm for an activity. The most dedicated half of Enthusiasts—that is, those putting in the highest one-half of days of participation among Enthusiasts—we call the Ultra Enthusiasts.

The first distinguishing trait of the Ultra Enthusiast participant in all activities in Tables 15.10 through 15.13 is that the lower bound on number of activity days encompassing the range of days of participation is much higher than for Enthusiasts in general. To be an Ultra Enthusiast in day hiking and mountain biking, a person must participate in these activities 52 and 50 days per year respectively. For Ultra Enthusiasts in horseback riding, driving motor vehicles off-road, and small game hunting, a person must participate at least 30 days per year.

Generally, Ultra Enthusiasts in the physically active land activities (Table 15.10, p. 282) are composed of much higher percentages who are male, White, and mostly under 25 than other Enthusiasts who participate less. An exception is day hiking, which is widely popular within the general population and among Hispanics. Orienteering and rock climbing are more activities of young, White urban males. More than half big game hunting Ultra Enthusiasts were defined as rural.

Table 15.10 Percentages of Ultra Enthusiasts for physically active land activities by demographic characteristic, 2000–2001

Activity	Minimum Days per Year to Qualify as an Ultra Enthusiast	Percent Male	Percent White, Non-Hispanic	Percent Ages 25 and Under	Percent Ages 45 and Older	Percent Earning $50,000 or More	Percent Who Live in Metropolitan Areas
Day hiking	52	42.7	41.7	14.8	35.8	35.6	85.0
Mountain biking	50	65.7	76.7	19.6	28.0	45.2	78.6
Horseback riding	30	45.6	85.0	25.0	33.7	41.2	58.6
Driving off-road	30	64.1	85.7	42.3	20.1	56.5	68.9
Small game hunting	30	97.6	87.1	27.4	28.2	25.1	55.1
Big game hunting	24	91.8	96.8	23.3	23.3	48.9	43.4
Migratory bird hunting	20	94.8	93.7	30.2	24.5	53.1	59.2
Orienteering	20	87.5	100.0	69.2	13.4	38.4	97.8
Primitive camping	14	70.7	86.5	27.5	25.4	41.9	72.7
Visiting a wilderness/primitive area	14	65.4	88.8	28.2	31.0	43.9	68.0
Backpacking	12	72.5	84.1	41.5	19.3	56.7	74.1
Mountain climbing	10	80.0	89.4	44.1	30.4	43.6	74.7
Rock climbing	9	83.1	96.2	61.7	9.1	41.7	89.0
Caving	4	35.7	55.7	37.0	9.5	62.6	80.7

Table 15.11 Percentages of Ultra Enthusiasts for passive land activities by demographic characteristic, 2000–2001

Activity	Minimum Days per Year to Qualify as an Ultra Enthusiast	Percent Male	Percent White, Non-Hispanic	Percent Ages 25 and Under	Percent Ages 45 and Older	Percent Earning $50,000 or More	Percent Who Live in Metropolitan Areas
Viewing/photographing birds	360	38.6	86.0	6.9	70.6	40.9	67.9
Walking for pleasure	250	46.1	67.9	21.9	54.1	43.6	79.7
Viewing/photographing wildflowers, trees	120	43.8	82.0	15.1	49.6	42.5	71.6
Viewing/photographing natural scenery	90	44.8	87.0	16.4	43.5	42.0	72.0
Viewing/photographing other wildlife	40	48.7	86.4	13.5	49.0	43.7	64.3
Driving for pleasure	30	49.2	78.5	21.9	41.8	43.1	70.1
Sightseeing	25	42.4	79.4	10.8	49.6	44.7	73.5
Visiting a farm or agricultural setting	20	53.8	89.2	22.6	44.2	47.8	58.9
Gathering mushrooms, berries	20	55.4	72.9	23.6	42.0	36.3	69.3
Developed camping	14	50.5	90.8	18.5	43.4	62.9	73.9
Picnicking	12	41.2	70.5	16.7	35.5	40.5	78.5
Family gathering	10	40.9	61.8	19.0	33.5	49.7	82.6
Visiting nature centers	10	49.5	78.3	20.3	31.8	57.2	85.7
Visiting historic sites	8	52.2	86.5	28.9	35.2	58.8	83.3
Visiting prehistoric or archeological sites	7	46.5	80.8	29.2	32.2	50.3	82.9

Table 15.12 Percentages of Ultra Enthusiasts for water activities by demographic characteristic, 2000–2001

Activity	Minimum Days per Year to Qualify as an Ultra Enthusiast	Percent Male	Percent White, Non-Hispanic	Percent Ages 25 and Under	Percent Ages 45 and Older	Percent Earning $50,000 or More	Percent Who Live in Metropolitan Areas
Swimming in an outdoor pool	45	38.1	83.6	30.8	28.3	59.5	85.4
Surfing	36	76.9	61.2	56.8	11.9	43.5	87.3
Warmwater fishing	30	77.1	81.6	18.3	41.5	36.3	69.3
Swimming in lakes, streams	25	49.9	83.5	33.6	23.9	50.8	76.8
Visiting other watersides (besides beach)	25	52.9	85.1	23.6	33.1	51.5	75.9
Motorboating	24	64.5	90.0	22.7	34.6	59.5	74.4
Visiting a beach	20	49.7	79.2	25.1	32.6	51.6	83.9
Coldwater fishing	20	76.9	80.2	23.8	37.5	33.1	70.5
Saltwater fishing	20	76.8	67.2	22.0	38.6	53.7	84.0
Jetskiing	15	60.1	84.0	46.5	14.1	59.9	75.9
Waterskiing	15	63.3	84.4	43.2	14.3	67.2	78.5
Anadromous fishing	12	81.5	86.7	11.7	60.8	48.7	74.3
Sailing	12	55.7	91.8	24.9	37.8	64.7	87.5
Scuba diving	12	82.9	79.9	23.3	25.4	65.6	86.1
Kayaking	10	62.3	88.3	27.4	29.2	62.7	77.3
Rowing	10	59.0	92.8	25.4	39.4	50.9	74.5
Windsurfing	10	67.6	71.3	39.3	27.3	59.4	82.2
Canoeing	9	63.1	91.4	32.4	31.9	55.8	75.5
Snorkeling	8	67.5	75.8	26.6	30.2	56.5	81.8
Rafting	6	36.9	93.4	45.8	11.1	34.7	73.7

Table 15.13 Percentages of Ultra Enthusiasts for snow/ice activities by demographic characteristic, 2000–2001

Activity	Minimum Days per Year to Qualify as an Ultra Enthusiast	Percent Male	Percent White, Non-Hispanic	Percent Ages 25 and Under	Percent Ages 45 and Older	Percent Earning $50,000 or More	Percent Who Live in Metropolitan Areas
Snowmobiling	15	76.3	87.8	40.1	20.0	40.4	59.0
Downhill skiing	14	57.7	92.1	49.5	11.1	63.0	90.5
Snowboarding	12	82.8	81.4	65.9	0.5	47.2	85.4
Snowshoeing	10	76.3	78.7	7.9	64.3	29.0	49.8
Cross-country skiing	10	62.3	94.2	19.0	38.2	52.2	55.6

Ultra Enthusiasts in some of the less physically active land activities shown in Table 15.11 (p. 283) must put in very large numbers of days to be classed as an Ultra Enthusiast. For the Ultra Enthusiast birder, the most active sixth of birders, the range of days is 360 to 365—virtually every day! Relatively small percentages of Ultra birders are male, under 45 or earn over $50,000 per year. Compared with less active Enthusiasts, the Ultra Enthusiasts for the passive activities in Table 15.11 are made up of much higher percentages female, smaller percentages who are under 25, and smaller percentages who are urban. Developed camping Ultra Enthusiasts are similar to other passive land activity Ultra Enthusiasts, except that much higher percentages earn over $50,000 per year.

As with Ultra Enthusiasts in land activities, water-based activity Ultras put in a relatively large number of days per year participating in their chosen activities (Table 15.12, p. 284). Pool swimming Ultra Enthusiasts spend a minimum of 45 days, surfing Ultra Enthusiasts spend 36 days and warmwater fishing Ultra Enthusiasts spend a minimum of 30 days per year. Percentages of Ultra Enthusiast pool swimmers, natural water swimmers, and rafters who are male are relatively low. Percentages of surfing, jetskiing, waterskiing, and rafting Ultra Enthusiasts who are under 25 are much higher than for other activities. Percentages of Ultra warmwater and anadromous anglers who are over 45 are higher than for other activities.

Table 15.13 (p. 285) describes snow/ice activity Ultra Enthusiasts. Minimum days of participation to be classified a snow/ice activity Ultra Enthusiast are lower than for most land and water activities. Except for downhill skiing, most snow/ice Ultras are male and White. Many Ultras, except for snowshoeing Ultras, are under 25, especially among the Ultra Enthusiast snowboarders. In contrast, almost two thirds of snowshoeing Ultra Enthusiasts are 45 or older. A percentage approaching two thirds of downhill skiing Ultra Enthusiasts earn $50,000 or more while just 29% of snowshoeing Ultra Enthusiasts do. Only about half of snowmobiling, snowshoeing and cross-country skiing Ultra Enthusiasts are urban.

Trends

Table 15.14 (pp. 288–290) presents data from both NSRE 1994–1995 (in parentheses) and 2000–2001 to identify trends in Enthusiast participation characteristics. This table is an update of an earlier table published in 1999 (Cordell et al., 1999). For most activities, the percentage of the population participating at levels putting them into the ranks of the most active one third of participants has gone up. This is true for walking, viewing/photographing wildlife, snow/ice (most activities), camping, hunting, fishing, boating, swimming, and adventure activities, as shown in Table 15.14. For some activities, however, the number of days of participation per year for an individual to qualify as an Enthusiast fell. This was particularly true for walking, viewing/photographing birds and swimming activities. The lower bound on days of participation for Enthusiasts in other groups of activities rose modestly for the most part. Notable among activities for which this lower bound of days for Enthusiasts fell is birdwatching (birding). Falling from a lower bound of 50 days per person per year in 1994–1995 to 31 days in 2000–2002 is quite a reduction (even though the number of participants overall has risen sharply).

For a number of activities as well, the percentage of total participation days fell modestly. These activities include visiting a beach, cross-country skiing, snowmobiling, developed camping, big and small game hunting, most fishing activities, sailing, rafting, swimming, backpacking, and off-road driving. This reflects the addition to the ranks of activity participants a sizeable number who are novices and who participate only a few days per year.

Across the activities listed in Table 15.14, percentages of Enthusiasts who are 16 to 24 years old has decreased somewhat, particularly in walking, viewing/photographing activities, snow skiing, camping, most fishing, most boating, swimming, and outdoor adventure activities. At the same time, percentages of Enthusiasts 50 years old or older have risen in almost all activities, especially for the activities of visiting prehistoric sites, anadromous fishing, sailing, kayaking, rock climbing, and horseback riding. Percentages of Enthusiasts 25 to 49 have mostly remained constant, except for snowmobiling, small game hunting, anadromous fishing, and kayaking.

Table 15.14 Percentage of population, days annually and percentages of total days by Enthusiasts by activity and age group, 2000–2001 (with 1994–1995 in parentheses)

Activity	Percent of Population Classified as Enthusiasts	Minimum Days per Year to Qualify as an Enthusiast	Percent of Total Participation Days by Enthusiasts	Percent of Enthusiasts by Age Group		
				16–24	25–49	50+
Fitness Activities						
Walking	26.3 (21.4)	101 (112)	77.8 (76)	11.7 (15)	44.7 (45.4)	43.5 (39.6)
Viewing Activities						
Visiting a prehistoric site	5.3 (4.3)	4 (3)	78.0 (75)	15.3 (17.2)	44.7 (53.1)	40.0 (29.7)
Visiting a historic site	13.2 (11.8)	5 (4)	79.6 (72)	13.5 (14.7)	49.0 (55.9)	37.6 (29.4)
Birdwatching	10.2 (9.1)	31 (50)	94.0 (91)	4.3 (4.9)	39.8 (44.3)	55.9 (50.8)
Viewing wildlife	13.7 (9.6)	13 (12)	92.1 (92)	10.1 (10.6)	52.7 (57.7)	37.3 (31.8)
Sightseeing	16.7 (17.4)	13 (12)	81.4 (78)	7.9 (13.1)	50.2 (50.5)	41.9 (36.4)
Visiting a beach or waterside	11.2 (19.7)	11 (15)	77.4 (84)	15.9 (20.4)	56.3 (57.6)	27.8 (22.0)
Snow and Ice Activities						
Downhill skiing	2.6 (2.6)	7 (6)	76.1 (74)	27.0 (35.8)	61.5 (53.6)	11.5 (10.6)
Cross-country skiing	1.2 (0.9)	6 (6)	72.2 (73)	8.8 (16.8)	57.5 (54.4)	33.8 (28.8)
Snowmobiling	1.7 (1.1)	8 (5)	82.1 (84)	28.7 (22.0)	53.0 (62.6)	18.3 (15.5)
Camping Activities						
Developed area	7.2 (6.3)	8 (8)	70.2 (76)	12.5 (15.0)	59.9 (59.7)	27.6 (25.2)
Primitive area	5.2 (4.1)	7 (7)	77.1 (76)	19.2 (24.2)	60.1 (60.0)	20.8 (15.9)
Hunting Activities						
Big game	2.6 (2.4)	15 (12)	69.9 (74)	18.2 (20.8)	59.7 (64.6)	22.1 (14.6)
Small game	2.2 (1.9)	16 (10)	76.8 (77)	24.1 (18.6)	55.6 (64.6)	20.3 (16.8)
Migratory bird	0.8 (0.6)	12 (7)	75.5 (71)	21.8 (20.2)	56.9 (57.1)	21.3 (22.8)

Table 15.14 Percentage of population, days annually and percentages of total days by Enthusiasts by activity and age group, 2000–2001 (with 1994–1995 in parentheses) *continued*

Activity	Percent of Population Classified as Enthusiasts	Minimum Days per Year to Qualify as an Enthusiast	Percent of Total Participation Days by Enthusiasts	Percent of Enthusiasts by Age Group		
				16–24	25–49	50+
Fishing Activities						
Saltwater	3.1 (2.6)	8 (7)	83.5 (85)	14.1 (17.2)	54.9 (57.4)	31.0 (25.4)
Warmwater	7.5 (6.2)	15 (14)	80.6 (82)	17.4 (18.7)	55.3 (54.7)	27.2 (26.5)
Coldwater	4.3 (2.3)	11 (10)	80.3 (76)	16.8 (13.2)	54.5 (55.9)	28.6 (30.9)
Anadromous	1.3 (1.0)	7 (6)	76.3 (80)	13.2 (16.6)	45.6 (57.2)	41.2 (26.2)
Floating/Boating Activities						
Sailing	1.4 (1.4)	6 (5)	80.2 (81)	14.1 (23.4)	48.2 (49.8)	37.7 (26.8)
Canoeing	3.2 (1.8)	5 (4)	80.5 (73)	19.7 (27.6)	56.0 (49.4)	24.3 (23.1)
Kayaking	1.2 (0.2)	5 (5)	84.2 (78)	20.3 (22.5)	54.0 (71.3)	25.7 (6.2)
Rowing	1.4 (1.1)	5 (3)	81.0 (79)	16.8 (15.5)	49.1 (51.3)	34.1 (33.1)
Rafting	2.9 (1.9)	4 (4)	72.7 (75)	32.9 (37.1)	57.1 (55.5)	10.0 (7.5)
Surfing	0.5 (0.3)	13 (15)	89.0 (89)	45.0 (54.2)	46.6 (38.6)	8.5 (7.1)
Windsurfing	0.2 (0.3)	6 (4)	78.9 (81)	25.6 (24.5)	48.9 (56.6)	25.6 (18.8)
Swimming Activities						
Swimming (pool)	11.8 (13.0)	21 (25)	76.6 (80)	20.8 (26.9)	56.9 (55.0)	22.3 (18.1)
Swimming (lakes, streams)	12.7 (11.9)	13 (13)	76.5 (78)	20.2 (27.0)	58.8 (58.7)	21.0 (14.3)

Table **15.14** Percentages of population, days annually and percentages of total days by Enthusiasts by activity and age group, 2000–2001 (with 1994–1995 in parentheses) *continued*

Activity	Percent of Population Classified as Enthusiasts	Minimum Days per Year to Qualify as an Enthusiast	Percent of Total Participation Days by Enthusiasts	Percent of Enthusiasts by Age Group		
				16–24	25–49	50+
Outdoor Adventure Activities						
Hiking	10.4 (7.1)	16 (10)	88.5 (83)	16.4 (24.4)	57.1 (58.3)	26.5 (17.3)
Orienteering	0.6 (0.6)	7 (5)	85.6 (75)	35.5 (32.2)	48.4 (55.0)	16.1 (12.8)
Backpacking	3.5 (2.4)	7 (5)	79.8 (81)	24.3 (33.4)	61.8 (56.0)	13.9 (10.7)
Mountain Climbing	1.8 (1.3)	5 (3)	82.0 (74)	21.9 (29.5)	58.3 (55.6)	19.8 (14.8)
Rock Climbing	1.4 (1.0)	4 (3)	82.4 (78)	37.7 (45.5)	49.3 (48.4)	13.0 (6.2)
Caving	0.9 (1.1)	3 (2)	58.0 (58)	36.0 (34.4)	46.0 (54.6)	18.0 (11.0)
Off-Road Driving	5.3 (4.5)	16 (14)	83.6 (87)	24.3 (25.6)	58.1 (57.0)	17.6 (17.3)
Horseback Riding	2.9 (2.3)	7 (6)	93.2 (94)	16.3 (36.8)	60.6 (52.6)	23.2 (10.5)
Social Activities						
Picnicking	15.6 (15.0)	7 (7)	74.2 (73)	10.1 (13.5)	58.8 (64.0)	31.1 (22.6)

Note: This table includes only activities for which the number of days participated was asked.

References

Cordell, H. K., Betz, C. J., English, D. B. K., Mou, S. H., Bergstrom, J. C., Teasley, R. J., Tarrant, M. A., and Loomis, J. (1999). Outdoor recreation in American life: A national assessment of demand and supply trends. Champaign, IL: Sagamore Publishing.

Cordell, H. K., Betz, C. J., and Green, G. T. (2002). Recreation and the Environment as cultural dimensions of contemporary American society. Leisure Sciences, 24(1), 13–41.

Cordell, H. K., Herbert, N. G., and Pandolfi, F. (1999). The growing popularity of birding in the United States. Birding, 31(2), 168–176.

Cordell, H. K., McDonald, B. L., Lewis, B., Miles, M., Martin, J., and Bason, J. (1996). United States of America. In G. Cushman, A. J. Veal, and J. Zuzanek, World leisure participation: Free time in the global village (pp. 215–235). Wallingford, Oxon, England: CAB International.

Cordell, H. K. and Overdevest, C. (2001). Footprints on the land: An assessment of demographic trends and the future of natural resources in the United States. Champaign, IL: Sagamore Publishing.

Cordell, H. K. and Tarrant, M. A. (2002). Forest-based outdoor recreation. In D. N. Wear and J. G. Greis (Eds.), Southern forest resource assessment. (GTR-SRS-53, pp. 269–282). Asheville, NC: USDA Forest Service Southern Research Station.

Cordell, H. K., McDonald, B. L., Teasley, R. J., and Bergstrom, J. C. (1998). Emerging markets for outdoor recreation in the United States. Athens, GA: USDA Forest Service. Retrieved December, 19, 2003, from http://www.srs.fs.usda.gov/trends/sgma.html

Douglass, R. O. (1999). History of outdoor recreation and nature-based tourism in the United States. In H. K. Cordell et al., Outdoor recreation in American life: A national assessment of demand and supply trends. Champaign IL: Sagamore Publishing.

Gibson, C. and Jung, K. (2002). Historical census statistics on population totals by race, 1790 to 1990, and by Hispanic origin, 1970 to 1990, for the United States, regions, divisions, and states (Working Paper Series No. 56.) Washington, DC: U.S. Census Bureau.

Harrington, C. (1975). The coastline of the United States. [Pamphlet]. Washington, DC: National Ocean Survey.

Leeworthy, V. R. (2001, May). Preliminary estimates from versions 1–6: Coastal recreation participation, national survey on recreation and the environment (NSRE) 2000. Silver Spring, MD: National Oceanic and Atmospheric Administration, National Ocean Service, Special Projects Office.

Leeworthy, V. R. and P. C. Wiley (2001). National survey on recreation and the environment (NSRE) 2000: Current participation patterns in marine recreation. Silver Spring, MD: National Oceanic and Atmospheric Administration, National Ocean Service, Special Projects Office.

National Survey on Recreation and the Environment (NSRE). (2000–2001). [A dataset]. The Interagency National Survey Consortium, coordinated by the USDA forest service; outdoor recreation, wilderness, and demographics trends research group: Athens, GA and the Human Dimensions Research Laboratory, University of Tennessee, Knoxville.

Natural Resources Canada. (1999). Forests for the future: Montreal process criteria and indicators. Ottawa, ON: Policy, Planning & International Affairs Office, Canadian Forest Service. Retrieved December 19, 2003, from http://www.mpci.org

Outdoor Recreation Policy Review Group. (1983). Outdoor recreation for America—1983. Washington, DC: Resources for the Future, Inc.

Outdoor Recreation Resources Review Commission. (1962). National recreation survey. Study report 19 to the Outdoor Recreation Resources Review Commission. Washington, DC: U.S. Government Printing Office.

President's Commission on Americans Outdoors. (1987). Americans outdoors—The legacy, the challenge, with case studies: The report of the President's Commission. Washington, DC: Island Press.

Smith, W. B., Vissage, J. S., Darr, D. R., and Sheffield, R. M. (2001). Forest resources of the United States, 1997 (General Technical Report NC—219). St. Paul, MN: USDA Forest Service, North Central Research Station.

Teasley, R. J., Bergstrom, J. C., Cordell, H. K., Zarnoch, S. J., and Gentle, P. (1999). Private lands and outdoor recreation in the United States. In H. K. Cordell (Ed.), Outdoor recreation in American life (pp. 183–218). Champaign, IL: Sagamore Publishing.

University of Texas at Austin. (2003). The Organization of Territories in the United States Since 1803 [map]. Retrieved from http://www.lib.utexas.edu/maps/historical/shepherd/us_expansion_shepherd.jpg

U.S. Bureau of the Census. (1993). 1990 Census of population and housing, population and housing unit counts, United States (1990 CPH-2-1). Washington, DC: Author.

U.S. Bureau of the Census. (2000). Profile of general demographic characteristics: 2000 (Summary file 1). Retrieved December 19, 2003, from http://www.census.gov

USDA Economic Research Service. (1999). Agricultural Resource Management Study. Retrieved December 19, 2003, from http://www.ers.usda.gov/briefing/FarmStructure/Gallery/sourcesofincome.htm

USDA Economic Research Service. (2002). Agricultural resource management survey, 2000 and 2001. Retrieved December 19, 2003, from http://www.ers.usda.gov/Briefing/ARMS

USDA Forest Service. (1989). Basic assumptions (General Technical Report RM-174.) Fort Collins, CO: USDA Rocky Mountain Forest and Range Experiment Station.

USDA Forest Service. (2001). 2000 RPA assessment of forest and range lands (FS–687). Washington, DC: USDA Forest Service. Retrieved December 19, 2003, from http://www.fs.fed.us/pl/rpa

USDA Forest Service. (2002a). Draft 2003 national report on sustainable forests. Washington, D.C. Retrieved December 19, 2003, from http://www.fs.fed.us/research/sustain/data.htm

USDA Forest Service. (2002b). National visitor use monitoring program. Retrieved December 19, 2003, from http://www.fs.fed.us/recreation/programs/nvum

USDA National Agricultural Statistics Service. (1999). Agricultural economics and land ownership survey. Retrieved December 19, 2003, from http://www.nass.usda.gov/census/census97/aelos/aelos.htm

U.S. Department of the Interior. (1986). 1982–1983 Nationwide recreation survey. Washington, DC: U.S. Government Printing Office.

Wipper, D. (1999, May/June). How to choose the right canoe hull. Paddler Magazine, 19(3), 23–24.

Other Books by Venture Publishing, Inc.

Other Books by Venture Publishing, Inc.

Experience Marketing: Strategies for the New Millennium
by Ellen L. O'Sullivan and Kathy J. Spangler

Facilitation Techniques in Therapeutic Recreation
by John Dattilo

File o' Fun: A Recreation Planner for Games & Activities, Third Edition
by Jane Harris Ericson and Diane Ruth Albright

Functional Interdisciplinary-Transdisciplinary Therapy (FITT) Manual
by Deborah M. Schott, Judy D. Burdett, Beverly J. Cook, Karren S. Ford, and Kathleen M. Orban

The Game and Play Leader's Handbook: Facilitating Fun and Positive Interaction
by Bill Michaelis and John M. O'Connell

The Game Finder—A Leader's Guide to Great Activities
by Annette C. Moore

Getting People Involved in Life and Activities: Effective Motivating Techniques
by Jeanne Adams

Glossary of Recreation Therapy and Occupational Therapy
by David R. Austin

Great Special Events and Activities
by Annie Morton, Angie Prosser, and Sue Spangler

Group Games & Activity Leadership
by Kenneth J. Bulik

Growing With Care: Using Greenery, Gardens, and Nature With Aging and Special Populations
by Betsy Kreidler

Hands On! Children's Activities for Fairs, Festivals, and Special Events
by Karen L. Ramey

In Search of the Starfish: Creating a Caring Environment
by Mary Hart, Karen Primm, and Kathy Cranisky

Inclusion: Including People With Disabilities in Parks and Recreation Opportunities
by Lynn Anderson and Carla Brown Kress

Inclusive Leisure Services: Responding to the Rights of People with Disabilities, Second Edition
by John Dattilo

Innovations: A Recreation Therapy Approach to Restorative Programs
by Dawn R. De Vries and Julie M. Lake

Internships in Recreation and Leisure Services: A Practical Guide for Students, Third Edition
by Edward E. Seagle, Jr. and Ralph W. Smith

Interpretation of Cultural and Natural Resources, Second Edition
by Douglas M. Knudson, Ted T. Cable, and Larry Beck

Intervention Activities for At-Risk Youth
by Norma J. Stumbo

Introduction to Recreation and Leisure Services, Eighth Edition
by Karla A. Henderson, M. Deborah Bialeschki, John L. Hemingway, Jan S. Hodges, Beth D. Kivel, and H. Douglas Sessoms

Introduction to Writing Goals and Objectives: A Manual for Recreation Therapy Students and Entry-Level Professionals
by Suzanne Melcher

Leadership and Administration of Outdoor Pursuits, Second Edition
by Phyllis Ford and James Blanchard

Leadership in Leisure Services: Making a Difference, Second Edition
by Debra J. Jordan

Leisure and Leisure Services in the 21st Century
by Geoffrey Godbey

The Leisure Diagnostic Battery: Users Manual and Sample Forms
by Peter A. Witt and Gary Ellis

Leisure Education I: A Manual of Activities and Resources, Second Edition
by Norma J. Stumbo

Leisure Education II: More Activities and Resources, Second Edition
by Norma J. Stumbo

Leisure Education III: More Goal-Oriented Activities
by Norma J. Stumbo

Leisure Education IV: Activities for Individuals with Substance Addictions
by Norma J. Stumbo

Leisure Education Program Planning: A Systematic Approach, Second Edition
by John Dattilo

Leisure Education Specific Programs
by John Dattilo

Leisure in Your Life: An Exploration, Sixth Edition
by Geoffrey Godbey

Leisure Services in Canada: An Introduction, Second Edition
by Mark S. Searle and Russell E. Brayley

Leisure Studies: Prospects for the Twenty-First Century
edited by Edgar L. Jackson and Thomas L. Burton

The Lifestory Re-Play Circle: A Manual of Activities and Techniques
by Rosilyn Wilder

Models of Change in Municipal Parks and Recreation: A Book of Innovative Case Studies
edited by Mark E. Havitz

More Than a Game: A New Focus on Senior Activity Services
by Brenda Corbett

Nature and the Human Spirit: Toward an Expanded Land Management Ethic
edited by B. L. Driver, Daniel Dustin, Tony Baltic, Gary Elsner, and George Peterson

The Organizational Basis of Leisure Participation: A Motivational Exploration
by Robert A. Stebbins

Outdoor Recreation Management: Theory and Application, Third Edition
by Alan Jubenville and Ben Twight

Planning Parks for People, Second Edition
by John Hultsman, Richard L. Cottrell, and Wendy Z. Hultsman

The Process of Recreation Programming Theory and Technique, Third Edition
by Patricia Farrell and Herberta M. Lundegren

Programming for Parks, Recreation, and Leisure Services: A Servant Leadership Approach
by Donald G. DeGraaf, Debra J. Jordan, and Kathy H. DeGraaf

Protocols for Recreation Therapy Programs
edited by Jill Kelland, along with the Recreation Therapy Staff at Alberta Hospital Edmonton

Quality Management: Applications for Therapeutic Recreation
edited by Bob Riley

A Recovery Workbook: The Road Back from Substance Abuse
by April K. Neal and Michael J. Taleff

Recreation and Leisure: Issues in an Era of Change, Third Edition
edited by Thomas Goodale and Peter A. Witt

Other Books by Venture Publishing, Inc.

Recreation Economic Decisions: Comparing Benefits and Costs, Second Edition
by John B. Loomis and Richard G. Walsh

Recreation for Older Adults: Individual and Group Activities
by Judith A. Elliott and Jerold E. Elliott

Recreation Programming and Activities for Older Adults
by Jerold E. Elliott and Judith A. Sorg-Elliott

Reference Manual for Writing Rehabilitation Therapy Treatment Plans
by Penny Hogberg and Mary Johnson

Research in Therapeutic Recreation: Concepts and Methods
edited by Marjorie J. Malkin and Christine Z. Howe

Simple Expressions: Creative and Therapeutic Arts for the Elderly in Long-Term Care Facilities
by Vicki Parsons

A Social History of Leisure Since 1600
by Gary Cross

A Social Psychology of Leisure
by Roger C. Mannell and Douglas A. Kleiber

Special Events and Festivals: How to Organize, Plan, and Implement
by Angie Prosser and Ashli Rutledge

Steps to Successful Programming: A Student Handbook to Accompany Programming for Parks, Recreation, and Leisure Services
by Donald G. DeGraaf, Debra J. Jordan, and Kathy H. DeGraaf

Stretch Your Mind and Body: Tai Chi as an Adaptive Activity
by Duane A. Crider and William R. Klinger

Therapeutic Activity Intervention with the Elderly: Foundations and Practices
by Barbara A. Hawkins, Marti E. May, and Nancy Brattain Rogers

Therapeutic Recreation and the Nature of Disabilities
by Kenneth E. Mobily and Richard D. MacNeil

Therapeutic Recreation: Cases and Exercises, Second Edition
by Barbara C. Wilhite and M. Jean Keller

Therapeutic Recreation in Health Promotion and Rehabilitation
by John Shank and Catherine Coyle

Therapeutic Recreation in the Nursing Home
by Linda Buettner and Shelley L. Martin

Therapeutic Recreation Programming: Theory and Practice
by Charles Sylvester, Judith E. Voelkl, and Gary D. Ellis

Therapeutic Recreation Protocol for Treatment of Substance Addictions
by Rozanne W. Faulkner

Tourism and Society: A Guide to Problems and Issues
by Robert W. Wyllie

A Training Manual for Americans with Disabilities Act Compliance in Parks and Recreation Settings
by Carol Stensrud

 Venture Publishing, Inc.
1999 Cato Avenue
State College, PA 16801
Phone: (814) 234-4561
Fax: (814) 234-1651